I, LIVIA

THE COUNTERFEIT CRIMINAL

I, LIVIA

MARY MUDD PhD

ISBN:
978-1-952874-66-6 (paperback - bnw)
978-621-95901-6-7 (paperback - colored)
978-621-95901-7-4 (hardback - colored)
978-621-95901-8-1 (ebook)

Published by:

 **OMNIBOOK**Co.

OMNIBOOK CO.
99 Wall Street, Suite 118
New York, NY 10005
USA
+1-866-216-9965
www.omnibookcompany.com

For e-book purchase: Kindle on Amazon, Barnes and Noble
Book purchase: Amazon.com, Barnes & Noble, and
www.omnibookcompany.com
Omnibook titles may be purchased in bulk for educational, business, fund-
raising, or sales promotional use. For more information please e-mail
info@omnibookcompany.com

www.marymudd.com

TABLE OF CONTENTS

BEGINNINGS

THE PUBLIC FIGURE

LIVIA THE MURDERESS:
THE ANATOMY OF THE STIGMA

THE PRIVATE LIVIA SEEKING
HER INTIMATE SIDE

EPILOGUE, APPENDICES, BIBLIOGRAPHY, AND INDEX

BEGINNINGS

Livia as a young woman
Louvre Museum, Paris
Photo credit: Erich Lessing/Art Resource, New York

DEDICATIONS 2022

The two previous editions were dedicated to the much honored and cherished memories of persons now deceased.

Let this current revision extol four persons very much living.

- My publicist Lui Monsanto for his unceasing confidence in the potential of *I, Livia*;
- My esteemed friend SKG whose inspiring, guiding, and comforting counsels enrich my life beyond measure;
- My grandsons James Lewis Mudd and Thomas Willem Mudd. May the lessons of history inspire them and their generation to identify and pursue best pathways in life.

MCMM
Somerset,
New Jersey
January 2022

DEDICATIONS 2011

The original version of this book was dedicated to the glory and memory of my dear friend, Byzantine scholar Constance Head, Ph.D. (1939—1985), who had insisted I stop grousing about the popular misrepresentations of Livia and write a corrective biography. Since that initial publication in 2005, three more very special individuals, who were integral to the book's preparation, progress and completion, have departed.

- My beloved husband John Edward Mudd, M.B.A., C.P.C.U., A.I.A.F. (1947—2005), who enthusiastically encouraged my writing of this study and made sacrifices both personal and financial to insure its completion. He read and corrected the galley proofs of the original edition while lying hospitalized in his final months;
- Surekha Dwivedi, M.D. (1969—2011) who answered many a medical question for me;
- My tuxedo cat Walker (1997—2008), who used to help by parking himself on my laptop while I was endeavoring to type the manuscript.

MCMM
Wall, New Jersey
November 2011

ACKNOWLEDGMENTS

My gratitude goes, in great depth, to the following individuals and institutions for their contributions to the preparation of this book.

- Reverend Anastasius Bandy of Saint George's Greek Orthodox Cathedral, Philadelphia, Pennsylvania: for assistance with the linguistic nuances of Dio Cassius.
- William Daniel Lee Pryor, Ph.D., of Houston, Texas, my longtime friend, mentor, and former English professor: for my writing style.
- Brookdale Community College in Lincroft, New Jersey; Rutgers University and the New Brunswick Theological Seminary in New Brunswick, New Jersey; Temple University and the University of Pennsylvania in Philadelphia: for access to their library collections.
- The Monmouth County, New Jersey, County Library System: for obtaining many obscure and obtuse items for me on interlibrary loan.
- Alessandra Corti of Alinari and, especially Michael Slade, Eileen Doyle, Ph.D., and Alison Slagowitz of Art Resource, New York City: for the splendid illustrations.
- Surekha Dwivedi, M.D. of Howell, New Jersey; Frank Navarro, D.M.D. of Point Pleasant, New Jersey; and Norman P. Einhorn, O.D. of Belmar, New Jersey: for assistance with medical questions.
- Marie DeFilippis, of Toms River, New Jersey: for proofreading.
- Publicist Scott Barrie and his team: for advice and guidance through the technical intricacies of the publishing process.

My most special thanks is nevertheless reserved, for

- John Edward Mudd and William Andrew Lewis Mudd, respectively my husband and son, who shared my interest in Livia, and assisted me with research and housework alike;

and for

- Walker and Teddy, our cats, who helped in their own way.

MCMM
Wall, New Jersey
December, 2004

INTRODUCTION

This biography has been many years in the making. Livia Drusilla has fascinated me ever since, as a geeky, history-obsessed teenager, I read Robert Graves' celebrated novel *I, Claudius*. Was Livia the murderous, power-hungry schemer this author depicts? Was she truly ready to slay anyone who threatened to obstruct her ambitions, and clever enough to obfuscate her crimes with consummate success? Or, was she actually the loving, supportive, wife and mother her polemicists insist she only pretended to be?

Meticulous and critical examination, of the historical records for Livia's life, eventually revealed her innocence. Livia most assuredly did not commit the crimes, of which she stands accused.

My studies yielded several other discoveries. Even when shown the falsity of Livia's purported criminality, some modern audiences cling to her villainous image with virulent intensity. I have been berated, belittled, even challenged to fistfights, by devotees of Livia's malevolent reputation. Not being a psychologist, I cannot even conceive of an explanation for this dogged adherence, to a patently false and libelous tradition. As a historian, however, I can show you why Livia does not deserve her evil representation, and offer reasons for its development.

Livia's position as an empress consort naturally made her a public figure; and Augustus publicized her as an icon of his regime. More than a passive symbol, however, Livia was an active and essential participant in the operations of her husband's administration. People accepted her as such, moreover, in a culture that traditionally restricted the responsibilities of women to homemaking and child rearing.

Repulsive imputations of murder and deception tend to combine, with the cold, aloof, delineation of a government functionary, to obscure

Livia's personal, human side. The ordinarily placid Livia could be surprisingly impulsive. For a span of at least three years, she lived in staunch loyalty to her first husband. Then she abruptly left him, while pregnant with his child, for love of the man who had driven her father to suicide and jeopardized her own safety in war. Decades later she nearly killed herself over the death of her son, and sought consolation in Greek philosophy—the ancient equivalent of psychotherapy. Livia was demure and dutiful, patient, forbearing and accommodating; but she could also be assertive, opinionated, and—especially late in her life—petulant. She was a dedicated homemaker, an accomplished intellectual, a profound political thinker, a connoisseur of art. Gracious, generous, and amiable, she was loved and respected by her family and countrymen alike.

My conclusions about Livia are based, rigorously, upon my readings of the ancient sources for her life. To minimize the inoculation of my opinions, by the attitudes and errors of other modern writers, I avoided the examination of contemporary analyses as much as possible. If an interpretation of mine parallels that of someone else, it is because we have arrived at the same point of view, and not because I have plagiarized. My failure to acknowledge any modern study means I have not consulted it.

All translations are my own, unless otherwise specified. Since I endeavored to preserve, as much as possible, the word orders and styles of the original documents, their renderings into English at times seem awkward and stilted. To highlight Latin and foreign phrases and terms, I have italicized them. Because proper names of humans, deities, places, months, and Roman magistracies, appear throughout English literature and historiography, many readers will already be familiar with them. These items were consequently left in roman type, unless particular emphasis was needed. In Latin the letter *i*, at the beginning of a syllable and before a vowel, was pronounced much like the English *j*. Although these Latin hard *is* are often written as *js*, to maintain orthographic consistency I have left them as *is*. The only exceptions are a few proper names—Julius, Julia, Janus, Jupiter, Juno, Justinian, and Sejanus—which readers more readily recognize in this format.

Space, time, and copyright restrictions prevented reproduction of all the images described in the text and appendices. The artifacts can nevertheless be found and viewed on a large variety of websites.

To those who prefer truth to malicious sensationalism, I dedicate this rehabilitation of a most unjustly maligned woman.

CORRIGENDA 2011

My most extensive revision is to the assessment of Marcus Livius Drusus Libo in Appendix I. In the 2005 edition I proposed this individual may have been the adoptive son of Livia's father; but after reexamining the epigraphic evidence, I discovered that inference is untenable. Other changes are slight but important nonetheless. These include the correction of Tiberius' age at the time of his retirement to Capri, a brief exposition on the falsity of allegations he engaged in sexual perversity during that retirement, a reconsideration of the significance of Capricorn in artistic renderings of Augustus, and a more precise identification of the Cyrenaican laser employed in medications.

Caesar Augustus
Uffizi Gallery, Florence
Photo credit: Alinari/Art Resource, New York

CHAPTER I

LIVIAS EARLY LIFE

On January 30, 58 BCE, in the city of Rome, Italy, an auspicious event took place. A daughter was born to the senator Marcus Livius Drusus Claudianus and his wife Alfidia. A brief ceremony followed the birth. After the baby was washed and swaddled, she was laid at her father's feet. Stooping over, he lifted her in his arms. This act was essential in ancient Rome, to establish a child's legitimacy. By performing it a father acknowledged that the child placed before him was his, and that he assumed responsibility for its upbringing. Claudianus gave his daughter the feminine form of his *gentilicum*, the name of his *gens*—his clan or extended family. To this he added a second appellation, the feminine diminutive of his *cognomen* or surname. And so the newborn was christened Livia Drusilla.

Little could her parents know, on that winter's day, that the infant they had welcomed into the world and their home was destined to be intimately associated with people and events which would profoundly affect the course of world civilization.

Livia's father belonged, by birth and adoption, to two of the oldest and most politically prominent families in Rome. In 79 BCE an Appius Claudius Pulcher held the executive office of *consul*—the Roman Republic's highest magistracy. Livia's father was most likely a son or brother of this man. Although the precise year of Claudianus' birth is unknown, it certainly occurred no later than 90 BCE. As an adult he held the office of *praetor* (trial judge) in 50 BCE. At that time, the minimum requisite age for tenure of this magistracy was forty years.

The *gens Claudia* was a patrician clan. Its members could trace their ancestry to the very founders (*patres*—fathers) of the Roman Republic. The cognomen *Pulcher* (Beautiful) designated a specific family within the clan. We may presume its progenitor was renowned for his good looks. The Claudii belonged to the *Sabini*, an Italian people that constituted some 20 percent of Rome's population. The remaining 80 percent, the *Latini*, had imposed their language on the city-state.

Plebeians were Romans of non-patrician origin; and patricians tended to look down upon them as inferiors. Still, a number of plebeian clans and families became as active and powerful in politics as patricians. Among such plebeians were the Livii Drusi.

The plebeian tribunes (*tribuni plebis*), a watchdog college of ten plebeian senators, prevented the passage of legislation deemed harmful to the interests of their class. Although they were elected solely by their fellow plebeians, the tribunes served, like the other Roman magistrates, for one-year terms.

A Marcus Livius Drusus was one of the plebeian tribunes for 91 BCE. Among the causes he promoted was reform of the court system. Another was enfranchisement of all Italians who were allies of Rome. Over the two preceding centuries, the Romans had formed alliances with the other indigenous peoples of Italy. Roman citizenship had been conferred on some of these allies, but not on others. Drusus now proposed that all of Rome's Italian allies be enfranchised. Before his term as tribune was over, Drusus lost his life to an assassin's dagger. In the subsequent Social War (90 – 88 BCE), the unenfranchised Italians took by force the privileges Drusus had aspired to give them freely.

The tribune Drusus was the man who adopted Livia's father. He may even have done so posthumously, since one could adopt an heir simply by bequeathing him one's estate. In the Roman ruling class, adoptions and marriages solidified political alignments between families. Appius Claudius Pulcher and Marcus Livius Drusus were members of the same senatorial faction.

There probably were practical considerations for the adoption as well. Drusus' need for an established heir was becoming increasingly urgent. In 91 BCE he was at least forty, the minimum age for tenure of the tribunate. By now he and his wife Servilia had very likely despaired of having a natural son, to perpetuate the family name and political philosophy. Growing hostility may also have led Drusus to suspect his life was in danger.

Law required the new heir to assume his adoptive father's name, and the adjectival form of his natal *gentilicum*. Hence upon his adoption, Livia's father became Marcus Livius Drusus Claudianus.

The children of Appius Claudius Pulcher matured into a flamboyant lot. The eldest son Appius (born about 97 BCE) was outwardly religious and proper; yet he was not above venality, as he struggled to support extravagant siblings in the face of dwindling family assets. Gaius (born 96 BCE) produced what Appius could not: an heir to the peculiar family *praenomen*. Publius (born 94 BCE) renounced his patrician heritage so he could stand for the plebeian tribunate as Publius *Clodius* Pulcher. He became a notorious demagogue and gangster with a following of thugs. The three daughters all assumed the name Clodia in support of their brother. The husband of the eldest provided some ribald entertainment in an ordinarily somber setting, when he detailed her sexual escapades during their divorce proceedings. The middle Clodia kept a salon and patronized the literary arts. Bold, racy, and promiscuous, she is the infamous Lesbia in the love poetry of her *protégé*, Quintus Valerius Catullus.

Livia's father by contrast appears to have grown up quite prim. Drusus had been a stern moralist; and Servilia probably raised her adoptive son in accordance with her late husband's principles. Moderation in all aspects of behavior, integrity, honesty, industry, chastity, and devotion to family, were traditional Roman *mores* that Livia eventually embraced. Adherence to these standards placed Claudianus in a minority. By the first century BCE, many Romans were disregarding and ridiculing such values as outdated and meaningless.

There was one scandal. Like many other senators, Claudianus often served private clients as a defense attorney. In 54 BCE a dissatisfied customer charged him with *prevaricatio*—the deliberate withholding of evidence that might bring about a defendant's acquittal. Claudianus was arraigned before the Senate, and defended by no less a personage than the great statesman and political philosopher, Marcus Tullius Cicero. Comments in some of Cicero's extant letters suggest he was not entirely convinced of his client's innocence. Cicero nevertheless managed to clear Claudianus by a narrow margin of votes. Claudianus' election to the praetorship three years later indicates the incident did not cling to his reputation.

The correspondence of Cicero with his friend, Titus Caecilius Atticus, provides a personal glimpse of Livia's father. Claudianus owned a formal garden, which Atticus wanted to purchase. Cicero reports that he pressured Claudianus to accept Atticus' offer, and Claudianus showed interest in the sale. The negotiations must have collapsed, however, because Cicero's final comment on the matter deprecates Claudianus as volatile and greedy.

In 63 BCE, at the age of twenty-seven, Claudianus was old enough to seek election as one of twenty *quaestores* (finance ministers). Tenure of the quaestorship, the lowest ranking Republican magistracy, brought automatic admission to the Senate for life. Although any Roman male citizen had the constitutional right to stand for the quaestorship, a special commission appointed by the Senate screened the candidates. For the most part, only the sons of senators were admitted to the roster. On occasion the board accepted a *novus homo*—new man—who lacked senatorial ancestors but possessed particularly impressive political qualifications.[1]

Three years after holding the quaestorship, Claudianus was eligible for the post of *aedilis* (public works administrator), the next highest public office. Probably around this time—certainly no later than the spring of 59 BCE—he espoused Alfidia. Roman women were customarily married at fourteen, men at about sixteen or seventeen. Claudianus' relatively advanced age at the time of his daughter's birth (he was at least thirty-two), suggests Alfidia was much younger than he, and probably not his first wife.

The mother of Livia Drusilla was not of senatorial stock. She was not, in fact, truly Roman but a native of Fundi (modern Fondi), an agricultural emporium on the coastal plain of Italy some sixty miles south of Rome. Alfidia was nevertheless an aristocrat within her own milieu. Her father Marcus Alfidius was a *decurio*—a member of his city's governing council.

Decurions as a class were extremely wealthy. Those who aspired to public careers at Rome usually found themselves lacking the name recognition and familial connections—the *auctoritas*, to use the proper Latin word, —necessary for acceptance as lawyers or candidates for the Senate.[2] To surmount this problem, the decurions married their daughters or other female kin to economically straitened senators. The resulting arrangements were usually quite satisfactory to everyone involved. In return for access to funds, the senatorial sons-in-law promoted the interests of their decurial fathers-in-law in all the right circles. The brides acquired noble status, along with entry into the high society of the capital.

There is no indication Alfidia's father ever gained admission to the Senate. His great-great grandson, the emperor Gaius Caligula, asserted he was never more than a decurion. Still, a Marcus Alfidius—perhaps Livia's maternal grandfather or his son—became a successful prosecution attorney. In 52 BCE he secured the conviction of Sextus Coelius, one of Publius Clodius Pulcher's ruffians.

Nothing specific is known about Livia's childhood. There are no references to siblings. Marcus Livius Drusus Libo, who was born no later than 48 BCE, appears from the recondite available evidence to have been a distant cousin rather than a brother by birth or adoption.

From general knowledge of the era we can make inferences, about the daily life of a young aristocratic girl growing up in the final years of the Roman Republic. That she would become a homemaker was a foregone conclusion. To women, the Romans maintained, belonged the most sacred and important of all social responsibilities: to produce and rear the next generation of the race. From this duty the women must not be distracted by the more mundane but dangerous responsibilities of earning a living, serving in the armed forces, or running the government. Such obligations were considered strictly the province of men.

Women lacked the legal rights of being able to vote and to hold public office. Since they could not stand for election to the quaestorship, women did not become senators. Surviving epitaphs do reveal the existence of female secretaries, accountants, teachers, doctors, and merchants; but these were rare anomalies. The only professional class of women in ancient Rome was that of the prostitutes, who were duly licensed and subject to income taxation. They were also the social and legal inferiors of female Roman citizens.

Such strictures did not prevent Roman women from taking interest and even sharing in the activities of their menfolk. Wall paintings from Pomepii reveal the presence of wives and daughters in the shops of tradesmen. Some women, like Livia's notorious relative Clodia Pulchra, promoted the careers of poets and other men of letters. Still other women became devotees of religious movements that eventually included Christianity.[3] Although they could not attend the sessions of the Senate, some women advised the activities of senators. Several women were among the planners of Lucius Sergius Catilina's unsuccessful *coup d'état* of 63 BCE. These interests must be purely secondary for women, never pursued in lieu of, or at the expense of, domestic responsibilities.

From earliest childhood, girls were taught to spin thread, to weave it into cloth, and sew that into garments. They learned to organize and clean their homes and to plan meals. Even parents who could afford servants made sure their daughters mastered household chores. The girls on reaching adulthood must supervise such tasks even if others performed them. Some wealthy matrons, including Livia, worked right along with their servants. Cooking, however, was one domestic activity Livia most likely avoided. The Romans considered the physical handling of food beneath a matron's dignity, although she was expected to oversee meal preparation. All but the very poorest of women employed cooks.

Girls of means and status underwent a finishing education, to prepare them for the social expectations of their *milieu*. They studied singing so that they might speak in well-modulated tones, and dancing to ensure they moved with grace and poise. Lessons in painting, embroidery, and sculpture fostered the ability to select with taste the furnishings and appointments of elegant homes. Professional artists and artisans, however, were invariably men, and considered menial laborers.

Because the Romans prized literacy highly in both sexes, the academic training of women was not neglected. Mothers began the education of their children, as soon as the latter were old enough to grasp and retain information. Fundamentals of reading, writing, and arithmetic computation—the proverbial **Three Rs**,—together with moralizing stories from Roman history, religion, and legends, were the usual components of home study. The amount of learning a child received depended upon the mother's own education and her ability to teach.

For more advanced education a child was entrusted to an academic tutor or sent to a school. The latter was usually a makeshift affair—a collection of stools and benches set up by a pedant in a corner of a public building or passageway. Latin grammar and rhetoric, Roman history, natural science, and more advanced mathematical computations, were the usual offerings. Many pupils also studied Greek language and literature. Although they had conquered the country of Greece, the Romans revered classical Hellenic culture as the basis of civilization. No Roman was considered truly educated unless he or she spoke and wrote Greek.

General education ended, for most children, when they were about fourteen. Boys began to learn their fathers' trades. The sons of senators studied law and military strategy. Some wealthy families sent their sons to universities, in Greece or in the Greek-dominated cities of southern Italy. Such institutions were off-limits to young women, who were expected to start devoting all their energies to homemaking. A woman must use her education to instruct her children, and to maintain the ledgers of household assets and expenses.

Some intellectually inclined women, especially those who could afford servants to relieve them of time-consuming household chores, pursued higher academics in private. They did so through self-study, the engagement of tutors, and attendance of public lectures offered by itinerant scholars. Among such self-taught women was Livia. As an adult, she was a renowned intellectual. Her knowledge and insights, especially in political matters, rivaled those of the most learned men of her day. There is every reason to assume these interests developed in her childhood. She apparently had no siblings to distract her. As the child of austere parents she had no opportunity—if, indeed, she ever had the inclination—to amuse herself with extravagant dress, gluttonous dining, or sexual promiscuity—all common pastimes of the idle rich in ancient Rome. As the daughter of an active politician, Livia had ample opportunity to observe, firsthand, the tumultuous events of the Roman Republic's final decades.

The last century of the pre-Christian era was, for the Romans, a period of great material prosperity but of serious political instability. During the preceding four centuries, Rome had conquered or subdued into client (i.e., vassal) alliances virtually all the principalities of the Mediterranean basin. Once the period of conquest was over, Rome's city-state government proved incapable of providing stable administration to far-flung dominions, in an era of slow, primitive communication. The Roman magistrates rotated annually. Once a provincial matter reached the capital for consideration, the entire administration could have changed—and often, policies with it. The inability to provide stable supervision allowed corruption to run rampant in provincial administrations.

Many conquered peoples were pressed into slavery and sharecropping. This source of cheap labor gave rise to truck farming, by Roman landowners in Italy and the provinces. Trade burgeoned as Roman businessmen extended their contacts and markets into conquered areas. The non-senatorial merchandising class increased in wealth and influence. Called *equites*—equestrians or knights because their order had once supplied the mounted divisions of the Roman army—these mercantilists began to demand a larger voice in the formation of public policy.

Meanwhile, falling prices undercut the small farmers and day laborers who had once formed the backbone of Italy's economy. Forced into bankruptcy and foreclosure, the dispossessed and unemployed drifted to the capital. There they became an angry and howling mob, demanding restitution from the government that had allowed them to come to such straits.

In earlier centuries, Rome had had a citizen army. Men who volunteered or were conscripted in time of war returned to their civilian occupations once a crisis was surmounted. Now the need to police provinces required the presence of standing armies, with specific terms of service and remuneration. Provincial troops, whose numbers included many indigents seeking relief, tended to become more loyal to their commanding officers than to the remote, ever-changing, and apparently indifferent central government.

The most highly ranked military officers, who were always senators, found themselves supported by fiercely loyal soldiers and veterans. This backing enabled commanders and former commanders to force the Senate to adopt their policies, by threatening and sometimes actually imposing martial rule on Rome.

Not all senators were indifferent to the plight of the impoverished, or to the importunity of the equestrians and allies for better representation. Those who sought reform—whether out of genuine altruism, or merely to obtain the political support of their beneficiaries—came to be known as *Populares*—Populists—and were deemed liberals. Conservatives who endeavored to restrict all the advantages to their *milieu* regardless of the cost to others, called themselves *Optimates*—The Best. Roman politics, once unified in purpose for the advancement of the state, now degenerated into virtually continual, often petty, and occasionally violent squabbling between these two factions.

The apparent solution to this variety of problems was a government that involved fewer personalities and changes. Kingship, however, was entirely out of the question. The Roman Republic had been established, in 509 BCE, to replace the Etruscan monarchy that had founded the city-state some 250 years earlier. The Romans were determined never again to be ruled by kings. Their Republic's constitution contained numerous safeguards, to prevent the concentration of power in the hands of any one person for extended periods of time. Furthermore the senatorial oligarchs, who had devised the Republican regime and dominated it since its inception, were loath to relinquish their control to a new system.

The Romans were nevertheless beginning to incline, perhaps unconsciously, toward the stability of monarchy. Some politicians attempted to establish one-man rule within the existing constitutional framework. Gaius Marius, a popular former commander, got himself elected to a series of successive consulships. Although the constitution specified a ten-year hiatus between tenures of the consulship by the same person, Marius' action was not unprecedented in Roman history. It was not his violation of the constitutional regulation, but the unscrupulous conduct of his political associates, that eventually forced Marius out of politics in 100 BCE.

Nearly twenty years later, in 82 BCE, a military strongman named Lucius Cornelius Sulla had himself proclaimed *dictator*. The dictatorship was a constitutionally authorized Republican office. It gave its holder supreme authority in both military and civilian affairs—the desired monarchic control. But the dictatorship was supposed to be held for no more than six months, and then only in times of dire national emergency.

Sulla managed to secure the office for as long as he wished to hold it; but he resigned in 79 BCE. He may have retired for reasons of health, for he died only a year later.

Both Marius and Sulla succeeded in introducing some order; but once either man withdrew from public life, Roman politics regressed immediately into the now familiar pattern of factional strife. In 60 BCE a new experiment was tried. Gaius Julius Caesar, the leader of the *Populares*, formed a private coalition with two predominant *Optimates*. The latter were wealthy financier Marcus Licinius Crassus, and former commander Gnaeus Pompeius Magnus whose name is consistently Anglicized as Pompey the Great. The goal of this alliance, which is known to history as the First Triumvirate, was to guide the respective factions toward unified constructive policies, and to secure political advantages for the Triumvirs themselves.

The strategy might have worked, had the Triumvirate remained intact. After holding the consulship for 59 BCE, Caesar secured an extended military command in Gaul for the purpose of subjugating the disruptive migratory natives. He consequently was not present in Rome to defend his interests. Crassus got himself killed in 53 BCE, while leading an abortive campaign against the Parthians. The desert empire of this Iranian people lay to the east of Rome's dominions, along a hotly disputed border. The enemy's capture of three legion standards was no less devastating to the Romans than the deaths of their soldiers.

Left alone with the Senate, Pompey was outnumbered and outmaneuvered by Caesar's Optimate enemies. When Caesar returned to Italy in 49 BCE, he faced an opposition army of which the reluctant Pompey had been placed in command. The result was a civil war, from which Caesar emerged the victor in August of the following year (47 BCE).

Now in a position to impose martial force on the Senate, Caesar followed the example of Sulla and demanded appointment to a dictatorship. An original term of ten years was subsequently extended to life. Caesar may have feared, after reviewing the experience of Sulla, that too short a tenure of this office would result in a renewal of factionalism. In his position, Caesar implemented many reforms and policies which were particularly advantageous to average and unprivileged Roman citizens. In the eyes of many aristocrats, however, Caesar's acceptance of the lifelong dictatorship, a perpetual consulship and other extraordinary honors, was unabashedly and unacceptably monarchic. Some sixty senators joined a conspiracy to overthrow Caesar. On March 15, 44 BCE, —the infamous Ides of March that inspired Shakespeare, —a small portion of the group confronted Caesar and stabbed him to death.[4]

At the inception of the First Triumvirate in 60 BCE, Livia's father was certainly an avid supporter of Caesar if not of the triple alliance itself. Both Claudii and Livii had traditionally been *Populares*; Claudianus was no exception. In the year of his daughter's birth (58 BCE) he served with integrity and enthusiasm on a commission, designed by Caesar to distribute government lands to qualified indigents.[5] But eventually Claudianus became an ardent enemy, if not of Caesar himself then certainly of the Dictator's successors.

Of these there were two: the one self-proclaimed, the other officially designated by Caesar. The former was Marcus Antonius—better known in the modern world as Mark Antony—who was one of the consuls for 44 BCE. Antony was thirty-eight years old. He may have acquired the consulship, prior to the requisite age of forty-three, through the special intervention of Caesar. Although brash and vulgar, Antony was keenly intelligent, cunning, and personable. Since his mother Julia was Caesar's cousin, Antony may have felt this relationship entitled him to the Dictator's personal and political legacy. By presenting the prospect of immediate intervention and uninterrupted leadership, Antony quickly rallied the support of Caesar's troops and veterans, and of the ordinary civilians whose interests the Dictator had furthered.

Caesar had nevertheless chosen someone else to succeed him. Gaius Octavius Thurinus was the Dictator's grandnephew, the son of Atia a daughter of Caesar's sister Julia. Octavius had been born on September 23, 63 BCE; and although young in years, he had already demonstrated a strong aptitude for statecraft. This had impressed Caesar, and prompted him to prepare the youth for a political career. Octavius was at Apollonia in northern Greece, furthering his academic education at the local university while studying the movements of troops stationed nearby, when he learned of his great-uncle's death.

Upon returning to Italy, Octavius discovered Caesar had

testamentarily adopted him. Following the accepted procedure, he changed his name to Gaius Julius Caesar Octavianus when he accepted the inheritance. Modern historians call him Octavian in this period of his life, to distinguish him from his great-uncle. He utilized the name Caesar, as much for name recognition as for legal entitlement.

Octavian knew he had not only accepted his great-uncle's name and material goods, but the responsibility of perpetuating Caesar's ideals and intentions. Antony knew this as well but was loath to surrender his newly found power to a rival, legitimate heir or not.

The Senate had begun to fear Antony might march on Rome, and place himself in control of affairs. Perceiving this concern, Octavian sought an alliance with the Senate early in 43 BCE. That body recognized Octavian's command over the army he had recruited with his own private funds. The Senate also augmented Octavian's force with troops commanded by the two consuls. This combined army routed Antony's near Mutina (modern Modena), but at the cost of both consuls' lives. Their demise left Octavian in command of the senatorial army along with his own.

The Senate ordered Octavian to relinquish its troops, and some of his own as well. What the consuls had died to keep Antony from achieving, Octavian now accomplished. With his enlarged army he occupied Rome, and demanded that he and his cousin Quintus Pedius be elected consuls in place of the deceased. The new chief magistrates established a court to try Caesar's assassins, and appealed to Antony to make peace.

Antony and Octavian met for talks at Bononia (modern Bologna). Together with Marcus Aemilius Lepidus, another former favorite of Caesar, they established the Second Triumvirate. Unlike the first of its kind, this coalition was not secret. The new Triumvirs coerced the Senate, to designate their alliance a legally constituted organ of the state with a term of five years. Now they could neither be accused of abusing a regular magistracy, nor of retaining power for extended or indefinite periods of time.

The Triumvirs proceeded to proscribe for execution, any opponents they considered potential threats to their control of the government. This measure was considered harsh by the standards of the day but not excessive. You were expected to be willing to die for your principles, especially if you were a public functionary like a senator. Marius and especially Sulla had promoted similar bloodbaths.

Among those who forfeited their lives to the Second Triumvirate was the great orator Cicero. He had attacked Antony in a series of bitterly caustic speeches called the **Philippics**, and dismissed Octavian as "exploitable and expendable." [6] Another, who was proscribed but not executed, was Livia's father.

Claudianus had introduced in the Senate the motion that demanded Octavian surrender his troops. Whether persuaded by this or by other adversarial conduct, the Triumvirs regarded Claudianus an enemy with sufficient influence to pose a danger to them. The Triumvirate did not automatically proscribe every opponent, just because he displayed some antagonism or disagreement. A senator named Tiberius Claudius Nero proposed the Senate publicly reward Caesar's assassins for their deed. Nero, however, was not indicated for death.

Claudianus fled to Greece, where the assassins were amassing an army of their supporters. On October 28, 42 BCE, this force was defeated by the Triumvirate's troops near the Macedonian city of Philippi. Claudianus survived the battle but took his own life to avoid capture, and to assure himself an honorable end. Octavian granted him a traditional Roman funeral.

It was not uncommon for Roman wives to follow their husbands in suicide. The fate of Alfidia, however, remains unknown.

Against this backdrop, of political upheaval and family tragedy, Livia matured and married. She reached the traditional matrimonial age of fourteen on January 30, 44 BCE. The husband her parents selected for her was the aforementioned Tiberius Claudius Nero, a distant kinsman. Nero served under the command of Julius Caesar between 46 and 44 BCE: first as a military *quaestor* (paymaster), then as a fleet commander in Egypt, and later as *legatus* (military governor) of Narbonnese Gaul (now the Provence section of France). For the excellence of his performance he was made a *pontifex* (high priest) of the Roman state religion.

Years earlier Nero had unsuccessfully sought the hand of Cicero's daughter Tullia, who had been born about 76 BCE. This chronology, and the year in which he held the praetorship (41 BCE), indicates Nero was at least twenty-three years older than Livia. The couple consummated their union no later than February of 42 BCE; for on November 16 of that year, Livia bore her husband a son. As was customary with firstborn Roman males, the baby was named Tiberius Claudius Nero after his father.

Now a wife and mother, Livia had fulfilled what had been, for generations of Roman women, the expectations of a lifetime. But the very forces that were transforming Roman politics, were shaping her personal destiny into channels unprecedented for one of her sex.

During the winter that followed the Battle of Philippi, each of the Triumvirs assumed responsibility for ruling a different geographic section of Roman dominions. Lepidus took North Africa, from which grain shipments to Rome had to be carefully supervised. Should they fall prey to pirates, the capital would immediately suffer food shortages. Antony went eastward, to concentrate upon reaffirming Rome's alliances with seven client kingdoms—Pontus, Cappadocia, Judaea, Commagene, Galatia, Cilicia, and Egypt—as well as independent city-states within the province of Asia Minor. All made sizeable tribute payments to the Roman treasury.

To Octavian fell Italy and Roman possessions in Europe. He faced the task of finding farmland, with which to reward the veterans of Philippi and other battles. Land grants were the traditional form of compensation for military service.

Octavian resorted to confiscations, taking great pains to target those who could best afford to surrender property: victims of the proscriptions, extremely large landowners, those who had acquired their holdings through fraud. Quite understandably, he incurred the opposition of those whose lands were forfeit. They found a champion in Lucius Antonius, brother of the Triumvir and one for the consuls for 41 BCE. Lucius' supporters included Mark Antony's outspoken wife Fulvia, as well as Tiberius Claudius Nero.

Livia's spouse was one of the praetors for 41 BCE. Two of these four judges, the *praetores urbani* (urban praetors), heard cases pertaining to the city of Rome itself. The other pair, called *praetores peregini* (wandering praetors) dealt with situations occurring outside the capital. A *praetor pereginus* might, if circumstances warranted, exercise a military command, or remain in his office beyond its one-year term. As Nero did both, he had to have been a *praetor pereginus*; and as such, he must have heard challenges to Octavian's land grabbing. This function quite naturally drew him into acquiescence with Lucius Antonius and Fulvia.

Later in 41 BCE, after legal maneuvering had failed to halt the land seizures, Lucius Antonius decided to try military force as a means of stopping Octavian. This endeavor proved unsuccessful as well. Octavian's army besieged the consular forces in the eastern Italian hill town of Perusia (modern Perugia). The fortress fell in February of 40 BCE.

Tiberius Claudius Nero was among the defenders of Perusia. His wife and young son were with him during the siege. The presence of Livia and little Tiberius represents a cultural anomaly. Traditionally the Romans took special care, to exclude woman and children from theaters of war. At Perusia this rule was emphatically broken, especially by Fulvia. She strode around the encampment girt with a sword, shouting orders at the fighting men as though she were a general. Whether Livia went to Perusia voluntarily, or at her husband's insistence, cannot be determined.

The Nerones fled first to Praeneste (modern Palestrina), and thence to Naples. Here the elder Tiberius attempted, without success, to recruit an army of slaves. With the arrival of Octavian's troops, the family made haste for Messina in Sicily. Twice, during this part of their flight, their whereabouts was almost betrayed by the younger Tiberius' crying.

Messina was the headquarters of Sextus Pompeius Magnus, the youngest son of Julius Caesar's former colleague-turned-adversary. Sextus was a bitter enemy of the Second Triumvirate, and champion of all who opposed that coalition. His *modus operandi* was piracy. With an aggressive fleet manned primarily by ruffians, he attacked the grain-laden ships that were bound from North Africa to Rome. Sextus sought, by creating food shortages, to cause public dissention for the Triumvirate to address.

There was some personal cordiality between Livia and the Pompeii Magni, who were related to her by marriage. Sextus' wife was the daughter of a senator named Lucius Scribonius Libo. He, as nomenclature indicates, was in some way connected to Livia's relative Marcus Livius Drusus Libo. At Messina, Sextus' sister Pompeia presented the younger Tiberius with gifts: a cloak, a clasp, and some gold studs. Livia and her son treasured these artifacts for the remainder of their lives.

Sextus nevertheless refused even to grant Tiberius Nero an audience, much less endorse Nero's retention of his praetorship beyond its one-year term. The rejected Nerones left Messina for the port of Brundisium (modern Brindisi), on Italy's eastern coast. They traveled across the mainland separately, to avoid detection by Octavian's agents. Their ultimate destination was the Greek city of Sparta.

It had long been customary for senators to patronize municipalities, tribes, or even nations which were Roman subjects or allies. The patrons pleaded the causes and needs of their clients before the Senate, or provided benefactions directly. The clients repaid their patrons with money, landownership, or the support of political causes. Livia's adoptive grandfather, the plebeian tribune Drusus, had patronized the town of Marruvium, the center of the Italian enfranchisement movement. Since her father bore the nickname *Pisareus*, he was possibly a patron of Pisaurum on Italy's Adriatic coast (modern Pesaro south of Rimini).

Generations of Claudii had been patrons of Sparta. Tiberius Nero knew he could expect a safe haven and a warm welcome. Nero may also have sought refuge in Greece because Mark Antony had his headquarters at Athens. To him the defeated defenders of Perusia now presented their grievances against Octavian.

Antony decided to visit Italy and survey the situation firsthand. In October of 40 BCE, the Triumvirs met at Brundisium. Questions were answered and differences resolved. As Fulvia had died, Antony now reinforced his bond with Octavian by marrying the latter's newly widowed sister, Octavia. The Triumvirs then repaired to Rome, for a winter of relaxation.

Although no dates are available, other evidence suggests Tiberius Nero and his family returned to Italy at this time. Perhaps they traveled in Antony's entourage. Our sources describe the Nerones' sojourn in Greece as short. While leaving Sparta, the family was caught in a flash forest fire that singed Livia's hair and clothing. Autumn, a dry season in Greece, is a likely time for such an occurrence. Nevertheless the Nerones may have extended their stay in Sparta until the spring of 39 BCE, when Octavian issued a general amnesty to those who had opposed him.

Octavian had become solicitous toward the former enemies of himself and his adoptive father. The Brundisium talks may have impelled him to soften his approach. Furthermore Octavian, who had proven himself ruthless but basically fair, was gaining the support of former opponents who had become disillusioned with the unsavory Sextus Pompeius as a champion.

In that spring of 39 BCE, the Triumvirs concluded a tenuous peace with Sextus. Antony then returned to Greece, and Lepidus to North Africa. In summer Octavian departed for Gaul, to oversee the installation of the governor. He returned to Rome sometime before mid-September, bringing with him several legions of troops. Angered by a dispute with Octavian over control of Sardinia, Sextus had resumed his raids on the grain shipments. Octavian saw war as the only way of stopping him.

September 23, 39 BCE was Octavian's twenty-fourth birthday. He marked it with a ceremony, which held political as well as personal significance. Having never shaved his first growth of beard, he now did so, and presented the refuse as an offering to the chief Roman god, Jupiter. This act, the *depositio barbae*—deposition of the beard—was customarily performed by a Roman youth on the birthday that immediately followed the first appearance of his beard. Octavian had postponed the rite, to indicate he was mourning and seeking retribution for the murder of Caesar. His performance of the ceremony at this time symbolized his reconciliation with his adversaries.

But in the fall of 39 BCE neither Sextus Pompeius nor the rethinking of relationships with former political foes, was foremost in Octavian's mind. His primary focus at this time was on making Livia his wife. He had fallen passionately in love with her, and she with him. Rumor suggested he had shaved his beard to make himself more attractive to her. Perhaps he did consider his appearance, when he performed the ceremony that affected it.

We cannot determine when or under what circumstances the pair first met. They very likely knew each other in childhood. The social circle of the ruling class was small and exclusive. The temporary alliance of Livia's father with Julius Caesar may have intertwined their families all the more.

Whatever their background history, Octavian and Livia must have become acquainted or reacquainted while Octavian was sojourning in Rome, during the winter and spring of 39 BCE. By September Livia was halfway through her second known pregnancy; and rumors of Octavian's paternity were spreading. For these to be credible, the two must have been associating with each other early in the year.

The lovers were not free to marry until a complicated set of preconditions had been satisfied. First, both had to be divorced from their current spouses. Octavian had married Scribonia, the sister of Sextus Pompeius' father-in-law, in the summer of 40 BCE. After persuading Sextus not to use Perusia as a pretext for declaring war, Octavian espoused Scribonia to solidify this agreement. The bride, who had already been twice married, was somewhat older than her new husband.

Sextus must have respected the non-aggression accord, at least for a time, if he rejected the overtures of Tiberius Nero after Perusia's fall. But in resuming his attacks on the grain transports, Sextus made clear his decision to disregard his pact with Octavian. The latter's union with Scribonia had become meaningless.

Octavian repudiated Scribonia on the very day she gave birth to their daughter Julia. Various writers, both ancient and modern, have erroneously attributed this concurrence to indifference or even cruelty on Octavian's part. Although he cared little for Scribonia's "contrary temper," [7] as he put it, Octavian had more to lose than gain by harassing her. He needed her cooperation. Divorce in ancient Rome required the assent of both partners, unless the one could prove he or she had suffered legal damages at the hands of the other. An accusation from Scribonia would have tarnished Octavian's reputation and furnished Sextus with propaganda. Since neither Octavian nor Scribonia made a complaint, their separation had to have been mutually acceptable. They must have agreed to remain married until Scribonia gave birth, so the legitimacy of their child could not be called into question.

Equally amicable was Livia's separation from Tiberius Claudius Nero. There is no evidence of friction between them at any time during their marriage. It is this author's suspicion that Nero readily released Livia because his health was failing. He did not resume active participation in politics after returning to Rome from Sparta; and he only lived another seven or eight years beyond that time. Nero may well have considered Octavian a more congenial spouse, for the young and dynamic Livia, than a declining invalid. Furthermore, Octavian must have agreed to promote the interests of Nero's children in return for their mother's hand. Octavian had blood relatives, who did not receive nearly the degree of political advancement he accorded his stepsons.

By the end of 39 BCE the divorces had been secured; but another obstacle remained. A divorced or widowed woman was expected to wait at least ten months before she remarried. If the woman bore a child during this interim, the waiting period guaranteed that the former husband was the father. Octavian, however, wanted to marry Livia at once.

There were precedents for such an action. Octavian's own sister Octavia had been pregnant by her late husband Gaius Claudius Marcellus, when she married Mark Antony in 40 BCE. Octavian, however, wanted a tangible, authority-based, sanction for his unorthodox nuptials. At this point in his career, he was particularly vulnerable to hostile criticism. He was preparing for war with Sextus who, for all his unsavory conduct, was still a Roman citizen. And simultaneously, Octavian was seeking the peace, trust, and cooperation of his former enemies: the senatorial aristocracy to which Livia and Tiberius Nero belonged.

Octavian turned to the college of high priests, of which his colleague Lepidus was the chief (*Pontifex Maximus*). Not wanting to cross either Triumvir, the pontiffs sanctioned an immediate marriage so long as the fatherhood of Tiberius Nero was indisputable. Encouraged by this vagary, Octavian took Livia to live in his house. There she bore her second son, whom Tiberius Nero duly acknowledged as his. The baby was named Decimus Claudius Nero.

The chronology surrounding Decimus' birth and Livia's remarriage is confusing and difficult to interpret. All ancient literary sources state Octavian and Livia were married some three months before Decimus was born. An official inscription gives their wedding date as January 17, 38 BCE. The third century author Dio Cassius places the marriage concurrently with political events of early 38 BCE.

This would indicate that Decimus was born in March of 38 BCE.[8] The second century writer Suetonius avers, however, that Decimus had the same birthday as Mark Antony. The very inscription, which provides the wedding date of Livia and Octavian as January 17, gives Antony's birthday as January 14. This would place Decimus' birth three days before his mother's remarriage.

Although his accuracy is sometimes suspect, Suetonius appears to be correct about this particular matter. The source he cites, for the concurrence of Decimus' birth date with Antony's, was a proclamation by the Roman emperor Claudius. The latter was Decimus' son by Antony's youngest daughter. Claudius urged his subjects to celebrate his father's birthday with particular diligence, because it coincided with that of Antony the emperor's maternal grandfather. Claudius may also have confirmed the parallel birthdays in his now lost autobiography, which Suetonius used as a source.

The chronological discrepancy has prompted some scholars to propose Octavian and Livia were betrothed three months before Decimus' birth, and married immediately after that event. The first-century writer Pliny the Elder mentions a betrothal, but does not indicate its duration. Octavian's own diary, which Suetonius quotes, nevertheless reveals that he and Livia were cohabitating at the time of her confinement.

It has also been suggested, that while the birthday of Livia's second son was celebrated on January 14, it actually took place on a different date. Livia's own birthday was January 30; but at Pergamon in Asia Minor (modern Bergamo, Turkey), it was feted on September 21. In this case, however, the celebration of Livia's birth was connected with the autumnal equinox, and with the commemoration of Octavian's genuine birth date of September 23. January 14 had no such ritual implications; it was not a major holiday. Suetonius specifies, moreover, that Claudius encouraged homage to Mark Antony's birthday because it coincided with that of the emperor's father—not the other way around. This particular emphasis lends credence to January 14 as the true date of Decimus' birth.

Octavian and Livia might have married ritually in the fall of 39 BCE, but waited until January 17 to consummate their union. This assumption, although conceivable, is tenuous. While sexual activity so soon after delivery is not impossible, it can pose an unpleasant prospect to both partners.

Another—and to this writer's mind the most believable—alternative concerns the *manus*.

Literally meaning hand, *manus* was the legal tutelage of a Roman husband over the persons and property of his wife and descendants. A son remained subject to his father's *manus* so long as the father lived. If the son married, his wife, children, and subsequent generations, all came under his father's *manus*. Once a father died, each of his sons assumed his own *manus* over his own household.

If a father died while his son was a child, a praetor appointed a *tutor*—guardian of the son's person in the creation of contracts—and a *curator*—supervisor of the child's property. A *tutor* and *curator* could be one in the same person, and usually was the late father's nearest male relative over twenty-five years of age. *Tutela*—the authority of the *tutor*—persisted until the son reached puberty. *Curatio*—the power of the *curator*—endured until the son reached legal majority at the age of twenty-five.

A woman of any age was subject to the *manus* of her father or guardian so long as she remained unmarried. Once she wed, she passed into the *manus* of her husband through one of three methods. *Confarreatio* was a religious ceremony, during which the nuptial couple offered a cake of barley (*far*) to Jupiter. Although originally practiced by all patricians, *confarreatio* by the first century BCE had become restricted to certain orders of priests.

Coemptio, a symbolic sale of the bride to her husband, had become the more common ritual for the transfer of *manus*. From *coemptio* arose the tradition of the engagement ring. It represented the prospective bridegroom's offer of earnest money in anticipation of his nuptial purchase. Either ceremony established the bridegroom's *manus* immediately.

The third mode of marriage, called *usus*, was simple cohabitation. A woman who lived with a man as his wife did not enter into his *manus* until a year had elapsed. If during that interval she absented herself from her mate's domicile for three consecutive nights, she remained under the *manus* of her prenuptial guardian.

The point of this entire discussion, is that Octavian and Livia may have lived together under the mandate of *usus* until after Decimus was born. Had Octavian's *manus* been instituted during Livia's pregnancy, questions could have been raised as to who was the father, and hence legal male guardian, of her child. Once the baby had been born—and duly acknowledged by Tiberius Nero—Livia and Octavian were free to undergo *confarreatio* or *coemptio*. Either rite would finalize the couple's union by putting Octavian's *manus* into effect at once. A story circulated that during the wedding ceremony, Tiberius Nero placed Livia's hand in Octavian's after the manner of a bride's father. This supports the contention that the marriage followed Livia's confinement. Nero's act symbolized the transfer of the *manus*. Had he performed it prior to Decimus' birth, Nero would have compromised his claim to the baby's paternity.

The new union was fraught with political implications, which were especially important to Octavian. He lacked a long, illustrious ancestry in the senatorial order on the basis of birth alone. His membership in the patrician *gens Julia* was strictly through his adoption by his great-uncle. In a memoir to which Suetonius refers, Octavian described the family from which he descended as ancient and wealthy, but of equestrian status. Suetonius further advises us that Gaius Octavius, Octavian's natural father, was the first in his branch of the *gens Octavia* to be a senator. His father had been a banker, but had also served as a decurion at Velitrae (modern Velletri, south of Rome).

Octavian's mother Atia was daughter of one of Julius Caesar's two sisters, and her husband Marcus Atius Balbus. The latter's family hailed from the town of Aricia (now Ariccia, near Castel Gandolfo). Suetonius identifies Balbus as a senator and descendant of senators, related through his mother to the Pompeii Magni. But, Suetonius continues, Balbus was also the grandson of an African-born tradesman, who had kept a perfumery and later a bakery at Aricia.

Octavian consequently contracted each of his three marriages, with women who possessed the sort of long, pedigreed background he lacked. His first wife had been Livia's cousin Clodia, the daughter of the infamous Publius Clodius Pulcher. Clodia's mother was Fulvia, who had married Mark Antony after Clodius was murdered. Octavian had ritually espoused Clodia in 43 BCE, to reinforce the establishment of the Second Triumvirate. Because of his bride's young age (she was only about ten), Octavian never consummated the union; and when his political relationship with Fulvia deteriorated in 41 BCE, he repudiated Clodia with her virginity intact. A year later Octavian married Scribonia to reinforce his short-lived peace with Sextus Pompeius.

By the autumn of 39 BCE, the turning of events and attitudes had made Livia an ideal political spouse for Octavian. She was a member of the very senatorial aristocracy he had once persecuted and was presently seeking to appease. After proscribing her father and precipitating his suicide, Octavian had pursued Livia and her first husband into voluntary exile. What better symbol of reconciliation for Octavian, than a wife who had once been his victim?

Marriage with Livia provided another advantage for Octavian, as he prepared for war with Sextus Pompeius. The latter's rebuff of Tiberius Claudius Nero after Perusia had left Livia and her family without protection, forced to endure hardships and dangers in their flight to Sparta. Now that Octavian had become the champion of the Roman people as they suffered food shortages from Sextus' raids on the grain shipments, he was also the personal guardian of a woman who had suffered firsthand from Sextus' callousness.

The political advantages of the marriage could hardly have been lost on Octavian, and must have encouraged him to make Livia his wife. First and foremost, however, the union was a rare love match. As such it created a furor, in a society where arranged marriage was essentially an absolute norm. To some Romans the coincidence of the nuptials with Livia's pregnancy was outrageous and immoral, even though it had pontifical approval and was not the first action of its type. Other observers found the unorthodox marriage a source of great amusement. The hardheaded, ruthless young Caesar, who had ordered men to their deaths without flinching, now seemed a lovelorn fool, so desperate to possess his darling that he could not endure the appropriate waiting period. Paraphrasing a verse from a Greek play, wits quipped that parents who had children after only three months were indeed fortunate. The implication, of course, was that Octavian was Decimus' natural father, and the efforts to confirm Tiberius Nero's paternity were all a vain charade.

One may wonder why Octavian, who was not unconcerned about his public image, chose to endure the consequent criticism and ridicule of rushing the marriage. Why did he not simply wait until the baby was born and the paternity undisputed?

Despite the improvement of his relations with the aristocracy, Octavian still faced serious troubles. His alliance with his fellow Triumvirs was uneasy. The province of Gaul, which fell within his jurisdiction, was both administratively disorganized and disrupted by restive marauding natives. Bellicose tribes in Illyria (roughly modern Austria, Slovenia and Croatia) were raiding Roman borderlands. War with Sextus Pompeius was inevitable. One or more of these factors could potentially call Octavian away from Rome on a moment's notice. It behooved him to marry Livia as quickly as possible, once essential legal and religious requirements had been satisfied.

The unusual marriage was not the only scandal imputed to Octavian at this time. Enemies impugned him with a variety of improprieties against which he had virtually no legal defense. The weak Roman laws regulating slander in political invective were seldom enforced. Lucius Antonius and Sextus Pompeius had charged Octavian with effeminacy and homosexuality. Accusations of womanizing were abetted, by the aggressive haste with which he had taken Livia.

Some adversaries complained of the passion for gambling, which Octavian would maintain throughout his life. Others sneered he was excessively fond of expensive furniture, and had proscribed some men simply to gain possession of their rare Corinthian bronze vases. On one occasion, Octavian hosted some sort of private celebration. The event became known as ***The Banquet of the Twelve Gods***, because the participants dressed as different divinities. Octavian's enemies maintained this affair squandered food at the very time the Romans were suffering shortages at the hands of Sextus Pompeius.

The newly married couple countered their critics by proceeding to live very decorously, in accord with traditional Roman standards of morality. Octavian was scrupulously faithful to his new wife, and she to him. Livia and her servants spun and wove cloth from which they fashioned the garments the family wore. Together they kept Octavian's home clean, well ordered, and comfortable.

The first house Octavian shared with Livia seems to have been situated in a commercial district. Suetonius describes it as a modest dwelling, located near the Forum and above the *Scalae anularii*—the Stairs of the Ringmakers. Two years later, in 36 BCE, Octavian and Livia moved to a residence on the Palatine Hill, Rome's most exclusive and fashionable district. Despite its prestigious location the second house was as unpretentious as the first.

During the first decade of his marriage to Livia, Octavian was almost continually engaged in warfare, political as well as military. He may have assumed the various public reactions to his unorthodox marriage would cease, once the next crisis erupted and the Romans' attention was refocused. This is precisely what happened in the summer of 38 BCE, after Octavian launched a disastrous naval attack against Sextus Pompeius. The unconventional nuptials were forgotten as Sextus strutted and plundered and the Romans cried for redress.

In 37 BCE the Triumvirate was renewed for a second five-year term, but only after disagreement between Antony and Octavian over the disposition of troops nearly precipitated civil war between the two. Thereafter Octavian focused his time and energy on developing a new military strategy against Sextus.

After another failed campaign, Octavian finally overpowered Sextus in 36 BCE. The Senate responded with a number of significant honors, one of which directly involved Livia. Octavian was permitted to host, in the company of his wife and children, a celebratory banquet for the citizens of Rome in the temple of the goddess *Concordia*. This was not a new concept, but a privilege many victorious generals had enjoyed. Ceremonial banqueting was associated with the *triumphus*, a festal procession that was Rome's highest military honor. A similar but somewhat less distinguished parade was the *ovatio*, which Octavian was now granted for having prevailed against Sextus.

Sextus fled into Syria, where Mark Antony had him hunted down and executed in the following year (35 BCE). To commemorate this achievement, Octavian had the banqueting privilege conferred upon his brother-in-law. This particular honor drew public attention to the women of Octavian's family. Octavian had earlier shared it with his little daughter Julia as well as with Livia. The wife associated with Antony's distinction was Octavian's sister Octavia. Two of the children, the daughters of Antony and Octavia, were Octavian's nieces.

Octavian obtained still other distinctions for his wife and sister. One of the honors he had received, in connection with his *ovatio*, was personal sacrosanctity. In 35 BCE he procured the same privilege for Livia and Octavia. Verbal or physical abuse of a person imbued with such protection violated a religious taboo. It had been traditionally reserved for Vestal Virgins to protect their chastity, and for plebeian tribunes to prevent their assault by patricians whose legislation they scuttled.

A year later (34 BCE), Livia and Octavia received exemption from *tutela*. The premise behind this guardianship of a woman's person, was that she lacked the necessary degree of *auctoritas* to induce participants to take contracts seriously and abide by their terms. Conversely, release from *tutela* implied the individual so honored possessed sufficient *auctoritas* to bind contracts without the intervention of a *tutor*. The only women routinely exempted from *tutela* were the Vestals. This meant, for Octavia and Livia, that the privilege had a divine quality.

It was more Octavia than Livia, whom Octavian wished to promote at this time. In 39 and then 37 BCE, the Triumvirate had issued coins bearing Octavia's likeness. She was the first woman in Roman history to receive such an honor. As the wife of one Triumvir and sister of another, Octavia was a significant unifying force in their relationship. She had been highly instrumental in diffusing the 37 BCE dispute between her husband and brother, which had almost destroyed the Triumvirate. Furthermore Mark Antony's association with the Egyptian client queen Cleopatra VII, which had begun in 41 BCE, was growing more and more serious. By drawing public attention to Octavia, her brother impressed upon the Romans as well as Antony and Cleopatra themselves, that Antony's sympathies belonged with his Roman wife and nation.

The legendary relationship of Antony and Cleopatra—for millennia a favorite topic of historical and literary writers—has been subject to considerable analysis, speculation, and distortion. That it was personal and sexual goes without question. The couple was formally married, under Egyptian and/or Macedonian[9] (albeit not Roman) law; and they had three children. Stories of debauchery and degeneration, which arose from Octavian's opposition propaganda, are exaggerations.

Cleopatra's political aspirations were clear enough. She wanted to restore Egypt—at present a tribute paying satellite of Rome—to her former glory, as an independent nation with vassals of her own. Antony seems to have regarded himself, not only as the Roman ambassador but as the personal patron of the Roman client states. Egypt was not the only eastern principality to which he had bound himself by marriage. Pythodoros was a nobleman of Tralles, one of the independent city-states of Asia Minor. His wife Antonia, if not Antony's own child, was the daughter of a retainer who had named his offspring for Antony. The daughter of Pythodoros and Antonia subsequently married Polemon, whom Antony had installed as client king of Pontus.

Despite Octavian's impugnation of his loyalty, Antony began to stress his commitment to Cleopatra more than ever. Antony invaded Parthia late in 36 BCE. He suffered a stunning defeat which forfeited yet more legionary standards to the enemy. Cleopatra and Octavia alike supplied food and clothing for the battered Roman survivors. Antony accepted Cleopatra's gift but rejected Octavia's.

Then, in 34 BCE, Antony staged an elaborate ceremony in Egypt's capital city. The event is known today as the ***Donations of Alexandria***. It granted Cleopatra and her descendants control over certain territories, which were currently claimed by Rome but had once been ruled by Egypt.

The alienation of Roman lands to client rulers was nothing new, and had been practiced by politicians other than Antony. His timing of the ***Donations***, however, caused the Romans to regard the action with suspicion. Octavian was engaged in a highly successful military campaign (35 – 33 BCE). He subdued the rebellious natives of Illyria, and rid the Adriatic Sea of pirates.[10] As a result of Octavian's efforts, the Romans' northeastern frontier became safe and open to trade. Back in the capital, the victor used confiscated enemy treasures to finance food distributions, entertainments, and public building projects that created jobs. Octavian's popularity burgeoned, and won him election to the consulship for 33 BCE. By contrast Antony had come to appear distant, indifferent to Roman affairs, but readily responsive to client interests.

In 32 BCE or possibly late in the previous year, the elder Tiberius Claudius Nero died. His namesake son delivered his eulogy. Tiberius, now aged nine, and Decimus, aged five or six, went to live with and be raised by their mother and stepfather. The boys' father had designated

Octavian as their legal guardian. Octavian had held custody of Julia, his daughter by Scribonia, since the day the girl was born. Julia was now about seven years old.

The Second Triumvirate expired in 32 BCE, and was not renewed. Antony formally divorced Octavia and proclaimed Cleopatra his lawful wife. Thereafter, he and Octavian began a war of propaganda. Octavian portrayed Cleopatra as a self-indulgent yet domineering siren, who aspired to rule the world from a court wholly given to sybaritic debauchery. He represented Antony as the queen's demoralized, infatuated lackey. Against this image of depravity Octavian contrasted the virtuous fidelity of Octavia—the longsuffering, supportive wife whose husband had deserted her for a dissolute and calculating, foreign queen. Octavia managed Antony's property interests, raised his children by Fulvia as well as the two daughters she had borne him, and offered aid to his beaten troops, only to be rebuffed and ultimately divorced.

Antony responded by bringing up *The Banquet of the Twelve Gods*, and other scandals associated with Octavian. Livia figured in several of these rejoinders. As Octavian's wife she was a natural target for retaliation in response to her husband's attacks upon Cleopatra. Antony reiterated the unconventional circumstances, under which Octavian and Livia began their marriage. He accused Octavian of adultery with men as well as with women. Antony also insinuated that Octavian was planning to divorce Livia so he could marry the daughter of Cotiso, the client king of a Thracian people known as the Getae. The parallel to Antony's relationship with Cleopatra is unmistakable. Antony further maintained, that Octavian had repudiated Scribonia because she complained of his attraction to a rival (Livia?). This was a logical rebuttal to Octavian's portrayal of Antony as Cleopatra's tool.

For some reason, Antony uses Livia's family name derogatorily. "Do you still embrace only Drusilla?" [11] he sneered after Octavian deplored the liaison with Cleopatra as adulterous. In a similar vein, Antony addresses his rival as Thurinus, utilizing the *cognomen* neither Octavian nor his father ever employed.

The surname Thurinus arises from Thurii Copia, a coastal town on south Italy's Gulf of Taranto. The site was that of ancient Sybaris, a Greek colony renowned for its extravagant luxury. Near this locale, Octavian's father as *praetor peregrinus* had subdued a band of renegade slaves.

Drusus derives from Drausus, the name of a Gallic enemy whom a Marcus Livius killed in hand-to-hand combat. To commemorate the achievement, the Senate decreed that Livius and his descendants should bear his adversary's name as a *cognomen*. The designation subsequently corrupted into its more familiar form.[12] As far as we can deduce from available evidence, Livia was the only woman of the line to use the feminine diminutive. Furthermore, she eventually dropped it. She is called Drusilla in only a few laudatory inscriptions which date from the early part of her husband's reign.

We can only speculate upon Livia's reasons for changing her nomenclature. There is no way to tell whether Antony lampooned her surname because she had ceased to use it, or if she relinquished the name because his ridicule clung to it. Evidently she did not dislike the appellation Drusilla; otherwise her grandson would not have given the name to his daughter. Nor does Livia's abandonment of the designation represent an effort to disassociate herself from her father, Octavian's former enemy. Inscriptions honor both her parents. Tiberius gave celebratory games in Claudianus' memory. Decimus commemorated his maternal ancestry by changing his name to Nero Claudius Drusus.

Livia's known acquaintances, in her later years, included a Livia Ocellina and a Livia Medullina. A Livia Orestilla was married, for a period of two days, to our Livia's deranged great-grandson Gaius Caligula. Livia Drusilla may have originally employed her *cognomen* to differentiate herself from relatives who bore the same *gentilicum*. Once people had begun to associate Livia with Caesar's wife, the need for the distinguishing Drusilla became obsolete.

Antony's unflagging adherence to Cleopatra ultimately turned the xenophobic Romans against him. Octavian easily won reelection to the consulship for 31 BCE. Municipalities throughout Italy and the western provinces, fearing the prospect of foreign domination, swore to him an oath of loyalty.

Early in 31 BCE, Octavian issued a formal declaration of war specifically against Cleopatra. (He thereby offered Antony one last opportunity to abandon her). On September 2 of the same year, Octavian's naval forces defeated Antony's near the promontory of Actium, on the northwestern coast of Greece. Antony and Cleopatra retreated to Alexandria. Octavian returned to Italy, where he disbanded and paid the majority of his troops. At Rome, the Senate made his birthday a religious holiday.

Since Cleopatra had not surrendered, Octavian led a force to Egypt in the following summer (30 BCE). He occupied Alexandria with ease; the few troops who had remained with Antony and Cleopatra after Actium, now deserted. The infamous couple committed suicide to avoid certain capture. Octavian claimed Egypt, not as a Roman province but as his personal duchy. He stayed for a year at headquarters on Rhodes, making sure the alliances of other eastern client kingdoms remained intact in the wake of Antony's death.

Livia most certainly did not accompany her husband to Actium or to Alexandria. It is recorded, that she never set foot in the Senate or the military camps, venues from which the Romans traditionally excluded women. Octavian had allowed resentment and disgruntlement, over Cleopatra's presence at the battlefields, to prompt desertions from Antony's forces. Similar attendance by Livia would have compromised this strategy. Livia may nonetheless have joined her spouse at Rhodes once the war was over. She would become famous for accompanying Octavian on his various junkets.

In August of 29 BCE, Octavian returned to Rome. There he celebrated a massive, three-day triumph for his victories in Illyria, at Actium, and at Alexandria. His reentry into the capital marked the beginning of a new phase in Roman and world history.

NOTES TO CHAPTER I

[1] Cicero was a *novus homo.*

[2] Although authority is its English cognate, *auctoritas* perhaps best translates as clout.

[3] See Saint Paul's greetings to women in Romans 16.

[4] The Roman calendar system—including the Ides—is fully explained in Appendix III.

[5] Recipients were usually those who were entitled to land in return for military service, or whose properties had been seized illegally.

[6] The Ciceronian **Philippics** are so called because they resemble the attacks of the Athenian orator Demosthenes upon the Macedonian king Philip II, the father of Alexander the Great.

[7] Suetonius, **Divus Augustus**, 62.

[8] Because the Romans did not understand the concept of zero, they would have counted January as the first month of this chronology. See Appendix III.

[9] Cleopatra was a Macedonian Greek, a descendant of Alexander the Great's general Ptolemy, who assumed control of Egypt after the dissolution of Alexander's empire.

[10] The descendants of the ancient Illyrians are the modern Albanians.

[11] Suetonius, **Divus Augustus** 69.

[12] In Latin no more than one vowel can occur between two consonants, except for the diphthong *ae* (as in the name Caesar).

Tiberius Claudius Nero
Louvre Museum, Paris
Photo credit: Herve Lewandowski/
Réunion des Musées Nationaux/
Art Resource, New York

THE PUBLIC FIGURE

Nero Claudius Drusus
Museo Lateranense, Vatican
Photo credit: Alinari/Art Resource, New York

CHAPTER II

THE EMERGENT EMPRESS

Octavian spent 28 BCE rethinking the position he had attained within the Roman political system. He had become immensely well liked, especially in the aftermath of his victory over Cleopatra. His popularity had combined with the Romans' now longstanding desire for governmental stability, to secure his election to the consulship for every year since 33 BCE. But Octavian had come to understand, from the usually violent experiences of predecessors in his situation, that he must circumvent the anti-monarchic provisions of the Roman constitution if he wished to retain his supreme authority permanently.

In January of 27 BCE he offered the Senate a solution in the form of a partnership. Octavian would continue to hold the consulship annually, retain control of Egypt, and govern Gaul, Spain and Syria for a term of ten years. This selection was not an arbitrary one. To insure his predominance could not be challenged, Octavian chose for himself the areas with the greatest concentrations of troops. The Senate would continue to debate and issue legislation and administer the rest of the provinces.

Cajoled by Octavian's agents—and presumably relieved it was not facing a worse proposition—the Senate readily accepted the arrangement. It also presented Octavian with an honorary *cognomen*. *Augustus*— Consecrated—is the designation by which he is best known to history. Although the Senate also voted to change the name of the month *Sextilis* to *Augustus*, Octavian did not accept this honor until 8 BCE. The new title was Octavian's alone; it did not automatically devolve upon the other members of his family. Livia did not assume the feminine form, *Augusta*.

Since 38 BCE Augustus had been calling himself *Imperator*— Commander. From this epithet arises the English word emperor. Although he retained this title, Augustus now sought a designation that would help belie the monarchic character of his station. In Latin the word *princeps* designates a leader, a premier, a foremost person, someone with a primacy more of honor than of rank. The *princeps senatus*, whose name stood first on the senatorial roster, enjoyed the privilege of speaking immediately after the consuls and consuls-elect had finished. A *princeps iuventutis* was a principal among youthful equestrians. Augustus would occasionally style himself *princeps civitatis*—Chief of State; but he preferred to be known simply as *princeps*. By itself, the word implied First Citizen. Our English word prince derives from *princeps*, as does the term principate with which historians describe Augustus' system of government.

In the summer of 27 BCE, Augustus departed for Gaul. He spent the remainder of the year in peacetime activities—reorganizing the provincial administrative machinery, planning a new system of roads, building schools, aqueducts, and other public structures. The emperor moved on into Spain early in 26 BCE, to inflict a war of subjugation upon the rebellious natives of the mountainous north.

Two young relatives accompanied the *princeps*. Livia's elder son Tiberius turned fifteen on November 16, 27 BCE. Customarily a Roman youth first donned the solid white toga of manhood, the *toga virilis*, on his fifteenth birthday.[1] The family marked the event with religious festivities and games. This coming-of-age indicated that the youth was pubescent, and ready for marriage. If his father was deceased—as was the case with Tiberius—the celebrant automatically became *sui iuris*. Meaning literally of his own right, the condition of *sui iuris* implied a man was free of *tutela*—guardianship of his person. He was now entitled to enter contracts, including marriage, without the interposition of a trustee. Legal majority—which allowed a male to vote, hold public office, and manage his property without a custodian—did not occur until the age of twenty-five.

Marcus Claudius Marcellus, Octavia's son by her first husband, had been born in the same year as Tiberius. Augustus was preparing both boys for extraordinary political careers. He had provided the best of Greek tutors for their academic education. In 29 BCE he gave the youths public exposure, by having them ride the trace horses that drew his chariot during his triumph. Now he provided them with intensive, firsthand administrative and military training.

We do not know whether Livia journeyed with her husband to Gaul. And if she continued with him to Spain, she must certainly have avoided the battlefields as off limits to women. She would have remained in Augustus' headquarters at Tarraco, on the province's Mediterranean coast.

Marcellus reentered Rome late in 25 BCE to marry his cousin, Augustus' fourteen-year-old daughter Julia. The *princeps* himself remained at Tarraco, too ill from his exertions in the wars to travel until the following spring. Livia may have preceded her husband to Rome. As the lady of his house she was responsible for preparing and mounting the wedding festivities. The bride herself was most likely made ready by her mother, Augustus' former wife Scribonia.

The Senate commemorated Augustus' eventual return by granting special privileges to his youthful *protégés*. Marcellus was inducted into the Senate, and granted the privilege of assuming the various magistracies ten years before he reached the requisite minimum ages. He was also made a pontiff. Tiberius was allowed to hold office five years early. Induced by propaganda and donatives, the Roman electorate duly responded. Marcellus won the aedileship and Tiberius the quaestorship for 23 BCE.

By now the Romans had started to surmise that Augustus was preparing his nephew to inherit, not only his personal assets but his unique political position as well. Augustus did not have a son. Much to his disappointment, his fifteen-year marriage to Livia had not produced a surviving child. Livia's only known pregnancy by Augustus ended in miscarriage. Marcellus was Augustus' closest male relative by blood. The *princeps'* two other nephews, Sextus and Marcus Appuleius, were the sons of his half-sister who was unrelated to the Caesar line. They were also too close to him in age to be viable choices for leaders of the next generation.

The emperor was probably motivated by more than just personal loyalty to his family. Despite the prevalence of adoption, the Romans were highly nepotistic. Augustus understood that his countrymen might not accept an adoptive successor if a blood relative was available.

23 BCE opened propitiously. Marcellus and Tiberius assumed their respective magistracies on January 1. As Livia's younger son Decimus turned fifteen on January 14, he very likely donned the *toga virilis* at this time.

Exuberance presently turned to calamity, however, when the emperor nearly lost his life to a conspiracy of disgruntled senators. The failed plot was followed by Augustus' struggle with a typhoid fever like illness, which nearly proved fatal. Both brushes with death prompted the *princeps* to revise the settlement he had made with the Senate four years earlier.

Although repeated consulships were certainly precedented in Roman history, they were nonetheless unconstitutional. Augustus now arranged to exercise, *ex officio*, several select functions of Republican magistracies. *Tribunicia potestas*—the power of the plebian tribunes—enabled him to convene the Senate, to veto legislation he considered detrimental, and to summon the general assembly of citizens for plebiscites. Because senatorial protocol gave the consuls and other magistrates precedence over the tribunes, a special *ius primae relationis*—right of first proposal—allowed Augustus to initiate motions and open debate. A *maius imperium proconsulare*—superior gubernatorial command—gave him supreme jurisdiction over the armies and provincial administrations.

These privileges were conferred in chronologically limited but renewable terms by decree of the Senate, and with the consent of the armies and general electorate.

There could be no abuse of public office, because Augustus was now able to govern without actually holding any elected position. Disordered or threatened provinces, in which the most troops were stationed, were placed under his jurisdiction. The remaining territories were still administered by the Senate, although Augustus' *imperium* gave him the right to intervene as necessary. This concept of power—approved by the

Senate and people but actually maintained by the armies—remained the constitutional basis of the imperial office for the duration of the Roman empire.

Livia, who had already enjoyed public eminence as the spouse of a Triumvir, was now all the more distinguished as the wife of the *princeps* and mother of a privileged son. Octavia, however, remained the most prominent woman of Augustus' house because she was the mother of his intended heir. Then disaster struck without equivocation. Augustus' heir-apparent Marcellus had fled to the resort of Baiae (modern Baia) on the Gulf of Puteoli (Pozzuoli). There he hoped to evade the ailment that had nearly killed his uncle. But despite this precaution the young man contracted the dreaded disease. Marcellus perished in the autumn of 23 BCE at the age of nineteen.

Construction of a large public portico, financed by the spoils of Augustus' Illyrian wars, was nearing completion. The *princeps* by way of consolation named the structure for his bereaved sister. She in turn dedicated the edifice to the memory of her deceased son. The *Porticus Octaviae* was lavishly adorned with marble facades. It housed a public assembly room, an art gallery, and extensive library collections in both Greek and Latin.

Octavia used her own resources to enlarge the building's artistic and literary collections and endow curators for each. She also presented a generous donative in gold to the poet Vergil (Publius Vergilius Maro). Vergil, who was composing the propagandizing epic **Aeneïs (The Aeneid)** on commission from Augustus, had included a description of Marcellus in the poem.

Marcellus' death did not alter the status of Livia or of Tiberius. The latter continued to advance in the advantaged political career his stepfather was arranging for him. Because he turned twenty in November of 22 BCE, Tiberius was eligible for the aedileship of the following year. It seems likely that in this capacity, he presented stage plays and lavish gladiatorial exhibitions. Augustus and Livia helped finance the presentations at great expense to themselves.

Tiberius dedicated the spectacles to the memory of his father Nero and of his maternal grandfather Drusus Claudianus. Furthermore at some time—perhaps now, in connection with his coming-of-age—Livia's younger son changed his name from Decimus Claudius Nero to Nero Claudius Drusus. This focus on Livia's father and ex-husband suggests Augustus felt a continuing need to stress his reconciliation with his former enemies. The conspiracy of the preceding year likely alerted the emperor to the persistence of this resentment. He entrusted the prosecution of Fannius Caepio, one of the plot's two ringleaders, to Tiberius. This seems like a mollifying gesture, since Tiberius was at once a son and grandson of Octavian's victims. Tiberius' suit succeeded admirably: the Senate found Caepio guilty of high treason.

Suetonius' description of Tiberius' early public activities reveals a distinctly privileged career. As a defense attorney Tiberius represented the client king Archelaus of Cappadocia, and two principalities: the city of Tralles in Asia Minor and the region of Thessaly in Greece. He secured an acquittal for each on differing charges, before no less a tribunal than that of Augustus himself. After being devastated by earthquakes, the cities of Laodicea and Thyatira in Asia Minor and the Aegean island of Chios asked Tiberius to solicit the Senate on their behalf. The young patron complied and obtained the desired relief. As administrator of Rome's grain supply (*praefectus annonae*), Tiberius alleviated a local food shortage. He also undertook the special assignment of investigating conditions in slave workhouses throughout Italy.

The emperor's partiality toward his stepson did not imply, however, he had chosen Tiberius to replace Marcellus as heir-apparent. Augustus desired a successor who shared his bloodline. Moreover his two recent brushes with death, while Marcellus was yet young and relatively untrained, had convinced the emperor he needed a regent. Marcus Vipsanius Agrippa was about the same age as Augustus.[2] They had been close friends since childhood. Agrippa's extraordinary military acumen caught the attention of Julius Caesar, who sent him to Apollonia to be trained at young Octavius' side. Agrippa had supported and advised his comrade through the Triumviral years. His brilliant military strategies had won Octavian's wars against Sextus Pompeius, in Illyria, at Actium, and in Alexandria. Agrippa had helped formulate and then implement the new system of government. Now by means of special senatorial grants, Augustus gave Agrippa powers of command second only to his own.

Agrippa had married Caecilia Attica, the daughter of Cicero's famous correspondent, in 37 BCE. For unknown reasons the union was short-lived. It nevertheless lasted long enough to produce Vipsania, who was betrothed to Tiberius while they were both yet children. Agrippa subsequently wed Marcella, the elder of Octavia's two daughters by her first husband. This marriage also resulted in a daughter, who eventually married a man named Quintus Haterius. Now, in 21 BCE, Augustus asked Agrippa to divorce Marcella and marry her brother's widow Julia. Agrippa was forty-one years of age; his bride was eighteen. At the behest of her mother Octavia the discarded Marcella espoused Iullus Antonius, the second son of Mark Antony and Fulvia. (The elder son Octavian had executed at Alexandria.)

Augustus had high hopes for his daughter's new marriage. If all went according to plan, Julia would bear her second husband a son. Father and grandfather would train and promote the heir to be the next *princeps*. Should anything befall Augustus before a grandson was ready to succeed him, Agrippa was able and available to step in as regent.

Except for an occasional trip to Rome, Augustus had been residing in Sicily since late in 23 BCE. Livia must certainly have been with him. The *princeps* had been making adjustments in the island's administration. Sicily was under his jurisdiction rather than the Senate's.

Sometime in 21 BCE, Augustus left Sicily for an extended tour of the empire's eastern possessions. This was to be primarily a working journey, designed to address administrative and diplomatic issues. Augustus made a point of visiting Sparta, and giving the city control of the island of Cythera (and hence of its tax revenue). The emperor's excursion to Sparta supports other evidence Livia accompanied her husband on his eastern junket. Dio Cassius asserts Augustus wished to reward the Spartans, for having sheltered Livia and her first husband after their flight from Perusia. Sparta, moreover, had consistently supported Octavian during the war with Cleopatra. Perhaps Octavian's new marriage to Livia, a member of Sparta's patron Roman *gens*, drove this particular loyalty.

After visiting mainland Greece, the emperor wintered on the Aegean island of Samos. The locale was at once pleasant, and strategically located for easy access to Roman interests in the eastern Mediterranean.[3] With the arrival of spring he crossed to Asia Minor, then journeyed southward to Syria and subsequently to Judaea. Augustus reformed the governments of imperial and senatorial provinces alike. He reaffirmed client alliances, and seized the chance to score a major diplomatic victory over Parthia. In return for Roman assistance against a pretender, the Parthian king Phraates surrendered his claim to Armenia. Phraates also agreed to restore the legionary standards captured from Crassus and Antony. Tiberius led an expeditionary force into Armenia, where he installed a loyal Roman client ruler and received the standards.

Upon returning to Rome in October of 19 BCE, Augustus met his first grandchild who was already a year old. Julia had presented Agrippa with a son, to whom they gave Augustus' forename of Gaius. In the early months of 19 BCE, Livia's younger son Drusus had married Augustus' youngest niece. Antonia Minor was the second daughter of Octavia and Mark Antony. We do not know when the union of Tiberius with Vipsania was solemnized. Augustus proceeded with the advancement of his stepsons' political careers. The day after his return to Rome, the *princeps* secured for Tiberius the honorary rank of ex-praetor, and for Drusus the right to stand for the elective magistracies five years before reaching the appropriate age.

17 BCE proved an auspicious year for the imperial family. On January 29 Julia bore Agrippa a second son, Lucius. By now adopting both his grandsons, Augustus took another step toward making them his legal heirs and successors. By this time, the minimum ages for tenure of the praetorship and consulship had been reduced by ten years. (The exact date of the change is unknown.) One could now be praetor at thirty, and consul at thirty-three. Exercising his right to hold public office five years early, Tiberius stood successfully for the praetorship of 16 BCE. Drusus, who enjoyed the same privilege with regard to age, was elected quaestor.

At harvest time in 17 BCE a unique religious festivity was held. As their designation indicates, the *Ludi Saeculares*—Centennial Games— were celebrated once every 100 to 110 years. Their current observance had been postponed since 49 BCE on account of continual warfare and civil strife. Augustus seized the opportunity to associate the event with the stability his new regime was bringing to Rome and her dominions.

In 16 BCE Augustus returned to Gaul. He would remain there, headquartered at the capital city of Lugdunum (modern Lyons), for the next three years. Augustus took Tiberius along to assist him, as he reorganized the provincial administration and fortified the frontiers. Drusus by a special senatorial decree took over his brother's praetorial duties in Rome. A year later Augustus appointed Tiberius to a one-year term as *legatus* (military governor) of Gaul; and Drusus joined the imperial entourage. The two brothers conducted localized military raids to keep native Alpine peoples from encroaching on Roman territory.

Archaeological evidence presents the possibility Livia and Octavia both accompanied Augustus. The Gallic city of Glanum (modern Saint Rémy, France) placed statues of both women in a civic temple complex. The facial features and hairstyles of the likenesses date from the period of Augustus' second junket to Gaul. Religious veneration of the emperor's family, —a subject that will be fully discussed in a subsequent chapter, —was not prevalent in Gaul during Octavia's lifetime. The statues consequently suggest that Livia and Octavia either visited the city, or collaborated in presenting it with some sort of entitlement.

Early in 13 BCE, Augustus and Tiberius reentered Rome. Tiberius, who had been elected consul *in absentia*, now assumed that office. Drusus remained in Gaul as the new imperial legate. He would spend the next four years in aggressive military action, against resistive German tribes in the region between the Rhine and the Elbe.

By now the women of Augustus' family had come to enjoy a variety of public honors at Rome. Back in 22 BCE, Augustus had named the *Porticus Octaviae* for his sister. The emperor further distinguished Octavia on May 7, 13 BCE, by dedicating a newly completed theater to the memory of her son Marcellus. The poet Krinagoras devoted epigrams to Antonia Minor, Octavia's youngest daughter. The Senate-controlled mint at Rome issued coins, honoring Augustus' daughter Julia as the mother of his designated heirs.

Similar acknowledgments for Livia in the capital were comparatively sparse. Two poetic references are the only distinctions we know she received at Rome, between the Triumviral period and her return from Gaul in 13 BCE. Neither poem mentions Livia in her own right, but in conjunction with Octavia. In an ode that celebrates Augustus' victories in Spain, the poet Horace (Quintus Horatius Flaccus) describes the conqueror's exultant wife and sister. Krinagoras prays to Hera for

Antonia's success in childbirth, over which her husband, mother, and mother-in-law may rejoice. Neither poet mentions Livia, or Octavia for that matter, by name.

Livia's frequent and prolonged travels may account, in part, for her relatively limited public recognition at Rome. She was physically absent from the city for most of the fifteen years between 27 and 12 BCE. Augustus may have seen little point in securing public honors for his wife until she could be present and influential in the capital. Octavia and Julia, moreover, had produced what Livia had not: heirs to Augustus' position. Honoring their mothers was one way in which the emperor drew public attention to his intended successors. Livia's barrenness must have posed somewhat of an embarrassment to her husband's focus on his progeny.

By 13 BCE, however, Livia's extended absences from Rome were over and the succession seemed secure. Augustus could now set about to remedy the deficiency in his wife's public stature. He began by associating Livia with a new and highly significant religious structure.

Augustus' reforms had rid provincial governments of corruption, violence, and ineffectiveness. The resulting stability had promoted prosperity, as residents turned from warfare and mere survival efforts to profitable agriculture and other productive pursuits. Supplementing public monies with funds of his own, the emperor constructed or restored a plethora of lavish public buildings—porticoes, theaters, basilicas, baths, granaries, aqueducts, bridges, and temples. His boast, that he had found Rome a city of brick and left her a city of marble, was entirely justified.

The emperor desired a religious symbol which, like the *Ludi Saeculares* four years earlier, would commemorate his achievement, and further justify the principate. The Senate was induced to authorize an altar to the *Pax Augusta*—the Augustan Peace. To initiate the project, Augustus conducted a solemn ceremony of consecration on July 4, 13 BCE. We discover from the friezes on the completed altar, that Augustus positioned Livia ahead of all the other women of his house. Whether she performed sacrifices or other rites connected with the consecration remains unknown.

Within a year the imperial family was back on the road. The Pannonians of Illyria were reported to be on the brink of revolt. The mere arrival of Agrippa with his troops prompted the rebels to sue for peace. Augustus departed for Athens and the *Panathanea*—the annual celebration of the city's namesake goddess. There the emperor exhibited contests of armed foot soldiers, in honor of his grandsons, the heirs-apparent. Little could the Caesars realize, at this time of familial prosperity, that bereavement and crisis loomed on their horizon.

TRAGEDIES AND FULFILLMENTS: 12 BCE TO 4 CE

In the summer of 12 BCE, after his return to Italy from his Illyrian expedition, Agrippa fell seriously ill. Before Augustus could arrive back home from Greece, the fifty-year-old Agrippa expired at his villa near Naples.

Agrippa's widow, the emperor's daughter Julia, was only twenty-seven years old at the time of her husband's death. Her sons Gaius and Lucius, respectively eight and five years of age, were far too young to assume the imperial office should something unforeseen happen to their grandfather. Augustus needed a new regent: his daughter must remarry. But as the emperor's only child and the mother of his intended successors, Julia was a person of unsurpassed political importance. Marriages reflected political alliances, so a union with Julia meant a direct alignment with the emperor. Who was worthy of Julia's stature, capable of administering the empire if necessary, and trustworthy enough to step aside once Gaius was old enough to assume control?

Augustus searched carefully for a new son-in-law/regent. He considered a host of candidates, from the equestrian as well as the senatorial order. At length, the emperor selected his elder stepson. Tiberius' wife Vipsania, already the mother of their son, was pregnant for a second time. Tiberius nevertheless agreed to divorce her and accept betrothal to Julia. The child Vipsania was carrying did not survive to adulthood.

News of Agrippa's death induced the Pannonians to resume their rebellious activities. After Tiberius hastened with an army to Illyria,

Julia gave birth to her third son. The boy was called Agrippa Postumus because he was born after his father's demise.

Drusus returned to Rome. He was elected urban praetor for 11 BCE, although he had completed his brother's unexpired praetorship five years earlier. The summer brought Drusus back to the German front, where his military successes earned him the honor of an *ovatio*.

Tiberius and Julia duly married in 11 BCE. The couple endeavored to put aside personal incompatibilities and make their marriage work. Julia accompanied her new spouse to his military headquarters at Aquileia, near the modern Italian border with Slovenia. There she bore her new husband a son; but the baby died shortly after birth.

Octavia expired later the same year, at the age of fifty-five. Augustus had her body placed in the temple of the deified Julius Caesar, where he pronounced her eulogy. Because the Senate ordered a period of public mourning, Drusus delivered a second funeral oration in the Forum. The Senate decreed other honors, the nature of which Dio Cassius does not specify. These Augustus declined for reasons we can only conjecture. Octavia was the first woman of the imperial family to die since the establishment of the principate. Augustus may have worried about an adverse public reaction to an excess of posthumous distinctions. Julia and Livia, moreover, had now surpassed Octavia in importance to the regime. The former was the mother of Augustus' intended heirs, the latter of his principal military leaders one of whom was now regent.

Augustus returned to Gaul in 10 BCE, to scrutinize Drusus' continuing military operations against the Germans. Tiberius accompanied his brother and stepfather, until new unrest in Illyria drew him back to that theater. Marauders were crossing the Danube to raid Pannonia; and Dalmatia was revolting against the tribute Tiberius had imposed on them.

Meanwhile, construction of the Altar of Peace was drawing to a close. The edifice was dedicated on January 30 of 9 BCE—Livia's forty-ninth birthday. Annual sacrifices, on anniversaries of this date, would perpetuate the altar's association with the empress.

In the summer of 9 BCE, Tiberius celebrated an ovation for his victory over the Pannonians. In keeping with the tradition of such occasions, the victor hosted a public banquet in the Temple of Jupiter. His guests were the men of Rome. Back in 36 BCE, on the occasion of Octavian's ovation, Livia had accompanied her husband to his celebratory banquet. Now she and her daughter-in-law Julia presided over a separate feast, at a location which remains unknown. Their guests were the women of Rome. This segregation honored the women in their own right, rather than as satellites of their men.

Livia's own maternity received particular recognition later in the same year, but under circumstances she would have preferred to avoid. Her younger son Drusus, now consul, had pushed the Roman frontier from the Rhine to the Elbe and created the new imperial province of Germania. But the young conqueror had little opportunity to savor his success. On the return march Drusus' horse slipped and rolled on him, crushing his hip and thigh. Drusus died on September 14, 9 BCE at the age of twenty-nine. His brother Tiberius escorted the body to Rome, for internment in Augustus' private mausoleum. In honor of Drusus' military victories, the Senate posthumously awarded him the *cognomen* of Germanicus.

Drusus left three small children by his wife Antonia: Nero, age six, Claudia Livilla (Little Livia) who was probably about four, and Tiberius who was a year old.[4]

The Senate ordered the erection of statues of the deceased, as a gesture of consolation to his grieving mother. Livia's name was also added to a public listing of matrons who had three or more children. Since Livia had borne only two living children, her inclusion in this tally was purely and honorary one. It nevertheless underscored the official emphasis on motherhood—Livia's own, and that of the other enumerated women.

Drusus' death prompted yet another enhancement of Livia's public representation. For the first time, she was the focus of a poet. Published late in 9, or early in 8 BCE, the **Consolatio ad Liviam (Consolation to Livia)** is a rambling panegyric that extols the empress and her late son. Its anonymous author was an imitator of the poet Ovid (Publius Ovidius Naso)—perhaps one of his pupils, whose ranks included his own stepdaughter Perdilla.

The poet of the **Consolation** praises Livia for her devotion (*pietas*) and demureness (*pudicitia*). Both qualities were considered essential characteristics of an ideal matron. The same writer calls Livia *princeps Romanae*. As *Romanae* denotes Romans in the feminine, *princeps Romanae* describes Livia as chief among Roman women—i.e. First Lady.

Within a year another poetic tribute addressed Livia by name. Gaius Maecenas died in 8 BCE. Maecenas, like Agrippa, had been Augustus' confidant since childhood. He was of Etruscan extraction and enormously wealthy, but of equestrian rather than senatorial rank. Maecenas never entered politics, preferring to use his immense resources to support the finest poets and writers of the era. His *protégés* included the poets Vergil and Horace, as well as the great historical chronicler Livy (Titus Livius). Maecenas used his artistic influence to become Augustus' unnamed minister of propaganda. In return for his sponsorship, Maecenas' literary charges sang the praises of the *princeps* and his new world order.

An unknown poet—most likely the author of the **Consolation**—composed two elegies in honor of this great patron of literary art. The second elegy ends with a prayer for the prosperity of the imperial family—of Augustus, Gaius and Lucius, Tiberius the new son-in-law/regent, and of Livia. May she be free from anxiety.

Augustus had built the *Porticus Octaviae* to show his commiseration for his sister after the death of her son Marcellus. Following the demise of Drusus, the emperor ordered and financed a similar structure which he named for Livia. The new edifice was completed in 8 BCE. In that same year, Augustus formally accepted the renaming of the month Sextilis in his honor. Tiberius had continued the task, begun by his brother Drusus, of subjugating the inhabitants of Germania. The Senate awarded him a military triumph; and he was elected consul for a second time.

Tiberius' triumph took place on January 1, 7 BCE, the same day on which he assumed his consulship. This was the feast of Janus, the Roman god of passing years, who looked simultaneously into the past and the future. As part of the festivities, the honoree and his mother dedicated the newly finished portico, which stood on the Esquiline Hill. Cool, shady, and aesthetically pleasing, the *Porticus Liviae* promptly became a favorite concourse to which the Romans came for relaxation. Ovid described the pleasures of its walkways in his **Ars Amatoria (The Art of Love)**, which he published in 1 CE. Pliny the Elder, writing between

69 and 79 CE, describes a great grapevine which not only festooned the portico, but yielded 14 *amphorae* (approximately 80.5 gallons or 304.73 liters) of wine per year.

Tiberius once again hosted a banquet for the men of Rome in the temple of Jupiter. As before, Livia and Julia feasted the women at an unknown site. A new *aedes* (shrine), to the goddess *Concordia*, had also been finished by the beginning of 7 BCE.[5] Since no trace survives today, of either the *aedes* or of the *Porticus Liviae*, their exact locations cannot be ascertained. Cryptic comments, however, by Ovid and Dio Cassius alike, suggest the shrine stood at the center of the portico. Livia's first association with public banqueting had been in the old temple of *Concordia*. Very conceivably, then, the women's banquet of 7 BCE took place in the new sanctuary.

The *Aedes Concordiae* was one of several building projects that Livia herself conducted, in the years that followed Drusus' death. She was not the first imperial woman to take an interest in building projects. Octavia had used her own resources to embellish her namesake portico. Sometime before 16 BCE, Octavia convinced her brother to bestow a comfortable pension upon an elderly military engineer named Marcus Vitruvius Pollio. He used his retirement to produce a monumental study of Roman architecture.

When Agrippa died he left unrealized plans for a portico to house an immense map of the empire. His sister Polla assumed responsibility for the project. She executed the financial provisions for the structure that her brother had left in his will. Polla then directed the construction of the edifice, until her own death in 7 BCE forced Augustus to supervise the completion of the *Porticus Vipsaniae*.[6] Polla also added adornments to the great Roman racetrack, the *Circus Maximus*.

Livia adorned her new shrine of *Concordia* with a collection of gemstones. One of these was the fabled Sardonyx of Polykrates, which reputedly brought misfortune to its owner. The empress also embellished the temple of Jupiter with a huge crystal, which weighed 150 pounds.

Another of Livia's new buildings was a source of nutrition. An immense meat market, the *Macellum Liviae*, was completed in 7 BCE. It stood between the present church of San Vito and basilica of Santa Maria Maggiore.

Like Octavia and Polla before her, Livia financed her structures with her personal resources, and oversaw their construction. The empress may have found these ventures emotionally therapeutic after the loss of her son.

By now Livia had begun to play an active role in provincial and foreign affairs. An inscription from Mytilene, the principal city on Lesbos, commemorates the return of envoys the Mytileneans had sent to Augustus. Although the mission of the embassy is unknown, it was clearly successful. After lavishing much praise and gratitude upon the emperor, the inscription extends greetings to Livia, to Octavia, their children, and kinsfolk. The reference to Octavia indicates the inscription predates her death in 11 BCE. A second inscription specifically thanks Livia, for mediating with her husband on the embassy's behalf.

Similar inscriptions show that Livia interceded with Augustus, for the city of Aphrodisias in Asia Minor. At first, the emperor declined the Aphrodisians' request, on the ground their city had already received its fair share of benefactions. Eventually he yielded to Livia's appeals and allowed the Aphrodisians the entitlement they sought.

An inscription from Athens calls Livia 'ευεργέτης—efergetys (benefactress). She is similarly addressed in an inscription from the island of Thasos, off the northeastern coast of Macedonia. This Greek word, meaning literally one who does good works, implies an individual who has rendered special service to the state.

On a separate occasion Livia asked Augustus to confer Roman citizenship on a Gaul. The reason for her interest in the Gaul is not known. Feeling that citizenship should be the exclusive privilege of Italians, the emperor rejected his wife's request. He must nevertheless have agreed with Livia's assessment that the Gaul deserved special consideration. In lieu of Roman citizenship, Augustus granted the Gaul exemption from the obligation of paying tribute. This suggests the Gaul was a *foederatus*—a chieftain whose tribe was permitted to settle on Roman lands for a fee. Livia very likely encountered him during one of Augustus' three sojourns in Gaul.

Two kings—Phraates of Parthia and Herod of Judaea—had sent their sons to Rome, to be educated under Augustus' direction.[7] The young charges most likely lived in the complex, which the emperor had constructed adjacent to his own mansion. The princes took their lessons in the company of Augustus' grandsons. Since Livia ran the household, the task of educating the youths fell to her. Tradition held Roman matrons responsible for educating the children under their care. As Livia was highly learned herself, she would have had no difficulty selecting even the most advanced and specialized curricula for her students.

Years earlier Octavia had agreed to rear the three children Mark Antony had fathered on Cleopatra, along with Juba the orphaned prince of Numidia. The fates of Alexander Helios and Ptolemy Philadelphus, the sons of Antony and Cleopatra, remain unknown. Juba married the couple's daughter, Cleopatra Selene. Their daughter espoused Antonius Felix, who as governor of Judaea would examine accusations leveled against Saint Paul.[8] In 25 BCE, Augustus installed Juba as client king of Mauretania (roughly modern Morocco). The Roman education and values that Octavia had instilled, in Mauretania's new royal family, strengthened Rome's influence over that country. Now Livia had pupils of her own, in whom to inculcate respect for Roman institutions and culture.

Strict, time-honored adherence to monotheism made Jews the one eastern people upon whom ruler adoration could not be imposed. The kingdom of Judaea, however, was strategically important to Rome as a buffer against Parthia; and Diasporitic Jews permeated the empire. Rather than risk certain insurrection, Augustus released Judaean and Diasporitic Jews alike from the obligation of venerating his person. The emperor and imperial family cultivated Jewish loyalty through *noblesse oblige*. Augustus perpetuated Julius Caesar's policies, which exempted Jews from Roman military service and allowed them to coin money without his image. He and Livia sent precious vessels and other adornments to the great Temple of Yahweh in Jerusalem. At Rome, Agrippa constructed a synagogue. Years later, in 1 CE, Augustus' grandson Gaius made a point of not offering pagan prayers when he passed through Jerusalem.

Augustus did not grant such indulgences without condition. In return for imperial munificence, Herod required his subjects to swear oaths in the emperor's name. The king offered daily sacrifices for the wellbeing of the imperial family. He included Augustus and Livia in his will and designated Augustus its executor. Herod also erected several temples in his realm, dedicated to the cult of Rome and Augustus. While these accommodated Greek and other non-Jewish inhabitants of Judaea, their very presence served to remind Jews of Roman suzerainty. One temple was located in Strabonis Turris, a port city that Herod expanded and embellished after the model of Alexandria. When he dedicated the edifice in 9 BCE, Herod established quinquennial games in honor of Augustus. In return, Livia sent Herod valuable furnishings to adorn his amphitheater.

Herod also adopted the policy of naming cities and other physical locales for members of the imperial family. The seaport became Caesarea. A massive tower in its harbor bore the designation Drusion. Herod called one wing of his palace at Jerusalem the Caesareum, and another the Agrippeum. He bestowed the same names upon buildings he erected at Jericho. The king rebuilt the war-ravaged town Anthedon as Agrippium. He constructed a grand new city, Σεβαστή—Sevaste (Greek for Augusta), on the heights of Samaria. Today the site is Savastiya, Israel.

After Herod died in 4 BCE, his sons pursued the same course. Shortly after his accession, Philip built the town of Julias beside the ancient city of Bethsaida, on the northern shore of the Sea of Galilee. The seaport became Caesarea Maritima, after Philip built the city of Caesarea Philippi near the source of the Jordan. Antipas rechristened the Sea of Galilee the Sea of Tiberias, and built a city of the same name on the southwestern lakeshore. Farther west, near Nazareth, lay Diocaesarea. Antipas also gave the city of Betharamphtha, east of the River Jordan from Jericho, the new name of Livias. The site is modern Tel'eilat el Ghassul, Jordan.

Around 8 BCE, Herod's widowed sister Salome aspired to marry Syllaeus, vizier to the king of the Nabataean Arabs. Livia obstructed the marriage because Syllaeus was an enemy of Rome. He had undermined Augustus' efforts to conclude a client alliance with Obadas the Nabataean king. Syllaeus hoped to exploit his marriage with Salome to compromise relations between Judaea and Rome.

The kingdom of the Cimmerian Bosporus (the Crimea, and coastal areas of southeastern Russia) lay on the northernmost shore of the Black Sea. The term *Bosporus*, which means Oxford, refers in this case to the

Kerch Strait that forms the entry to the Sea of Azov. The Cimmeri were the indigenous inhabitants of the region. Their king Asander was a loyal vassal of Rome; but when he died in 17 BCE, an anti-Roman party threatened to assume control of his realm. To forestall this, Agrippa placed the Cimmerian Bosporus under the jurisdiction of Pontus in 14 BCE. The Pontine king Polemon, another devoted Roman client, owed his throne to Mark Antony. The realm of Pontus (now in Turkey) stretched along the southeastern seaboard of the Black Sea.

To reinforce Agrippa's arrangement, Polemon married Asander's widow Dynamis. They quarreled and eventually separated. Dynamis returned to the Cimmerian Bosporus. Here she helped organize a movement to reestablish the kingdom's independence from Pontus and install herself as queen. Polemon remarried. His new wife Pythodoris was the daughter of Antony's retainer, Pythodoros of Tralles. Pythodoris bore Polemon three children: two sons and a daughter.

Dynamis apparently aspired to overthrow Polemon and appropriate direct control over both realms for herself. Her claim to Pontus was not without legitimacy. Dynamis' paternal grandfather had been Mithridates VI. This famous king of Pontus had tried to wrest control of Asia Minor from the Romans some eighty years earlier. Mithridates had conquered the Cimmerian Bosporus, and installed his son Pharnaces—Dynamis' father—as king.

In 8 BCE, Polemon endeavored personally to infiltrate the Cimmerian rebels. He was discovered and put to death. The event left Dynamis in a highly precarious position. When she divorced Polemon, she abrogated the agreement she had made with the Romans. Now his death meant her followers had captured and killed a Roman appointee. Augustus agreed to leave Dynamis in control of the Cimmerian Bosporus, so long as she demonstrated an unflagging loyalty to Rome. The queen complied. She remained scrupulously Roman-friendly (as she described herself) until she died at about the age of seventy in 7 or 8 CE. Nor did she molest Pythodoris, whom Augustus installed as queen of Pontus. Pythodoris subsequently married Archelaus of Cappodocia, her fellow client ruler and neighbor to the southeast. Pontus had originally been a part of Cappadocia.

Extant honors associate Livia with the politics of the region. A Pontic city bore the name of Liviopolis. Pontic coins represented Livia as the goddess Aphrodite. Particularly notable is a pair of Cimmerian inscriptions, in which Livia appears as benefactress to Dynamis and Pythodoris alike. We can understand an offering from Dynamis, whose inscription duly calls her queen; but why does a tribute to Livia from Pythodoris appear in Dynamis' kingdom? Did Livia suggest the terms under which Augustus granted Dynamis and Pythodoris control over their respective jurisdictions?

This may be the time in Livia's life at which she arranged, to have a great gold Greek letter *epsilon* placed in the sanctuary of Apollo at Delphi in Greece. At Augustus' suggestion, Livia had taken up the study of Greek philosophy to help herself cope with the death of Drusus. The Greeks regarded the number five, to which the letter *epsilon* corresponded, a manifestation of the creative harmony of nature. The divine representative of this principle was Apollo, a god to whom Augustus was particularly devoted. Moreover one philosophic school, the Pythagorean, held that two represented masculinity and three femininity. Their union—five—was marriage, the very institution Livia and Augustus were urging upon their fellow Romans.

But even as Livia sought solace for the loss of her younger son, his elder brother brought chagrin to his family and discomfiture upon himself. In October of 6 BCE, Tiberius abruptly abandoned the powers and privileges that were second only to his stepfather's. Leaving behind his wife, family, and friends, Tiberius retreated to the Greek island of Rhodes as a private citizen. Fatigue was the only explanation he offered for his action.

Augustus refused to accept his stepson's excuse. The emperor had little tolerance for insubordination; and he was furious at losing the support of so very important and essential an assistant. His grandson Gaius at fourteen years of age was still too young and untrained to assume any real political or military authority. To command the peacekeeping armies, which were needed to restrain the still restive Germans and Pannonians, Augustus had to rely upon generals whose abilities and loyalty he did not entirely trust. And finally, Tiberius' abandonment of his wife Julia flew in the face of imperial policies glorifying family unity. Nothing could induce Tiberius to change his mind and return to the public and familial positions he had forsaken. Augustus ranted and Livia pleaded; but Tiberius refused to budge.

Meanwhile Augustus began to augment the honors, privileges, and responsibilities of Gaius and Lucius. This move was inevitable. Since the boys were growing older, their grandfather must further their preparation to become his successors.[9]

Within a year of Tiberius' departure, Gaius turned fifteen and assumed the *toga virilis*. Augustus used the present occasion to make his grandson a pontiff, and introduce him to the Senate. That body at once gave Gaius the right to attend its meetings, to attend games and banquets in the company of senators, and to hold the consulship at the age of twenty. The men of the equestrian order, to whom Augustus had given new purpose as civil servants, proclaimed Gaius a *princeps iuventutis*. The entire routine was repeated three years later (2 BCE) for Lucius' fifteenth birthday. Both youths received the consuls' right to consecrate religious structures.

Augustus' familial difficulties deepened. In Tiberius' absence Julia took lovers. Her indiscretions directly violated her father's legislation of 18 BCE, which had made adultery a capital felony. As if to repudiate the staid domesticity Augustus was so aggressively endeavoring to promote, Julia repeatedly appeared publicly in the company of drunken revelers. To show her defiance of her father, she placed a wreath on a statue of Marsyas. Legend held that this flute-playing god of merriment had challenged Apollo, Augustus' patron deity.

Eventually Augustus' agents gathered sufficient evidence for him to bring an indictment against his daughter. The storm broke late in 2 BCE. The Senate's bestowal of the designation *Pater patriae*—Father of [his] Country—on Augustus earlier in the same year now compounded the emperor's embarrassment. While Augustus sat weeping the Senate convicted Julia on three counts of adultery. Her father made sure the penalties of his law were applied to their fullest extent. One of Julia's paramours—Iullus Antonius the husband of her cousin Marcella—was sentenced to death. The others were banished from Rome. Julia was formally divorced from Tiberius and remanded to Pandataria (modern Ventotene), one of the Pontic islands off the southwestern coast of Italy.

Julia's downfall brought Tiberius to his senses. He bombarded Augustus with apologetic, conciliatory letters—but to no avail. Angrier than ever, the emperor sharply denied his stepson's request to return home.

People throughout the empire had begun to view Tiberius with undisguised contempt. As early as 4 BCE a private citizen of Alexandria erected an altar that honored Augustus, Livia, Julia, Gaius, and Lucius—but not Tiberius. The city of Nemausus in Gaul (modern Nîmes, France), where Tiberius had lived while imperial governor, now overthrew public statues of him. Archelaus of Cappadocia openly snubbed his former benefactor by refusing to visit him at Rhodes.

The situation was aggravated by the conspicuous ambivalence of Gaius toward his former stepfather. In 1 BCE the young prince arrived at Samos on the first leg of a diplomatic mission to the Parthians. When Tiberius paid a visit, Gaius gave him an icy reception. Sometime later one of Gaius' dinner companions offered to visit Rhodes and return with the head of *the exile.*

Livia had quite understandably become anxious about her son's public image; and Augustus reacted to her concerns. After the powers of Tiberius' regency expired in January of 1 BCE, the emperor at his wife's request gave Tiberius the ambiguous designation of *legatus* (legate) to Rhodes.[10] Augustus subsequently warned Tiberius about a report, which suggested the latter had incited some military personnel toward sedition. Tiberius responded by making sure all his actions and comments were witnessed.

Augustus also made clear to the public, that recent difficulties had not compromised the unity of the Caesar family. Coins depicting Livia together with Gaius and Lucius appeared in Asia Minor. Before sending Gaius to the East, Augustus married this grandson to Livilla the young daughter of Livia's son Drusus. On May 24 of the following year (1 CE), the elder son of the late Drusus assumed the *toga virilis.* Although this youth's given *praenomen* was Nero, he preferred to be known publicly by his father's honorary *cognomen* Germanicus.

Presently the Roman-educated Phraacetes, who had succeeded his father Phraates as king of Parthia, informed Gaius his chief of staff

Marcus Lollius had been slandering Tiberius as well as betraying Roman state secrets. The treacherous Lollius ended his life by suicide.

The choice for Lollius' successor, a man who must suit Augustus and Gaius alike, reveals both were softening toward Tiberius. Publius Sulpicius Quirinius Cyrenius was distantly related to Livia and married to a cousin of hers. He was one of the few allies who had patently refused to desert Tiberius. While antipathy toward the exile was at its acme, Quirinius had defied popular opinion by visiting his kinsman at Rhodes.

Augustus and Gaius finally relented to some extent, in the late summer of 2 CE. Tiberius could return to Rome on condition he took no part in public affairs. On October 7 of that year, Tiberius supervised the assumption of the *toga virilis* by his son, Drusus Claudius Nero. For eighteen months thereafter Tiberius lived reclusively. He tended to personal issues, but upheld his agreement not to engage in political activities.

By 2 CE, Livia was the only woman of the imperial house who held a high degree of public prominence. Octavia and Polla were dead; Julia was in disgrace. Augustus' four nieces appeared at state functions such as the consecration of the Altar of Peace. Nevertheless no record specifically indicates any these daughters of Octavia enjoyed special honors. The two Antonias may have cooperated in sponsoring construction of a basilica; but firm association of the *Basilica Antoniarum* with this pair of sisters is inconclusive.[11] Augustus' aunt Atia and Marcia her daughter confined their civic activities to patronage of the arts.

The imperial granddaughters were still comparatively young, and just emerging into public notice. Vipsania Julia, the elder who turned nineteen in 2 CE, had married Lucius Aemilius Paullus. He was the son of the elder Julia's half-sister Cornelia, daughter of Scribonia by a husband who preceded Octavian. Agrippina the younger princess was around fourteen in 2 CE. She was betrothed to Livia's grandson Germanicus, whom she would marry in 5 CE. Germanicus' sister Livilla, the bride of Gaius, was around the same age as Agrippina.

But Livia's singular exaltation would soon increase all the more, as the result of another grievous tragedy for the Caesar family. Gaius and Lucius both perished, within eighteen months of each other. In the summer of 2 CE, eighteen-year-old Lucius departed for military training in Spain. At Marseilles he contracted the fever to which he succumbed. Having persuaded Phraacetes to maintain Parthian neutrality toward Armenia, Gaius entered that disputed nation and crowned a new Roman client king in the summer of 3 CE. Gaius was preparing to depart for Arabia, perhaps hoping to undo the damage Syllaeus had inflicted on Roman interests there, when an Armenian nationalist stabbed him. The wound refused to heal. Gaius became despondent as he struggled against lingering pain and infection. He resigned his various positions and titles, and announced his intention to remain in Syria as a private citizen. His grandfather, however, pressured him to return home; so the former prince began a long and agonizing journey back to Italy. After reaching Limyra in Lycia (a section of Asia Minor), Gaius Caesar died on February 21 of 4 CE.

Augustus presumably discussed his prospects for the succession with Livia as well as other advisers.[12] The emperor's nearest male relatives by blood were his third grandson Agrippa Postumus who was not yet fifteen, and his grandnephew Germanicus who was seventeen. Augustus at the age of sixty-five could not afford to wait for either youth to gain in years and experience. A qualified and capable person, ready to assume power the moment the *princeps* died or became incapacitated by age, was more urgently needed than ever.

The *princeps* put his antipathy aside, and on June 26, 4 CE formally adopted Tiberius as his heir and intended successor. Although he simultaneously adopted Postumus, Augustus clearly did not expect this grandson to become *princeps*. The emperor had misgivings about Postumus' mental capabilities. To insure the principate would eventually revert to the Caesar bloodline, Augustus obliged Tiberius to adopt Germanicus.

Livia at sixty-one had become an uncrowned queen—the wife of a ruler, the *materfamilias* of her people, the founder of a dynasty. From this point in her life the historical record begins to reveal, more than ever, the impact her position allowed her to produce on the lives and fortunes of individual people.

NOTES TO CHAPTER II

1   Boys too young for the coming-of-age rite wore the purple-bordered *toga praetextata*.

2   Since Agrippa was fifty when he died in the summer of 12 BCE, he was born no earlier than the summer of 63 BCE, and no later than that of the following year.

3   The same geographic advantage impelled Hitler to make Samos the base for German operations in the eastern Mediterranean during World War II.

4   Drusus' elder son was born on May 24, 15 BCE, the younger on August 1, 10 BCE. Livilla came between the two boys, most likely in 13 BCE. See Chapter VIII for a fuller discussion of their personal chronologies.

5   Livia's shrine (*aedes*) should not be confused with a new temple (*templum*) to *Concordia*, which Tiberius consecrated to the memory of his brother Drusus in 10 CE.

6   Polla's actual name was Vipsania of course. *Polla* is the Latin equivalent of the English sobriquet Babe.

7   The princes were essentially sent as hostages. Parthia and Judaea alike were suffering internal dissentions. Herod and Phraates wanted to be sure Augustus would not support usurpers.

8   Felix' Jewish wife Drusilla, whom Saint Luke mentions in Acts of the Apostles 24.24, was not a granddaughter of Antony and Cleopatra but a member of the royal Judaean house of Herod. Felix was thrice married.

9   Scholars have debated (pointlessly, I feel) over whether Augustus planned to have Gaius and Lucius rule jointly, in a diarchy. We cannot discern what Augustus' precise intentions were. If we assume, however, that later emperors modeled their succession provisions on the arrangements Augustus had made for his grandsons, then Gaius was to become emperor with Lucius held in reserve, to assume power immediately should anything happen to his brother.

10   The word *legatus* could refer to a military officer (roughly the equivalent of a modern lieutenant), to the governor of an imperial (as opposed to senatorial) province, or to an especially appointed envoy of the Senate or emperor. Since

Rhodes was under senatorial jurisdiction (as part of Asia Minor), Tiberius must have served in the third-mentioned capacity.

11   The edifice may date from the reign of Claudius, 41 – 54 CE.

12   Dio Cassius claims Julia was restored from exile, and thereafter strongly urged Augustus to adopt Tiberius. This statement is patently untrue. When Augustus considered designating Germanicus his direct successor, Livia urged her husband to indicate Tiberius because he was the more experienced. Consulting his sources, Dio must have confused Augustus' daughter with her own namesake daughter. This younger Julia was banished, recalled, and then banished anew.

CHAPTER III

THE YEARS OF ASCENDANCY

The Queen Consort: 4 to 14 CE

Livia was an accessible empress. Her laudatory contemporary the historian Velleius Paterculus, praises her as a woman "whose power was not felt unless for the alleviation of distress or the promotion of rank." [1] People were free to seek her help with problems they could not surmount without aid. She responded readily to cases she deemed worthy of assistance, taking care to comply both with the policies of her husband's regime and the cultural conventions of her era.

Roman tradition expected women of position and means to engage in charitable activities. Epitaphs still extant extol matrons who divided their lives between rearing their children and performing charitable activities. Livia donated, out of her sizeable personal resources, financial assistance to parents of large families and dowries to indigent brides. By doing so she supported Augustus' efforts to encourage marriage and childrearing by Roman citizens. The empress also appeared at the scenes of fires, where she exhorted the firefighting brigades her husband had established and provided assistance to the victims.

Marcus Salvius Otho was an orphan whom Livia raised in her own home. The rearing of orphans was a traditional charity for wealthy women. Otho's father was an equestrian, perhaps an imperial civil servant; but his mother was a woman of extremely low socio-economic status, possibly even a slave. Livia procured admission to the Senate for Otho, as well as a wife (identity unknown) from a highly distinguished family. Although Otho never advanced in public office beyond the praetorship, his son became consul (33 CE), and his grandson emperor (69 CE).

The practice of *patrocinium* was deeply rooted in the culture of ancient Rome. Patronage was a contractual arrangement between two individuals, one of whom was in some way more powerful than the other. The stronger partner, the patron, performed actions beneficial to the weaker party, the client. In return the client provided whatever services he was able, along with considerable deference, to the patron. This type of reciprocal arrangement was known as *obsequium* (compliance). Although an *obsequium* was not legally binding, both patron and client were socially and morally obligated to uphold it.

People from all walks of life engaged in patronage; but its incidence fell heaviest on politicians. Their positions of power enabled them to accomplish what most clients could never hope to achieve on their own. Clients in return became retainers and supporters of their patrons' political aims and strategies. We have already seen something of political patronage, in relations between the Roman state and vassal principalities.

Patronage was by tradition strictly the province of men. With the exception of destitute widows dependent on the charity of patrons for subsistence, women never entered into *obsequia* either as patrons or clients. No restriction, however, prevented a woman from privately influencing a man's decision about a patronage agreement. And nothing stopped a politician's wife, mother, or other female relation, from helping to lighten his workload by screening the pleas that came before him.

Inscriptions from the Greek East confirm the wives of Republican senators influenced their husbands' decisions about client individuals or political entities. Cleopatra knew this. When she surrendered to Octavian, she claimed she had kept back part of the Egyptian treasury as a gift for his wife and sister:

> "Is it not something terrible," she said, "O Caesar—
> since you have deemed it worthwhile to come to me
> and address me thus undone—that my slaves make

accusation because I lay aside feminine things, not indeed for me the wretched one; ornaments, however, that to Octavia and Livia I may give baubles, so from their propitiation I may find you yet more gentle?" [2]

Livia probably started to examine solicitations for Augustus' intervention on this informal yet well-accepted basis. Her travels with her husband might have encouraged her to intercede on behalf of foreign entities. At home in Rome, Livia reviewed appeals from her fellow citizens. The best known and documented is that of the poet Ovid.

Concupiscent and extravagant, Augustus' granddaughter Vipsania Julia followed in the wayward footsteps of her mother. In 8 CE the younger Julia was implicated in some sort of illegal activity and punished with banishment from Rome. Ovid seems to have been connected to this scandal in some manner. Scholars have speculated Augustus felt Ovid's erotic poems—the **Ars Amatoria (Art of Love)** and **Remedia Amoris** (**Remedy for Love**)—had contributed to the corruption of Roman morals, including those of the emperor's family.

Ovid was punished with relegation, a milder form of banishment. *Exsilium* entailed permanent expulsion from Rome, forfeiture of all civil rights, and relinquishment of up to two thirds of one's property to the state. *Relegatio* consisted of eviction without loss of property or citizenship, and usually for a specified number of years. Augustus remanded the poet to the pleasant port city of Tomis (modern Constanza, Romania), on the western shore of the Black Sea in the client kingdom of Thrace. The details of the incident, especially the precise nature of Ovid's offense, remain a mystery.

Ovid's wife, whose name may have been Fabia, was given permission to reside with her husband in Tomis. Fabia chose, however, to remain in Rome and seek a pardon for the poet. One of the avenues she explored was an appeal to Livia.

Ovid's most likely allies, among women who had access to the emperor, were the latter's aunt Atia and her daughter Marcia. Both patronized the literary arts, and were acquainted with Fabia. Nonetheless, Ovid does not indicate whether Atia or Marcia ever approached Augustus on the poet's behalf. Nor does Ovid advise his wife to seek help from any woman in the imperial family other than Livia.

Ovid coaches Fabia in the comportment and deference she must show, should indeed the empress grants her an interview at all. Fabia must also seek spiritual protection for the outcome of her appeal, with prayers, sacrifices, and attention to omens. An audience with Livia was a significant privilege.

Augustus did not reserve weighty issues to himself and his staff, and restrict Livia's attentions to relatively insignificant matters. The pleas of cities and foreign princes were certainly not trivial. Nor was Fabia's, which sought reversal of a relegation the emperor himself had mandated. Ovid nevertheless cautions his wife not to irritate Livia—and thereby endanger his cause—by approaching the empress while she is considering matters of greater import than his.

Fabia's particular petition clearly failed, for Ovid was never recalled. We do not know whether Livia or Augustus rejected the plea—assuming Fabia presented it at all. Ovid's wife was shy about approaching Livia. The poet warns Fabia not to let her timidity compromise her work on his behalf.

Although Livia's intermediary role was innovative in a society that excluded women from professional or government responsibilities, the Romans accepted and exploited it. This is evident from the high volume of petitions Livia reviewed. "For care of her own body," Ovid remarks, "there is scarcely time." [3] The empress' intervention very possibly encouraged the requests of applicants who might otherwise not come forward. Some petitioners, particularly women, very probably felt more comfortable approaching Livia than entreating Augustus or one of his male secretaries.

As early as 38 BCE, one of the consuls was Livia's kinsman Appius Claudius Pulcher. He was a nephew or grandnephew of Livia's father. Marcus Livius Drusus Libo held the consulship in 15 BCE. Appius' son was Marcus Valerius Messalla Barbatus Appianus. (His collection of names, of course, signifies his adoption by one of his father's fellow senators.) Barbatus married the younger Claudia Marcella, the second of Augustus' four nieces. Barbatus' sister Appia Claudia married Publius Sulpicius Quirinius, whom we met in Chapter II. The brothers-in-law,

Barbatus and Quirinius, were colleagues in the consulship for 12 BCE. Barbatus died shortly after the start of his term.[4]

While Livia may have encouraged some of the aforementioned marriages, she probably exercised little influence upon her kinsmen's public careers. Augustus for the most part limited preferential treatment to his heirs-apparent, his regents, and his stepsons. Although he could and sometimes did assert his *auctoritas* on behalf of a candidate, the emperor usually let elections to the traditional Republican magistracies run a natural course. His relatives and friends had to stand their electoral chances along with all the other senators.

Eventually Augustus began to promote *protégés* of Livia to high office. Quintus Ostorius Scapula, also an equestrian, was *praefectus praetorianus* (praetorian prefect—commander of the imperial guards) in 2 BCE, and thereafter *praefectus* (military governor) of Egypt. These were privileged positions whose occupants were selected by the emperor himself. That Scapula owed his exalted career to Livia's influence is suggested by his bequest to her of his slaves.

The Plautii Silvani, plebeians of senatorial rank, had been retainers of the Claudii for generations. Aulus(?) Plautius Silvanus and his wife Urgulania were clients of Livia. The 2 BCE consulship of the couple's son Marcus was made special by the fact Augustus was his colleague. This same Marcus Plautius Silvanus served as *proconsul* (governor of a province that was administered by the Senate) of Asia (western Turkey) for 4 CE. Two years later Augustus made him imperial legate (another emperor-designated military governor) of Galatia (central Turkey). His son, who was also called Marcus, married Fabia Numantina the daughter of Augustus' first cousin Marcia. The elder Marcus Silvanus' daughter Plautia Urgulanilla became the wife of Livia's grandson Claudius, the youngest child of her son Drusus.

Livia's influence upon the career of Publius Sulpicius Quirinius is somewhat more difficult to assess. Quirinius was *novus homo* from the town of Lanuvium, to the southeast of Rome. Lanuvium had special meaning for the Livii. It was here, in the fourth century BCE, that the members of the *gens* first acquired Roman citizenship. Quirinius was either unrelated to, or from an undistinguished branch of, the senatorial *gens Sulpicia*. He was a kinsman in some way to Marcus Livius Drusus Libo.

We do not know whether Livia or one of her Claudian cousins impelled Quirinius' union with Appia Claudia. Early in his career, military successes against African marauders in Cyrene won Quirinius the honorary *cognomen* of Cyrenius by which he was known to Saint Luke. Following his consulship, Quirinius began to receive appointments directly from Augustus. Between 8 and 4 BCE, Quirinius held some sort of position of power in Syria, an important province under the administration of the emperor. Quirinius was imperial legate of Galatia sometime prior to 2 CE.

Quirinius' steadfast loyalty to Livia's son Tiberius, during the latter's exile on Rhodes, occasioned his next promotion. If Livia did not instigate Quirinius' 2 CE appointment as chief of staff to Augustus' grandson Gaius, she certainly must have encouraged it. In his new post Quirinius worked to dispel the prejudice his predecessor, the treacherous Marcus Lollius, had instilled in Gaius toward Tiberius. Appia must have died, for Quirinius entered a second politically significant union in 4 CE. His bride Aemilia Lepida, a granddaughter of the former Triumvir, had been betrothed to Augustus' now deceased grandson Lucius. Quirinius was imperial legate of Syria when he supervised the creation of the Roman province of Judaea in 6 CE.

If Livia did not actively promote Publius Quinctilius Varus, she certainly accepted him as her retainer. The pairing of Varus with Tiberius as consuls in 13 BCE suggests an early alignment between Varus and the Claudii. Varus had married a daughter of Agrippa. Claudia Pulchra, the daughter of Barbatus and Marcella, either became Varus' wife subsequently or married his son. This union bound Varus to Augustus and Livia alike, since Pulchra was the emperor's grandniece as well as Livia's third cousin.

Varus was proconsul of Africa (the Roman province, now Tunisia and the Tripolitania section of Libya), perhaps in 7 BCE. From 6 to 4 BCE he served Augustus most competently as imperial legate of Syria. In 9 CE the emperor gave Varus the highly privileged command of the peacekeeping armies in Germany. But the task of controlling the rebellious natives was proving to be beyond the Romans' capabilities.

Varus took his own life after German commandoes ambushed and slaughtered three of his five legions. The *débâcle* convinced Augustus to abandon the conquests of his stepson Drusus and restrict the empire's northern frontier to the Rhine.

Augustus' appointee for imperial legate of Sicily in 4 CE was a Publius Alfidius Sabinus. Nothing more is known about him. His *gentilicum* does not necessarily confirm a kinship with Livia's mother, or even an acquaintance with the empress. Nor is there evidence that Livia was either a relative or promoter of the historian Titus Livius despite their common *gentilicum*. Livia's *protégés* are few in number. This suggests Livia herself was highly selective about individuals she commended to her husband for special promotion.

Augustus resumed his administrative duties in the summer of 4 CE after dispatching his new successor-designate to the German front. Tiberius was about to invade Bohemia, for the purpose of establishing a more defensible Roman frontier, when Augustus informed him that all Pannonia was in revolt. It took three years (6 – 9 CE) for Tiberius to crush the insurrection, after which he hastened back to Germany on the news of Varus' disaster. Tiberius organized and maintained frontier garrisons along the Rhine until 12 CE, when he delegated the task to his nephew and adopted son Germanicus.

The mental instability of Agrippa Postumus, Augustus' only surviving natural grandson, continued to increase. In 7 CE Augustus rescinded the youth's adoption and banished him. Postumus' disinheritance left Livia's descendants the undisputed successors to the imperial office. If all went as planned the position would pass from Augustus to Tiberius, and subsequently from Tiberius to Germanicus. The latter was Augustus' grandnephew as well as Livia's grandson. Moreover his marriage to Augustus' granddaughter Agrippina by 12 CE had produced three sons.

The succession would devolve upon Tiberius' son, Drusus Claudius Nero, should something unforeseen tragedy befall Germanicus. Drusus had married Germanicus' sister Livilla. As Augustus' grandniece she partook of the Caesars' bloodline and would transmit it to her children. The eventual reversion of the principate to mutual descendants of Augustus and Livia now appeared secure.

In January of 12 CE, Germanicus assumed the consulship at the age of twenty-six without having first served as praetor. His cousin Drusus received the right to hold the same magistracy in two years, also without a preliminary praetorship. On October 23 Tiberius celebrated a triumph at Rome, for his victories in Pannonia and Germany.

Augustus was now seventy-five years old and in seriously failing health. The following January he had the Senate grant Tiberius military and civilian authority equivalent to his own. For the next eighteen months, Tiberius carried out his new responsibilities under his predecessor's watchful supervision. Augustus wanted to make sure his successor had no questions or uncertainties; the transition of power must not be jeopardized by confusion. Then in the summer of 14 CE, Caesar Augustus began to relax for perhaps the first time in his adult life.

Tiberius set out for Illyricum, to investigate whether the peacetime administration he had established was running smoothly. Eager for a pleasure trip, Augustus insisted on accompanying Tiberius as far as Beneventum (Benevento) in south-central Italy. The emperor had started back toward Naples, perhaps with the intention of continuing to his villa on Capri, when his weak health deteriorated critically. Augustus took to his bed in the villa of his natural father Octavius at Nola. Acting very possibly upon instructions from her husband, Livia increased the guard around the house, had the approaching roads blocked off, and sent for her son. Augustus was still alive when Tiberius arrived; the two conferred privately for a day. Then, on the nineteenth day of the month that still bears his name, Caesar Augustus died peacefully in Livia's arms. They had been married for fifty-one years.

An order was at once dispatched for the execution of Agrippa Postumus. No one knows for sure who issued this directive; it has been attributed to Tiberius, to Livia, to their counselors, to Augustus himself. So long as Postumus remained alive, he could become a rival to Tiberius as the figurehead of an opposition party. Conscience and emotional attachment had to retire in the interests of national security. The transition of the principate had never before been attempted. No risk must be allowed to imperil its success.

The funerary cortege traveled to Rome by night, to avoid exposing the corpse to the warm summer weather. While Augustus' body lay in state in the vestibule of his home on the Palatine Hill, Tiberius convened the Senate for the reading of the deceased emperor's will. Over the course his lifetime, Augustus had amassed a vast fortune from a variety of sources: the patrimonies of Gaius Octavius and Julius Caesar; property confiscations during the proscriptions; conquest and control of Egypt; gifts from foreign potentates such as Herod; bequests from Roman citizens. Most of this wealth—upwards of 2 billion *sesterces*—the emperor had spent before his death, on the establishment of new government programs. In his will Augustus named Tiberius and Livia as his heirs. His bequests to them were comparatively small: 100 million *sesterces* to the former, and 50 million to the latter. The balance of the late ruler's assets was worth at least another 100 million *sesterces*. These monies he divided, into a gift of 43 million *sesterces* to the Roman state, donatives to each soldier under arms, and legacies to various relatives and retainers.[5]

When a Roman husband died his wife legally ceased to be a member of his family. For this reason a widow could not be her husband's lawful heir. Roman law defined an heir as a deceased's natural or adoptive descendant, who had been under the decedent's paternal authority at the time of death. This stipulation restricted ownership of an estate to successive generations of the same family. A man could provide his widow with property, in the form of a *legatum* (legacy) or a *fideicommissum* (trust). Either term refers to a portion of an estate, which the testator obliges his heirs to relinquish to a third party. An heir was legally bound to cede a *legatum* but not a *fideicommissum*. Property surrendered under either arrangement necessarily left the testator's family.

Because the private assets of the emperor were used to sponsor state programs, Augustus could ill afford to alienate any portion of them from the Caesar family. By testamentarily adopting Livia as his daughter, he enabled her to be his heir. With this method Augustus managed to provide for Livia while keeping his patrimony intact.

Augustus also mandated Livia assume the feminine form of his honorary *cognomen*. Some eastern venues had already applied this designation—*Augusta*—to Livia as well as to her stepdaughter. Now under the terms of her husband's will, Livia Caesaris officially became Julia Augusta. She was seventy-one years of age.

THE DOWAGER: 14 TO 29 CE

All Rome turned out for Augustus' funeral, the actual date of which remains unknown. Members of the Senate carried the emperor's coffin from the Palatine to the Forum, where Tiberius' son Drusus delivered a panegyric. The procession proceeded to the temple of the deified Julius Caesar, at which Tiberius pronounced the primary eulogy. The cortege continued to ancient Rome's famous park, the *Campus Martius* (Field of Mars) where the funeral pyre stood ready. After all was over, Livia remained at the cremation site for five days, in the company of the most distinguished members of the equestrian order. Then barefoot and ungirt to signify her mourning, she gathered her husband's ashes into their urn. This she placed in his mausoleum, a great domed structure he had built beside the Altar of Peace near the Tiber's bank. The building already held the remains of Marcellus, Agrippa, Octavia, the elder Drusus, and an infant son of Germanicus and Agrippina.

On September 17, 14 CE the Senate formally deified Augustus, accepted Tiberius as the new *princeps*, and executed the provisions of the late emperor's will.

Livia became one of the wealthiest, if not *the* wealthiest of Roman women, once her inheritance from Augustus was conjoined with properties she already owned. Ancient evidence—primarily in the form of inscriptions—gives us a glimpse at some of her assets. Her new name of Julia Augusta, etched on water pipes, reveals she inherited Augustus' mansion on Rome's Palatine Hill. She was co-owner (possibly co-heir) with Tiberius, of a villa at Tusculum (later called Tuscolo, now in ruins) and of properties on the Italian islands of Capri and Lipari. With Germanicus as partner Livia co-owned agricultural estates in Egypt. She also possessed tracts of land in Asia Minor near Thyatira (modern Akhisar, Turkey). Livia's slaves and freedmen, who ranged in their vocations from menial laborers to skilled artisans and administrators, numbered nearly 1,000 souls.

Livia's possessions included two monopolies, which guaranteed raw materials to state facilities. Pliny the Elder mentions a copper mine in Gaul. Its product, called *aes Livianum* rather than *Julianum Augustanum*, suggests Livia acquired the mine before Augustus died. Pliny describes the *aes Livianum* as a third-rate quality of copper, best suited for the coining of *sesterces*. This comment suggests the Gallic mine supplied the imperial mint at Lugdunum (Lyons). In Tiberius' reign Livia owned a brickyard in Campania, the region in which Naples is located. The brickyard provided municipalities throughout Italy with construction materials for buildings and other public works.

Her vast assets enabled Livia to continue the charitable projects, which she had initiated during her husband's reign. She arranged for the distribution of foodstuffs to needy families. In 16 CE Tiberius joined her in assisting victims of great fire, which had devastated areas of Rome in the vicinity of the Caelian Hill. A year later mother and son aided residents of Asia Minor in the aftermath of a devastating earthquake.

Tiberius declined many of the titles and honors the Senate voted him upon his accession. He accepted the positions of *princeps senatus* and *Pontifex Maximus* because they were essential to the execution of his office. Designation as Augustus was his by inheritance. Otherwise Tiberius allowed only the celebration of his birthday, and the erection of portrait statues provided these likenesses were not used to signify his personal divinity. Through a lifetime of hard-won achievement, Augustus had earned the titles of *Imperator* and *Pater patriae*, the renaming of a month in his honor, the right to place an oak leaf civic crown over his front door.[6] Tiberius felt he would appear overbearing and obviously monarchic, if he accepted the same honors by *fiat*.

The new emperor similarly refused honors the Senate proposed for Livia. He forbade the renaming of October in her honor, the erection of an altar in recognition of her adoption, the titles *Mater patriae* (Mother of [her] Country) of *Parens* (Parent) and the proposal that he be called *Juliae filius* (son of Julia) as well as *Augusti filius* (son of Augustus). In the provinces, however, acknowledgements of this nature flourished. An inscription from Macedonia commemorates the accession of Tiberius and Julia Augusta. This terminology cannot refer to a joint rulership between mother and son since there was none. The caption honors Livia's adoption.

In a similar vein the Jewish tetrarch Herod Antipas, who had changed the name of the Perean city Betharamphtha to Livias, rechristened the locale Julias. Coins of Leptis Magna in North Africa represented Livia as *Mater patriae*. At Gythium the port of Sparta in the Peloponnese, an annual festival commemorated Tiberius' accession. Celebrants carried Livia's statue beside that of Augustus and ahead of her son's. The implication was that the ruling emperor's parents preceded him.

Tiberius was amenable to his mother's accepting these provincial distinctions. In 15 CE he allowed her to consider the honors an embassy from Gythium proposed for her and select whichever she liked.

Tacitus, Suetonius, and Dio Cassius all maintain Livia began to dominate the operations of the principate as if she were Tiberius' co-ruler if not his superior. This is certainly exaggeration. Dio Cassius avers Tiberius' official letters bore his mother's name as well as his own; but the archaeological record disproves this assertion. Texts of Tiberius' correspondence with Gythium, preserved in inscriptions from that city, do not bear Livia's name.

The prerogatives Livia exercised after Tiberius became emperor had been conferred upon her during Augustus' reign. Dio maintains she received senators and others in her home. This implies she continued to hear petitions for her intervention, like the plea Ovid's wife had prepared years earlier. One of those who sought her assistance was Quintus Haterius Agrippa. His mother was the daughter of the elder Marcus Agrippa and Augustus' niece, the elder Marcella.

Haterius derided Tiberius before the Senate, during the hearings to confirm Tiberius' installation as emperor. Aspersions of this sort could result in the capital punishments of execution or banishment. Augustus had included slander of the head of state and his family in the legal definition of treason.

After Tiberius denounced him before the Senate, Haterius proceeded to make matters worse for himself. Seeking reconciliation with Tiberius in person, Haterius went to the palace. Here he attempted to seize Tiberius about the knees in a gesture of supplication, and ended up causing him to fall over backward. Physical assault did more than jeopardize the emperor's safety: it violated the religious sacrosanctity of his person. After barely escaping a violent death at the hands of Tiberius' bodyguards, Haterius turned to Livia for intervention. With urgent pleas, Tacitus writes, she convinced Tiberius to overlook the incident.

Tiberius' strong reaction to Haterius' affront was definitely an anomaly—if indeed it was actually as intense as Tacitus insinuates. In this early period of his reign, Tiberius exhibited considerable forbearance toward hostile public opinion. When questioned about Augustus' interpretation of slander as treason, Tiberius replied that the law must be upheld. Nevertheless at the very time of Haterius' *gaffe*, the newly installed *princeps* ignored the derision of several other senators. A year later, in 15 CE, Tiberius encouraged the acquittal of several defendants. One had been arraigned for denigrating Tiberius, two others for desecrating the memory of Augustus.

The 17 CE trial of Appuleia Varilla reveals that Livia too embraced an indulgent policy toward derision. An informer accused Appuleia, the granddaughter of Augustus' half-sister, of having ridiculed the late ruler along with Tiberius and Livia. Tiberius agreed Appuleia should face trial for belittling his predecessor, but asserted he did not want her arraigned for what she had said about himself. When the consul asked him how the Senate should proceed with regard to Appuleia's slurs against Livia, Tiberius did not reply. The consul's inquiry, and Tiberius' failure to answer, imply both Senate and emperor were awaiting Livia's own response to the issue; otherwise Tiberius would have spoken for her at once.

Any Roman citizen who had suffered legal damages at the hands of another had the right to prosecute the malefactor. Under the strict letter of Roman law a *tutor*—guardian of the person—must serve as proxy for any woman involved in the suit whether as plaintiff or defendant. Livia had enjoyed exemption from *tutela* since 34 BCE. But although she had the right to make her own decision regarding Appuleia's derision of her, Livia could not address the Senate directly. That body's sessions were off limits to women; and Livia respected the restriction. The next time the Senate met, Tiberius asked in his mother's name that no deprecations of her be construed as criminal. Although Tiberius cleared Appuleia of the treason charge, the Senate found her guilty of adultery. She was remanded to the custody of her immediate family, who exiled her to a locale some 200 miles from Rome.

Dio Cassius maintains Livia's *auctoritas* exceeded that of any other woman in history. Yet intervention by Livia was not always successful, because it depended upon the willingness of others to accept it. A case in point was her failed endeavor to extricate her client Urgulania from a lawsuit. Lucius Calpurnius Piso brought charges against Urgulania in 16 CE, alleging she had failed to repay him a debt. Urgulania appealed to Livia, who in turn tried to pressure Piso into dropping his suit. Presumably Livia expected Piso to capitulate out of respect for her *auctoritas*. She was mistaken. Posturing, and complaints she felt insulted and belittled, were to no avail. Once Livia realized Piso was not going to back down, she settled the matter by paying him the monies he sought. Tacitus makes the comment that Livia's surrender kept Piso from suffering dishonor. Had Livia persisted in opposing Piso, her formidable influence might have devastated his reputation and made him a social outcast among his fellow Romans.

In 17 CE Tiberius turned his mother's intercessory power to his advantage. He entrusted Livia with the delicate diplomatic task of summoning the client king Archelaus of Cappadocia to stand trial before the Senate. Roman intelligence had discovered that Archelaus, probably unwittingly, had allowed the Parthians to use Cappadocia as their staging ground for an intended invasion of Roman territory. The Cappadocian monarch was elderly, stricken with gout, and subject to increasingly frequent lapses of mental competence.

Tiberius had good reason for not wanting to confront Archelaus directly. Early in their respective political careers, Tiberius had successfully defended Archelaus at a legal hearing before Augustus. Later, when Tiberius was languishing in exile at Rhodes, Archelaus had breached the *obsequium* between them by refusing to visit his patron. Now some fifteen years later, Tiberius did not wish Archelaus or anyone else to construe the summons as a *vendetta* for that slight. The emperor nevertheless wanted the king to obey the directive to appear in Rome. On receipt of a letter from no less a person than Livia, Archelaus hastened to comply. The Senate found him innocent.

In 19 CE the imperial family faced a far more difficult and tragic situation. Tiberius had sent Germanicus, fresh from a triumph for victories against the Germans, on a special junket to the East. Archelaus had died, as had the client kings of Cilicia and Commagene. Germanicus now annexed the three realms as Roman provinces, and relieved the incidence of taxation in Syria and Judaea. Meanwhile the Parthians had attempted to reestablish control in Armenia by ousting the unpopular pretender Vonones. Germanicus placed Zeno, a son of Queen Pythodoris of Pontus, on the Armenian throne to the satisfaction of the Parthian king and Armenian people alike. But Germanicus began to quarrel with Gnaeus Calpurnius Piso, the intransigent imperial legate of Syria. He was an older brother of the Lucius Piso who had sued Urgulania. Following a vacation in Egypt, Germanicus arrived in Antioch to find the elder Piso had countermanded adjustments the Roman crown prince had mandated for the administration of Syria. Bitter arguments ensued. Germanicus removed Piso from office; and the ex-legate departed for Rome. Germanicus thereafter became fatally ill. The dying prince and his volatile consort Agrippina were insistent that Piso and his wife Munatia Plancina had administered poison.

Tiberius arraigned Piso and Plancina before the Senate. The senators found the couple innocent of Germanicus' murder, but guilty of insurrection and other offenses. Piso committed suicide; but Plancina threw herself on the mercy of Livia. At Livia's request, Tiberius asked the Senate to commute Plancina's sentence. The Senate complied quite readily.

Rumors began to spread—with angry Agrippina's sanction if not her help—that the trial had been fixed; that Piso and Plancina had actually poisoned Germanicus with Tiberius' knowledge if not at his behest. People were insinuating the emperor envied his nephew's immense popularity, and aspired to clear the succession for his son Drusus. Livia may have hoped her display of compassion toward Plancina might allay the growth of popular suspicion, if not put the whole matter to rest. The pardon caused some to speculate whether Livia herself had endorsed her grandson's death; but it nonetheless accomplished its objective of forcing the issue to a conclusion.

The text of the senatorial decree pardoning Plancina has been preserved. Its pronouncements shed light on the new-old nature of Livia's public position. The Senate honors Livia's request because the state owes her that favor. She brought the reigning *princeps* into the world; and she has assisted many people of different ranks. Legal right and personal deservedness have given her a *plurimum posse* (supreme influence) which she exercises sparingly; therefore the Senate feels obliged to grant her petition.

Throughout Roman history, meritorious public service had been ascribed to women as well as to men. Political writers of the Roman Republic, including Cicero and Julius Caesar, employ the phrase *plurimum* (or *plurumum*) *posse*. This expression describes the overwhelming *auctoritas* of a *princeps*, in the latter term's pristine sense as a first among equals. Livia's preeminence like the principate itself, was based upon antecedents in Roman culture and political theory. The manner in which these attributes were combined gave Livia an unprecedented and unique status.

Tiberius' interaction with Livia was cordial until about 22 CE. Thereafter the relationship of mother and son deteriorated rapidly into conflict and alienation. The emperor tried to discourage his mother's intervention in public matters, insisting such behavior was overbearing and unbecoming a woman. Tiberius ordered Livia to forego further public appearances and direct her activities from home. He reprimanded her for appearing at a fire near the temple of the goddess Vesta, although she had engaged in her customary practice of exhorting the firefighters and offering aid to the victims. When she asked Tiberius to allow a man who had not been born a Roman citizen to become a juror, he agreed on the condition the official list of daily events show his mother had forced the decision upon him.

Tiberius may have been concerned about Livia's age and health. She turned eighty in January of 23 CE. Less than a year earlier she had been seriously ill. But Lucius Aelius Sejanus, whom Tiberius had appointed praetorian prefect in 17 CE, may have instigated at least some of the emperor's enmity toward his mother.

Sejanus had an appreciable reason for wanting to discredit Livia in Tiberius' eyes. The unscrupulous prefect aspired to usurp the principate for himself. He planned first to ingratiate himself to Tiberius, while disparaging all other influences upon the emperor including Livia. Then through murder or disgrace, the prefect would eliminate all contenders for the succession. Once Tiberius decided Sejanus was the most qualified person remaining to assume control of the empire, the prefect's future as heir-apparent would be secure. Sejanus could then bide his time until

Tiberius died naturally, or hasten the transfer of power by assassinating the emperor.

In 23 CE Sejanus seduced Germanicus' sister Livilla, who had married Tiberius' son Drusus. With her paramour's help, Livilla poisoned her husband. Three years later Sejanus persuaded the sick and sorrowing, sixty-six-year-old Tiberius to seek solace in retirement from Rome. While the *princeps* lived on Capri, away from the persuasions of his family and advisers, Sejanus managed imperial affairs as the emperor's alleged trustworthy deputy.

The prefect's next targets were Agrippina and her eldest son Nero, who was twenty when Tiberius quit Rome in 26 CE. Now that Tiberius' son Drusus was dead, Nero was next in line for the succession. Agrippina had continued to insinuate Tiberius had arranged the death of her husband Germanicus. Her accusations had inflamed a large and vocal following of supporters who regarded Tiberius with suspicion, hostility, and contempt. Sejanus fanned her suspicions, persuading her Tiberius intended to kill her and her children with her. She began to accuse Tiberius of aspiring to clear the succession for his own grandchild, the young son of Drusus and Livilla.

Hitherto Tiberius had considered Agrippina an annoyance. Sejanus proceeded to represent her as truly dangerous. The prefect and his agents convinced Tiberius that Agrippina was plotting to overthrow him and enthrone Nero in his stead. Sejanus persuaded Tiberius to accuse Agrippina and Nero, in letters which the prefect would read to the Senate. Tiberius prepared the letters; but Sejanus held off presenting them so long as Livia remained alive.

Despite their increasing estrangement, Tiberius and Livia continued to interact with one another. Sejanus felt a need for agents, to intercept and censor correspondence intended for the emperor at Capri. Tiberius and Livia jointly financed an aqueduct, for the town of Forum Cassii in southern Etruria. The project's dedication in 28 CE shows that mother and son cooperated on it during Sejanus' hegemony.

Livia, moreover, could still sway the Senate. So irresistible was her influence, it kept at least one of her favorites untouchable. Gaius Fufius Geminus, a man reputed for his wit, would openly ridicule Tiberius. Fufius and his wife Mutilia Prisca nevertheless enjoyed the friendship and protection of Livia, who advanced Fufius to the consulship for 29 CE. Sejanus understood that Livia would use her influence to oppose the destruction of Agrippina.

DIVA AUGUSTA: 29 TO 43 CE

Late in 28 CE or early in 29, the aged Livia once again fell ill. She died at Rome, in the home she had shared with Augustus for half a century. Since Tacitus and Dio Cassius mention her death as the first event of 29 CE she may well have expired sometime around her eighty-sixth birthday. From his retreat in Capri Tiberius directed the arrangements for her funeral; but he did not attend the simple, unpreposing ceremony. Mourners awaiting the emperor found themselves forced, by the deterioration of the corpse, to conduct the obsequies without him. Livia's great-grandchild Gaius, the sixteen-year-old third son of Germanicus and Agrippina, delivered the eulogy. Her ashes were interred beside those of Augustus in the imperial mausoleum.

Favorites Livia promoted toward the end of her life reaped the benefits of her partiality for several years after her demise. Born in 3 BCE, Servius Sulpicius Galba was a scion of the senatorial Sulpicii. Galba's stepmother, who eventually adopted him, was a beautiful and wealthy woman named Livia Ocellina. She must have been related to the empress; for Galba repudiated his adoption, and hence his connection with the Julio-Claudian family, when he overthrew Nero in the spring of 68 CE.

As Lucius Livius Ocella Sulpicianus, Galba "esteemed before all Livia Augusta, whose favor greatly benefited him while she lived, and by whose testament when she died he was almost made rich." [7] Suetonius neglects to mention what advantages Livia procured for her adoptive cousin. One may have been his well-connected marriage. Galba's wife, who predeceased him along with their two sons, was another Aemilia Lepida. She was a great-granddaughter of the Triumvir, and cousin to the second wife of Quirinius.

Although Livia died in 29 CE, Galba held the consulship of 33 CE as the result of her intervention. Livia also bequeathed Galba a fortune valued at 50 million *sesterces*. This figure is significant, since it equals the amount that Livia inherited from Augustus. Suetonius may have exaggerated. He adds that Tiberius reduced the award to 500,000 *sesterces* and subsequently neglected to pay it.

After Galba had reigned as emperor for seven months, Marcus Salvius Otho deposed him. The usurper owed his family's political prominence to Livia, who had raised and promoted Otho's orphaned grandfather.

Livia in her later years had employed a young man from the Gallic city of Vasio (modern Vaison, France), to administer some of her private lands. Sextus Afranius Burrus eventually rose, through the various ranks of the imperial service, to become praetorian prefect under Claudius in 51 CE.

The eventual fate of Munatia Plancina further illustrates the great weight a recommendation from Livia could carry, even long after she had made it. In 33 CE Tiberius prosecuted Plancina anew. All that is known about the second charge is that it was serious enough to warrant Plancina's suicide, and that it was unrelated to the Germanicus affair. Livia's satisfaction that Plancina had deserved her pardon was never challenged, even while Plancina was under indictment on other charges.

Citing his mother's own wishes, Tiberius strictly forbade the Senate to deify her. He did allow the Senate to impose a year of mourning upon the women of Rome. Tiberius accepted the authorization of an arch to commemorate Livia's benefactions, an honor unprecedented for a woman. The arch, however, was never built. Although he promised to finance the construction from his own resources, Tiberius failed to supply the necessary funds.

Tiberius also neglected to carry out the provisions of Livia's long and generous will. His indifference may not have stemmed so much from hostility toward his mother's memory, as from preoccupation with Sejanus and the consequences of the prefect's eventual exposure.

Once death had removed Livia's leverage, Sejanus took control of the Senate. Almost immediately after Livia's demise, the Senate decided Fufius Geminus' jests at Tiberius' expense were excessive and met the criteria for sedition. Fufius and his wife Mutilia Prisca committed suicide. They may have had two daughters who joined them in self-inflicted death. Shortly thereafter, Sejanus secured the banishments of Agrippina and Nero. Agrippina's second son—another Drusus—had accompanied Tiberius to Capri. After inducing the emperor to send the twenty-three-year-old youth to Rome, Sejanus had him incarcerated in the palace.

At length Germanicus' mother Antonia managed to get a letter exposing Sejanus' treachery, past the prefect's blockade and into Tiberius' hands. Tiberius sent a denunciation of the prefect, which was read in the Senate on October 18, 31 CE. Sejanus was promptly executed; but the intervention came too late to prevent the self-imposed death of Nero. Sejanus' estranged wife Apicata exposed the adulterous, murderous Livilla, who was put to death—intentionally starved, according to one tradition, by her own mother Antonia. Tiberius inflicted the same penalty on Agrippina's son Drusus, after learning that the youth had collaborated with Sejanus.

Shaken, embarrassed, and embittered by the Sejanus affair, Tiberius remained in seclusion on Capri. Unable to forgive Agrippina for her efforts to implicate him in Germanicus' death, Tiberius left her to commit suicide in exile (33 CE).[8] From his island refuge the emperor directed intensive, methodical investigations and prosecutions of Sejanus' accomplices. The relentlessness with which Tiberius authorized his agents to pursue their targets prompted critics to complain he was perpetrating a reign of terror. Tiberius died on March 16, 37 CE at the age of seventy-seven.

The Senate confirmed Gaius, now twenty-five and the sole surviving son of Germanicus, as the new emperor. The Romans affectionately called their new ruler *Caligula* (Little Combat Boot) because of the minute legionary uniform he had worn as a small boy.[9] Gaius ruled magnanimously until he fell ill in October of 37 CE. On recovering he embarked upon a blatant, oppressive despotism that drove Romans, provincials, even Gaius' own sisters, to rebellion. After a number of conspiracies had failed, the praetorian guards finally killed Gaius on January 24, 41 CE.

Gaius' attitude toward Livia reflects the pattern of his rule. At the beginning of his reign, Gaius promptly paid the bequests of Livia's will that Tiberius had neglected. Suetonius sweepingly declares that upon his accession, Gaius granted his grandmother Antonia all the distinctions

Livia had acquired over the course of her life. Writing more specifically, Dio Cassius indicates Gaius honored each of his female relatives with some of Livia's privileges. The emperor made Antonia priestess of the deified Augustus. He offered her the designation *Augusta*; but this she declined. And while he did not utilize every one of Livia's honors, Gaius granted his womenfolk some that Livia herself did not enjoy. The Arval Brethren, a college of aristocratic lay priests, said regular prayers for the emperor's wellbeing. Gaius had his sisters Agrippina, Drusilla, and Julia included in these petitions. He allowed the three women to sit with him during circus spectacles, and required that oaths of loyalty be sworn to them as well as himself. Gaius conferred, on grandmother and sisters alike, all the prerogatives of the Vestal Virgins. Livia had held only four of these.[10]

During his tyranny Gaius often described Livia as *Ulixes stolata*—a stola-clad Odysseus. The *stola* was the traditional garb of a Roman matron. Gaius' motive for equating his great-grandmother with Homer's hero cannot be determined. In general the young madman was intent upon degrading Livia. He attempted to belie her senatorial pedigree. In a letter to the Senate Gaius ascribed a lowly origin to Livia, solely on the ground her maternal grandfather Alfidius had been a decurion of Fundi.[11] Rumor also maintained Gaius abducted a bride from her new husband, and afterward crowed he had acquired a wife in the manner of Romulus and Augustus.[12] Statues of Livia dating from Gaius' reign depart from the idealized model that had prevailed since the reign of Augustus. They portray Livia as aging, fat, and decrepit.

There is no evidence, however, that Gaius rescinded Livia's public honors in Rome or in the provinces. Nor, apparently, did his obloquies alter public opinion of Livia. In 39 CE the fractious Greek and Jewish populations of Alexandria sent delegations to Gaius, each carrying complaints against the other's faction and the imperial authority in Egypt. A noted rabbi and philosopher named Philo headed the unsuccessful Jewish embassy. In his address to the emperor, Philo praises Livia as a unique woman and profound intellectual.

Gaius' assassins enthroned his uncle, the crippled younger brother of Germanicus. Although his family had always called this youngest grandson of Livia by his *praenomen* of Tiberius, he preferred to be known by his *gentilicum* Claudius. The new sovereign initiated various public celebrations of his relatives, perhaps to suppress hostility toward the dynasty in the aftermath of Sejanus and Gaius. At Rome he commemorated with circus spectacles, the birthdays of his late parents and of his maternal grandfather Mark Antony. The latter had the same birthday (January 14) as Claudius' father Drusus. Upon his mother Antonia, Claudius posthumously conferred the designation Augusta and the inclusion of her likeness in circus processions. To honor Germanicus, Claudius established a prize for comedy at the annual theater competition in Naples. And finally, Claudius asked the Senate to declare his grandmother Livia a goddess.

We do not know precisely when the ceremony of deification took place. The most likely date seems January 30, 43 CE, the centennial of Livia's birth. The Senate established an annual horserace to commemorate the event. The emperor placed Livia's statue in the temple to the divine Augustus, the construction of which she had mandated personally. Henceforth on circus days, Livia's image would be displayed in a chariot drawn by elephants. The Arval Brethren now invoked the Diva Augusta in their annual prayers for the emperor's well being.

And so Livia, who had begun her life as a typically reticent Roman matron, became an active and influential civil servant, the symbol of a new system of government, and eventually a divinity. This unprecedented prominence for a Roman woman resulted, as we have seen, from Augustus' careful adaptation of traditional practices. The empress was part of the new and beneficial system of government. Her role, like that system itself, had its roots in time-honored custom.

NOTES TO CHAPTER III

1   *Historia Romana* 2.130.
2   Plutarch, *Antonios* 83; cf. Dio Cassius 51.13. Shakespeare, who used Plutarch's *Antonios* as his source for *Antony and Cleoptra*, paraphrases the cited quotation in Act 5, scene 2:

> Some nobler token I have kept apart
> For Livia and Octavia, to induce
> Their mediation;

3   *Epistulae ex Ponto* 3.1.142.
4   The genealogies of Livia and her relatives are discussed in Appendix I.
5   The *sestercius* was the smallest denominated Roman silver coin, worth roughly the equivalent of the modern American dollar in purchasing power. See Appendix III for a conversion table.
6   The *corona civilis* commemorated the saving of Roman citizens' lives in battle.
7   Suetonius, *Galba* 5.
8   Agrippina perished on October 18, 33 CE, precisely two years after the overthrow of Sejanus. The timing of her suicide may have been intentional.
9   *Caligula* is the diminutive of *caliga*, the nail-studded half boot of the Roman legionary.
10   Livia enjoyed the Vestals' exemption from *tutela*, personal sacrosanctity, use of a *carpentum*, and special seats at the theater. The remaining privileges, which Gaius granted his grandmother and sisters, were the right to give court testimony without taking an oath, to be accompanied by a *lictor* at all times, and to be buried in the Forum.
11   See Appendix I for Suetonius' confusion about Alfidius' name.
12   The reference to Romulus alludes to the celebrated Rape of the Sabine Women. This frequent subject of artistic renderings was supposedly the means, by which the legendary founder of Rome and his companions acquired their wives. The legend explains the 20% Sabine element of the Roman population. The comment about Augustus refers to the criticism that he had inappropriately usurped Livia from her first husband. It also alludes to Augustus as a neo-Romulus, founder of a new Roman political system.

Il Banchetto di Ottaviano e Livia (Livia in Renaissance imagination)
Domenico Passignano (1558 – 1638)
In situ: Salon Pubblico, Villa Medici, Artimio, Italy
Photo credit: Scala/Art Resource, New York

LIVIA THE MURDERESS: THE ANATOMY OF THE STIGMA

Julia, daughter of Caesar Augustus
Uffizi Gallery, Florence
Photograph by the author

Marcus Vipsanius Agrippa
Uffizi Gallery, Florence
Photograph by the author

CHAPTER IV

ASSESSING LIVIAS CRIMINALITY

A distinctly unsavory impression of Livia confronts anyone who investigates her personal history. Tacitus in his **Annals** and Dio Cassius in his **Roman Matters** portray her as a vicious dynastic murderess. They insinuate Livia procured the deaths of Marcellus, Gaius, Lucius, Augustus himself, and finally Agrippa Postumus, to secure the throne for her son Tiberius. Both authors maintain Livia rejoiced at the death of her grandson Germanicus, a demise Tacitus implies she may have arranged. Additionally, Tacitus insinuates Livia persecuted Germanicus' wife Agrippina, and may have precipitated the banishment of Agrippina's sister Julia.

This has been a popular view of Livia in modern times. Historians embraced it in the eighteenth and nineteenth centuries. While virtually all contemporary scholars of Roman history dismiss Livia's criminal reputation, purveyors and devotees of literary and television fiction perpetuate, extend, and embellish it. Popular lore has added the elder Agrippa and Augustus' daughter Julia to Livia's targets, even though no ancient testimony imputes their destructions to her.

Careful study proves this disparaging tradition about Livia to be a myth. To understand its fallacies, we must scrutinize the circumstances under which each alleged victim met his or her ruin.

MARCELLUS

Marcus Claudius Marcellus, the son of Augustus' sister Octavia by her first husband, met his end in 23 BCE at the age of nineteen. The only imputation of his demise to Livia is from the **Romaïka** of Dio Cassius:

> Livia was suspected of [having caused] Marcellus' death because he was preferred above her sons. This assumption, however, was rendered questionable by that year and the following, because in them sickness developed so greatly that many perished.[1]

The polemical conclusion is that Livia used the epidemic as a cover for Marcellus' murder.

Marcellus and Livia's elder son Tiberius were both born in 42 BCE. Marcellus appears to have been a few months Tiberius' senior. Augustus clearly treated the boys as equals in their childhood and early youth. They took their lessons together, rode the trace horses of Octavian's triumphal chariot, and shared military service under Augustus' supervision in Gaul and Spain.

Augustus subsequently began to procure greater privileges for Marcellus than for Tiberius. In 25 BCE the Greek propagandist poet Krinagoras celebrated Marcellus' *depositio barbae*. A year later, Marcellus was made a pontiff. He was inducted into the Senate, where he enjoyed the special honor of sitting among the ex-praetors. Marcellus was also allowed to stand for the magistracies ten years before attaining the requisite age. Tiberius by contrast received only a single and lesser privilege: the right to hold office five years early.

Marcellus, moreover, received the hand of Augustus' daughter Julia. This union created the closest possible alliance between the emperor and his nephew, short of outright adoption.

Why would Augustus promote Marcellus so aggressively, unless the emperor expected his nephew to succeed him as *princeps*? But why, then, did Augustus fail to take the final, decisive step of confirming Marcellus as successor-designate by adopting him? Marcellus' marriage to Julia was no obstacle; an adoption would not have rendered the union technically incestuous. When she married, Julia legally passed out of her father's family. In other words she had ceased to be Augustus' daughter.

The principate was still young. Augustus may have felt that the Romans were not yet ready to accept his theoretically temporary position as hereditary. Too premature an imposition of this concept could smack blatantly of monarchy. Perhaps Augustus planned to adopt his nephew testamentarily, as Julius Caesar had adopted him. The emperor may also have been holding out hope that Livia, who was only in her thirties, would still bear him a son of their own.

Meanwhile, Augustus continually faced the prospect of untimely death. His health was chronically poor. Political enemies had made several attempts on his life. What if he should die before Marcellus had received sufficient training to become *princeps*, or before the idea of hereditary transfer of authority had gained adequate acceptance? The situation called for an interim successor—a regent. He must have experience in government, familiarity with Augustus' ideas and intentions, the acceptance of the Senate and armies, the loyalty of the populace, and the willingness to abdicate his powers in favor of Augustus' chosen heir.

The emperor had already selected such a person in the spring of 23 BCE. During a nearly fatal bout with the malady Dio Cassius describes, Augustus had handed his signet ring—the symbol of his personal authority—to his childhood friend Marcus Agrippa.

Agrippa's marriage to the elder of Marcellus' two sisters had already created an alliance between the regent and the emperor's presumed successor. Should Marcellus become *princeps*, Augustus would have the familial succession he desired. If Augustus' premature death brought Agrippa to power, Marcellus would still occupy a position of special prominence as the new ruler's brother-in-law. Their descendants could intermarry, and thereby transfer Augustus' bloodline to future *principes*. Agrippa might even adopt Marcellus, especially if Claudia Marcella failed to bear sons.

The sons of Livia were part of this marital network. Tiberius' wife was Vipsania, Agrippa's daughter by his first wife Caecilia. Drusus was betrothed to Octavia's youngest daughter, Antonia. She was half-sister to Marcellus and to Agrippa's present wife. No one, however, was more closely bound to Augustus than Marcellus, by virtue of his union with Julia.

If Livia presumed Marcellus' death would prompt Augustus to adopt one or both of her sons and marry one of them to Julia, she certainly miscalculated. The emperor adopted neither stepson, but presented his widowed daughter to Agrippa. For a brief time Tiberius, as Agrippa's son-in-law was that regent's most likely successor. Livia nevertheless failed to strengthen Tiberius' prospects by murdering or disabling Augustus, thereby forcing Agrippa into the principate. She also apparently ignored the certainty Agrippa would give preference to sons of his own. This was precisely what came about, once Julia bore Gaius in 20 BCE.

THE ELDER AGRIPPA

Because Tiberius replaced Agrippa as the husband of Julia and regent for her sons Gaius and Lucius, modern polemicists of Livia have speculated she precipitated Agrippa's early death in 12 BCE. No ancient testimony supports this contention. Agrippa's mental and physical health were failing. The elder Pliny asserts the fifty-year-old Agrippa was suffering from severe depression, brought on by his awareness of Julia's marital infidelity and by Augustus' implacable demands for service to the principate. Pliny also reveals that Agrippa had a chronic and particularly virulent case of gout, which he endeavored to alleviate by plunging his feet into scalding vinegar.

If Livia intended to eliminate Agrippa all along, why did she wait until he had fathered five children on Julia, three of them males and hence potential competitors to Tiberius and Drusus? A detractor might argue that Livia was holding out until Tiberius had gained sufficient maturity and experience to be regent. Had she acted too soon, Augustus would have given the position to someone else. But Tiberius reached the age of legal majority (twenty-five) in November of 17 BCE. He had been learning and performing principate operations for a decade. There was no reason for Livia to postpone the destruction of Agrippa for five more years.

Furthermore if Livia did eliminate Agrippa, she at best gave Tiberius a chance of attaining the regency. The possibility of Augustus selecting Tiberius may have been a strong one; but it was still only a possibility. Augustus took a year to scrutinize a variety of candidates in both the senatorial and equestrian orders.

Let us examine some of those whom Augustus may have considered for the regency in lieu of Tiberius. We cannot determine, from our fragmentary records, how seriously Augustus contemplated any of these individuals as potential successors to Agrippa—if the emperor did so at all. These persons simply appear, from our perspective, to have been his most logical alternatives to Tiberius.

Agrippa's death left Gaius Maecenas, the great patron of writers and poets, as perhaps the emperor's closest friend and adviser. Another equestrian, Gaius(?) Sallustius Crispus, was second only to Maecenas in Augustus' esteem if we can believe Tacitus. In a letter written after he became emperor, Tiberius asserts Augustus had considered giving Julia's hand to an equestrian named Gaius Proculeius. He was half-brother to Maecenas' wife Terentia. Proculeius had long been a faithful supporter of the principate. He had helped negotiate the surrender of Cleopatra in 30 BCE. Four years later Proculeius successfully prosecuted Gaius Cornelius Gallus, Augustus' first appointee to the prefecture of Egypt. Gallus proved to be seditious and corrupt.

There were blood relatives. Marcus and Sextus Appuleius were Augustus' nephews, the sons of a much older half-sister of Octavia and himself. Sextus had been Octavian's colleague in the consulship of 29 BCE. The emperor also had cousins, descended from the Caesar family through his grandmother's sister. Quintus Pedius had served Caesar the Dictator as legate of Gaul. Later, as proconsul of Nearer Spain, Pedius conducted a military campaign that won him a triumph in 45 BCE. Pedius, or possibly his son, was Octavian's colleague in the short-lived consulship of 43 BCE. Lucius Pinarius Scarpus had commanded Triumviral divisions at Philippi, and then entered the service of Mark Antony. As governor of Cyrene in 31 BCE, Pinarius had handed his province and its four legions over to Octavian.[2]

Livia's kinsman Marcus Livius Drusus Libo might have presented a possibility. Other members of the inner circle included Publius Sulpicius Quirinius, Paullus Fabius Maximus, and Publius Quinctilius Varus.

Quirinius was distantly related to Livia, and had married her cousin Appia Claudia. Fabius wed Augustus' first cousin Marcia, the patroness of the poet Ovid. Like Tiberius, Varus had espoused a daughter of Agrippa (we do not know by which wife). One of Varus' female relatives must have married Augustus' nephew Sextus Appuleius, because Sextus' daughter was known as Appuleia Varilla.

There were also the husbands of the emperor's nieces, the daughters of Octavia. Iullus Antonius, the younger son of Mark Antony and Fulvia, had wed the eldest after her divorce from Agrippa. The younger Claudia Marcella had espoused Appia Claudia's brother, Marcus Valerius Messalla Barbatus Appianus. Their daughter Claudia Pulchra would marry a Quinctilicus Varus—either the aforementioned or his son. Octavia's older daughter by Mark Antony had espoused Lucius Domitius Ahenobarbus. The younger Antonia was the wife of Tiberius' brother, Drusus.

Now: no pattern of deaths, disgraces, or similar efforts to diminish Augustus' retainers emerged while the emperor was contemplating a new regent. Only Marcus Barbatus Appianus, the husband of the younger Claudia Marcella, died in 12 BCE, and apparently earlier than Agrippa. In other words, nothing suggests Livia endeavored to remove Tiberius' competitors for Agrippa's post. She may have urged Augustus to select Tiberius and assumed he would; but she did not force her husband's hand with criminal manipulations.

The regency actually portended a dead end for Tiberius. Augustus was not about to let Tiberius or anyone else compete with Gaius and Lucius for the succession. To be sure, Tiberius would assume Augustus' public responsibilities should the emperor die or become incapacitated during Gaius' minority. Once Gaius reached an appropriate age (presumably his legal majority), Tiberius must necessarily surrender the imperial office to him. Augustus assuredly committed Tiberius to this arrangement. How, then, can we attribute Agrippa's death to Livia if that event backed Tiberius into a hopeless situation?

During Tiberius' regency his brother Drusus stood a chance of becoming Augustus' successor. Drusus was a remainderman of his stepfather's will. Should Gaius and Lucius both fail to accept Augustus' bequest, the legacy would then devolve upon Drusus. This was a contingency, not a firm commitment of the succession to Drusus. The latter's death in 9 BCE ultimately left Livia's only living offspring mired in his marriage and the regency.

And finally: why should Livia bother maneuvering her son into the regency at all? Gaius and Lucius were the real obstacles to Tiberius' attainment of the succession. Only by removing them could Livia force Augustus to seek a new heir.

JULIA

In October of 6 BCE, Tiberius left Rome for the southern Aegean island of Rhodes. He cited fatigue as the reason for his withdrawal. Many Romans nevertheless suspected his five-year marriage to Augustus' daughter had become unbearable.

Four years later, the Senate found Julia guilty on several accounts of adultery. Augustus' law of 18 BCE had made this offense a capital felony, subject to the penalty of banishment, or under some extreme circumstances to death.

Julia was formally divorced from Tiberius. She was then remanded to Pandataria (Ventotene), one of the beautiful but remote Pontine islands that lie in the Tyrrhenian Sea west of Capri.

Some modern polemicists contend that Livia deliberately exposed Julia, leaving Augustus no choice but to press charges. But as in the case of Agrippa's death, no ancient source attributes Julia's downfall to Livia's intrigues.

What would Livia expect to accomplish by disgracing Julia? We cannot assess any motives from our sources, because none of these connects Livia with Julia's ruin. If we assume for the sake of argument that Livia did engineer her stepdaughter's conviction, we find the empress' purported efforts repeatedly detrimental to her son.

Suetonius writes that after learning of Julia's disgrace, Tiberius endeavored to reconcile Augustus to his daughter. At the same time, Tiberius asked permission to return home so he could visit the family he so sorely missed. Augustus responded by ordering his stepson to remain on Rhodes, and forget the kindred he had so eagerly abandoned.

Back in 6 BCE, Augustus and Livia had pleaded with Tiberius not to leave Rome. The emperor even made a formal complaint to the Senate about his stepson's intention. Tiberius adamantly defied his family's efforts to keep him at home. Eventually he got his way, after refusing food for four days.

In the aftermath of Julia's disgrace the tables were turned. Tiberius had become acquiescent; but Augustus as well as Julia's eldest son Gaius had grown defiant. Gaius' hostility abetted Augustus' determination to restrict Tiberius to Rhodes. Did insightful and intuitive Livia fail to discern the developing disaffection, of her husband and his grandson toward Tiberius?

If Livia had perceived getting rid of Julia would induce Tiberius to return to Rome, why did she take four years to accomplish this task? A detractor might argue Livia took time to compile evidence against Julia, convince Augustus of his daughter's guilt, secure an indictment, and then await the outcome of the trial. But suppose Julia were acquitted? What if Augustus should decide to pardon her? He did eventually make the terms of her confinement less harsh, by moving her to the southern Italian city of Rhegium (modern Reggio Calabria). Was Livia unable to find a quicker and more permanent means of ruining Julia—murder, for example?

Julia's trial took place in the autumn of 2 BCE. The *tribunicia potestas* and *maius imperium* of Tiberius' regency were due to expire a mere few months later, on January 1 of the following year. All the more reason, a detractor might argue, for Livia to ruin Julia before Tiberius' regency ended, freeing Augustus to bestow it upon someone else. But by the time Livia's alleged machinations finally brought Julia to trial, Augustus had decided his grandsons no longer needed a regent. Livia's presumed interference, moreover, cost her son a very singular privilege. Had Tiberius stayed married to Julia, he would have at least retained special distinction as the emperor's son-in-law after the heirs-apparent had assumed their full share of powers. Following Julia's fall, Tiberius was neither regent nor husband of the *princeps'* daughter.

Augustus did not have legal grounds for confining his stepson to Rhodes. Tiberius was of age and consequently free of his stepfather's guardianship. Nor had Tiberius been sentenced to banishment for having committed a crime. When the powers of the regency expired in 1 BCE, Augustus at Livia's request gave Tiberius the position of imperial legate to Rhodes; and a convicted felon could not hold a public office. Clearly, Tiberius stayed on Rhodes in deference to Augustus' wishes.

A legate by definition was a governor, adjutant, or ambassador whom the emperor assigned to a specific region. The fact that Tiberius commissioned centurions shows his command was no fiction. The position was an exalted one; but it confirmed Tiberius' geographic restriction to Rhodes by making the island his jurisdiction. If Livia was working to bring Tiberius back to Rome, why did she procure him a position that reinforced his detention?

According to Suetonius, Livia hoped the legate position would conceal the fact that Tiberius was living on Rhodes against his will. The ruse failed: Tiberius became the laughingstock of the empire. Although no court of law had formally sentenced Tiberius to banishment, people everywhere referred to him as *exsul*—the exile. Statues of Tiberius were overthrown in Gaul, where he had once been governor. Tiberius' former retainer, the king of Cappadocia, broke the rules of patronage by refusing to visit him. A dinner companion of Gaius offered to sail for Rhodes and return with Tiberius' head.

Livia begged Augustus to release Tiberius, but to no avail. Fortuitously in the summer of 2 CE, Gaius discovered his traitorous chief of staff had misrepresented Tiberius. Augustus let Tiberius return to Rome, but with the stipulation Tiberius stay out of the political arena.

Eventually the deaths of Lucius and Gaius forced Augustus to change his attitude toward Tiberius. As we know, the emperor adopted Tiberius as his son and successor on June 26, 4 CE. Livia's detractors detect her hand again; surely she brought Julia's sons to their untimely ends. For once, it would seem, Livia's alleged manipulations worked to Tiberius' advantage.

If Livia ruined Julia, she concealed her intrigues so thoroughly that no source records them. She also managed to hoodwink Augustus, so that he failed even to suspect her of destroying his daughter. But if Livia was intrepid enough to hide her machinations so effectively, why did she bungle poor Tiberius into one predicament after another?

GAIUS AND LUCIUS

Tacitus writes:

> After Agrippa had relinquished life, either fate or the treachery of their stepmother Livia brought quick death to Lucius Caesar while *en route* to our forces in Spain, and to Gaius while returning from Armenia and ill from a wound, and Drusus having already been destroyed, Nero (i.e., Tiberius) was alone among the stepsons, [and] everything devolved upon him.[3]

And Dio Cassius:

> Straightway resigning all his powers [the wounded Gaius] sailed to Lycia in a merchant ship, and subsequently passed away at Limyra. By the time this happened to him, Lucius had already expired at Massilia...He died suddenly of illness; yet people suspected Livia, especially since at that very time Tiberius returned to Rome from Rhodes.[4]

Throughout their brief lives, the sons of Agrippa and Julia stood between those of Livia and accession to Augustus' throne. By the time Lucius was born on January 29, 17 BCE, Augustus felt the Romans were inclined to accept a hereditary principate. The emperor formally adopted his grandsons as his legal offspring and intended heirs. If Augustus survived until Gaius and Lucius were sufficiently experienced to rule, at least one of them would certainly succeed him as *princeps*. Should Augustus' premature death bring Agrippa to power, he would eventually surrender that power to Gaius and Lucius because they were his natural sons.

Livia's detractors expect us to believe she waited until Lucius was eighteen and Gaius twenty-two before striking them down. What advantage did she expect to gain from this delay? Suppose some unforeseen occurrence obstructed her ability to perpetrate the murders before the time she had chosen carry them out arrived? Surely she must have known her husband's plans for his grandsons. From virtually the moments of their births, Augustus had aggressively promoted Gaius and Lucius as his heirs-apparent: to Roman citizens, to provincials, and to foreign potentates. As the princes grew older and their renown increased, the more notable their deaths stood to be.

Infant mortality was rampant in ancient Rome. Perhaps one child in ten survived to adolescence. In today's developing countries, sanitation and food preservation techniques approximate those of ancient Rome. Modern children living under such conditions suffer a plethora of unnamed sniffles, fevers, and gastric distresses.

Dynastic murders consequently stood less chance of detection if perpetrated on children rather than adults. Did the shrewd, intrepid Livia fail to perceive this fact? She must have had direct, personal interaction with Gaius and Lucius during their childhood and youth. Augustus closely supervised his grandsons' upbringing and education, especially after Agrippa's death. The boys certainly frequented if not resided in their grandfather's townhouse and country homes. Suetonius describes how they dined and traveled with him. Why not strike them in this period of their lives? Then they were close at hand, easily deceived, and too naive to realize they were in danger.

If Livia meant to annihilate her sons' rivals all along, why did she allow them to be born in the first place? Why not arrange to have some unscrupulous doctor or midwife strangle the newborns, or cut their umbilical cords too close? Why not have Julia injured, so that she persistently miscarried or failed to conceive at all? For that matter, why not simply eliminate Julia herself? Then she would no longer be available to contract marriage alliances potentially detrimental to the advancement of Tiberius and Drusus.

Lucius died at Marseilles and Gaius in Asia Minor. Did Livia hope to evade suspicion by striking her targets while they were absent from Italy? She could only have done so through long chains of agents, any one of whom might incriminate her by confession or a botched attack on an intended victim. Why not eliminate this potential for discovery by perpetrating the murders herself, while the princes were in Rome and in immediate contact with her?

The fact Tiberius remained regent until January 1, 1 BCE produces the detracting argument, that Livia felt no real urgency to remove Gaius and Lucius prior to this deadline. Tiberius could become emperor no matter where he was, so long as he held the regency. Presumably its expiration caught Livia off guard, if she had to take several years thereafter to arrange the princes' assassinations. Did Livia not know, or at least suspect, Augustus would not renew Tiberius' powers? Why did she neglect to devise the murders before the regency ended? Augustus was still the target of conspirators. His advancing years were taking their toll on his persistently weak health. Livia might lose her husband at any time. If he died before she intervened, her son's chances would be lost forever.

Tiberius' own behavior came under suspicion several times, over the course of his seven-year sojourn on Rhodes. When he first left Rome in 6 BCE, Tiberius sailed hastily from Ostia the port of Rome. He then put in somewhere along the Campanian coast upon learning that Augustus was ill. The delay prompted rumors: was Tiberius waiting to see whether Augustus' ailment would prove fatal? Once apprised of these speculations, Tiberius immediately embarked for Rhodes in spite of contrary winds.

By the time the regency expired, Gaius had grown distinctly ambivalent toward his erstwhile stepfather. Gaius had come to view Tiberius as a threat to the political statures of the two heirs-apparent. Dio Cassius writes that Gaius and Lucius alike felt slighted when Augustus renewed Tiberius' regency in January of 6 BCE. Although they were only in their early teens, the brothers clearly appear to have felt entitled to powers greater than what they already enjoyed. Suetonius and Dio both claim Tiberius began to insist he had retired to Rhodes, specifically to avoid political competition between the two crown princes and himself as their regent.

Another suspicion about Tiberius centered upon messages—perhaps military orders[5]—that Tiberius allegedly sent to an unspecified number of persons. The *communiqués* were purportedly ambiguous and intended to incite subversive activities. Some centurions who were obligated to Tiberius for their appointments, were suspected of having delivered the incriminating instructions while returning to active duty from furlough.

Augustus notified Tiberius about these suggestions of sedition and misuse of military authority. Tiberius responded by arranging to have someone witness all his actions and utterances.

Tiberius' keen interest in astrology prompted conjectures about his motives. A man who knew the future could manipulate his own destiny and those of others. The Romans consequently looked with suspicion, upon those who practiced occult arts for non-religious purposes. Dio Cassius claims Tiberius divined the fates of Gaius and Lucius as well as his own. This author also asserts Tiberius' expectations of becoming emperor prompted him to cultivate an enduring friendship with the noted astrologer Thrasyllus.

Gaius relented, as we know, after learning his chief of staff Marcus Lollius had slandered Tiberius. With Gaius' approval, Augustus allowed Tiberius to leave Rhodes and return to Rome in the summer of 2 CE. Tiberius' exoneration was nevertheless incomplete, because he was forbidden to resume a public career. We do not know the reason for this proviso. Did Augustus intend it as punishment, for Tiberius' abandonment of Julia? Did the emperor have some lingering doubts about Tiberius' loyalty? Or was Augustus afraid Tiberius might yet become a figurehead, if only an unwilling one, around whom opponents to Gaius might form an opposition party?

This restriction on Tiberius' activities might have continued indefinitely, had not the death of Gaius forced Augustus to change his arrangements for the succession.

If Augustus did not attribute foul play to Livia after one of her sons was dead and the other in a state of terrible uncertainty, he would hardly have done so while both men were at the heights of their careers. Livia could have eliminated Gaius and Lucius, without fear of incrimination, years before 4 CE. She had more to lose than gain from delay.

AUGUSTUS AND THE YOUNGER AGRIPPA

When elder Agrippa died in the summer of 12 BCE, Julia was pregnant with their fifth child. The boy was very likely born sometime after June 26 of the following year. When his grandfather adopted him on this date in 4 CE, the youth had not yet assumed the *toga virilis*; therefore, he had to be less than fifteen years of age.

We do not know the full name, of Augustus' youngest surviving grandchild.[6] Velleius Paterculus and Suetonius use only the paternal *cognomen* Agrippa, to which Tacitus and Pliny the Elder append the epithet *Postumus* (Latest or Last Born). Gaius and Lucius, predestined from birth as their grandfather's successors, bore traditional forenames of the Caesar family.[7] Since Augustus originally did not plan to adopt their younger brother, the latter very likely received his father's *praenomen* of Marcus. His full name, then, would have been Marcus Vipsanius Agrippa Postumus. Possibly, but less grammatically correct, he was called Postumus Vipsanius Agrippa.[8] Modern writers utilize Postumus (often but wrongly spelled Posthumus) to differentiate the younger Agrippa from his father.

We encounter the schoolboy-aged Postumus in 2 BCE, at the dedication of Augustus' temple to Mars the Avenger. His older brothers, the crown princes, marked the occasion by presenting elaborate circus games. During these festivities, Postumus participated with other boys of noble rank in a traditional equestrian exercise called *Lusus Troiae* (The Game of Troy).

Then came the fateful year of 4 CE. Lucius and Gaius, the anticipated future *principes*, were dead. Augustus must resecure the succession. On June 26 the emperor adopted his stepson Tiberius, who had already adopted his nephew Germanicus. On the same occasion Augustus adopted Postumus.

Under the new arrangement the principate would pass from Augustus to Tiberius, and then from Tiberius to Germanicus. Augustus never intended to bestow the imperial office upon Postumus. Desire for a personal heir of his own bloodline, not an additional successor to his political position, had moved the emperor to adopt his sole surviving grandson. After his adoption, Postumus was treated like an ordinary young nobleman. In 5 CE his name was added to the list of aristocratic youths who were eligible for training as military officers. Augustus neither provided Postumus special schooling in government, nor procured for him the extraordinary honors and privileges of successor-designates.

Postumus would inherit his grandfather's name, property, and physical bloodline—but not the principate.

Postumus created problems for his family, even in the relatively private station they had chosen for him. The youth was boorish, insolent, highly irascible, and potentially violent. He possessed great physical strength in which he exulted; and he showed little interest in anything apart from fishing. Postumus resisted efforts and inducements to improve his conduct. This incorrigibility prompted Augustus to revoke his grandson's adoption and remand him to exile. Initially Augustus restricted Postumus to a villa at Surrentum (modern Sorrento), on Italy's splendid Amalfi Coast. Very likely the estate was the villa Postumus had inherited from his father, located at modern Boscotrecase.

Postumus' behavior only worsened until, in 7 CE, Augustus decided a firmer confinement was needed. The emperor procured a senatorial decree that relegated Postumus to Planasia (modern Pianosa), one of the rock pinnacle islands lying between Italy and Corsica.[9] Augustus bolstered the locale's natural inaccessibility by installing an armed garrison. He also instructed the Senate never to allow Postumus' release. The emperor was determined to keep his grandson on Planasia, and visitors away.

So how does Livia figure in all this?

Tacitus attributes Postumus' banishment to her mischief. This author insists Livia, taking advantage of Augustus' advancing age, cajoled him into exiling his grandson without due process of law:

> [Livia] dominated the aged Augustus to the point that he banished, to the island of Planasia, his sole grandson Agrippa Postumus, rude without good qualities and brutishly ferocious with a strong body, yet convicted of no criminal action.[10]

No writer except Tacitus claims Augustus was senile and Livia exploited this weakness to ruin Postumus. Plutarch maintains Postumus' exile was the result of false accusation but does not impute this to Livia. In a strictly juridical sense, the banishment was unlawful because

Postumus had not been formally convicted of a crime. Banishment was a form of capital punishment.

Tacitus continues:

> Augustus' health worsened and some suspected the wickedness of his wife. For a rumor maintained that a few months earlier, Augustus, with the knowledge of a chosen few and Fabius Maximus as his one companion, sailed to Planasia to see Agrippa. There were many tears and signs of affection on both sides, and hope emerged that the youth would be returned to the grandfather's family. Maximus disclosed this to his wife Marcia, and she to Livia. Caesar was made aware of the matter; and when not long afterward Maximus perished, perhaps from an unnatural death, the groans of Marcia were audible at his funeral as she blamed herself for having been the cause of her husband's demise.[11]

Dio Cassius' account omits Fabius, but otherwise parallels that of Tacitus:

> So Augustus, having taken ill, died; and some suspected that Livia caused his death, after he had sailed secretly to Agrippa on the island [of Planasia] and appeared to become totally reconciled to him. Fearing, so they say, that [Augustus] would restore the monarchy to him (i.e. Postumus) she placed on figs, still on the tree from which Augustus was accustomed to gather fruit with his own hands, poison. She then ate the unanointed while at the same time directing him to the poisoned.[12]

Neither Pliny the Elder nor Plutarch attributes Augustus' death to Livia. Pliny maintains that Fabius' indiscretion incited Livia and Tiberius to some sort of unspecified skullduggery:

> [The] exile of Postumus Agrippa after the adoption, longing [for him] after the banishment, then the

suspicion that Fabius had betrayed secrets, whence the designs of his wife and Tiberius, gave [Augustus] the greatest concern.[13]

Plutarch writes that Augustus aspired to recall Postumus, and Livia reacted with hurt feelings:

> Fulvius (i.e. Fabius), a companion of the aged Caesar Augustus, once happened to hear [the emperor] lamenting the devastation that had befallen his family: two grandsons having perished, Postumius (sic.), the one remaining, was in exile from false accusation, forcing [Augustus] to confer the succession to the empire on his wife's son. Being merciful, however, [Augustus] planned to recall the grandson. Fulvius, having heard this confided it to his wife, and she to Livia. Livia bitterly reproached Caesar because, if he felt as he did, he did not summon the grandson long ago, but cast her into hatred and hostility toward the successor of the state. Consequently when Fulvius came to him in the morning, according to custom, and said, "Greetings, Caesar," he (Augustus) replied, "Farewell, Fulvius." The latter, perceiving the meaning, went home at once, and after sending for his wife said, "Caesar has discovered that I have not kept his secret; because of this I intend to destroy myself." The wife said, "Rightly, since after living with me for this time you have not learned to guard against laxity; only let me die first." And seizing the sword, she predeceased her husband.[14]

Hatred and hostility is a puzzling phrase. Does it imply that Livia had disparaged Postumus as an exile, and was now embarrassed because Augustus was planning to honor her victim with the succession? Or does it suggest Livia, offended by public antipathy toward Tiberius, realizes that she would have escaped such discomfiture had Augustus pursued his original inclination of exonerating Postumus. Whatever his intention, Plutarch imputes neither Postumus' exile nor Augustus' death to Livia.

Although he gives a differing account of Marcia's eventual fate, Plutarch agrees with Tacitus on two points. By disclosing Fabius' comments to Livia, Marcia got him into trouble with Augustus. Marcia thereafter recriminated herself, for having occasioned her husband's predicament.

Velleius and Suetonius say nothing of all this. They do not mention Fabius, Marcia, the Planasia junket, nor any kind of reaction on Livia's part. Velleius pontificates that Postumus "acquired the consequence his madness deserved." [15] Suetonius declares Augustus dubbed his banished descendants—his daughter Julia, Postumus her son, and Vipsania Julia her namesake daughter—his "three ulcers and three cancers." [16]

The **Liber de Caesaribus** of the fourth century Sextus Aurelius Victor appears to be a gloss of a more comprehensive history. Victor describes Augustus as "altogether lucky (except in children and indeed as well in marriage)…" [17] An anonymous epitomist, who apparently summarized the same narrative Victor condensed, cites the tradition that blamed Livia for Augustus' death:

> On reaching seventy-seven years, he (i.e., Augustus) entered death at Nola. Notwithstanding, others write that by the treachery of Livia he attained extinction: indeed, because he was planning to recall her stepdaughter's son Agrippa, whom she had removed to an island out of stepmotherly hatred, she gave him to be overtaken by the greatest of punishments.[18]

Whose stories, then, should we believe—and to what extent?

The journey to Planasia lacks credibility, in view of Augustus' deteriorated physical condition. By 12 CE the emperor had ceased to attend the sessions of the Senate. His voice had so weakened, that he could no longer make himself heard in the meetinghouse. He was blind in one eye, and prone to chills even in summer. The contraction of one such affliction, in mid-August of 14 CE, would lead him to his deathbed. Reaching Planasia from Ostia entailed negotiating some 200 miles of turbulent waters, without the aid of modern navigational or meteorological instruments. The voyage portended an arduous and risky venture, especially for a septuagenarian in ill health. The emperor did not need to visit Planasia in person to keep track of his grandson's mental condition; he could have done so by studying the reports of agents.

Paullus Fabius Maximus' name is absent from the **Acts of the Arval Brethren** for May of 14 CE; but all this indicates is that Fabius failed to show up for a religious rite he was scheduled to perform. The absence does not automatically imply Fabius accompanied Augustus to Planasia. Fabius may have been ill; he would only live a few more months. He may have been away from Rome on vacation, on a family matter, on personal or governmental business.

On the other hand, the story of Fabius' indiscretion does have some plausibility. Augustus very conceivably did mourn the fates of his grandsons. Furthermore the *princeps* would have lost his temper on learning, from Livia or anyone else, that a relative such as Fabius had disclosed the musings Augustus considered strictly personal and private. The emperor did not tolerate breaches of confidence, lest they compromise the security of the principate. He severely punished members of his staff who leaked government information. Postumus' exile was more than a family misfortune. It was a touchy political and legal issue, because Postumus as Augustus' direct descendant had a legitimate claim to the succession. His banishment, moreover, was technically unlawful. A sufficiently irate reaction on Augustus' part might have driven Fabius to suicide. Or if Fabius suffered a sudden but natural demise—a heart attack, for example—the emperor's anger could have spawned rumors the death was self-inflicted.

Why should Augustus have wished to conceal his feelings about Postumus from Livia, especially if he trusted her as implicitly as our sources unilaterally contend? Had Augustus finally become suspicious and fearful of his wife after half a century of marriage? Did he assume she would at once resort to deception and treachery, to keep him from rehabilitating Postumus?

Let us suppose that in the summer of 14 CE, Augustus decided Postumus was entirely healed of his aberrations and in his right mind. Recovery notwithstanding, the aged, sick, dying emperor would scarcely have entrusted the system he had founded to an utterly inexperienced young man, who had never been trained for the principate, had been living in strict isolation for seven years, and bore a history of mental illness. Even Tacitus, who comes closer than any other writer to being an apologist for Postumus, acknowledges the youth's incompetence.

No arrangement had been made by this time, to set Tiberius aside and allow Germanicus to succeed Augustus directly. If Germanicus was not yet deemed sufficiently prepared to become the next emperor, how much less so was Postumus? Who, moreover, would succeed Postumus? He had never been married; he had no descendants.

This deduction, that Augustus would never have indicated Postumus for the succession, produces a second. Livia had no need to murder her husband. Tiberius was never in danger of losing or having to share the succession.

The twenty-five-year-old Postumus did not long survive his grandfather. Augustus expired in his family's villa at Nola, on August 19, 14 CE. Very soon afterward the tribune commanding the guard on Planasia received written instructions to execute Postumus.

Did Livia issue the death warrant? Was this the intrigue, which Pliny claims she shared with Tiberius? Suetonius is undecided:

> [Tiberius] did not at first make Augustus' death public, until the youth Agrippa had been destroyed. The tribune appointed commander of the soldiers killed him after reading instructions, by which he was ordered to do so. There is uncertainty about those instructions, as to whether the dying Augustus left them to eliminate a pretext for insurrection after him; or if Livia dictated [them] in Augustus' name, and whether Tiberius was aware or ignorant thereof.[19]

Dio Cassius places the responsibility for Postumus' death on Tiberius, but reports that some attributed the execution directive to Augustus, and others to Livia:

[Tiberius] straightway sent from Nola and had Agrippa put to death. Afterward he said this was not done on his orders, threatened the perpetrator, and subsequently made no reprisal but allowed men to speculate. Some [hypothesized] that Augustus eliminated [Postumus] before his [own] demise, some that the centurion of the guard, acting on personal responsibility, slew [Postumus] for being involved in revolution, and others that Livia rather than the former (i.e. Tiberius) ordered the latter's (Postumus') execution.[20]

The Elder Pliny records a tradition, which maintained Augustus had eliminated his own descendants to secure the succession for Tiberius. This lends credence to the notion Augustus himself issued the execution order. Tacitus disputes this proposition. He imputes the execution to Tiberius and Livia jointly, in a thorough and damaging treatment of the circumstances under which Postumus met his end:

> The first crime of the new principate was the killing of Agrippa Postumus who, although surprised and unarmed, was nevertheless overcome with difficulty by a centurion of resolute spirit. Tiberius mentioned nothing of these matters in the Senate. He invented a command from his father [Augustus], which ordered the tribune entrusted with the watch not to hesitate in putting Agrippa to death once he himself (i.e. Augustus) had fulfilled his final day. Without question, Augustus had frequently and bitterly brought complaint about the conduct of the youth, so that the exile would be sanctioned by senatorial decree. Otherwise, he was in no way callous to his kindred at any time; nor was it credible, that the death of a grandson was perpetrated for the security of a stepson. More likely Tiberius and Livia, the former from fear, the latter with stepmotherly hatred, hurried the slaughter of a youth they suspected and detested. When the centurion announced,

according to military procedure, that the matter stood as commanded, [Tiberius] responded that he never issued the command and that an account of the facts must be rendered to the Senate. Sallustius Cripsus, a participant in the secret, —he had sent the directive to the tribune— subsequently learned of this. Fearing the matter may incriminate him, since fiction or truth promised equal danger, he admonished Livia not to disclose the secrets of her household, the counsels of friends, or the activities of the soldiers, lest Tiberius diminish the power of the principate by reporting everything to the Senate...[21]

Tacitus' Roman readership would view stepmotherly hatred not so much as personal acrimony, than as a second wife's aspiration to alienate her husband's inheritance from his own offspring to hers.

Innuendo aside, Tacitus' assessment of the reasons for Postumus' execution appear to be accurate. Tiberius and Livia had good reason to fear Postumus, although the latter could hardly have led a successful rebellion by himself. Postumus' behaviors suggest he suffered from autism, a condition not understood in his era. He had passed all of his brief adult life in restrictive, well-scrutinized captivity. Nevertheless he did present a viable menace, as a potential figurehead for dissidents to rally around.

Postumus' blood descent from Augustus gave revolutionaries a convenient pretext for supporting the exiled prince, in opposition to Augustus' legitimate but adoptive heir Tiberius. Suetonius reports that Augustus himself uncovered a plot, to remove Postumus and his mother Julia from their respective island prisons and carry them to the armies. A similar *scenario* would surely have emerged had Postumus survived his grandfather. Tacitus writes that Clemens, a former servant of Postumus, set out to bring the latter to the disgruntled soldiers on the Rhine. Only the slowness of the merchant vessel on which he traveled kept Clemens from reaching Planasia prior to Postumus' execution.

Because he strongly resembled Postumus in age and appearance, Clemens decided to exploit his ex-master's identity to challenge Tiberius' claim to the principate. Tacitus and Dio Cassius describe his endeavor.

Between 14 and 16 CE Clemens cultivated devotees, first in Gaul and subsequently in Italy. Although neither Tacitus nor Dio clarifies whether Clemens actually entered Rome, both writers aver he enjoyed strong support there. Tiberius responded by infiltrating Clemens' following with spies, who captured the imposter. Once he had ensnared Clemens, Tiberius decided not to make any further inquiries. There were no suspects to investigate: Clemens would not reveal the identities of his accomplices even under torture. Once the authorities had put Clemens to death his following fell apart.

The transience of Clemens' movement may prompt a detractor to suggest opposition to Tiberius was an ephemeral fad, and the death of the real Postumus consequently was not necessary. But Tiberius had no way of foreseeing such evanescence. If he tolerated a pretender, he risked assassination for himself and civil war for his country. Tiberius was particularly vulnerable in this respect immediately after Augustus' demise. As *princeps*-designate Tiberius had to obtain the Senate's confirmation, and either pacify or subdue his opponents. A potential usurper stood the best chance of accomplishing his goals before Tiberius had obtained the security of formal or at least tacit acceptance.

Prompt elimination of Postumus, then, was clearly essential to the stability of the principate. But did Livia impose the death sentence? Did she act on her own authority, or at the behest of another—her husband, her son, an adviser like Sallustius Cripsus? We cannot deduce firm answers to these questions, from the vague and recondite testimony of our sources. But it is nevertheless clear, that whoever ordered Postumus' execution had sound reasons of state for doing so. His—or her— intervention kept a precursor of Caligula from claiming and possibly acquiring the succession Augustus had intended for Tiberius.

Germanicus

Handsome, flamboyant, personable, and generous, Livia's eldest grandson was the darling of Romans and provincials alike. He died in Antioch, Syria on October 10, 19 CE at the age of thirty-three. His decease—the result of a mysterious recurring illness—produced intense and widespread mourning.

Germanicus' body was cremated at Antioch. His grief-stricken widow—Augustus' granddaughter Agrippina—braved the dangers of a late autumn voyage to bring the ashes to Rome for a formal state funeral. Germanicus' mother Antonia made the arrangements for this event. Then apparently to the surprise of everyone, neither Tiberius nor Livia nor Antonia attended the obsequies. Tiberius' son Drusus pronounced the panegyric.

Detractors ancient and modern construe Livia's absence as evidence of her hatred for her late grandson. Tacitus writes:

> Tiberius and Augusta (i.e. Livia) kept away from the public, [either] because they felt it inferior to their majesty if they lamented openly, or because hypocrisy would be discerned if everyone's eyes focused on their countenances. I do not discover, in the works of authors or in the record of the daily activities, that [Germanicus'] mother Antonia took any significant part in the ceremony; although in addition to Agrippina, [Tiberius' son] Drusus, and [Germanicus' brother] Claudius, other blood relatives are recorded by name. [Antonia] was either hindered by ill health, or because her spirit, conquered by grief, could not bear to endure the sight of such great evil. I can more easily believe that Tiberius and Augusta, who did not leave home, confined her (i.e. Antonia), so that grandmother and uncle appeared to match the mother's example with equivalent mourning.[22]

Dio Cassius, far more tersely:

> Tiberius and Livia were thoroughly pleased when Germanicus died, while everyone else was terribly sorrowed.[23]

There is no direct evidence Livia disliked Germanicus. On the contrary, their relationship appears to have been indisputably cordial. After a son of Germanicus died in early childhood, Livia dedicated a statue of Cupid the divine son of Venus, in that goddess' temple on Rome's Capitoline Hill. The Cupid bore the likeness of Germanicus' deceased boy.[24] Germanicus subsequently named two of his three daughters—Drusilla and Julia Livilla—after his grandmother.

Even Tacitus admits Germanicus took inspiration from Livia. The night before he launched an attack upon the Germans, the prince was offering a sacrifice as spiritual preparation for the forthcoming campaign. When the blood of the sacrificial victim stained his *praetexta* (the purple-bordered, upper-body garment worn by a magistrate), Livia stepped forward and presented him with one more beautiful.

Tacitus describes Germanicus as "anxious about the secret hatred of his uncle and grandmother." [25] But if Germanicus considered Livia treacherous, why did he neglect to expose her on his deathbed? Tacitus writes that the dying prince whispered some words of warning to Agrippina, but maintains they applied to Tiberius.

Livia was not inclined to conceal disaffection with her relatives. She disliked her awkward grandson Claudius so intensely, that she avoided having to converse or dine with him. She picked arguments with Agrippina, both before and after Germanicus' death. (We shall scrutinize these disagreements more closely in subsequent chapters.)

Tiberius bore the brunt of Livia's wrath as well. The empress maintained a harmonious relationship with her elder son for most of his life. She started to quarrel openly with Tiberius, once the unscrupulous praetorian prefect Sejanus began to create friction between mother and son. Tacitus maintains Livia frequently taunted Tiberius with the reminder he owed his position to her intervention. Augustus had originally planned to make Germanicus his successor after Gaius died. Livia, however, persuaded her husband to implement the arrangement he ultimately employed: Tiberius as successor to Augustus, and Germanicus to Tiberius.

Suetonius describes another clash. Tiberius granted Livia's request to make a non-citizen a juror, but insisted the official jury list show that his mother had forced the decision upon him. Livia thereupon retaliated by reading in public some of Augustus' correspondence with her, in which the late *princeps* complained of Tiberius' acerbic and recalcitrant disposition. The effect was apparently quite stinging. Suetonius claims Tiberius' embarrassment over this incident was one of the principal reasons for his retirement to Capri in 26 CE.

Tacitus maintains Livia's amiability toward Germanicus and Tiberius was hypocritical, the consequence of an aversion very effectively concealed. This premise implies Livia maintained a *façade* of congeniality toward some of the relatives she disliked, but not toward the others. Behavior of this nature was utterly uncharacteristic of Livia. She was never known for being inconsistent or indirect, even in her old age.

THE GRANDDAUGHTERS OF AUGUSTUS

The year 28 CE saw the demise of Vipsania Julia, the elder of Augustus' two granddaughters. She was about forty-five years of age and living in exile at the time of her death. Tacitus writes of the occasion:

> About the same time Julia met death, the granddaughter convicted of adultery whom Augustus condemned, and deported to the island of Trimerus (modern Tremiti in the southern Adriatic Sea), not very far from the coast of Apulia (Puglia). There for twenty years she tolerated exile, sustained by the assistance of Augusta, who after secretly overthrowing her prospering stepsons, openly displayed mercy toward the afflicted.[26]

Here, surely, is grist for a detractor's mill. Tacitus leads his readers to suspect Livia incriminated Julia. He then assures us Livia's charity to the victim, in the form of financial aid, was purely hypocritical.

Vipsania Julia was born in 18 BCE. She married her cousin Lucius Aemilius Paullus, the son of Scribonia's daughter Cornelia. Paullus was Gaius Caesar's colleague in the consulship of 1 CE. Julia bore her husband two children, a son and a daughter. The son eventually married Drusilla, the middle daughter of Germanicus and Agrippina. The daughter of Paullus and Julia was betrothed for a time to Germanicus' brother Claudius. She eventually married a youth named Marcus Junius Silanus.

Julia and her husband were subsequently involved in a scandal, the details of which remain highly obscure. Suetonius writes that Paullus conspired against Augustus, but does not provide the date or details of the plot. The emperor had Paullus executed sometime between 1 and 8 CE. In the latter year, Augustus banished Julia for adultery.

The second-century poet Juvenal maintains Augustus relegated Julia shortly after Paullus' death, recalled her, and then sent her into exile a second time because she failed to mend her profligate ways. Tacitus names Julia's only known paramour. Decimus Junius Silanus was the uncle of Julia's young son-in-law. Silanus was not actually convicted nor sentenced to banishment by a court of law. Augustus renounced him as a personal enemy; whereupon Silanus withdrew from Rome voluntarily.

Why would Livia want to frame Julia?

The husband of a princess was necessarily a man of considerable political importance. We could theorize Livia feared a partner of Julia, be he Paullus or Silanus, might rival or eclipse the empress' descendants in influence and prestige. But for Livia deliberately to destroy Julia in such a situation, would be to throw the baby out with the bathwater. Julia could be turned into a valuable asset, were she to wed a loyal adherent of Livia's family. Julia's presumed lover Silanus appears to have been just such a potential partisan. His brother Marcus, whose son married Julia's daughter Aemilia, was a retainer of Augustus and Tiberius alike. After he became emperor, Tiberius granted Marcus Silanus' request that Decimus be allowed to return to Rome. If Julia and Decimus were innocent, then Livia vitiated two people of whom she could have made good political use.

Was Livia afraid Julia might deliberately convince Augustus to name Paullus or Silanus to the succession in lieu of Tiberius or Germanicus?

Substantiated proof that Julia advocated the overthrow of Tiberius and Germanicus would have given Livia a legitimate legal case against her husband's granddaughter. To attempt or encourage disruption of the emperor's regime was to engage in treason. Julia's banishment would then have been appropriate—not fraudulent, as Tacitus implies.

By the time of Julia's banishment in 8 CE, Augustus' arrangements for devolution of the principate upon Tiberius and Germanicus had been in place for four years. Considerable effort and expense had been invested in those measures. Methods of propaganda—inscriptions, altars, artworks, and coins—were preparing the public to accept the chosen heirs. Germanicus was being readied, to undertake the special responsibilities that one day would be his. He had assumed the quaestorship for 7 CE, five years before attaining the requisite age of twenty-seven. Later that same year, Augustus sent Germanicus to the Pannonian front for firsthand lessons, in military strategy and command protocol from the expertise of Tiberius.

Augustus would hardly have altered his strategy and begun training Paullus or Silanus for the succession, unless some drastic event—for example, the simultaneous decease of the established heirs—forced him to do so. In 8 CE, the year in which he banished the younger Julia for the second time, the emperor reached the age of seventy. He assumed that each day would be his last. On his sixty-third birthday back in 1 CE, Augustus had sent his grandson Gaius a letter, in which the *princeps* expressed surprise at already having lived as long as he had. By 8 CE it was too late to make voluntary changes.

Had Julia tried to persuade Augustus to change his mind about the succession, she would not have faced resistance from Livia alone. Julia's younger sister Agrippina, the obsessively ambitious wife of Germanicus, would surely have opposed any challenges to her husband's destiny. The same would hold true for Germanicus' sister Livilla, who had married Tiberius' son Drusus. Already Livia had successfully convinced Augustus to place Tiberius, rather than Germanicus, next in line for the throne. Now she could count on two other voices to support any necessary opposition to the *status quo.*

Livia, then, had no need to malign the younger Julia. Suppose Julia did try to promote her menfolk as potential replacements for Tiberius and Germanicus? Her efforts would have proven futile, and made her justifiably liable for prosecution.

A detractor might speculate Julia was about to expose Livia as the murderess of Gaius and Lucius. Why would Livia perpetrate the deaths of the two princes, and then go out of her way to keep a potential revelator of those crimes alive? Banishment on a trumped-up charge is a clumsy way to silence a potential accuser. Even in exile, Julia could not exist without some contact with the outside world. She had to be supplied with food and other necessities; ships must ply the island. Suppose Julia managed to get a letter, in which she incriminated Livia, to Augustus or anyone else who might heed the accusations? Maintaining an embargo, year after year, on communications from or about Julia had to be a formidable if not impossible undertaking. *Communiqués* must be intercepted, then suppressed or altered, without detection by Augustus' intelligence agents.

Murder would silence Julia and, as a one-time event, be easier to conceal. Suetonius informs us Julia was pregnant at the time of her banishment. Augustus, questioning the paternity of the child, would not let it be acknowledged or reared as legitimate. Would not Julia's death in childbirth have provided a plausible cover for her murder? Did Livia miss yet another opportunity? And if she did, why did she not arrange for Julia to perish from some accident or supposed illness?

There is no record of Livia providing assistance to the elder Julia or to Agrippa Postumus during their exiles. Augustus' daughter might have benefited from such relief. Suetonius maintains Tiberius worsened the conditions under which she lived. Tacitus and Dio Cassius assert Tiberius allowed his former wife to starve herself to death in hopelessness, neglect, and despair. Why, then, did Livia single out the younger Julia for an allowance?

This question, like so many others from this era, cannot be answered with certainty. Appalled, perhaps, by the conditions under which the elder Julia had perished, Livia may have aspired to spare the daughter a similar fate. Or maybe Livia agreed to supply, from her personal assets, the funds necessary for the younger Julia's upkeep. Augustus habitually took seed money, for the establishment of new state programs, out of his private reserves: hence he may have been cash poor at the time of Julia's sentencing. Whatever Livia's reasons were for supporting her charge, they were neither to conceal an injustice nor salve a guilty conscience.

Tacitus complains further, that Livia deliberately antagonized Augustus' younger granddaughter Agrippina:

Womanly frictions increased because of Livia's stepmotherly sniping at Agrippina.[27]

...and without doubt, Augusta admonished Plancina to impugn Agrippina with womanly rivalry.[28]

The historian avers Sejanus took advantage of this antipathy to pit Livia and her friends, as well as Germanicus' sister Livilla, against Agrippina:

He therefore inveighed against her (i.e., Agrippina's) haughtiness, exciting Augusta's old hatred and Livia's (i.e., Livilla's) recent sense of guilt, so they would persuade Caesar (i.e., Tiberius) that, proud of fecundity and confidant of popular support, she (Agrippina) aspired to reign. And the latter (Livilla), by means of expert calumniators—from among whom she singled out Julius Postumus, who owing to [his] adultery with Mutilia Prisca was among the intimates of her grandmother and suitable to her designs, because Prisca was influential upon the mind of Augusta—made the old crone, by nature anxious about her power, hostile to [her] granddaughter-in-law.[29]

The guilt of Livilla to which Tacitus refers, was her adultery with Sejanus and complicity in the murder of Tiberius' son Drusus her husband.

Tacitus admits quite candidly that Agrippina was exasperating. Throughout his narrative he refers to her excitability, her ferocity, her ill-conceived ambition, impetuosity, and stubborn rage. "But Agrippina, intolerant of equality, greedy for dominance, with masculine concerns laid aside the weaknesses of women." [30] The author describes several occasions, in which the volatile princess provoked Tiberius. Tacitus nevertheless blames Livia, entirely, for the rancor between herself and Agrippina.

Looking beyond Tacitus' innuendo, we find Livia did not injure

Agrippina in the legal sense of that verb. The dowager did not cause the younger woman any physical harm. Nor did Livia deprive Agrippina of her home, the custody of her children, her properties, or any personal rights or freedoms. Had Livia inflicted such criminal or tortious damages upon Agrippina, Tacitus would surely have mentioned them.

Sejanus eventually convinced Tiberius that Agrippina should be banished. The prefect persuaded the emperor to prepare denunciations of Agrippina and her eldest son Nero as dangerous and depraved. Tiberius complied; but Sejanus deliberately held off presenting these letters to the Senate until after Livia had died. Tacitus writes:

> Meanwhile, hereafter there followed indeed a severe and driving despotism: for while Augusta was alive there was still a refuge, since compliance to his mother was ingrained in Tiberius, and Sejanus did not dare exceed the authority of a parent. Now, as if unbridled by reins they broke forth; and letters sent against Agrippina and Nero, which the public believed had been delivered earlier and suppressed by Augusta, were certainly read openly not long after her death. The words were extraordinarily harsh: not with armed rebellion or revolution, but with desire for young men and sexual excess he impugned his grandson. Not having dared fabricate anything against his daughter-in-law, he reproached her for insolence of mouth and impudence of spirit...[31]

If Livia knew about the letters, why did Sejanus wait until she was dead before he revealed them to the Senate? A detractor might well argue, that Livia insisted the letters be read after her death so she could not be blamed for engineering Agrippina's downfall. But if Livia wanted to evade such suspicion, why did she escalate Agrippina's mistrust and anger by harassing her for over a decade?

Let us assume, on the other hand, that Livia did not know about the letters. We must then conclude Sejanus suspected Livia would protect Agrippina. He consequently concealed the letters until after the dowager was dead.

These lines of reasoning support our earlier conclusion. While she may have bickered with Agrippina, Livia did not wish any genuine harm to befall her grandson's widow.

THE DEMENTED LIVIA

One detracting tradition maintains Livia did not originally intend to eliminate her husband's chosen successors. She nevertheless became so obsessed, with not having given Augustus an heir, that she eliminated his blood descendants so he would have to accept hers. Poor Livia! She held out as long as she could, but eventually proved unable to endure her failure to produce the next *princeps*. Thereafter she simply had to do away with her sons' rivals.

The assumption Livia procrastinated with the murders while she wrestled with her conscience, aspires to explain why her alleged victims were relatively mature when they met their deaths. It also tries to justify Tacitus' contention, that Livia alternately persecuted and cosseted Augustus' granddaughters.

When the demise of her son Drusus in 9 BCE left her stricken with grief, Livia sought solace in Greek philosophy. Under the tutelage of a Stoic philosopher, Areus Didymus of Alexandria, Livia found consolation and psychological healing. But then—according to the premise under consideration—Livia still found herself inexorably driven to destroy her husband's grandsons. Either she neglected to discuss her frustrations about the succession with Areus, or his counsels failed to aid her.

This image represents an indisputably disturbed mentality. It portrays Livia as torn between morality and wifely devotion, and an irrepressible craving for specific recognition as the mother of the next *princeps*. Presumably she was not even satisfied with her unique position as the spouse of the reigning emperor.

Mental illness of such intensity reveals itself in a variety of extreme behaviors. Deceitfulness, impulsivity, consistent irresponsibility, and irritability, are anti-social traits that criminals often exhibit. Repressed desires find expression in chronic anxiety, attention deficits, indecisiveness, severe depression, compulsion, memory impairment, bewilderment, and confabulation. Low self-esteem, guilt, and the sense of failure can trigger alcoholism, eating disorders, excessive shyness, accident-proneness, narcissism, asceticism, or masochism. A frustrated need to exercise power can induce delusions and fantasies.

No author—not even Tacitus—attributes any such characteristics to Livia. Had she exhibited even some of them, she would have proven an embarrassment to her family. Augustus would have felt the necessity of secreting her from the public eye, as he did Postumus. True, Tiberius endeavored to restrict Livia's public activities; but he only did this in her extreme old age.

Furthermore an individual, troubled and distracted by a severe, pathological obsession such as the one just described, could not have made the sound political and social decisions that Augustus and Tiberius alike entrusted to Livia.

In Summation

Dear reader, the information we have examined leads us to an inescapable discovery. Looking through and beyond the pretentious posturing and innuendo of hostile tradition, we find that Livia could not have committed the crimes of which she has stood accused for two millennia.

NOTES TO CHAPTER IV

1   *Romaïka* 53.33.
2   A statement by Suetonius (*Divus Julius* 83.2) suggests the possibility of a younger Pedius. The author says Caesar the Dictator divided his estate among the grandsons of his two sisters. Three quarters went to Octavius; the remainder was split between Pinarius and Pedius.
3   *Annales* 1.3.
4   *Romaïka* 55.10a.
5   Suetonius' word is *mandata*—mandates, orders, commissions.
6   Augustus' sixth and youngest grandson, born to Julia and Tiberius sometime between 11 and 9 BCE, died in infancy.
7   Gaius was the *praenomen* of Caesar the Dictator, and of his father. Augustus' first name was Gaius as well; but he was called after his natural father Octavius. Lucius Julius Caesar was the name of Mark Antony's maternal uncle, who was a cousin and fellow senator of the Dictator.
8   Being an adjective, *Postumus* is more correctly employed in Latin as a *cognomen* than as a *praenomen*.
9   This group of seamounts includes Elba—the site of Napoleon's first exile—as well as Monte Cristo. Look for references to Pianosa in Alexandre Dumas Pere's classic novel, *The Count of Monte Cristo*.
10   *Annales* 1.3.
11   *Annales* 1.5.
12   *Romaïka* 56.30.
13   *Historia natura* 7.150.
14   *Peri adolesxias* 11.
15   *Historiae Romanae* 2.112.
16   *Divus Augustus* 65.
17   *Liber de Caesaribus* 1.
18   *Epitome de Caesaribus* 1.
19   *Tiberius* 22.
20   *Romaïka* 57.3 My profound thanks to Reverend Anastasius Bandy, for assistance with the translation of this passage.

[21] *Annales* 1.6.
[22] *Annales* 3.4.
[23] *Romaïka* 57.6.
[24] Venus, through her mortal son Aeneas, was the legendary ancestress of the Julian house.
[25] *Annales* 1.33.
[26] *Annales* 4.71.
[27] *Annales* 1.33.
[28] *Annales* 2.43.
[29] *Annales* 4.12.
[30] *Annales* 6.25.
[31] *Annales* 5.3.

CHAPTER V

EXPLAINING THE SINISTER TRADITION

Since the record of Livia's dynastic crimes is spurious, how do we explain its origin? What constitutes the proverbial smoking gun—the root cause of the malignant tradition?

Actually the plural combination smoking guns more aptly describes the basis of Livia's criminal reputation. Various factors have united to create the corrupt image we have of her.

APPARENT PLAUSIBILITY

When considered superficially, the accusations against Livia do seem highly credible. Augustus uncannily lost one blood heir after another, until he had no choice but to make Tiberius his successor. The pattern of deaths appears wholesale and systematic, until one carefully examines the events that surround each occurrence. Only then do we perceive that the timings, antecedents, and consequences of the incidents are too random and illogical to be premeditated.

Neither the demise of Marcellus, nor that of the elder Agrippa, promised the throne to Livia's offspring. Postumus was never a threat in the first place. Only the deaths of Gaius and Lucius forced Augustus to select Tiberius. But the clumsy, haphazard, ill-timed procedures by which these princes were supposedly murdered hardly characterize an incisive and cunning thinker like Livia.

Other family misfortunes, such as the disgraces of Augustus' daughter and granddaughter and the death of his grandnephew Germanicus, give the impression of having been premeditated to protect Tiberius' tenure of the succession. Scrutiny nevertheless reveals that if Livia perpetrated these tragedies, she wound up worsening conditions for herself and her son. Once again, such bungling fails to befit an intrepid schemer.

THE LITERATURE OF THE OPPOSITION

Not all publications dating from Augustus' reign were complimentary. Some writers were highly critical of the emperor, his family, his associates, and his regime.

One offending author was Cassius Severus, a lawyer who routinely produced denunciations of Augustus and other notables. Paullus Fabius Maximus, himself one of Severus' targets, successfully prosecuted the writer for treason. Another muckraker was Timagenes, an Alexandrian Greek who taught rhetoric at Rome and published diatribes of the imperial family. Misrepresentations of Livia originated with these contemporaneous insinuators. Seneca the tutor and regent of Nero writes that Cassius Severus attacked distinguished women as well as men, and that Timagenes aimed disparagements specifically at Livia.

None of this hostile literature is extant today, largely because Augustus and later Julio-Claudian emperors suppressed it. Roman writers like Tacitus, however, had access to this invective—if not to the actual material then to people's recollections of it.

RHETORIC

Imputations of murders and other crimes to Livia abound in the narrative of our muckraking friend Tacitus. Although less vituperative, Dio Cassius's account closely parallels that of Tacitus in detail and depth. Tacitus actually does not mention Livia in connection with the death of Marcellus; Dio does but dismisses Livia's guilt as questionable. Tacitus writes that Livia may have arranged the murders of Gaius and Lucius. Dio attributes those princes' deaths to natural causes; but he adds that some believed Livia engineered Lucius' demise because it coincided with Tiberius' return to Rome from Rhodes. Tacitus asserts Livia persuaded Augustus to remand Postumus to exile. Dio hints at this, writing that Postumus' slanders of Livia were among the principal reasons his grandfather banished him.

Tacitus and Dio alike maintain Augustus visited Postumus on Planasia in the summer of 14 CE. Tacitus adds that Livia learned of the journey from Marcia, the wife of Augustus' indiscreet traveling companion Paullus Fabius Maximus. Both writers suggest Livia murdered Augustus lest he change his mind about bequeathing the throne to Tiberius. Tacitus writes that after Augustus' decease, Livia demanded Postumus' execution to satisfy her stepmotherly hatred for him. Dio claims Tiberius ordered Postumus' death, but adds that some believed the mandate came from Livia.

Tacitus challenges the popular assumption Germanicus died of poisoning, but goes on to create the impression Gnaeus Calpurnius Piso and his wife Munatia Plancina certainly did try to poison the prince. Tacitus also insinuates Livia encouraged the couple's malfeasance and then obfuscated their guilt. Now differing sharply, Dio asserts Piso and Plancina definitely poisoned Germanicus. He adds that Tiberius, hoping to diffuse the suspicion he had instigated the murder, personally arraigned Piso before the Senate. Dio does not connect Livia with Piso and Plancina at all. He nevertheless joins Tacitus in claiming Livia took pleasure in her grandson's death.

Both authors question the reliability of their source material for Livia's criminality. They repeatedly employ such combinations as, *some say,* or, *it was suspected that.* And yet by simply reproducing damaging if spurious information about Livia, Tacitus and Dio focus their readers' attention upon it. Tacitus, moreover, employs the rhetorical device of double entendre, which gives particular emphasis to the suspicions he raises. He makes a strongly factual statement, then immediately contradicts it with innuendo. He writes that Gaius and Lucius perished from natural causes, or perhaps from their stepmother Livia's treachery. Antonia absented herself from Germanicus' funeral because of ill health, or because Tiberius and Livia restrained her to conceal their own hypocrisy. While some of Agrippa's offspring certainly perished by the sword, others were believed to have been starved or poisoned. Livia rendered assistance to the younger Julia after having secretly ruined the latter's family.

Tacitus admits to citing rumors, but presents these insinuations as if they were verifiable truths. Livia and Tiberius hastened the execution of Postumus, Tiberius acting from fear and Livia from stepmotherly contempt. Germanicus was troubled by the secret hatred of his grandmother and uncle. Surely Livia urged Plancina to impugn Agrippina. Livia and Tiberius boycotted Germanicus' funeral because they felt attendance would belittle their majesty or betray their insincerity. Livia's defense of Plancina provoked the contempt of all decent men. Livia considered Agrippina a threat.

In one notable description of Livia, Tacitus employs an adjective that carries various meanings. After deploring Augustus' rise to power as the development of despotism, Tacitus calls Livia *gravis* to the world as a mother (i.e., of Tiberius), and *gravis* to the Caesars as a stepmother. Translators, looking at the context in which Tacitus uses the adjective, tend to give *gravis* the pejorative connotation of terrible, dreadful, or horrendous. *Gravis*, however, in Latin can simply mean important or significant.

Tacitus uses another double entendre in his description of Augustus' feelings for Livia. "Then Caesar, with desire for her person, wrested [her from her] marriage." [1] One meaning of the Latin word *forma*, translated here as person, is physical visage or appearance. When read from this standpoint, Tacitus' words suggest that Augustus, in his eagerness to satisfy his visceral infatuation for Livia, married her without regard for her intentions or integrity. *Forma*, however, can also denote attitude, demeanor, or character. We shall see in our next chapter, that these were the very aspects of Livia's personality Augustus respected and loved. Tacitus combines ambiguity with innuendo, to incline his readers toward negative views of Livia and her kindred.

Tacitus' narrative is clearly contradictory in places. At the beginning of the **Annales**, Livia so dominates the senile Augustus that he banishes Postumus to Planasia without due process of law. Two paragraphs later,

Augustus has sufficient presence of mind to evade Livia's scrutiny and visit Postumus without her knowledge. The supposedly incompetent emperor then deduces that Paullus Fabius Maximus disclosed the secret of the voyage.

Tacitus expresses doubt Germanicus was poisoned, but subsequently calls Plancina his murderess. The author assures us Livia, intent on persecuting Agrippina, succumbed readily to Sejanus' efforts to exacerbate friction between the two women. Tacitus subsequently insists Livia protected Agrippina from Sejanus, and the prefect was afraid to countermand the dowager's intentions.

Making matters even worse for Livia, no extant ancient writer specifically rejects her criminality. The obsequious Velleius Paterculus describes the empress as "a woman most remarkable, and in every respect more like the gods than men." [2] Philo Judaeus praises her intellectualism. The younger Seneca extols Livia's self-control, her acumen in political matters, and her companionable relationship with Augustus. Still, none of these apologists systematically challenges derogations of Livia's character.

Neither Plutarch nor Suetonius comments on Livia's integrity at all. Pliny alludes to some sort of collusion between Livia and Tiberius at the time of Augustus' death, but does not provide any specifics. Dio Cassius waffles. He disputes the contention Livia murdered Marcellus and attributes, to rumor, suspicions she engineered the deaths of Lucius, Gaius, Augustus, and Postumus. But by charging Livia with plausible motives, Dio leaves his readers with the feeling she might be guilty after all. Furthermore, he definitely sullies her character by maintaining she was thoroughly pleased when Germanicus died.

The anonymous author of the **Epitome de Caesaribus** adds to the damage. He (or she) emphasizes, but does not rebuff, prior writers' assertions that Livia murdered Augustus because the emperor intended to recall Postumus.

Let us consider, for the sake of contrast, a derogatory tradition which attributes dynastic murders to Augustus. Notice it does not persist, like that of Livia, in the popular imagination. The allegations about Augustus appear in four references. Three of these contain sharp rebuttals. Tacitus, rather indirectly, charges Augustus with the murder of the elder Drusus:

Utter truths about Drusus the old men spoke: displeasing
to the ruling are the civic temperaments of sons; nor are
they cut off for anything, other than because they agitate
to embrace the Roman people with equal rights through
restored liberty.[3]

Suetonius reports the same tradition, but zealously discards it:

[Drusus] did not equivocate at any time that he would
restore the pristine condition of the Republic, should he
ever be able. Consequently I believe some have dared
to insinuate that, suspected by Augustus and recalled
from his province (Gaul), upon tarrying he was removed
by poison. This I mention not to pass it by, rather than
because I think it true or close to true; for Augustus
cared for him so greatly while he lived, that he always
named him coheir with [his] sons, as once he declared in
the Senate; and when he was dead, so praised him before
the assembled people, and prayed the gods that they
make similar to him his Caesars [Gaius and Lucius],
and give to him so honorable an exit whenever he should
die. Not content with having a eulogy in verses of his
own composition sculpted on his tomb, [Augustus]
also composed a memorial of [Drusus'] life in a prose
oration.[4]

The elder Pliny maintains Augustus resented a rumor, suggesting
he murdered his grandsons to secure the throne for Tiberius. One of
the emperor's many vexations, Pliny writes, was the "imputed deaths
of [his] children."[5]

Tacitus stridently rejects the same notion:

He (Augustus) was in no way callous to his kindred at
any time; nor was it credible, that the death of a grandson
was perpetrated for the security of a stepson.[6]

In short, Livia's criminal reputation endures because it receives considerable embellishment, but virtually no denial, in the historic record.

Augustus' Contribution to Livia's Criminal Reputation

Suetonius writes that at the mention of Postumus and the two Julias, Augustus would sigh deeply, and sometimes exclaim, "Would that I had remained unmarried, or perished childless!" This is a paraphrase of a line in Homer's **Iliad**. Hector curses Paris with the words, "Would that you had remained unborn, or perished unmarried!" [7] Childless and unborn are designated in Greek by the same word; the context of use changes the meaning.

Writing a century after Augustus' death, Suetonius makes clear the emperor only intended to deprecate his disgraced daughter and grandchildren. The marriage Augustus regrets, in this narrow and specific implication, is his espousal of Scribonia which led to the birth of Julia. Later authors appear to have missed the emperor's point, and assumed he was deploring the fact he had married at all. Dio Cassius maintains Augustus quipped his variant on Homer, "because he was unfortunate in marriage and in the waywardness of his children." [8] Sextus Aurelius Victor characterizes Augustus as fortunate in all ways, except in marriage and with his children.

The assumption which consequently evolved, is that Augustus was unfortunate in marriage for the duration of his wedded life—hence in his union with Livia. Additionally he was unhappy with his children.

The Evil Stepmother

There is no evidence of personal friction between Livia and her husband's daughter. Julia was well respected for her gentleness and humanity. We presume she engaged in the charitable activities that were expected of aristocratic women. The northern Aegean island of Thasos honored her as benefactress. Julia was fond of literature and, like

Livia, extremely well educated. Here, however, the similarity between the women's lifestyles ended.

Livia was demure and unassuming. She preferred recognition as a chaste and devoted housewife who kept her husband's home orderly and comfortable. From cloth she wove herself she fashioned his garments. Her own dress was simple and free of adornment. She seldom appeared in public. When she did venture forth, she surrounded herself with matrons and mature men of impeccable reputation. Her comments and responses to personal questions were forthright, dignified, and uncontroversial.

Julia contrastingly reveled in notoriety. She wore revealing, sexually explicit clothing. She frequented public venues, at which she preferred the company of rakish, sophisticated young men.

So long as a husband was part of her life, Julia was discreet about her sexual habits. With flippant and provocative evasions she deflected criticisms and malicious gossip about her alleged infidelities. After Tiberius abandoned her in 6 BCE, Julia became unabashedly dissolute. She took at least five lovers. By night in the Forum, she participated in orgies of wine drinking and group sex. In what seems likely a gesture of filial defiance, Julia placed a wreath on a statue of Marsyas. This lusty, lute-playing, Phrygian god had once challenged Apollo—Augustus' patron divinity—to a contest of musical proficiency.

Over the course of his reign, Augustus imposed a variety of moralizing regulations on the citizenry of Rome. His legislation prohibited abortion, criminalized adultery and homosexuality, and placed penalties on marriages with non-citizens. One law imposed tax penalties on unmarried persons, and on couples with fewer than three children. Another condemned extravagant personal expenditures, so family assets were not depleted before they could be bequeathed to subsequent generations. Additional legislation restricted the manumission of slaves, and their consequent dispersal among the free populace. Augustus' rules aspired to protect, preserve, and proliferate the pure Italian stock from which the ancient families and clans of Rome descended. Foreign peoples, who had entered Italy as the result of Roman conquests and trade, now threatened to outnumber and dilute the native population.

Despite the lofty intentions of Augustus' ethical legislation, many Romans resented it. Some regarded it as an infringement upon personal freedoms and rights. Marriage—frequently loveless and virtually always arranged—could present a distasteful prospect. Other citizens found the expenses of rearing three or more children prohibitive and financially damaging, despite government subsidies and tax abatements. Furthermore the laws raised an ethical question of a different sort. What other forms of self-determination was the new regime going to restrict?

Opponents of the moral laws discovered, in Julia's brazen hedonism, a refreshing form of protest. The princess' sympathizers coalesced into a distinct and sharply dissident political faction.

Livia embraced and exemplified the conventional domesticity from which Julia and her adherents recoiled. Augustus, moreover, approved and promoted his wife and her conduct as the paradigm of ideal Roman womanhood. Livia, consequently and understandably, became the dissidents' ideological enemy. She was the instrument through which Augustus disseminated the measures his own daughter rejected as repressive.

People had other reasons for hating Livia. Like most societies of its era, Roman culture was male chauvinistic. Its traditions held that women should manage their homes and children, leaving government operations to their men. Along came Livia, whose *auctoritas* exceeded that of many politicians. Similar situations ruffle masculine feathers in our present era.

Augustus' enduring affection for Livia was no secret. Most ancient writers—including the polemic Tacitus—allude to the imperial couple's happiness and compatibility. This visible devotion conceivably grated upon Romans who were chafing in loveless arranged marriages. It also must have irritated designing females, who aspired to usurp Livia's place in her husband's heart, home, and political system.

Relatives and retainers of the Scribonii Libones, the family of Julia's mother, joined the protest faction. When the Senate sentenced Julia to banishment from Rome for the capital crime of adultery, Scribonia voluntarily accompanied her daughter into exile. One of Julia's codefendants in her trial of 2 BCE was Publius Cornelius Scipio. He was her half-brother, Scribonia's son by a husband prior to Octavian. Scipio was never indicted for adultery with Julia, for no ancient writer mentions incest. Nor was Scipio sentenced to the prescribed penalty for adultery: *exsilium*, with its forfeiture of property and constitutional rights. Scipio was nevertheless found guilty of having contributed to Julia's corruption. He suffered the lesser penalty of *relegatio*, which allowed him to retain his privileges and goods.

Back in Rome, Julia's partisans clamored and demonstrated for her release. The Libones likely spearheaded this movement. Augustus eventually agreed to transfer Julia from the island of Pandataria to the mainland city of Rhegium. The Scribonii were patrons of this pleasant municipality, located at the toe of Italy's boot.

Scribonian hostility to Livia's family predates Augustus' divorce of Julia's mother. Sextus Pompeius, the husband of Scribonia's niece, had refused asylum to Livia and the elder Tiberius Claudius Nero, after their flight from Perusia in 40 BCE. The animosity is puzzling, in light of the Romans' traditional respect for kinship. Livia was somehow related to the Libones. We have already encountered Marcus Livius Drusus Libo. Pompeia, the daughter of Sextus Pompeius and his Scribonia, married a kinsman of her mother and aunt. Pompeia's sons were called Lucius and Marcus Scribonius Libo Drusus.

But the Libones apparently were enemies of the Claudii Nerones. After Julia married the younger Tiberius Nero, she disparaged her new husband as an inferior. Julia could hardly have scorned Tiberius' membership in the aristocratic *gens Claudia*. Furthermore, an ancestor of Tiberius was a military hero of the Second Punic War (218 – 201 BCE). As one of the consuls for 207 BCE, Gaius Claudius Nero led the campaign that expelled the Carthaginian forces from Italy. These credentials made Tiberius' pedigree certainly more distinguished than that of Julia's former husband, the *novus homo* Agrippa. Her condescension is therefore difficult to explain, unless it arose from the attitude of her mother's relatives. Years later Lucius Libo Drusus would extol his descent from Pompey the Great, as well as his relationship to Julia's mother and to cousins within the imperial family. This Libo, however, was clearly no friend of the Nerones. In 16 CE he hatched an abortive plot to strike down Tiberius, Germanicus, and Tiberius' son Drusus, and establish himself as *princeps*.

The Libones came to have reason for resenting Livia as well. Although she agreed to an amicable divorce, Scribonia apparently begrudged Octavian's preference for his new wife. Suetonius reports that while she and Octavian were still married, Scribonia objected to her husband's interest in another woman. But for Livia's intrusion, Scribonia might have been empress. Moreover as Octavian's new spouse, Livia introduced the hated Nerones into his household. The Libones could only watch and fume, while Augustus bestowed special political privileges and marital connections upon their enemies. But for Livia, these advantages might have gone to the Scribonii. Then came the crowning devastation. Augustus appointed Livia's son and grandson—both Nerones—to be his successors. But for Livia, a Scribonius Libo might have been Rome's second emperor.

Julia's sons enjoyed their own coteries of followers. Dio Cassius writes that some adherents were genuine admirers. Nevertheless many others were sycophants, who apparently had good reason to assume adulations would be rewarded. Dio's description of their personalities suggests Gaius and Lucius responded readily to flattery. Much to Augustus' disappointment, his grandsons inclined toward self-indulgence and arrogance which their adulators intensified. Aggrieved when Gaius was elected consul prior to military age (sixteen), Augustus uttered a reverential hope no forthcoming circumstance should require a man to hold the consulship before the age of twenty.

The toadies' hopes died with the young princes. Tiberius the new successor-designate despised both flattery and the people who endeavored to exploit it. Those who had once hoped to profit, from ingratiating themselves to Gaius and Lucius, now joined the ranks of the disgruntled who attributed their misfortunes to Livia.

Some displaced supporters of Gaius and Lucius might have looked upon Livia as an enemy even before the princes died. Since Gaius and Lucius were the grandsons of Scribonia, their retinue must have included relatives and retainers of the Libones.

One might think Tiberius would have come under suspicion of having arranged the assassinations of Augustus' grandsons. Tiberius was the principal beneficiary of the princes' deaths. He had already been scrutinized for purportedly engaging in seditious activities while living in exile on Rhodes. Why does criminal tradition exempt Tiberius from accusation, but impute the deaths of Gaius and Lucius to Livia?

When Augustus adopted Gaius and Lucius in 17 BCE, Livia became their legal stepmother. This fact eventually created and reinforced presumptions she had engineered the princes' deaths. The concept of the malevolent, scheming stepmother pervaded Roman cultural, folkloric, literary, and even legal traditions. Remarriage after widowhood or divorce was common in ancient Rome. While stepfathers were held to be generally benign, well-intentioned stepmothers were looked upon as rare anomalies. It was presumed that, on becoming a stepmother, a woman developed a natural and inexorable urge to abuse and ultimately eliminate her stepchildren. This specifically misogynist prejudice was more socio-economic than psychological. If a stepmother destroyed her husband's children from his prior marriage, the stepmother's own offspring stood to inherit the husband's estate without competition. A stepfather, by contrast, had no reason to harbor similar hostility toward his stepchildren. His assets would devolve upon his natural children whether the stepchildren survived him or not.

When Augustus indicated Tiberius for the succession in 4 CE, Livia became a stepmother whose offspring had profited from the deaths of her stepsons. As a consequence she fit one aspect of the evil stepmother stereotype. Detractors could now, with credibility, accuse her of mistreatment and murder—the other stock elements of the stepmother image. Postumus the younger brother of Gaius and Lucius definitely embraced this attitude. Dio Cassius maintains the youth maligned or slandered Livia as a stepmother. The same view of Livia produced rumors, attributing Postumus' banishment to her stepmotherly machinations.

The chronology in which Livia's evil-stepmother characterization emerged explains why she was not blamed for the disgrace of Augustus' daughter. Once Julia became a married woman upon espousing Marcellus back in 25 BCE, she legally ceased to be Livia's stepdaughter. Julia' banishment occurred in 2 BCE, five years before the death of Gaius catapulted Tiberius to the succession. Livia's reputation as a malevolent stepmother to Julia's children had not yet developed.

Aggrieved members of the armed forces began to champion Julia and her children. Augustus suppressed a plot to free his daughter and her son Postumus from their island prisons and transport them to the armies. Germanicus regained control over mutinous troops on the Rhine frontier by invoking their loyalty to his wife Agrippina: Julia's daughter.

Any hopes Julia's partisans might have entertained, about persuading Augustus to alter the succession, disappeared with his death in the autumn of 14 CE. The execution of Postumus a few days later destroyed the possibility of forcibly enthroning Augustus' youngest grandson.

The death of a husband who had made a stepson his heir, followed immediately by the deliberate killing of the ostensibly rightful heir: surely these were the doings of a stepmother! The events of 14 CE, like those of 4 CE, matched preconceived expectations of stepmotherly malfeasance. If Livia murdered Gaius and Lucius so Augustus would convey the succession to Tiberius, she must have destroyed her husband to keep him from retracting that decision. Tacitus cites a stepmother's hatred as Livia's specific reason for demanding the death of Postumus. This statement implies that so long as Postumus was alive, Livia considered him a threat to Tiberius. Remember, Tacitus' Roman readers would have interpreted stepmotherly animosity as the intent to purloin a stepchild's legacy.

The adherence of dissidents to Julia and her kindred persisted into Tiberius' reign. Clemens, the slave who impersonated the late Postumus in 16 CE, garnered a large if short-lived following. Lucius Libo Drusus, who conspired against Tiberius later the same year, touted his relationship to Julia's mother Scribonia and to his cousins within the imperial family. Libo, however, did not attract adherents. Either his plans were uncovered before he could cultivate devotees, or he was truly as ridiculous as Tacitus makes him out to be.

The majority of disaffected centered their allegiance upon Germanicus. He certainly had the right genealogy to be their hero. Germanicus was the son of Julia's cousin Antonia, the husband of Julia's younger daughter Agrippina, and the father of Julia's grandchildren. He also enjoyed a reputation for liberality. Many supporters believed Germanicus would restore freedoms they felt the prevailing policies of the principate had suppressed.

After Germanicus died, his adherents rallied about his widow. Agrippina was emotionally unstable by nature, and overwhelmed with grief at her husband's demise. She was easily persuaded—if not by her own convictions, then by the dissidents who exploited her—to insist Germanicus' death was no accident. Suspicion fell upon Gnaeus Calpurnius Piso, the recalcitrant imperial legate of Syria, and his wife Munatia Plancina. Tried by the Senate, Piso was found guilty of insurrection but cleared of Germanicus' murder. After finding Plancina guilty of undisclosed crimes, the Senate proceeded to commute her sentence at Livia's behest.

Agrippina and her party refused to accept the verdicts. The dissidents also insinuated Tiberius had encouraged the elimination of Germanicus, so the succession would devolve upon his own son Drusus. Why else would the Senate exonerate so guilty a couple, except for fear of alienating the emperor? Lucius Aelius Sejanus, Tiberius' unscrupulous praetorian prefect, furthered the suspicions of Agrippina. His suggestions led her to insist Tiberius intended to destroy her children as well. So long as descendants of Augustus lived, they could legitimately challenge Tiberius' progeny for the succession.

Livia must have defended Tiberius against Agrippina's imputations, because the princess and her followers cast the empress-mother as their enemy. The detractors capitalized upon Livia's emergent reputation as an evil stepmother. Tacitus their apologist writes that Livia bore a stepmother's enmity toward Agrippina. He also complains Livia verbally harassed Agrippina with stepmotherly invectives.

Agrippina was never Livia's legal stepdaughter. Nor did the younger woman stand to receive an inheritance the dowager might have coveted for her own descendants. The transfer of the succession to Tiberius' son Drusus, on the heels of Germanicus' sudden and suspicious demise, admittedly resembled the stepmotherly objective of alienating a legacy from its rightful heir to an interloper. Drusus was not, like Germanicus, a blood relative of Augustus. Germanicus, however, had not been Livia's stepchild but her own grandson, and undisputed heir to the principate. How could Agrippina's partisans assert, with credibility, that Livia desired Germanicus' destruction? By alleging Livia hated Germanicus— and secretly, too, since the overt interactions between grandmother and grandson had been consistently harmonious.

Just when Agrippina's supporters were endeavoring to embellish

Livia's reputation for malevolence, Livia herself committed two acts that substantiated the dissidents' insinuations. Firstly she did not attend Germanicus' funeral. Subsequently she demanded a legal pardon for Munatia Plancina, Germanicus' suspected murderess.

Did Livia fail to foresee that her enemies would malign her for her deeds? Was there some truth to Agrippina's accusations of hate and malfeasance? Or did Livia have political objectives that outweighed the consequences of hostile response?

GERMANICUS' FUNERAL

Livia's detractors, ancient and modern, want us to believe she avoided Germanicus' funeral because she hated him. In our last chapter we established the absurdity of this proposition. Livia was neither indirect nor evasive about her feelings towards her kinfolk and their actions. When she disapproved of a relative, she expressed her opinion in unequivocally certain terms.

We must also remember Livia was not the only member of the imperial family who shunned the obsequies for Germanicus. Tiberius and the decedent's mother Antonia abstained as well.

Unfortunately we cannot deduce any precise explanation for which the absentees stayed away. Nor can we tell whether the three concurred, or if each followed his or her own incentives for remaining at home. We can nevertheless consider some plausible possibilities. Let us review Tacitus' comments about the absences:

> Tiberius and Augusta kept away from the public, [either] because they felt it inferior to their majesty if they lamented openly, or because hypocrisy would be discerned if everyone's eyes focused on their countenances…[Antonia] was either hindered by ill health, or because her spirit, conquered by grief, could not bear to endure the sight of such great evil. I can more easily believe that Tiberius and Augusta, who did not leave home, confined [Antonia], so that grandmother

and uncle appeared to match the mother's example with equivalent mourning.[9]

The three absentees conceivably preferred to grieve in private, as Tacitus begrudgingly suggests. Livia, as we know, sought comfort from Greek philosophy after her younger son Drusus was killed. Tiberius was similarly forbearing. When his son died in 23 CE, the emperor went about his usual routine without betraying any apparent sorrow. He smiled and even joked when a deputation from Ilium offered him condolences.[10]

Antonia quite possibly stayed away specifically because Livia did. The personal bond between the two women was very strong. After marrying Antonia in 19 BCE, Drusus lived with her in his mother and stepfather's home. Antonia and her children continued to reside with Augustus and Livia after Drusus was killed.

Since Germanicus' funeral took place in winter, ill weather and consequent ill health may have kept some if not all of our defectors from attending. The three were no longer young: Livia was seventy-seven years old; Tiberius was sixty and Antonia fifty-four. Tacitus admits Antonia may have been sick. Livia's health was possibly in decline as well. In two years she would suffer a nearly fatal illness.

The trio conceivably remained home to ease Tiberius' worries, about the monarchic implications of excessive attention to a death in the imperial family. Tacitus writes:

> He (i.e., Tiberius) proclaimed by edict that many illustrious Romans had died for the sake of the state, none honored with such intense grief. And that was special, both to himself and to everybody, so long as moderation was exercised. Certainly, conduct did not become leaders of men and an imperial people, which did [suit] ordinary homes or communities. Grief and the solace of mourning may befit initial grief; but now the soul must be restored to firmness, as once Divus Julius having lost his only daughter, as Divus Augustus bereft of his grandchildren, pushed away sadness. There was

no need for time-honored examples, of how often the
Roman people had resolutely endured the slaughter of
armies, the annihilation of generals, the complete loss of
noble families. *Principes* are mortal; the State is eternal.[11]

The boycott may also have indicated the absentees' distaste for
Germanicus' insolent and insubordinate behavior as heir-apparent. There
is absolutely no evidence to suggest he aspired to overthrow Tiberius. On
the contrary, Germanicus' conduct at the time of his uncle's succession
demonstrated an unassailable loyalty. Since Germanicus was then
governor of Gaul, the responsibility of pacifying the mutinous troops
on the Rhine frontier fell to him. He staunchly rejected the dissenters'
efforts to proclaim him emperor in Tiberius' stead.

Germanicus was nevertheless ambitious and impetuous. His
grandiose but unrealistic designs caused the Roman populace to
admire, and Tiberius to fret. After quelling the mutiny of 14 CE,
Germanicus spent the next two years running punitive and invasive
raids into German territory. He aspired to extend the Roman frontier
from the Rhine to the Elbe, as his father Drusus had done, even though
Augustus had ordered the region abandoned as impossible to patrol.
Germanicus was largely victorious, but by the proverbial skin of his
teeth. His complicated and arduous campaigns endangered and depleted
Roman personnel and equipment. Citing the proven impracticality of
the project, Tiberius recalled Germanicus in the autumn of 16 CE.
Germanicus insisted victory was imminent and refused to comply. The
emperor managed to lure his nephew back to Rome with the promise
of alternative glories. Tiberius guaranteed Germanicus a triumph for
victories already achieved, plus the consulship for 18 CE.

By the time Germanicus entered upon his consulship, he was
already *en route* to the East as Tiberius' special envoy. Just before the
prince departed on his eastern mission, Tiberius designated Gnaeus
Piso to be imperial legate of Syria. Gossip maintained—perhaps with
justification—that the emperor had secretly assigned Piso to oversee
Germanicus' activities in the region. Germanicus chafed at the notion
of being subject to a watchdog and quarreled bitterly with the legate.
Tacitus maintains retainers of Germanicus increased his anger by

casting unfounded aspersions against Piso, his wife Plancina, and their two sons. The author adds that Plancina nevertheless did her part to heighten frictions, by hurling insults at Germanicus and Agrippina.

The prince competently executed the tasks his uncle assigned to him. Germanicus placed a Roman puppet on the throne of Armenia without precipitating war with the Parthian empire. He converted the former client kingdoms of Cappadocia, Cilicia, and Commagene into Roman provinces, implemented tax relief measures in Syria and Judaea, and negotiated trade agreements with caravan cities.

But as in Germany, Germanicus began to conduct himself inappropriately. He and Agrippina visited the Nabatean Arabs, whose king hosted a banquet in their honor. During the festivities the Nabatean ruler presented Germanicus and his wife with a pair of heavy gold crowns. He then gave lighter crowns to the members of Germanicus' retinue, including Piso. The latter carped that the entertainment was not for the son of the king of Parthia, but for that of the Roman *princeps*. Casting away his crown, Piso proceeded to launch a diatribe against profligacy.[12] The legate's message was that Germanicus, in accepting the banquet and crown, had behaved like an eastern monarch. This was the very image the Augustan system assiduously sought to avoid.

Germanicus subsequently departed for Egypt, to revel in the Pharaonic antiquities. By doing so he violated a ruling, which Augustus had insisted must be stringently obeyed. No senator or equestrian might enter the duchy unless he first obtained permission from the emperor. Germanicus took his disregard of the regulation a step further. He relieved a food scarcity at Alexandria, by ordering a special distribution of grain. The mistakes, very possibly, were honest ones. In anticipation of his eastern junket, the Senate had given Germanicus *maius imperium* over the senatorial and imperial provinces "that were separated [from Italy] by the sea." [13] Germanicus may have assumed this delineation included Egypt.

Tiberius made a formal complaint in the Senate about this apparent indifference to protocol, and sent a sharp reprimand directly to Germanicus. There is no record, however, that Germanicus ever apologized to emperor or Senate for having overstepped his authority. Tiberius also chided his nephew more gently for dressing in Greek costume and sandals at Alexandria. It was improper for Germanicus to forego his toga and shoes in public so long as he was exercising the powers of a Roman official.

Agrippina gave her relatives cause for vexation as well. Tacitus describes her as "a little excitable," then continues "with chastity and love of husband [her] wild spirit turned toward good." [14] The princess had maintained a high profile among the armies on the Rhine frontier. Germanicus exploited this visibility to his advantage. During the mutiny of 14 CE he expressed his dismay at having to send his family away: because the troops were refusing to fight, the area was no longer safe for women and children. The mutineers allowed Agrippina to depart, but insisted she leave her youngest son Gaius behind in the camp. The sight of Augustus' granddaughter, weeping and embracing her little boy before she departed, mollified many mutineers and enabled Germanicus to reassert control.

During her husband's subsequent maneuvers against the Germans, Agrippina remained in his base camp at Vetera (modern Xanten, Germany). When a rumor spread that Germanicus was trapped and the Germans were descending on the Rhine, the defenders of the base garrison recommended destroying the bridge over the river. They feared the structure would allow the approaching enemy army to enter Roman territory. Agrippina defied the decision; and her assessment presently proved correct, as Roman legionaries rather than Germans soldiers began to cross the bridge. Agrippina proceeded to supply the battle-worn Roman troops with clothing, and dressings for their wounds. She visited divisions, tended the legionary standards, and distributed donatives. She provided entertainment by parading young Gaius in the homuncular legionary uniform, which led him to be called Caligula (Little Boot).

Agrippina was not the first Roman woman to assume command prerogatives. During the siege of Perusia in the winter of 41 BCE, Mark Antony's wife Fulvia wore a sword and barked orders at the combatants. Nevertheless the Romans held in general that women should take no part in military affairs. Octavian's propaganda, criticizing the presence of Cleopatra at Actium and in Alexandria, prompted serious desertions among Antony's troops. Dio Cassius praises Livia for never entering the camps. Tacitus defends Agrippina's interaction with the army as the diligence of "a lady of immense spirit," [15] and attributes Tiberius' grumbling about her military intervention to jealousy rather than justified disapproval. The author then proceeds to complain that Piso's wife "Plancina did not hold herself within the propriety of women, but attended the exercise of the cavalry, [and] maneuvers of the [infantry] cohorts." [16]

Furthermore, Germanicus had accepted the endorsement of the dissident party. This could account for the defections from his funeral. Tiberius could hardly have condoned his nephew's adherence to opponents of the regime; quite plausibly Livia and Antonia shared his view.

Germanicus had tried to separate his association with the dissidents from his interaction with his relatives. Tacitus writes:

> The court was divided and discordant, with unspoken preferences for either Drusus or Germanicus. Tiberius cherished Drusus as his offspring and bloodline: [and] because Germanicus had been separated from his uncle's love, the opposition acclaimed him…But the [adoptive] brothers (i.e., Drusus and Germanicus) were singularly concordant, and unshaken by the rivalries of their supporters.[17]

On his very deathbed, Germanicus expressed worry about the way Agrippina would behave once she was back in Rome. Tacitus maintains the dying prince exhorted his wife to "abandon ferocity, submit [her] spirit to the severity of fortune and, on returning to the capital, not to irritate the stronger with competition for power." [18] Nonetheless, Germanicus never renounced the support of the dissidents; and after his death, Agrippina enhanced their antagonism toward Tiberius and Livia.

Tacitus neglects to tell us whether Livia attended the funeral for Tiberius' son, which took place in 23 CE. None of our sources, in fact, discloses this information. Writers could have determined from public records whether or not Livia was present. Suppose we assume, for the sake of argument, that Livia did attend the obsequies for Drusus. Then her detractors unanimously failed to cite her presence as proof that she preferred this grandson to Germanicus.

On the other hand if Livia abstained from Drusus' funeral, she accorded both grandsons identical consideration under the same circumstances. Were Livia's detractors to admit this, they would vitiate their insistence upon her hatred for Germanicus. We presume that she was absent from Drusus' funeral, and not merely from the silence of the detractors. Livia was eighty years old in 23 CE; and she had only recently recovered from a life-threatening illness.

MUNATIA PLANCINA'S PARDON

Livia's criminal image gains considerable impetus from her defense of Gnaeus Piso's wife Munatia Plancina. There is no way to deny Livia demanded a senatorial pardon for a clearly disreputable woman.

With his usual omissions, ambiguities, and invectives, Tacitus distorts the nature of Livia's association with Plancina. He leads his readers to suspect Plancina at least tried to poison Germanicus with Livia's approval if not at her behest. Subsequently, Livia worked to prevent disclosure of her collusion with Plancina.

Tacitus writes of secret interviews in which Livia purportedly urged Plancina to harm Germanicus and Agrippina. Gossip maintained that Livia encouraged the acrimony between her grandson and Piso:

> At Rome, after the state of Germanicus' health became well known—and everything was exaggerated for the worse since it came from afar—sorrow, anger, and complaint broke forth. No doubt for this reason [Germanicus] was relegated to the ends of the earth, for this reason Piso was ceded a province; this is what clandestine conversations of Augusta with Plancina had occasioned.[19]

This is purely speculative innuendo. From the experience of Ovid's wife we know any citizen might approach Livia with a petition on any issue. These encounters were truly secret interviews, since their contents were kept confidential. The simple fact that Livia granted Plancina an audience does not automatically imply the women were friends. Nor does it indicate that the dowager encouraged the harassment of her own grandchildren.

Upon his return to Syria from Egypt in the autumn of 19 CE, Germanicus received an unpleasant surprise. In his capacity as imperial legate, Piso had countermanded the military, administrative, and diplomatic measures the prince had implemented before departing. The enraged Germanicus sent the Senate a complaint about Piso, who responded by vehemently defending his actions. Then Germanicus fell ill. Convinced Piso and Plancina had administered poison, Germanicus removed the legate from office and ordered him back to Rome.

Suetonius and Dio Cassius insist Germanicus' corpse exhibited clear indications of death by poison. Tacitus disagrees sharply, writing that the condition of the body presented no conclusive evidence of poisoning. The discrepancy arises from the conflicting arguments presented at Piso's trial. Lucius Vitellius, one of the prosecutors, maintained Germanicus must have been poisoned because his heart did not burn when his body was cremated. Piso responded that certain diseases could also prevent the heart from burning, citing a prevalent medical theory the elder Pliny corroborates. Indeed, Germanicus' symptoms—recurrent fever, drooling, and splotchy skin—are consistent with acute arsenic poisoning; but they also characterize Rocky Mountain spotted fever. The prince could very well have contracted, in the course of his travels, a localized disease or parasite for which he lacked native immunity. Nevertheless he and Agrippina were certain that poison had precipitated his affliction; and they convinced many of their fellow Romans to share their belief.

Suspicions of foul play were heightened by the discovery of artifacts related to the practice of necromancy, between the walls and under the floors of the house Germanicus and his family had occupied in Antioch. These items included dismembered human remains, half-burnt cinders of cremations smeared with blood, and lead tablets linking Germanicus' name with incantations and spells. Neither Tacitus nor Dio Cassius (who describes the items) attributes them to Piso or anyone else. Suetonius' testimony nevertheless suggests Germanicus suspected Piso of planting the articles. The author writes that Germanicus hesitated to renounce his relationship with Piso until the prince found himself the target of potions and spells.

While in Syria, Plancina had consorted with a local woman named Martina. Gnaeus Sentius Saturninus, who was appointed interim legate of Syria after Piso's departure, sent Martina to Italy for interrogation. Tacitus calls Martina a *venefica*, which in Latin means a poisoner or witch. He would have us suspect she was privy to an attempt on Germanicus' life. Martina's profession, however, did not necessarily make her a murderess. In Greek, Martina's native tongue, there are two equivalents to *venefica*: φαρμακίς—*pharmakis*—and φαρμακεύτρια—*pharmakeutria*. Both terms signify a woman who administers drugs, potions, or spells. Taken in an evil context they do connote a sorceress. In a benign sense, however, they simply designate a folk healer like a Granny of rural England or Appalachia.

Piso and his family had gotten as far as the Aegean island of Cos, when they received the news of Germanicus' death. Tacitus reports that Piso rejoiced extravagantly, visiting temples and offering sacrifices of thanksgiving. Plancina, who had been lamenting the death of her sister, now exchanged her mourning garments for her gayest attire.

Piso proceeded to raise a military force, with which he endeavored to recover control of Syria. After being repulsed by Saturninus, Piso began a leisurely journey back to Rome. Meanwhile it was discovered Martina had died suddenly upon reaching the Italian port of Brundisium. Although a vial of poison was found in a knot of her hair, her body did not exhibit any indication her death was self-inflicted. Here Tacitus leaves us with the impression of a cover-up. What incriminating information did Martina have to disclose?

Piso reached Rome shortly after Germanicus' funeral. Although facing indictment for murder and misconduct in public office, Piso hosted banquets and feasts. He and Plancina strolled the Tiber's riverbank, with joy on their faces and numerous retainers at their sides. They festooned their house, which towered visibly over the Forum, with banners and festive decorations. Tacitus asserts that since the city was still in mourning, Piso's blatant displays of merriment sharply offended public sentiment.

Because Piso's case involved a member of the imperial family, Tiberius referred it to the Senate instead of considering it at his own tribunal. The senators found Piso guilty of attempted insurrection but innocent of Germanicus' murder. People standing outside the Senate house began a series of protests against the exoneration. These so increased in violence that Tiberius had Piso sent home under armed escort. Frightened by the public outcry against him—and anticipating severe penalties for the offense of which he had been convicted—Piso took his own life. He revealed his fears in a suicide note, in which he also begged clemency for his youngest son Marcus.

Tiberius proceeded to win acquittal for Marcus Piso from a charge of complicity in his father's insurgence. At the same time the emperor asked the Senate to pardon Plancina, on the ground Livia had interceded with him on Plancina's behalf. Tacitus asserts Tiberius made the plea with obvious shame, and that public opinion turned sharply against Livia:

> It was therefore a grandmother's prerogative to face a grandson's murderess, address [her], and snatch [her] from the Senate. That which the laws maintain for all citizens, to Germanicus alone was not applied. While by the voice of Vitellius and of Veranius (the prosecutors) the Caesar was bewailed, by the emperor and Augusta Plancina was defended. Now the poisons and artifices, so successfully proven (against Germanicus), might be turned against Agrippina, against her children, that an extraordinary grandmother and uncle with the blood of a most miserable family might be satiated.[20]

As Tacitus continues, he gives the impression the outcome of Plancina's trial was inconclusive:

> Two days were expended on this pretense of an inquiry, with Tiberius urging Piso's sons to defend their mother. After both accusers and witnesses competitively presented their cases, and no one responded, pity rather than ill will was intensified. The consul Aurelius Cotta,

called first to the vote…proposed that Piso's name be stricken from the public register, part of his property be confiscated, part conceded to his son Gnaeus Piso who must alter his *praenomen*; that [Marcus] Piso, deprived of rank and having received 5 million *sesterces*, be relegated for ten years, [and] that Plancina's security be allowed because of Livia's entreaty.[21]

The younger Gnaeus Piso changed his *praenomen* to Lucius.

The senatorial decree containing the proceedings against Piso and his family is extant today. Portions of it strikingly parallel Tacitus' narrative, proving the historian used the document as his source. The decree does not disclose the indictments against Plancina that the Senate examined. This omission implies Plancina was arraigned for the same charges as her husband.

The segment of the decree devoted to Plancina reveals Tacitus obfuscated a highly significant detail. The missing information places Livia's demand for Plancina's pardon in a perspective quite different from that which Tacitus presents. The Senate not only tried Plancina but convicted her as well. What Livia requested was not Plancina's immunity from prosecution but commutation of her sentence. Livia's intervention was not intended to prevent Plancina from coming to trial.

The decree is written in stilted, legalistic Latin, analogous to the affected English of a modern Congressional or Parliamentary resolution:

With regard to the issue of Plancina, to whom many and very serious crimes have been imputed: whereas she acknowledges to have all hope in the mercy of our *princeps* and Senate, and our *princeps* has often and accurately petitioned, of its ranks, that the satisfied Senate withdraw the punishment of Gnaeus Piso the father from his wife as from Marcus [his] son; allow for Plancina the appeal of his (i.e., Tiberius') mother; inasmuch his mother desired that this be accomplished, accept the issues most justly explicated to him by her: the Senate determines, both that Julia Augusta, superlatively deserving of the state, not alone for the bearing of our *princeps*, but also because of many and large benefactions to the ranks of every sort of people— she with [legal] right and supreme influence, of which she scarcely makes use—ought to have this matter granted by the Senate; and that in consideration of the supreme devotion of our *princeps* to his mother, it should be voted and conceded that the punishment of Plancina be rescinded.[22]

The pardon could not have been designed to obfuscate connivance between Livia and Plancina in the elimination of Germanicus. Were Livia afraid the proceedings might expose her as an accomplice, she would have contrived to keep Plancina from coming to trial in the first place.

Nor did the pardon reward Plancina for maintaining silence about Livia's presumed involvement in Germanicus' destruction. The death penalty finally overtook Plancina in 33 CE. Tacitus writes that, "charged with crimes by no means unknown," [23] Plancina took her own life. Since Dio Cassius avers Tiberius ordered her execution, Plancina may have committed suicide before a death sentence could be carried out. Dio adds that Plancina's end had nothing to do with the Germanicus matter. Indeed, Plancina could not be sentenced anew for charges from which she had obtained reprieve through Livia's intervention. The pardon had been granted by a senatorial decree, which the emperor lacked legal authority to overturn.

Were Plancina concealing incriminating information about Livia, Tiberius would have left her alone. A new prosecution and the prospect of an unpardoned conviction might impel Plancina to expose her secrets. Tiberius could not afford to take a risk of this nature. A disclosure by Plancina, implicating Livia in Germanicus' death, would have verified the allegations of Agrippina and discredited the accusations and penalties Tiberius had brought against her.

Why, then, did Livia seek clemency for Plancina?

Livia may have offered the pardon as an inducement for Plancina to testify. Tacitus indicates Plancina was promised her amnesty before she came to trial, and this assurance prompted her to abandon her husband's cause:

> And she herself, so long as hope for Piso remained, was promising him an ally in fortune of any kind, and if it should be brought about, a companion in death; but once by the secret pleas of Augusta she obtained pardon, gradually she began to separate from [her] husband, and divide the defense.[24]

Plea-bargaining could explain why the senatorial decree omits the crimes of which Plancina was convicted. The Senate conceivably agreed to withhold the specifics against Plancina from the public record in return for her cooperation.

Although the Senate had exculpated Piso of Germanicus' murder, Agrippina refused to accept the verdict. She resolutely maintained that her husband had been poisoned; and she enjoyed the support of a vocal, potentially violent following.

The members the imperial family, like all Roman citizens, were legally obligated to accept and abide by the Senate's decisions. The pardon gave Livia an opportunity to display distaste for and opposition to the conduct of Agrippina and her adherents. A comment by Dio Cassius supports the assumption this was Livia's purpose. The author writes that Tiberius, who detested Plancina, would like to have had her executed sooner than he did. He nevertheless held off purposely, so Agrippina could not rejoice at Plancina's death.

What would have happened had Livia not intervened? Plancina's sentence would have been carried out while Agrippina and her supporters exulted in a moral victory. Vindication of the dissidents' cause might have proven detrimental to the public image of the new crown prince. As we have noted, opponents to Agrippina and her party had begun to rally about Tiberius' son Drusus while Germanicus was yet alive. Drusus had now replaced Germanicus as the emperor's designated successor. By securing defeat for the Agrippina faction, Livia insured the heir-apparent enjoyed the support of the winning side.

And finally, Livia may have felt personally obligated to the memory of Lucius Munatius Plancus. He was either Plancina's father, or her grandfather. Plancus, who held the consulship in for 42 BCE, was a friend of Cicero. He sided with Antony and Cleopatra for several years, but eventually deserted to Octavian. Plancus proposed, in 27 BCE, that the Senate honor the victorious Octavian with the honorary *cognomen* of Augustus.

A Confusion of Names

There was a Livia, who proved to be a poisoner. She was the granddaughter of our subject, the daughter of the elder Drusus and sister of Germanicus. The younger Livia married Tiberius' son Drusus. She bore him a daughter sometime before 14 CE, and in 19 CE a pair of twin boys. In 23 CE the praetorian prefect Sejanus seduced the younger Livia, and persuaded her to assist in the poisoning of her husband. Sejanus' wife Apicata eventually exposed the murderess.

We know this notorious woman by the name Livilla, the diminutive her family used to distinguish her from her grandmother. Roman public records and inscriptions nevertheless referred to her as Livia—as does Tacitus.

How many people, who lived in Roman times, accidentally attributed the granddaughter's *modus operandi* of poison to the grandmother because the two women had identical names? Casual acquaintances frequently confuse my spouse's forename with that of a famous newscaster, a distant relative with the same surname. Add the fact the elder Livia was a stepmother and *Voila!* With a method to match the alleged motives, our Livia's reputation as a criminal becomes all the more credible.

Of Medicines and Poisons

Six medications, of which Livia made frequent use, have come down to us. These include a digestive, dentifrice, cough syrup, a formula for wound plasters, and two salves for the relief of aching joints. For the most part these would have been produced in the Caesars' residences, rather than purchased from an external apothecary. Pliny the Elder's analysis of Roman medical practices reveals remedies were for the most part prepared at home.

Some scholars consequently attribute Livia's murderous reputation to her use of homemade curatives. To a large extent this logic is flawed. Livia's creation and application of home medications should not be any more suspect than the similar activities of other Roman housewives. Octavia's favorite recipe for toothpaste has survived: does this imply she poisoned her first husband with that substance?

The notion of Livia chasing after each relative with a different brew for every ache and sneeze—or administering poisoned prescriptions to Marcellus, Gaius, and Lucius from hundreds of miles away—is difficult to extrapolate from repeatedly employed remedies, half of which were applied externally. Furthermore the authors who record Livia's medications—the aforementioned Pliny, and Claudius' personal physician Scribonius Largus—indicate quite clearly she had these prescriptions prepared for herself.

Tacitus does not connect Livia with poisoning as a *modus operandi*. Dio Cassius does so in only one instance, the death of Augustus; and in this case the author purports that Livia used figs, not medicine, to administer the fatal toxin. Furthermore if Livia was an expert in poisonous medications, why did she fail to discern that her grandson Drusus was succumbing to just such a formula? To accomplish the murder of Drusus, Livilla elicited the expertise of her personal physician, Eudemus. He administered Drusus a poison that simulated the action of natural disease.

Livia's use of home-produced medications does not account for the origin of the homicidal tradition about her. The polemics of Tacitus and Dio Cassius lead us to believe Livia committed murder. They do not indicate she concocted her murder weapons like some mad scientist in her kitchen.

Granted once Livia's reputation as a murderess emerged, detractors may have embellished that stigma by proposing she used homemade medications to accomplish her dirty work. The idea of women disseminating poison in the guise of home curatives was not unprecedented in Roman history. A high incidence of deaths in 334 BCE was most likely the result of an unidentifiable epidemic. The authorities in Rome nevertheless attributed the deaths to a mass hysteria, which impelled matrons to administer lethal medical preparations to their families. Rumor held the intrepid general Publius Cornelius Scipio Aemilianus, who concluded the Third Punic War with the destruction of Carthage (146 BCE), met his own end at the hands of his fractious Sempronia. Livia's notorious relative Clodia—the patroness of the poet Catullus—was suspected of poisoning her husband Quintus Caecilius Metellus Celer. And finally the revelation of Livilla's connivance with her physician in the murder of the younger Drusus, may have helped engender speculation that Livia used poisoned medications.

OF POISONS, MUSHROOMS, AND FIGS

A red fig named in Livia's honor may help explain why Dio Cassius accuses her of poisoning Augustus with this particular type of fruit. Pliny writes the *ficus Livianus* acquired its designation because Livia introduced it to the Roman public. The method by which she did so is not known. Livia may have promoted the fig by favoring it for her personal use. Another possibility is that horticulturists developed and raised the strain at orchards Livia owned.

The *ficus Livianus* itself could not have been used as the instrument of Augustus' death. Lucius Junius Moderatus Columella, who produced an exhaustive study of Roman agriculture about 60 CE, asserts the ripening of the Livian fig coincided with the rising of the star Arcturus. In antiquity, Arcturus appeared in dawn skies around the end of September. (Today this star rises on mornings in mid-October.) When Augustus met his end in the middle of August, the fruits of the *ficus Livianus* were not yet edible.

Forty years after Augustus' death, the emperor Claudius died suddenly after consuming a dish of mushrooms. Our principal sources for his reign concur, that most people assumed the younger Agrippina had her husband/uncle poisoned. Fortunately the bilious accounts of Tacitus and Suetonius, detailing how Claudius had to be poisoned anew after ejecting the mushrooms from both ends, need not concern us here. Of interest, however, is Dio Cassius' version of the event. He maintains Agrippina induced Claudius to eat the poisoned mushrooms by offering them to him on a platter, from which she had selected and eaten untainted ones. Dio uses the same rhetorical formula to describe Livia's alleged method of poisoning Augustus. The author claims Livia smeared poison on some of the figs while they hung on the tree. She then directed her husband to them while she picked and ate untainted fruits.

A detractor of Livia would accept Dio's account as true. Never mind that Livia's namesake fig was not yet producing fruit; she could have poisoned a different, earlier yielding variety. Four decades later, Agrippina presumably took inspiration from the great-grandmother she so ardently admired, and substituted mushrooms for figs.

Let us now look a bit more carefully at our source material. First and second century writers, including Livia's polemicist Tacitus, omit the fig story from their narratives but include Claudius' death by mushrooms. Only Dio Cassius, writing in the third century, mentions the fig-poisoning incident. He records it as a rumor, not an established fact.

The mushroom-poisoning story appears to have engendered the fig-poisoning account, rather than the other way around. Greco-Italian folklore associated figs, and their close botanic relatives the pomegranates, with death and its deities. Sprigs and fruits of both species appear in Etruscan tomb paintings. Some fruit-yielding branches of both trees emerge directly from the ground, the realm of the dead. The myriads of tiny seeds, hidden within the sweet flesh, are suggestive of fertility, conception, and rebirth. Pluto (Greek Hades) the god of the underworld, married Proserpina (Greek Persephone) the goddess of ripening fruits and grains, by feeding her the seeds of a pomegranate. Proserpina/Persephone was the daughter of Ceres/Demeter, the goddess of agriculture, whose manifestation Livia was frequently represented to be.

The *ficus Livianus* helped form a connection between Livia and figs in the popular imagination. The younger Agrippina, renowned for aspiring to emulate Livia, served Claudius poisoned mushrooms after eating uncontaminated ones from the same serving dish. Detractors combined the two traditions, to produce the tale of Livia and her selectively poisoned figs.

TACITUS' LIVIA: THE PREQUEL TO AGRIPPINA THE YOUNGER

Tacitus was a parallelist historian. He perceived and recorded similarities, between the events and human activities of different chronological eras.

Born about 55 CE, Publius (or possibly Gaius) Cornelius Tacitus was a senator during the reign of the emperor Domitian (81 – 96 CE). Although a conscientious ruler, Domitian had strongly autocratic ideals. To emphasize that the real power of the principate lay with the emperor, Domitian scorned and belittled the Senate as an impotent figurehead. This policy quite understandably alienated the senatorial nobility to which Tacitus belonged.

In 88 CE an abortive coup galvanized Domitian's authoritarianism. He was now determined to repress not only the senatorial aristocracy, but anyone else who could be considered guilty of demeaning the emperor's majesty. Treason trials, especially of senators, abounded. The slightest derogation of the emperor's person, image or reputation resulted in the capital punishments of death or banishment.[25] Domitian's readiness to pursue leads with little regard for their severity or plausibility, elicited accusations from informers seeking favor or compensation. Since Rome lacked an official public prosecutor, authorities had to rely on accusations that citizens brought against one another. When an accusation led to a conviction, the informer was entitled by law to a reward.

Domitian's brutal and repressive methods understandably embittered Tacitus toward the principate. The historian had endured painful firsthand encounters with the system's potential for abuse. His researches into the history of the Julio-Claudian dynasty reinforced his antipathy. Tacitus focused his **Annales** (published in 109 CE) upon the repression of personal freedoms, mere lip service to the Republican constitution, the enforced servility of the Senate, and prosecutions for crimes against the state.

The praetorian prefect Sejanus persuaded Tiberius that Agrippina's hostile attitude was a threat to the stability of the principate. Tiberius accordingly sanctioned arraignments of Agrippina's friends and supporters for treason. Sejanus' machinations culminated in the incarcerations and deaths of the princess and her two eldest sons. The prefect may have trying to maneuver Tiberius into designating him regent for Livilla's son, if not as heir-apparent outright. To achieve his goal the prefect had both murdered Tiberius' son Drusus and exacerbated the emperor's variance with Agrippina.

Once apprised of this treachery, Tiberius authorized reprisals. Sejanus and his children were executed; his estranged wife committed suicide. Anyone accused or suspected of having ties with the prefect was aggressively investigated. Proven associates were prosecuted for treason and promptly convicted. Tiberius endeavored to insure those who suffered death or banishment for seditious behavior were genuinely guilty. He dismissed frivolous charges and punished informers whose accusations proved to be groundless.

The subsequent Julio-Claudian rulers—Gaius, Claudius, and Nero— were far less discriminate. If an emperor or one of his favorites took a dislike to you or coveted your wealth, you were in certain danger. Claudius (41 – 54 CE) personally tried to avoid making arbitrary treason charges; but he gave his wives and courtiers free reign to do so.

What has any of this to do with Livia?

Augustus had represented his wife to the public as an embodiment of feminine qualities he wanted people to associate with the principate— peace, prosperity, and nurturing maternalism. Livia was consequently a very conspicuous symbol of the regime Tacitus detested so intensely. The historian's dislike for Livia was nevertheless personal as well as political. Tacitus championed those whom he considered victims of the principate—Augustus' daughter Julia, her children, their spouses, and their apologists. Among the latter was Agrippina's namesake child.

Julia Agrippina was the oldest of Germanicus' three daughters. She was born in 15 CE at Forum Ubii, a Roman *canaba* (military settlement} on the Rhine, during the course of her father's maneuvers in the area. Years later she established a colony for Roman veterans and their families at her birthplace. The town was renamed Colonia Agrippinensis in her honor. Today we know the place as Cologne, Germany.

Little Agrippina was four years old when Germanicus' death necessitated his family's retirement to Rome. She consequently grew up an eyewitness to the tensions and quarrels that alienated her mother from Livia and Tiberius. The younger Agrippina later detailed these dissensions in memoirs which Tacitus used as a source.

Agrippina the Younger was thirteen when Tiberius bestowed her hand upon her father's first cousin. Gnaeus Domitius Ahenobarbus was the son of Antonia Major, the first daughter whom Augustus' sister Octavia bore to Mark Antony. (Germanicus was the second daughter's son.) The younger Agrippina gave birth to Lucius Domitius Ahenobarbus on December 15, 37 CE. Two years later Gnaeus Ahenobarbus died of dropsy. Agrippina promptly married her one-time brother-in-law, Passienus Cripsus. He had been the husband of Domitia, one of Gnaeus Ahenobarbus' two sisters. Agrippina did not bear Passienus any children.

The younger Agrippina's adult life was turbulent and sordid. Her brother, the deranged emperor Gaius Caligula (37 – 41 CE), maintained an incestuous relationship with her as well as their two younger sisters Drusilla and Julia Livilla. Drusilla died in 38 CE. A year later her cousin and widower, Marcus Aemilius Lepidus, attempted to lead the armies of Germania Superior (the northern Rhenish frontier) in rebellion against Gaius. The emperor suppressed the insurrection and executed Lepidus. Because Agrippina and Julia had been sharing Lepidus as a lover, Gaius banished both sisters to the Pontine islands. Before implementing this sentence, Gaius compelled Agrippina to transport Lepidus' ashes from Germany back to Rome.

Praetorian guards killed Gaius in January of 41 CE and hailed Germanicus' younger brother Claudius as emperor. The new *princeps* promptly rescinded the banishments of Agrippina and her sister. Sometime between her return to Rome and the year 48 CE, Agrippina had her husband Passienus murdered. Apparently she was after the more than two million *sesterces* he left her in his will.

At the time of his accession Claudius was married to his third wife Valeria Messallina, the daughter of Gnaeus Domitius Ahenobarbus' sister Domitia Lepida. In 47 CE the young empress participated in a plot against her husband. After executing Messallina, Claudius and his advisers considered three women as potential replacements for her. Eventually they chose Agrippina, even though the emperor was her father's brother. The strongest argument for selecting Agrippina was the ancestry of her son. Lucius was a direct male descendant, both from

Augustus' side of the dynasty and from Livia's. Agrippina helped sway the choice in her favor by exciting Claudius' sexual interest in her.

The Senate passed special legislation to exclude marriage between an uncle and his fraternal niece from the definition of incest. Claudius and Agrippina celebrated their nuptials in 48 CE. A year later the emperor had the title of *Augusta* bestowed upon Agrippina.

At this point we begin to see strong parallels between Tacitus' portrayal of Agrippina the Younger and his depiction of Livia. Claudius has a son of his own, called Tiberius Claudius Britannicus in commemoration of his father's conquest of Britain. Agrippina, however, convinces the emperor to adopt her son Lucius as his intended successor.

Livia similarly manipulates Augustus, into bestowing the principate upon his stepson Tiberius in lieu of his natural heir Agrippa Postumus.

Four years after Claudius has adopted Lucius as Nero Claudius Caesar Drusus Germanicus, Agrippina begins to fear her uncle/husband will reconsider the arrangement for the succession. Before Claudius can change his mind in favor of Britannicus, Agrippina hastens the emperor's death by poison. She stations soldiers at the approaches to the palace to prevent anyone from entering or leaving. Agrippina sends out bulletins alleging Claudius' health is improving, until she is ready to present Nero as the next emperor.

Livia is correspondingly suspected of precipitating Augustus' demise. Having learned of her husband's secret visit to the exiled Agrippa Postumus, she fears Augustus will make that grandson his heir in lieu of Tiberius. Livia has military roadblocks placed around the villa at Nola where Augustus lies on his deathbed. After sending for Tiberius, who is en route to Illyria (Pannonia), Livia submits favorable reports about Augustus' condition until her son arrives and assumes control.

To perpetrate Claudius' murder, Agrippina relies on a skilled poisoner named Locusta. Somewhat similarly, Livia and Tiberius supposedly obfuscate Plancina's association with the alleged poisoner Martina.

Because she aspires to exceed Livia in magnificence, Agrippina patterns Claudius' funeral after that of Augustus. Claudius like Augustus is deified; and Agrippina like Livia is heaped with honors and declared priestess of the new divinity.

Both new reigns, which have been secured by maternal shenanigans, begin with dynastic murders. Agrippina opens her son's regime with the destruction of Marcus Junius Silanus. As a grandson of Augustus' granddaughter Julia, he is a potential claimant to the throne. Anxious about competition from a natural descendant of Augustus, Tiberius and Livia promptly have Postumus put to death.

Both empress-mothers are dominant figures in the early years of their sons' regimes. Here the parallels are somewhat imprecise. Agrippina destroys those who would keep her from controlling everything her son does. Nero's aunt Domitia Lepida is banished after trying to exert some influence of her own upon her nephew. Narcissus, an important government administrator who also encouraged Nero's independence, is imprisoned and driven to suicide.

Livia's manipulation of Tiberius is more embarrassing than dictatorial. At the outset of her son's reign she insists he pardon Quintus Haterius Agrippa for heckling Tiberius before the Senate. Two years later, Tiberius agrees to indulge Livia by defending her arrogant friend Urgulania in a lawsuit over a personal debt. In 20 CE Tiberius acquiesces with undisguised discomfiture to Livia's demand for the pardon of Plancina. And finally until the day of her death, Livia protects Gaius Fufius Geminus from prosecution for making jests at Tiberius' expense.

Even as they cosset their mothers, our emperors place some restrictions on the women's privileges. While Nero is hearing the plea of an Armenian embassy, he refuses to let Agrippina join him on the dais where he sits. Tiberius rejects some of the honors which the Senate offers Livia in 14 CE. Subsequently he endeavors to curtail her public activities, like her personal appearances at building fires to encourage firefighters and aid victims.

Eventually each ruler reaches a juncture at which he ceases to tolerate maternal interference. Nero resolves to free himself from Agrippina's control, after she opposes his decision to make a slave girl his mistress. Agrippina retaliates by confessing she poisoned Claudius to secure the throne for Nero. She threatens to replace Nero with Britannicus, who is now old enough to assume power as Claudius' rightful heir.

Tiberius' relationship with Livia starts to deteriorate after she places her name before his on a new statue of the Divine Augustus. Livia begins to taunt her son with the reminder she secured the principate for him. After Augustus' grandson Gaius died in 4 CE, the emperor considered making Germanicus his successor. Livia, however, persuaded her husband to confer the succession upon Tiberius.

Eventually the favored sons turn against the domineering mothers to whom they owe their sovereignty. So Agrippina cannot exploit Britannicus to further her own plans, Nero with the aid of Locusta has the youth poisoned. To keep Agrippina from holding secret interviews with her friends (as Livia allegedly did with Plancina), Nero restricts his mother to the residence of her grandmother Antonia. Nero continues to associate with Agrippina, but in an aloof and unsubmissive manner. Agrippina tries various maneuvers to regain control of her son—intimidation, persuasion, even seduction. Eventually Nero decides to divorce his wife—Britannicus' sister Octavia—and marry his new mistress Poppaea Sabina. Agrippina begins to remonstrate as usual. Perceiving his mother will never stop attempting to dominate him, Nero has her killed.

Tiberius would like to remove Livia from power; but this he does not do because he realizes he owes his position to her. He withdraws to Capri, leaving his mother to live out her days in Augustus' house without him. He ignores her in death as in life by neglecting to attend her funeral and execute her will.

Tacitus' parallels raise some intriguing if unanswerable questions. We have already noted the author's reference to Agrippina's imitation of Livia at Claudius' funeral. Did Agrippina deliberately mimic other actions, including dynastic murders, which she wrongly attributed to Livia? Did Agrippina include in her memoirs a representation of Livia based on Agrippina herself? Did Tacitus model his portrait of Livia on what he knew about Agrippina? Or did Tacitus extrapolate his view of Agrippina from what he suspected about Livia?

Whether Tacitus patterned Livia after the younger Agrippina or Agrippina after Livia is actually irrelevant. The purpose of the **Annales** is to impute wickedness to successive generations of Julio-Claudians. Tacitus wants his readers to believe the criminal tradition about Livia. His parallelism presents Livia as a precursor to Agrippina the Younger, just as it exemplifies Tiberius as harbinger of Domitian. The matching maternal portraiture offers another explanation, as to why the deaths of Gaius and Lucius are imputed to Livia but not to Tiberius. Without the intervention of his mother, Nero would never have become emperor. The same presumption was applied to Tiberius.

LIVIA'S OWN CONTRIBUTION

Livia herself may have unwittingly perpetuated her unsavory reputation, simply by neglecting to counteract it. She had little incentive to do so. Dissidents' efforts to malign her failed to diminish her influence and leverage. When she died in 29 CE her favorite Fufius Geminus was consul. He was so untouchable as a result of the dowager's patronage, that the Senate could not prosecute him for deriding Tiberius until after her demise. Livia's *auctoritas* remained not only formidable but enduring, for it brought Servius Sulpicius Galba to the consulship four years after her demise.

Even Sejanus found he could not oppose Livia. Agrippina's propaganda attacking Tiberius and Livia slandered members of the imperial family. Livia would have been entirely within her rights, had she allowed Sejanus to prosecute Agrippina for treason. Instead, Livia protected her adversary. Again, we repeat a passage cited earlier:

> ...while Augusta was alive there was yet a refuge, since compliance to his mother was ingrained in Tiberius, and Sejanus did not dare exceed the authority of a parent... letters sent against Agrippina and Nero, which the public believed had been delivered earlier and suppressed by Augusta, were certainly read openly not long after her death.[26]

Tacitus' words suggest Livia was more concerned about the hegemony Sejanus was gaining over Tiberius, than about damages to her reputation from innuendo and invective.

NOTES TO CHAPTER V

1.   *Annales* 5.1.
2.   *Historia Romana* 2.130.5.
3.   *Annales* 2.82.
4.   *Divus Claudius* 1.
5.   *Historia natura* 7.150.
6.   *Annales* 1.6.
7.   *Divus Augustus* 65; Homer, *Iliad* 3.40.
8.   *Romaïka fragment* vii. 108.
9.   *Annales* 3.3.
10.   Ilium was the Roman city that Julius Caesar had founded on the site of ancient Troy. Tiberius responded to the city's condolences on the death of his son Drusus, by offering his own sympathies for the Ilians' loss of the Trojan hero Hector.
11.   *Annales* 3.6.
12.   Tacitus uses the word *luxus*—luxury, debauchery, reveling, or sensual excess. The Romans associated such conduct with the courts of oriental or Hellenistic monarchies.
13.   *Annales* 2.43.
14.   *Annales* 1.33.
15.   *Annales* 1.69.
16.   *Annales* 2.55.
17.   *Annales* 2.43.
18.   *Annales* 2.72.
19.   *Annales* 2.82.
20.   *Annales* 3.17.
21.   *Ibid*.
22.   *Das senatus consultum de Cn. Pisone patre* 109-120.
23.   *Annales* 6.26.
24.   *Annales* 3.15

25   Acts of treason under Domitian included undressing or bathing before a likeness of the emperor, and the carrying of a ring or coin bearing the ruler's portrait into a brothel or latrine.

26   *Annales* 5.3.

Garden painting from Livia's Villa Ad Gallinas Albas at Prima Porta
Museo Nazionale delle Terme, Rome
Photo credit: Nimatallah/Art Resource, New York

THE PRIVATE LIVIA SEEKING HER INTIMATE SIDE

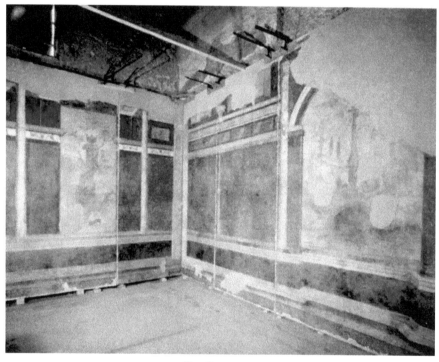

Rustic scenes
Wall paintings in situ, Casa di Livia, Rome
Photo credit: Scala/Art Resource, New York

CHAPTER VI

THE WIFE OF CAESAR AUGUSTUS

All we have established so far about Livia's character, is that she was not a devious scheming criminal. What was she really like in private? How did she interact with her family? Who were her friends? What insights into her personality do the anecdotes in our sources provide?

We may well begin by studying Livia's relationship with the most significant person in her life—her second husband.

There was a kindly, congenial aspect to Caesar Augustus' disposition. He once put a nervous petitioner at ease by commenting the man was behaving as though he were offering a coin to an elephant. The emperor enjoyed gently embarrassing those who took themselves too seriously. A military tribune whom Augustus discharged for insubordination, demanded to know how he might explain the dishonor to his father. "Say you did not like me," [1] the *princeps* quipped. During his last cruise down the Campanian shoreline in the days immediately before his death, Augustus invented some hackneyed Greek verses. He then asked Thrasyllus, Tiberius' erudite astrologer friend, to identify the poet who had composed them.

Augustus loved to gamble. He cast dice with friends and family members on special occasions and chuckled about his losses. The emperor liked to watch boxing matches. He enjoyed fishing, and passed his angler's gene to his unfortunate grandson Postumus.

The *princeps* cherished his family intensely. Suetonius writes that Augustus showed profound devotion to his mother Atia. The signet ring the emperor used in the earlier part of his political career commemorated Atia. The ring was a sardonyx engraved with a sphinx. He discovered the ring while examining Atia's personal effects, after her death in 43 BCE. Although he later used an image of Alexander the Great whom he admired, and subsequently his own likeness for his signet, Augustus never abandoned the sphinx as a personal emblem. It can be observed on the shoulders of the famous armored statue of the emperor, from Livia's villa at Prima Porta on the outskirts of Rome.

Suetonius also mentions Augustus' fondness for Octavia his sister. After her son Marcus Marcellus died in 23 BCE, Augustus by way of consolation named his newly constructed portico for the sorrowing mother. Ten years later he christened a grand new theater after his deceased nephew.

The emperor's extant letters betray his affection for his daughter Julia, his grandson Gaius, his granddaughter Agrippina, even his recalcitrant stepson Tiberius. He reportedly wept upon learning his cousin and former friend Mark Antony had committed suicide. Augustus grieved bitterly over the untimely deaths of his nephew Marcellus, his son-in-law Agrippa, his sister Octavia, his stepson Drusus, and his confidant Maecenas. He shed tears anew when his daughter Julia received her conviction for adultery.

This benevolent and sensitive side of Augustus engendered his intense love for Livia and her reciprocated affection for him. Evidence of her love comes from an unlikely source: her polemicist Tacitus. "Then Caesar, with desire for her person, wrested [her from her] marriage, unlikely against her will…" [2] Writing half a century after Tacitus, Suetonius avers Livia kissed Augustus as he bade her farewell on his deathbed.

Augustus' character nevertheless had its darker elements. He was often relentless, unremittingly intense, demanding, controlling, intractable, self-centered, and inconsiderate. These qualities made him an effective king, but took their toll on his private relationships. To further the development of the principate, Augustus imposed formidable social, political, and military responsibilities—not to mention strained marriages—upon the members of his family. Such treatment drove

Agrippa to despair, Tiberius to self-imposed exile, and Julia to reckless rebellion. The emperor may have precipitated the death of his grandson Gaius, by demanding the young man travel from Asia Minor back to Italy in a wounded and debilitated condition. Augustus nevertheless resented family members' resistances to his importunities as indications of their insubordination or weakness.

Livia did not let Augustus' peremptory nature compromise their relationship. She willingly married the man who had marked her father for death and placed her own life in jeopardy at Perusia. She accepted her husband's desire to bestow the succession upon his blood descendants, in lieu of on her own eminently qualified sons whom he had helped raise. Livia saw Drusus die and Tiberius suffer in his miserable marriage with Julia, both in service to her spouse. She watched Tiberius retire to Rhodes, angering his stepfather while becoming the butt of people's jokes. She also understood that Augustus appointed Tiberius to the succession as a last resort.

Still, Livia was hardly a reticent wife. She urged her husband to grant the requests of petitioners, such as the cities of Aphrodisias and Mytilene. She persuaded him to advance the political careers of her *protégés*. When Augustus ordered Tiberius to remain on Rhodes in the aftermath of Julia's disgrace, Livia induced her husband to conceal her son's degradation with the position of *legatus* to the island. Livia eventually convinced Augustus to make Tiberius his successor in lieu of her far younger and less experienced grandson Germanicus.

Augustus placed a high value on Livia's opinions and sought them frequently. Suetonius has preserved some of the emperor's correspondence with his wife. These letters address the personal development and potentially embarrassing public image of Livia's crippled and awkward grandson Claudius. The imperial couple discussed affairs of state as well as familial concerns. Augustus often organized his ideas in writing before presenting them to Livia, a practice he employed when consulting his male advisers.

The younger Seneca provides a moralizing story, which indicates the type of guidance Livia provided her husband. The action takes place in Gaul. Augustus is over forty years of age. He is therefore in that province on his second junket of 16 – 13 BCE, or on his brief third tour of 10 BCE.

The emperor is upset because he has learned Lucius Cornelius Cinna is plotting against him. Augustus is in a quandary. He is loath to have Cinna executed. With the civil wars at an end and peace in their place, a renewal of bloodletting seems excessive and harsh.

On the other hand, would leniency toward Cinna endanger Augustus even more? Augustus has already suppressed several conspiracies that were formed against him. Would the prospect of ready pardon encourage renewed attacks? That Cinna is a grandson of Pompey the Great adds to Augustus' distress. The emperor regrets the prospect of having to destroy the scion of so distinguished a family.

After Augustus spends several sleepless nights pondering this dilemma, Livia intervenes. She points out the very emergence of this new conspiracy confirms, the violence Augustus inflicted on his enemies in the past is not deterring others from plotting against him. She suggests he try the new approach of befriending Cinna by forgiving him. The emperor follows his wife's suggestion; and Cinna, impressed by the *princeps'* clemency, becomes a loyal retainer. When Cinna hesitates to stand for the consulship, the grateful emperor sponsors his new ally's election.

Dio Cassius relates virtually the same tale, but identifies the hapless conspirator as Gnaeus Cornelius Cinna Magnus. Lucius Cornelius Cinna, the staunchly anti-Caesarian praetor of 44 BCE, was his father; and Pompeia, a daughter of Pompey the Great and half-sister to Octavian's enemy Sextus Pompeius, was his mother. Dio places the confrontation with Augustus at Rome in 4 CE, perhaps because Gnaeus Cinna was consul the next year.

Since no other ancient author corroborates the tale, determining whose version is the more accurate is impossible. The lengthy and wordy dialogue Dio attributes to Augustus and Livia must be an invention: it is characteristic of the dialectic exercises which were employed to train students of rhetoric in Dio's day. The differences between the versions of Seneca and Dio do not affect the *nexus* of the story. Livia urged her husband to replace severity with benevolence, and he profited from her advice.[3]

Livia's ability to influence her husband has prompted ancient and modern detractors to represent her as a domineering virago—and

Augustus the master of the western world as an emasculated milquetoast in private life. Some cite another anecdote from Dio Cassius as proof of Livia's obstreperousness. When he introduced his laws to protect family life, Augustus urged his fellow senators to command and admonish their wives as he did. His audience in return pressed him to disclose the admonitions he administered to Livia:

> And he, albeit against his will, said some things about dress and other adornments, about goings out [of the house] and modesty therewith, not caring whether these [comments] lent credence to the issue.[4]

The passage hardly establishes Livia as a shrew. If anything, the story indicates that the Caesars valued their privacy. Augustus was reluctant to reveal information about his personal relationship with his wife. He very likely did order and admonish her at times. His letters to her, regarding her ungainly grandson Claudius, betray his insistence upon decisive action. Augustus was demanding by nature; and the structure of his political system mandated his family's subordination and cooperation.

Livia consequently tempered her assertiveness with deference. Seneca and Dio Cassius concur, that before advising Augustus on the matter of Cinna, Livia asked her husband if he would accept her womanly recommendations. Elsewhere in his narrative, Dio writes of Livia:

> When somebody asked her how and by what means she prevailed upon Augustus, she replied that she stayed scrupulously discreet, did cheerfully whatever he desired, did not meddle in any of his concerns, and made a point neither to hear about nor to notice his erotic playthings.[5]

Livia's final comment does not imply that Augustus was unfaithful to her, in the Roman sense of that word. The emperor's own law defined adultery as the sexual intercourse of a married female citizen with any man other than her husband. Augustus had to avoid illicit relationships, lest he make himself liable to prosecution under his own moralizing legislation. As this regulation was highly unpopular, many Romans would have relished a chance to see the emperor caught in his own trap. But although the seduction of a Roman woman married or otherwise constituted a capital offense, a Roman male was free to take his pleasure with a slave, a non-citizen, or a licensed courtesan. Prostitution was legal in ancient Rome, where practitioners of the world's oldest profession had to register with the aediles and pay income tax on their earnings.

Suetonius joins Dio in representing Augustus as a womanizer; but Suetonius also asserts that the emperor "cherished and esteemed [Livia] solely and persistently." [6] Note that in the quotation Dio cites, Livia describes Augustus' love-interests as *playthings*. One preposterous story, which even the scandal-mongering Suetonius dismisses as hearsay, alleged Livia provided her husband with virgins to deflower. These tales are illustrative of Livia's attitude toward Augustus' sexuality. She did not take his amours any more seriously than he did. Flirting probably gave Augustus respite from the intense pressures he faced day after day.

The emperor took particular interest in a woman named Terentia. Her brother was Lucius Terentius Varro Murena, who conspired with Fannius Caepio against Augustus in 23 BCE. Terentia married Augustus' friend Gaius Maecenas, the great patron of the literary arts. Augustus' infatuation with Terentia may date from Triumviral days. In the letter that defends his relationship with Cleopatra, Mark Antony scoffs:

> So farewell, if you, when you read this letter, have not embraced Tertulla, or *Terentilla* (my emphasis), or Rufilla, or Salvia Titisenia, or all of them.[7]

Terentilla is the diminutive form of Terentia.

Dio Cassius writes that when Augustus departed for Gaul in 16 BCE:

> … some suspected him of leaving home because of Terentia the wife of Maecenas—since much about them was being said at Rome—so that abroad he might have access to her without rumor. For indeed, he so intensely desired her, that once he made her enter into a competition of beauty with Livia.[8]

Augustus may have found Terentia enticing; but he could hardly have maintained a surreptitious relationship with her in Gaul any more than in Rome. The statues of Livia and Octavia, which the Gallic city of Glanum erected at this time, suggest that both women may have accompanied the emperor to the province. Let us suppose, for the sake of argument, that we are misinterpreting the archaeological record, and that Livia and Octavia remained behind in Rome. Augustus was still surrounded by a staff that included his two stepsons. How could he have carried out a secret love affair?

Dio's reference to the beauty competition, moreover, reveals Livia as the standard against whom Augustus judged other women.

Maecenas' relationship with his beautiful, patrician wife was not as idyllic as their *protégé*, the poet Horace, would have us believe. Maecenas and Terentia were not compatible spouses. They divorced several times, only to reconsider and remarry. The imperial family may have taken Terentia to Gaul, to give her a change of perspective during a period of estrangement from her husband.

Livia, moreover, most likely did accompany Augustus to Gaul in 16 BCE. She appears, in fact, to have been a rather avid traveler. Her grandson Drusus would one day exclaim to the Senate, "How often did the divine Augustus travel to the West and the East accompanied by Livia?" [9] For Augustus such excursions were business as usual; but for Livia, they served as introductions to cultures and customs few Roman women had the opportunity to encounter. While wintering on Samos in late 20 or early 19 BCE, during the course of his eastern tour, Augustus received embassies from a variety of different peoples. One group of delegates came from as far away as India. They brought along the first tigers Romans had ever seen, as well as an armless boy who used his feet to shoot arrows and play a trumpet.

Emperor and empress traveled for pleasure as well. Like most Romans of means, they had several country homes. Livia owned a retreat some nine miles north of Rome, near the old Etruscan town of Veii: the villa's remnants stand in what is now the Roman suburb called Prima Porta. From his father Octavius, Augustus had inherited an estate at Nola in the hills east of Naples. From the city of Naples, Augustus purchased the entire island of Capri. He and Livia used this locale as a base for the yacht in which they would cruise the beautiful, island-studded waters off Campania (the Amalfi Coast).[10] The couple also owned villas at Praeneste (Palestrina), at Tibur (Tivoli), and at Lanuvium (Lanuvio).

The buildings of these rustic havens were simple and unpretentious. Their interiors were adorned with wall paintings. This type of decoration was considered conventional and relatively unextravagant— the Roman equivalent of wallpaper. Like their modern counterpart, Roman wall paintings varied in quality and price. Those of the imperial family exhibit superlative artistic and technical standards. Golden leafy tendrils against a black background give a sense of filigree delicacy to panels from Agrippa's villa near Pompeii. On a white wall from a bedchamber, two slender red columns are depicted amid the same type of filigree. A cameo portrait of Livia atop the left column faces a similar rendering of Julia on the right. Surely this bedroom was reserved for Augustus' use.

A large room was discovered, almost completely intact, at Livia's Prima Porta villa. The painted walls give the occupant the sense of being in a garden. Plants, shrubs, trees, and birds, —all of exquisite detail, — fill the four walls. The grounds of this villa, and of the Caesars' other estates, were elaborately landscaped with groves and terraces. Augustus and Livia were fond of natural settings. On pleasant evenings they were often found strolling together through the public gardens of Rome.

Home in the capital was the modest mansion on the northwest corner of the Palatine Hill. It had once belonged to Quintus Hortensius Hortalus (114 – 50 BCE), a distinguished orator and a political enemy of Cicero. Augustus came to acquire the house in a somewhat roundabout way. In 36 BCE he purchased a piece of property on the Palatine with the intention of building a new house thereon. Before construction could begin, lightning struck the lot.

Augustus was terrified of lightning. While traveling in a thunderstorm, he had barely missed being struck; his torchbearer received the fatal blow. At the time his residential plot on the Palatine was hit, Augustus was engaged in his campaign against Sextus Pompeius. Regarding the lightning strike as an omen from Apollo, Augustus donated the property to the Senate, with the stipulation a temple to that deity be erected on the site. The Senate compensated Augustus with the Hortensius house, which lay adjacent to the Apollo property.

The Caesars' city dwelling was as unassuming as their country homes. The Palatine house incorporates construction materials, which in their day were commonplace and cheap. The walls are of mortar and volcanic tuff, finished with plaster overlay. Suetonius writes that a short colonnade of gray, easily worked volcanic stone from the Alban hills adorned the structure's exterior. The same material was used in the entrance-hall stairway, and remains intact today. The original roof, which no longer exists, most likely consisted of terracotta tiles spread over a wooden frame. The interior surely had vaulted ceilings, which the Romans believed gave protection from lightning. The surviving portions of the house reveal such comfortable amenities as a heated bath and running water. Furnishings, however, were modest. Couches and tables were plain and inexpensive.

Archaeologists excavated the remains of the house in 1869. Lead water pipes, etched with the name Julia Augusta, facilitated identification of the house, and gave rise to its modern Italian designation as *La Casa di Livia*—The House of Livia. The rectangular structure, which faces northwest, is a typical example of Roman residential architecture. Because the house is nestled against the hillside, the narrow street that runs along the building's northernmost side is level with what was the second story. The main entrance opens from the street into a stairway, which descends into the *atrium*.

Unlike most rooms of its type, this *atrium* has no *impluvium*—a sunken decorative catch basin in the floor. The roof may have been solid, lacking a *perpluvium*—an opening that let air and sunlight into the *atrium* and rainwater into the *impluvium*. Vertical windows near the top would have replaced the *perpluvium* as the source of light and air. Alternatively, what we are calling the *atrium* may have been an open courtyard, with a covered walkway skirting its perimeter to provide shelter from the weather.

The *atrium* section is the best-preserved portion of the house. This was the public area, in which fellow citizens were greeted and entertained. Suetonius writes that the Palatine residence lacked costly adornments, such as marble facades and elaborate mosaics. The stairway is lined with gray stone the author describes. The floors of the *atrium* area are covered with black and white *tesserae*—irregularly shaped bits of marble—a type of paving that was commonplace in ancient Italy.

The *atrium* and its adjoining rooms are replete with wall paintings. As lady of Augustus' household, Livia was responsible for selecting and supervising the appointments of his homes, and the artists who produced them. The extant wall paintings reveal she possessed discriminating artistic standards, sensitivity to her husband's tastes, and knowledge of literature. The entrance hall and *atrium* of the Palatine townhouse are adorned with geometric panels, painted to simulate marble inlays. The wall at the base of the stairs, beside the entranceway, is adorned with a painting of scales. Libra was Augustus' birth sign.

Doorways on the atrium's southeastern wall—that facing the entryway—open into three reception rooms of essentially equal size. The extant paintings in the northeasternmost reception room—that closest to the street (to the viewer's left as he or she faces the three rooms)—consist primarily of fanciful architectural patterns, with simulations of marble columns and porphyry panels. In small ivory-colored panels on the rear wall sit caryatids, one on either side of stylized foliage designs resembling candelabra. Another panel contains a pair of griffins. These fabulous creatures, with their birds' heads, lions' bodies, and snakes' tails, represented the heavens, the earth, and the underworld.

The paintings on the left wall of the central reception room have been destroyed. Those on the other two walls are devoted to themes of mythology. In a large panel on the rear wall, the sea-nymph Galatea rides upon a seahorse to escape her pursuer the Cyclops Polyphemus. Eros the god of sexual desire encourages Polyphemus while other nymphs watch the action. Mount Aetna the celebrated volcano of Sicily erupts in the background. The painting depicts a Sicilian legend, for which George Friedrich Handel would compose a masque nearly two millennia later. Polyphemus loved Galatea; but she rejected him for the beautiful mortal Acis. After Polyphemus crushed Acis with a rock, Galatea turned her beloved into the Sicilian river that still bears his name. Philoxenus and Theocritos, Sicilian poets of the fourth century BCE, recounted the story in antiquity. Both men were active at Syracuse, when that city was in its heyday as a center of Greek power and culture. Livia would have known their works and recognized the story the wall painting represented.

A larger panel on the southeastern wall shows the multi-eyed Argos, guarding the captive princess Io while the messenger-god Hermes approaches. The painting is based upon an original by Nicias, a Greek artist of the fourth century BCE. Beautiful Io was priestess of Hera, the queen of the gods. After Hera's husband Zeus loved Io, the jealous Hera imprisoned the girl, and sent the monster Argos to guard her. Argos seemed the perfect warden. With his 100 eyes he saw everything. He could close half his eyes in sleep, while the other half remained awake and observant.

Zeus ordered Hermes to find a way of freeing Io. By telling a long, dull, pointless story, Hermes managed to bore Argos to the point that he dozed off, shutting all of his eyes. After Hermes released Io, Hera turned her into a heifer and sent a gadfly to torment her. Io, whose name means Wanderer, crisscrossed Europe in search of relief. After she swam to Asia Minor from mainland Greece, the straits she crossed came to be known as the Bosporos—Cow's Crossing or Oxford.[11] Io eventually reached Egypt, where she resumed human form and bore Zeus a son.

The many-eyed Argos represents the starry heavens, and Io the wandering moon, which changes position in the sky from night to night. The heifer's horns, which protrude from Io's brown hair in Livia's painting, correspond to the moon's crescent. Io's purple garment represents the hue of the night sky as well as her royal birth. Because it rises later and grows smaller every night, the waning crescent moon seems to be journeying toward the East—and Egypt, from a Roman perspective. Io's eventual settlement in Egypt suggests an association with that land's earth-goddess Isis, who is always represented with a heifer's horns. The Egyptian connection could have had special meaning for Livia. She was the wife of Egypt's conqueror; and the Egyptians venerated her as a manifestation of Isis.

Various versions of Nicias' Io appear at Pompeii, indicating it was a popular design. We cannot tell, unfortunately, whether Livia chose a pattern already fashionable, or if her selection set a trend Pompeians followed.

Architectural motifs of plinths and columns, similar to those of the northeasternmost reception room, surround the mythologic panels. The viewer has the sense of looking through windows and doors. The Galatea panel is surmounted by a pediment, which is decorated with a frieze of urns and topped by the bust of a winged Gorgon. Beside the Galatea scene, in a small panel to the viewer's right, a man and woman perform oblations at an altar. Above this picture, through a simulated window adorned with a drape, a statue appears atop a column.

On either side of the Io panel, caryatids holding swords stand on the edge of pediment. The decorations to the viewer's right are mostly destroyed; but the remnants indicate they were similar to those on the left. At the center of the pediment, another small panel represents a religious scene similar to that on the other wall. A woman and child execute a ritual at a small altar while a seated adult watches. Farther to the left a winged sphinx—the symbol on Augustus' signet ring—reclines in profile. Through a simulated doorway, other surreal structures beckon. Another candelabrum-like ornament stands atop the doorway. The frieze on the roof above the street scene contains smaller versions of the same ornament.

The solid panels, above and beside the pictorial ones, simulate red marble. These give way, below the Galatea scene, to blue panels bordered in red. A similar blue/red combination beneath the Io panel is flanked by golden squares.

Architectural ornamentation continues in the southwesternmost reception room. Here a garland evocative of the Altar of Peace appears suspended between narrow columns. Bucolic objects—a lyre, an ox' head, and a basket with a shepherd's crook—hang from the garland's swags. A painted frieze above the garland represents scenes of country life: men and women perform a religious rite; fishermen ply a boat while others draw their nets; a farmer pushes a loaded donkey. A man leading a camel reveals the setting as Egyptian or Asiatic. Above this frieze runs a border of more candelabra-like forms, with calyxes, tendrils, caryatids, and griffins.

On the *atrium's* southwestern wall—that which faces the foot of the stairway—a doorway leads to a small plain alcove, and thence into a large room. This combination suggests the great room may have been a *triclinium* (formal dining room) and the smaller room the pantry from which the meals were served. To reduce the risk of fire, and to keep smells and smoke from reaching the guests, the kitchen would have been located elsewhere. Although the original excavators of the house named this room the *triclinium*, its identification as a dining room is not incontrovertible. The so-called *triclinium* might have been a large reception room, in which sizeable groups of people were greeted and addressed. The alcove could have served as a station for a servant or bureaucrat, who maintained appointment lists and checked the identities of visitors.

The white tesserated floor of the *triclinium* is embellished with inserts of alabaster and pastel colored marble. The paintings are pastoral. Only those on two walls are extant. The rear wall displays a rustic shrine amid a grove of trees. A sacrificial urn surmounts a column. A bird—perhaps a magpie—sits at the column's base; goats graze in the foreground. The scene on the main wall, opposite the door, depicts another sacred grove. A tall tapering wood column, clearly fashioned from a tree, dominates the center of the scene. The column stands on a culvert under which ducks are swimming. A shepherd sits at the column's base, playing his pipes. Heads of animals—a stag, a boar, and a wild goat—adorn the column. These trophies of the hunt identify the column as an offering to Diana.

Diana was an ancient Italian goddess of the open air, and of the countryside with its hills, streams, and forests. Originally she was venerated as a female counterpart of Janus, the god of elapsing solar years. Diana was a personification of the moon, by the phases of which the progression of months was reckoned. Hunters, moreover, used moonlight to detect and pursue their quarry. The Romans consequently came to identify Diana with the Greek Artemis, goddess of the moon and chase, and sister of Augustus' divine benefactor Apollo. Diana's lunar sense creates a thematic link between the trophy scene in the *triclinium* and the portrayal of Io in the central reception room.

Roman matrons petitioned Diana *Lucina*—Shining, as when the moon is full—for happiness in marriage and success in childrearing. Menstrual cycles are monthly; and children tend to be born at night. Such maternal attributes made Diana particularly significant to Livia, the premier matron of Rome. In the painting a portico rises behind the trophy, to the viewer's left. Three figures of women in the act of worship stand on the portico's roof. Their larger-than-life size suggests that they are statues. Could this be a fanciful rendering of the *Porticus Liviae*?

A hallway, running along the southwestern wall, links the house's *atrium* region with the private living quarters. Two doors—one on either end of the hallway's northeastern side—connect that passage with a quadrangle of small rooms. These open onto a peristyle garden. Suetonius writes that on hot summer nights, Augustus often slept on a cot, in the garden near a fountain. A single door on the opposite side of the hallway gives access to a linear series of interconnected rooms. Portions of the second floor are extant in this area. The house originally had a basement, two full above-ground storeys, plus a partial third floor that opened onto a roof garden. Italian townhouses still follow this architectural pattern.

Literary evidence indicates Augustus often shared his home with others. After fire destroyed their own Palatine residence in 23 BCE, Agrippa and his second wife Marcella lived for a time in the emperor's house. Drusus never left the home in which he was raised, and brought his bride Antonia to live there. The widowed Antonia and her children continued to occupy the rooms they had inhabited before Drusus' death. Client princes, with their entourages, often resided with the emperor as well.

Augustus had his house connected, by a series of vaulted hallways, to a complex of buildings that he had constructed on adjacent properties. The compound included the administrative offices of the principate, staging areas for visiting dignitaries, and apartments for guests. This arrangement allowed for comfortable accommodation of multiple households. Since it was located on the Palatine Hill, this center of imperial government came to be called the *Palatium*: whence our English word palace.

Augustus' general health was poor. A chronically nervous stomach forced him to consume plain, easily digestible foods. He drank goat's milk, which the Romans prized for its digestibility as we do today. When he sailed for the East in 21 BCE, the emperor had a milch goat placed aboard his ship. Augustus also relied upon complex herbal potions to settle his stomach.

Livia attributed her long life to the wine of Pucino (modern Pizzino, near Trieste). The vines grew on a rocky hillside, where sea breezes from the Adriatic Gulf ripened the grapes. Pliny the Elder calls Pucino the most medicinal of all wines, and adds that Livia drank none other. Augustus nevertheless found he could not tolerate his wife's preference. Wine tended to upset his stomach. Consumption of more than a pint caused him to vomit. His favorite wine was Rhaetian, from the foothills of the Austrian Alps. Almost exclusively, however, the emperor drank Setinum, produced at Forum Apii (Foro Apio) on the northern outskirts of Rome. Sentium did not disturb his digestion as readily as other wines.

In addition to his volatile stomach, Augustus endured poor dentition, dermatitis, and bladder stones. He could not tolerate long exposure to sunshine even in winter. His eyes were often irritated: the formula for an eye salve he used, based on aloe, opium, and frankincense, has survived. In later life he was partially blind in his left eye. He was subject to seasonally recurring lower respiratory congestions. Rheumatism ached and weakened his limbs and made them stiff in cold weather. He found respite from this ailment in baths of sulphur and hot saltwater.

Livia had her own set of favorite medications. We cannot tell if she experimented with original concoctions, or relied upon the tried and true recipes of others—her mother, her friends, her servants, professional apothecaries, or practicing physicians such as Augustus' personal doctor Antonius Musa. The mixing of established formulae to replenish depleted supplies would have been delegated to servants.

Pliny writes that Livia's menus included daily servings of elecampane. The Romans cultivated this hardy perennial herb of the aster family (*Inula helenium*) for the medicinal properties of its roots. Modern Europeans raise elecampane (which is also known as starwort) for the same purpose. Pliny comments that virgin elecampane is bitter, and induces an upset stomach. He continues that once dried, pulverized, mixed with fruit juice, and then flavored with quince, sorbs, plums, pepper, or thyme, elecampane becomes an effective remedy for a weak digestion. Elecampane, Pliny asserts, strengthens the teeth. The extract of the boiled root expels worms. When dried in the shade and powdered, it remedies coughs, convulsions, flatulence, and animal bites. The leaves steeped in wine relieve lumbago and tracheal difficulties.

Livia used a toothpaste, of which the primary ingredients were rock salt and pellitory. The latter is a variety of nettle with which the Romans polished glass pitchers. For quinsy Livia endorsed a medicine based on honey, opium, and a lengthy list of aromatics. The latter include cinnamon, saffron, coriander, anise, and alum—items, again, that are common to modern kitchens. Please note the similarities between Livia's preparation and modern cough remedies. My grandmother used to administer a heated mixture of honey, lemon juice, and cinnamon. The opium derivative codeine is a principal ingredient in modern prescription cough syrups; and these, like honey, are viscous and sweet so they can be easily swallowed.

For rheumatic symptoms, Livia favored two ointments. Both acted much like modern mineral ice, bringing warmth and flexibility to arthritic joints. One salve was a mixture of fenugreek, marjoram, rosemary, vegetable oil, wine, and wax. The other, more complex, combined pork or goose fat with wine, cinnamon, cinnamon wood, cardamom, cypress, *schoenus* (an aromatic reed), rose petals, clover, Syrian and Celtic nard, *amomus* (a balsamic shrub), cassia, and myrrh.

Although Livia's remedies addressed afflictions from which Augustus suffered, one should not be tempted to assume she developed the medicines specifically for him. Both Pliny and Scribonius Largus (personal physician to the emperor Claudius) distinguish between medications Augustus favored and those that Livia endorsed. Scribonius also writes that Livia's daughter-in-law Antonia utilized the lard-based salve for relief of joints stiffened and aching with cold. "A pain reliever," Scribonius calls the balm, "which almost always Augusta and Antonia employed." [12] Scribonius specifies that Livia used the joint salve. He does not write she commended it to Antonia or had it concocted especially for her. Scribonius also distinguishes between Livia's dentifrice, and that which her sister-in-law Octavia preferred.

From the descriptions of Livia's favorite curatives we can, of course, discern the ailments from which she suffered—indigestion, throat infections, and rigid painful joints that were susceptible to cold. Since she found two salves essential for alleviating the last-mentioned affliction, she must have had a chronic arthritic or neuralgic condition.

We learned in our previous chapter of the autumn-ripening fig, which came to bear Livia's name because she popularized it. Athenaeus, a food writer of the second century, asserts that the *ficus Livianus* was cultivated near Rome. Perhaps Livia's namesake fig grew at her villa near Prima Porta. This estate was definitely associated with two other agricultural commodities: laurel and chickens.

Pliny and Suetonius recount a legend, which Livia may well have created herself. She was traveling from Rome to Prima Porta, shortly after her betrothal (Suetonius says marriage) to Augustus. An eagle (the symbol of Roman political authority), flying overhead, dropped a white hen (the symbol of divination or prophecy) into Livia's lap. The hen held a laurel twig (the symbol of victory) in her beak. Perceiving the event as an omen, Livia resolved to rear the hen and plant the sprig. Both flourished: the hen into a flock and the laurel into a grove. Suetonius adds—as do Dio Cassius and Aurelius Victor—that the sudden, simultaneous demise of flock and grove foretold the death of Nero and the extinction of the Julio-Claudian dynasty.

Suetonius relates another bit of family propaganda, which reveals Livia was raising chickens before she married Augustus. Aspiring during her first pregnancy to divine the type of child she would bear, Livia removed an egg from under a setting hen. She and her serving maids took turns warming the egg with their own hands, until a young cockerel with a fine crest was hatched. The event foretold the birth of Tiberius, the future emperor.

White fowl were essential to the peculiarly Roman practice of divining omens and future events from patterns in the creatures' entrails. Chickens were also a source of food. They laid eggs; and they themselves were eaten. Recipes for chicken and other fowl abound in the writings of Livia's contemporary, the gourmand Marcus Gavius Apicius. His **De re coquinaria** (**On the Matter Culinary**) is the world's oldest extant cookbook. Modern chefs study Apicius' entries. One of these is a version of *pollo Tetrazzini* that predates its operatic namesake by nineteen centuries.

The laurel tree was symbolic not only of victory, but of Augustus' patron deity Apollo. Members of the imperial family, female as well as male, wore laurel wreaths on festal occasions. These adornments are clearly apparent, on the Altar of Peace, on the *Grande Camée de France*, and on individual portraits.

Pliny the Elder attributes a wide variety of uses to laurel. Its foliage made good animal fodder. The light strong wood was good for good tools, especially levers. Dried laurel sprigs made effective matches. Dyes could be extracted from laurel. A combination of rue, honey, alum, and laurel remedied testicular flux. Laurel berries mixed with anise made an effective emetic. Pomegranate rind warmed in laurel oil was effective for paralysis, convulsions, sciatica, bruises, headache, chronic catarrh, and ear infections.

Pliny was not the only writer who extolled the medical properties of laurel. Hippocrates, the great Greek physician of the fourth century BCE, included laurel in many of his medications for gynecological problems. Livia suffered at least one miscarriage in the course of her futile efforts to bear Augustus a child. Her difficulties may have prompted her to experiment with laurel-related remedies.

Laurel is ubiquitous in the recipes of Apicius. The Romans used the berries and leaves as food seasonings, just as we do today.

Pliny describes Livia's laurel as "of minimal height, with curled (or trembling) leaf—in short, seldom encountered." [13] This implies the laurel was a rare dwarf and quaking variety. The laurel and chickens were connected with family traditions and associated with a single farm. These factors combine to suggest both commodities were raised at Prima Porta for the family's private use and not for retail sale.

Excavations at Prima Porta have yielded *ollae perforatae* (terracotta pots punctuated with apertures). Such containers were used for the cultivation of seedlings, the openings allowing for crucial ventilation of the developing root systems. The plots lined the perimeter of a peristyle garden. When planted, this arrangement created a living colonnade. Unfortunately we cannot tell if Livia or a subsequent occupant of the villa, placed the pots in this pattern. Nor do we know whether the *ollae* actually held laurel seedlings or those of other shrubs.

The laurel grew in terraced groves, some of which commanded a view of Rome's Capitoline Hill. Perhaps the famous frescoed room, mentioned above, is a rendering of the villa's actual grounds. This chamber, measuring roughly nineteen by thirty-eight feet (six by eleven and one half meters) was probably a hot-weather retreat, for it is offset from the rest of the villa and sunken to preserve coolness. A clerestory originally shed natural illumination on the garden scene which fills all four walls. A low fence of willow wood appears to enclose the foreground. A ceramic balustrade parallels the fence to create an *ambulatio* (grassy walkway). Etched panels decorate the balustrade. Irises, hartstongue ferns, and ivies, regularly spaced along the balustrade's base, decorate the *ambulatio*. Blooming violets decorate some of the ivies.

The balustrade has six salients—two on each long side of the room, and one on either narrow end. Spruce trees stand in the pair of salients on each of the room's longer walls. On the narrow wall to the right of the door, a pine fills the salient. An oleander rises in the far right corner, a laurel in the near. The salient on the opposing narrow room wall (to the left of the door) contains an oak. Here a laurel stands in the far corner and an oleander in the near. The laurels and oleanders consequently oppose each other from across the room.

Immediately behind stone balustrade, along its outer perimeter, fruit-bearing pomegranate trees alternate with fruiting quinces. A single oak bisects this array, in the center of the long wall opposite the doorway. Interspersed among these trees are oleander, viburnum, arbutus, laurel, boxwood, and myrtle bushes. Flowering plants—daisies, poppies, roses, periwinkles, and chrysanthemums— grow beneath the shrubs.

Birds, at rest and in flight, fill the entire panorama. Some twenty avian species are represented—buntings, finches, larks, linnets, sparrows, flycatchers, martins, thrushes, warblers, wagtails, nightingales, blackbirds, orioles, jays, magpies, doves, pigeons, and quail. On the narrow wall to the right of the doorway a large golden domed birdcage— strikingly modern in appearance—rests on the balustrade. The cage is home to a nightingale.

In the background we see the groves of laurel. The trees are in various stages of growth. Scattered among them are cypresses, pines, spruces, and palms. The vibrantly active scene, with its birdlife and fruiting flowering plants, conveys a sense of freshness and joy. A Wedgwood-like frieze, pale blue and white, skirts the perimeter of the room just below the vaulted ceiling. Candelabra-like tendrils reminiscent of those in the Palatine house adorn the panels of the frieze.

When relaxing in private, Augustus liked to wear the homespun clothing that Livia, Octavia, Julia, and the other women of his family made for him. The pleasantly scratchy, loose-fitting comfort of the garments was not the only reason for his partiality to them. A frugal and efficient Roman housewife, devotedly spinning, weaving, and sewing her family's clothes from the wool and flax produced on their estates, was a traditional Roman ideal.

Slaves and freedmen nevertheless performed the majority of tasks in the Caesars' various residences. Large staffs of domestic attendants were common in ancient Rome and not considered extravagant. Centuries of conquest had provided an abundant source of cheap labor in the form of subjugated peoples; and all but the very poorest of Romans had servants.

Furthermore since Augustus and Livia were public figures, their lifestyle embraced a sophisticated side that required the assistance of a staff. Special elaborate clothes were reserved for state occasions. This attire was not gaudy, but elegant, tasteful, and costly. In the manner of an ordinary Republican magistrate, Augustus wore a purple-bordered toga over a knee-length tunic with a vertical purple stripe on its front. Although this trim was not ostentatiously broad, it was dyed with Tyrian purple—the most expensive and fashionable coloration of the ancient world. Selection, manufacture, and care of the Caesars' dress garments were delegated to exclusive tailors, cobblers, and wardrobe supervisors. Livia utilized the expertise of hairdressers and *parfumiers*. The couple hosted formal dinners, which required the services of cooks, waiters, and a scullery staff. Chamberlains oversaw domestic activities, making sure household needs and problems were addressed.

Responsibility for domestic operations ultimately rested with Livia. She appears to have been an effective but good-natured supervisor. Even her enemy Tacitus describes her as,

> In principles of the household toward old-fashioned values inclined, with an affability immensely beyond that by ancient women approved,...[14]

Domesticity was hardly the focus of the Caesars' private lives. The imperial couple laid great stress upon academic pursuits. Augustus relished Greek prose, poetry, and drama, as well as the literature of his own people. He would jot down passages he thought interesting or instructive and then share these with the members of his family. The emperor dabbled in letters of his own. He wrote treatises on philosophy and political theory, a verse epitaph and prose biography of his stepson Drusus, and a history of his own life up to the end of his wars in Spain (25 BCE). The *princeps* attempted but eventually abandoned a tragedy. He composed a book of hexameter poems about Sicily. In the spirit of those of us who sing in the shower, he improvised epigrams while relaxing in his bath.

Augustus took an interest in art as a form of therapy. His cousin Quintus Pedius had a grandson, who was fretful and intractable because he could not speak. After some observation, Augustus discerned the child had an aptitude for drawing and painting. The emperor suggested education in these media might calm the boy, focus his attention and interests, and make him easier to handle. The remedy showed great promise. Pedius reported the child responded readily to his instruction, and made great progress in comportment as well as artistic skill. The family anticipated a productive adulthood for the mute; however his death in his teen years squandered their hopes.

Augustus was an avid collector of "things notable for their age and rarity." [15] Among these was an acquisition of historic weapons. The emperor occasionally gave foreign or ancient Roman coins as gifts. At his villa on Capri he displayed what Suetonius describes as "the immense limbs of sea creatures and wild beasts, which are called the bones of giants." [16] These animal relics—fossils—were and still are easily discovered in southern Italy's granular soils.

Livia was somewhat of an antiquarian herself. The *Porticus Liviae* housed a collection of precious gemstones. Livia donated the so-called Sardonyx of Polykrates to this congeries. She indicated her reverence for the gem by having it set in a golden horn. Her esteem for the stone was founded on an intellectual rather than a monetary appraisal.

Pliny writes that the sardonyx' gemological quality was the poorest of all the jewels in the collection. The stone nevertheless possessed immense historic value on account of the legend attached to it. Polykrates, who was king of Samos about 540 BCE, considered himself a most prosperous man. He began to fear that Fortune was due to turn against him, because she had granted him such bounty. Polykrates decided to offer the ring in which the sardonyx was set as propitiation to the goddess. He put out to sea in a boat and cast the ring into the deep. Fortune proceeded to show Polykrates she could not be bought. A fish which swallowed the ring was caught for Polykrates' table; and the ring, "as if made an omen, in food was returned to the ruler by Fortune's insidious hand." [17] Fortune eventually balanced Polykrates' account with her, and in a manner beyond his ability to control. The king was deposed and crucified.

Livia's signature hairstyle reveals her appreciation for the cultural history that surrounded her. In the Triumviral period she followed the current trend in hair fashion. This entailed pulling the hair uniformly to the back of the head, and twisting the tresses into a rounded or pointed chignon. Women sometimes softened the severity of this look with bangs or raised hairpieces.

As empress, Livia wore an Etruscan coiffure. Her hair, parted along the center of her head was gathered at her temples into two long plaits. Each of these ran along her hairline and just above her ears to the nape of her neck. Sometimes she wore a third plait along the top of her head, from the center of her forehead to her nape. Here the plaits were bound together into a club-shaped ponytail, which rested against her neck. In some portraits, long ribbon-like tresses cascade over her shoulders. Livia's hairstyle became a hallmark of Julio-Claudian women. Julia, Antonia, Livilla, and the elder Agrippina are all represented with the same arrangement

With a chauvinistic admiration typical of his era and culture, Philo Judaeus attributes Livia's keen political insights to her erudition:

> For by all means, the judgments of women are weaker, not capable of acquiring perception except from the senses. She (i.e., Livia) nevertheless completely differed from the gender in everything else as well as this, [and] developing character and attention with pure learning, masculinized her reasoning, which so engendered quick comprehension, that it grasped things of the mind better

than things of the senses and judged the latter to be shadows of the former. [18]

Livia complemented her intellectualism with an earthy self-effacing, sense of humor. It was apparent while she and Octavian were celebrating their wedding. During the *cena nuptialis*, the dinner-feast that followed the marriage ceremony, one of Livia's servants approached her as she reclined beside her new husband. "What are you doing here, Mistress?" the boy queried. "For your man," he said, pointing to Tiberius Claudius Nero, "reclines over there." [19] The comment reflects the opinion, prevalent in some circles, that Livia's new marriage was spurious and Tiberius Nero was her rightful spouse.

Dio describes the servant as "a boy of the whisperers, which the women keep, naked for the most part, to amuse." [20] This representation identifies the slave as a *delicium*—a comrade, playmate, or jester. The Romans were fond of such youthful companions. Augustus enjoyed the prattle of *delicii*, for whom he would roll dice, marbles, or nuts.

No servant would have been permitted to embarrass Livia, without her assent, on so auspicious an occasion as her wedding. Disconcerting disparaging banter, then, must have been the type of humor Livia expected from the *delicium*. Indeed the word Dio uses for whisperers— ψιθύρων—*psithyron*—can also mean slanderers.

Livia once encountered a group of naked men. The indiscretion placed the offenders' lives in peril. Dio Cassius does not reveal whether Livia's bodyguards converged on the hapless nudists, or the latter were found guilty in a court of law. The Senate had conferred personal sacrosanctity upon Livia in 34 BCE. Exposing oneself to an individual who enjoyed this honor was both a religious and a treasonable offense. By making light of the incident Livia saved the nudists' lives, and propagandized the principate's devotion to virtuous femininity in the process. She remarked that to discreet women, such men were no different from statues.

Dio's story of the beauty contest between Livia and Terentia suggests both women had raucous sides. If they flaunted their charms for Augustus' pleasure, they did so voluntarily. Augustus was not the type of husband who would force his wife to humiliate herself for his amusement. He was conscientious of her feelings and emotional health.

Augustus' tenderness is apparent in his treatment of Livia at the time of her younger son's death. Livia's reaction to the passing of Drusus reveals that emotionally she could be quite vulnerable. On this occasion she nearly took her own life. She refused to eat or drink, until her vital condition became precarious. The **Consolation to Livia** reads:

> You would have been scarce of life in hours
> When against your will Caesar provided you succor.
> He applied entreaties and with them mingled legal
> privilege (or soup—see footnote)
> *The Latin text of the preceding line is ambiguous.*
> Then your parched throat decanted water moistened.[21]

The younger Seneca continues the story. Augustus and Livia were in Rome when, in September of 9 BCE, when they received the sad news that Drusus was dying. The imperial couple braved bad weather to reach Ticinum (Pavia) in northern Italy. Here they awaited the funerary cortege, which they escorted back to the capital.

At her husband's suggestion, Livia sought the counsel of a Stoic philosopher named Areus. Philosophers and their writings served the Romans, in the way that psychotherapists and self-improvement manuals aid us today. Areus Didymus of Alexandria was one of many learned Greeks who were important and valued functionaries of Augustus' household. These men served as secretaries, emissaries, tutors, publicists, traveling companions, counselors, and confidants.

Areus advised Livia to revel in her pleasant recollections of her son, rather than dwell on the terrible catastrophe that had taken place. He recommended she seek the company of her friends, and encourage conversation about Drusus. Areus urged Livia to focus her attention on her surviving son Tiberius, and on the grandchildren whom Drusus had given her.

> On the long journey (from Ticinum to Rome) the
> remains of her Drusus she accompanied, by the many
> pyres glowing throughout all Italy distressed, as though
> she were losing him with each; yet once [he was] buried

in the tomb, at the same time him and her sorrow she laid away, mourned no more than what was honorable to Caesar or equitable for Tiberius, [as they were] alive. Lastly, she did not cease to celebrate the name of her Drusus, to picture him to herself everywhere in private and public, to speak of him most willingly, to hear of him: with his memory she lived...[22]

Livia later confessed that loving as the solicitations of Augustus and Tiberius were, they did not help her to surmount her grief as effectively as the guidance of Areus.

She, in initial fervor, when the wretched are most impatient and wild, having approached Areus, the philosopher of her husband, allowed and admitted that he helped her greatly in this matter, more than the Roman people, whom she was unwilling to sadden with her sadness; more than Augustus, who was staggering from the loss of a support (i.e., Drusus), and not poised to be distracted by the lamentation of his kindred; more than [her] son Tiberius, whose devotion was sustaining, so in that funeral bitter (or untimely) and bewailed by the human race, she felt nothing was lost to her except the number (i.e., of sons).[23]

Drusus was not the only child Livia lost. A third baby, of whom Augustus was the father, did not survive a premature birth.

We have no way of knowing the extent to which Livia grieved for her newborn. Its demise would not have engendered the fanfare that marked the passing of Drusus. The baby was not a public figure; and infant mortality was common. Roman parents tended to avoid developing strong affection for extremely young children, because the latter were very apt to die. We see similar psychological defenses today among parents in Third World countries, where medical care is minimal and child death rates are high.

Although their union proved sterile, Augustus and Livia did not lack a nuclear family. It consisted of their offspring by prior spouses. They also had an extended family of kindred. And like the rest of us, the Caesars found their relatives at once a source of joy and chagrin.

NOTES TO CHAPTER VI

1   Quintilian, *De institutione oratoria* 6.64; cf. Macrobius, *Saturnalia* 2.4.
2   *Annales* 5.1
3   The emphasis on clemency in the Cinna story became the inspiration, for Pierre Corneille's 1641 moralizing drama, *Cinna*.
4   *Romaïka* 54. 16.
5   *Romaïka* 58.2.
6   *Divus Augustus* 62.
7   *Divus Augustus* 69. *Ita valeas*—so farewell—in this context is an expression of contemptuous rejection. It is essentially the Latin equivalent of the English invective, "Bully for you!"
8   *Romaïka* 54.19.
9   *Annales* 3.34.
10   In Augustus' day, the contour of the coastline south of Naples differed significantly from its present delineation. The eruption of Mount Vesuvius in 79 CE effected the change.
11   This is the Turkish Bosporus, the strait between the Sea of Marmora and the Black Sea. Please do not confuse it with the Cimmerian Bosporus or Kerch Strait, at the entrance to the Sea of Azov.
12   *Compositiones medicamentorum* 271.
13   *Historia natura* 15. 130.
14   *Annales* 5.1.
15   Suetonius, *Divus Augustus* 72.
16   *Ibid.*
17   *Historia natura* 37.4.
18   *Presveia pros Gaion* 319-320.
19   *Romaïka* 48.44.
20   *Ibid.*
21   *Consolatio ad Liviam*, 419 – 422.

   The Latin text reads,
   Vix etiam fueras paucas vitalis in horas,
   Obtulit invitae quom tibi Caesar opem;

Admovitque preces et ius immiscuit illis
Aridaque affusa guttura tinsit aqua.

The poet makes a play upon the Latin homonym *ius*. To revive Livia physically Augustus brought her a container of broth—*ius*. In demanding she come to her senses, the emperor exercises the legal prerogative—*ius*—of a husband.

22   Seneca Minor, **Consolatio ad Marciam** 3.2.
23   **Consolatio ad Marciam** 4.2.

Antonia the Younger
Capitoline Museum, Rome
Photo credit: Alinari/Art Resource, New York

Hermes rescuing Io from Argos
Wall painting in situ, Casa di Livia, Rome
Photograph by the author

CHAPTER VII

LIVIAS FAMILY
AND FRIENDS

THE IMPERIAL CHILDREN

When Augustus espoused Livia in November of 39 BCE, he already had custody of his infant daughter. Julia had been born earlier that same year, on the very day her father divorced her mother Scribonia.

Augustus insisted Julia receive traditional instruction in domestic activities, which included spinning and weaving. Responsibility for this training fell upon Livia. As a proper Roman wife she was accountable for the practical education of the children in her family. Julia shared Livia's appreciation for academic learning. The fourth century writer Macrobius remarks Julia was endowed "with a love of letters in general and knowledge of much—since such was readily available in her home…" [1]

Julia had asymmetrical eyes and prematurely graying hair. Augustus needled her about her prospects of going bald, when once he came upon her while her serving women were pulling out her faded strands. She matured into a pleasant, witty, urbane woman who shared her father's love for gambling.

But although gentle and kind, Julia displayed a flippant rebelliousness that often distressed Augustus. She wore racy clothing, socialized with a fast set, and defended her behavior with teasing defiance. Augustus once praised her for a modest costume that contrasted sharply with her *risqué* attire of the preceding day. "Is not this garb more appropriate to the daughter of Augustus?" he inquired. She retorted "Today indeed for my father's eyes I adorned myself, [but] yesterday for my husband's." [2]

Julia apparently failed or refused to understand her father's reasons for wanting her to live as simply and unobtrusively as he did. Augustus was a monarch who was trying to avoid the appearance of being a monarch. Julia saw only the rank and entitlement her father's position engendered for her. "He forgets he is Caesar," she remarked, "but I remember I am Caesar's daughter." [3]

Nonetheless, Augustus doted on Julia. She was his only surviving child; and her good-natured high spirits made her an amiable if exasperating companion. The emperor once exclaimed he had two spoiled daughters—Julia, and the Roman state.

Livia's association with Julia seems to have been friendly, despite the stark differences in their lifestyles. Julia's flamboyance contrasted blatantly with Livia's demureness. The divergence made the two women the foci of opposing political parties. There is no specific record, however, of personal acrimony between Livia and Julia. Nor do our sources indicate Julia's partisans attributed her eventual corruption and disgrace to Livia's malice. This minimal evidence suggests Livia and Julia agreed to disagree about their socio-political differences, and interacted with civility if not cordiality.

Julia's first husband was her cousin Marcus Claudius Marcellus, the only son of her father's sister Octavia. We have no idea of how Julia got on with him. Her union with her second spouse Agrippa had its congenial aspects. She accompanied him on his travels, and bore him five children in the nine years they were married. In other respects their relationship was strained. Julia had at least one lover: Tiberius Sempronius Gracchus. Chagrin over Julia's wantonness contributed to the deep depression that haunted Agrippa. He nevertheless neglected to invoke Augustus' own law, which gave a cuckolded husband the legal right and responsibility to press charges against an unfaithful wife.

The sons of Livia joined the Caesar household upon the death of their father Tiberius Claudius Nero, in 33 or 32 BCE. Tiberius was nine years of age, Decimus five or six. The frequency with which Livia saw her children prior to her ex-husband's demise cannot be determined. As their legitimate father, Nero had retained custody of the boys after he divorced Livia. He consequently had the right to restrict or even prevent their association with their mother. If Nero did limit Livia's access to their sons, he certainly recanted before he died; for he entrusted the boys' guardianship to Augustus.

Some people conjectured that Decimus—later Drusus—was Augustus' natural son. Suetonius declares Augustus so dearly loved Drusus, the emperor in his will named Drusus testamentary remainderman. This designation placed Drusus third in line for the succession. If Gaius and Lucius both failed to accept their inheritance, then Augustus' position and patrimony would devolve upon Drusus.

Augustus' failure to contrive some means of bringing Drusus closer to the succession strongly suggests the emperor was satisfied he was not Drusus' father. To marry Livia while she was pregnant, Octavian had to disclaim paternity of the child she was expecting. The pontiffs absolutely refused permission for the pair to wed unless Tiberius Nero's fatherhood was undisputed. Augustus never recanted this denial, even after Nero was long dead and the uproar over Livia's unorthodox divorce and remarriage long gone. Nor did Augustus ever adopt Drusus. Augustus' inclusion of Drusus in his will is not an indication the emperor suspected he might have begotten his stepson. Had Drusus inherited the principate under his stepfather's testamentary provisions, he would have occupied the position of stopgap successor that Tiberius eventually filled. Drusus' wife Antonia was Augustus' niece. As soon as one of their descendants ascended the throne, the principate would revert to its founder's bloodline.

Augustus gave his stepsons the sort of upbringing that was typical for the sons of senators. Their curriculum included law, government procedure, military science, and such purely academic subjects as mathematics, literature, and rhetoric. Tutors supplied what erudition Augustus and Livia did not. Tiberius' first active military duty under Augustus' supervision was as a cavalry tribune in the Spanish wars of 26 and 25 BCE. We have no specific information about Drusus' first service; but we can safely conjecture it occurred in 21 BCE. Drusus, who turned seventeen that year, was likely a member of the military force Tiberius led into Armenia.

In public life the imperial stepsons enjoyed special considerations and advantages. Each received and exercised the privilege of holding the regular magistracies five years prior to reaching the requisite age. As a budding attorney Tiberius undertook high profile cases—prosecution of the conspirator Caepio; patronage of earthquake victims in Asia Minor; defense of the king of Cappadocia, of the city of Tralles, of the people of Thessaly. The emperor assigned Tiberius the special responsibilities of relieving a grain shortage at Rome, and investigating the conditions of Italian slave workhouses. When Tiberius accompanied Augustus to Gaul in 16 BCE, Drusus completed his brother's unfinished praetorship. During the course of his Gallic junket Augustus appointed Tiberius, and subsequently Drusus, to the position of imperial legate of the province.

Augustus invested both stepsons with special military commands. In 21 BCE at the age of twenty, Tiberius headed the expedition to enthrone a Roman puppet in Armenia and receive the captured Roman standards from the Parthians. In 15 BCE the brothers cooperated on a pincer movement to halt the inroads of Alpine natives into Gaul. Between 12 and 9 BCE Tiberius subdued the rebellious Pannonians and pushed the Roman frontier to the Danube. During the same period of years, Drusus conquered the German dominated region between the Rhine and the Elbe.

Tiberius and Drusus rendered more service to the principate than the successors Augustus had selected for their ties of blood. The emperor's chosen heirs—his nephew Marcellus, and later his grandsons Gaius and Lucius—received the lion's share of accolades; but none lived long enough to match the achievements of Livia's sons. Tiberius and Drusus appear to have been content with their public lives despite their secondary status with regard to the succession. They conscientiously and diligently executed the tasks their stepfather delegated to them.

Tiberius was aloof and diffident. His reticence arose not so much from condescension as from nervous self-consciousness. Livia's elder son was nearsighted. He was left-handed. His complexion was disfigured by acne. An inclination to stutter prompted him to speak slowly and deliberately, gesticulating all the while with his fingers. Augustus, having reared Tiberius, vigorously insisted these speech mannerisms were natural and unintentional. Nonetheless the gestures made Tiberius seem obstinate and arrogant. Theodoros of Gadara, Tiberius' instructor in rhetoric, once described his charge as "mire with blood mingled."[4]

Had he lived in our era, Tiberius might well have made a successful contestant on a television quiz program. He loved to cull obscure information from literary sources. Augustus would tease Tiberius for employing pedantic and obsolete Latin phrases, which made his prose compositions in that language difficult to understand. Fluency in Greek enabled Tiberius to become an *aficionado* of trivia about figures in Greek mythology and legend. Tiberius enjoyed writing Greek verses, particularly in imitation of three little-known poets of that nationality. He also tried his hand at Latin poetry, and produced a lyric **Lament on the Death of Lucius Caesar.**

There was a streak of male chauvinism in Tiberius. Julia became romantically attracted to him while she was still the wife of Agrippa. Tiberius recoiled from her attention as inappropriate for a married woman. He also apparently chafed at the degree of public visibility Augustus granted Livia. At the time of his accession Tiberius rejected some of the honors the Senate proposed for Livia, maintaining excessive distinction was unbecoming a woman. He also tried to restrict the civic activities Livia had pursued while Augustus was alive. Tiberius' attitude may be one reason Augustus testamentarily adopted Livia as an heir, instead of following the customary procedure of providing her with a widow's trust. Under Roman law, an heir could refuse to cede a trust to its intended recipient; but one heir might not obstruct another heir's receipt of a designated bequest.

Tiberius had a hedonistic side. He was a heavy drinker. His love of winebibbing earned him the nickname of Biberius Caldius Mero. The sobriquet derives from *bibendum*—inclined to drink; *caldus*—hot: the Romans heated some wines to improve bouquet and taste; *merum*—wine unmixed with water and drunk only by the intemperate. Far later in his life, Tiberius acquired an unjustified reputation for lechery. Stories of voyeurism and pedophilia—which Suetonius describes in lurid detail— date from Tiberius' retirement to Capri. They are a mixture of baseless innuendo and exaggerations of common Roman sexual practices.[5]

Astrology fascinated Tiberius. His intense pursuit of the subject while living on Rhodes prompted conjectures about his political motives.

Virtually all Romans—including Augustus himself—believed in personal horoscopes and indications of the future in the stars. Excessive interest was nevertheless regarded with suspicion, especially by governments and persons in positions of power. One who felt he had divined forthcoming events might endeavor to alter them in his favor, to the detriment of an established ruler or society.

In the interests of national security, Augustus in 11 CE ordered a general expulsion of astrologers and soothsayers from Rome. But Augustus never insisted Tiberius cease practicing astrology, or maintained Tiberius was setting a bad example for the people he would someday rule. An astrologer friend of Tiberius was a member of the entourage that accompanied Augustus on his last vacation in the summer of 14 CE. Augustus must have viewed Tiberius' pursuit of the subject as a harmless hobby.

Tiberius eventually moved out of the Palatine home of his mother and stepfather and into a house of his own. The dwelling he acquired had once belonged to the Pompeii Magni—the multi-generational enemies of the Caesars. The house was located on the western section of the Esquiline Hill, overlooking the Forum. The Romans called the area *Carinae* (The Keels) because its topography resembled the backbones of ships. The Church of San Pietro in Vincoli stands in this region today.

Drusus was as personable and popular as his brother was not. He was sensitive to adverse public opinion, of the principate as a form of monarchy. In a letter to Tiberius, Drusus suggested the brothers urge Augustus to restore *libertas* (civil liberty). Suetonius maintains Drusus "did not equivocate at any time that he would restore the pristine condition of the Republic, should he ever be able." [5] Tacitus concurs:

> "Indeed great among the Roman populace was Drusus' memory, and it was believed that if he had become master of the state, he would have reinstated *libertas*." [6]

These comments have prompted some authors to conclude Drusus aspired to reestablish the Roman Republic. The argument is flawed, because Drusus certainly took advantage of personal prerogatives that the principate guaranteed him. He duly held public offices, including two praetorships, while underage. He served as military commander in service to Augustus' regime, but also to bring special glory upon himself. Suetonius continues:

> He was believed to be no less of glory-hungry than of gracious disposition; for in addition to victories over enemies he sought superlative trophies and earnestly, often impetuously, chased German leaders all over the field.[7]

Drusus must have contemplated the unpopularity of measures Augustus had enacted to sustain the principate—the moralizing laws a prime example. Instead of fanning opposition by defying and mocking such provisions—the tactics Julia employed—Drusus urged conciliation. Concluding Augustus had moved too far too fast in the direction of undisguised monarchy, Drusus encouraged a reinstatement of modes and appearances more characteristically Republican.

Drusus' outspoken endorsement of *libertas* suggests he was somewhat of a demagogue. His attitude produced the rumor Augustus had him murdered. Tacitus supports this allegation; but Suetonius dismisses it with good reason. Drusus did not expect to become *princeps*. Augustus never directly indicated him for the succession. Drusus could promise his adherents whatever they wanted to hear without fear of crossing his stepfather.

In the summer of 9 BCE, Drusus conducted a military campaign into German territory, which brought him to the banks of the Elbe. Both Suetonius and Dio Cassius write that during the course of this operation, Drusus saw an apparition of a larger-than-life barbarian woman. Speaking in Latin she admonished him not to pursue the conquest he had begun.

The female figure is a Walküre, one of nine warrior daughters of Wotan, the chief god of the Germanic pantheon. The Walküries' primary responsibility was to intercept the souls of soldiers who had died valiantly in battle. The goddesses transported their charges to Wotan's heavenly fortress Walhala. There the fallen soldiers enjoyed immortal honor as defenders of Walhala against the enemies of the gods. The warrior who beheld a Walkürie before a battle was certain to die and receive this hero's reward.

The story of Drusus' encounter suggests he acquainted himself with German folklore, or became the subject of local legend, —or both.

Drusus died on September 14, 9 BCE, at his military staging ground on the Rhenish frontier of Gaul. He was twenty-nine years of age. Suetonius attributes Drusus' demise to a fall from his horse while he was returning with his army to their base camp. Dio Cassius claims Drusus perished from disease. Complications from gangrene and trauma, arising from an equestrian catastrophe, could certainly have produced such disease-like symptoms as fever, vomiting, delirium, and convulsions. Drusus' accident occurred while he was on the march in a German wilderness, where he had access only to the most rudimentary medical care.

Tiberius' response to the news of Drusus' impending end shows Livia's sons were deeply devoted to one another despite their sharply differing personalities. Tiberius was at Ticinum in September of 9 BCE when he learned Drusus' death was imminent. Determined to reach his brother before the latter expired, Tiberius set out on horseback. Changing mounts at military way stations, he covered 200 miles of rugged Alpine terrain in twenty-four hours to accomplish his goal. Drusus died as Tiberius was embracing and kissing him. Tiberius escorted the funerary cortege back to Ticinum on foot.

The brothers commemorated their mutual affection with a building project. Drusus proposed or initiated construction in the Roman Forum of a temple to Castor and Pollux. The originally Greek cult of these heavenly brothers had been practiced in Italy for centuries. Castor and Pollux represented bravery and dexterity in battle as well as ideal brotherly love. Legend maintained their divine father Jupiter rewarded their fraternal fidelity by placing them in the night sky as the constellation Gemini. When Tiberius eventually dedicated the completed temple in 6 CE he made sure Drusus' name was inscribed thereon, although legally they were no longer members of the same family. Augustus had adopted Tiberius two years earlier.

Both men were fond of the wives Augustus selected for them. Tiberius married Agrippa's daughter by his first wife Caecilia Attica. Her father was Titus Caecilius Atticus Pomponianus, the famous correspondent of Cicero. Since Suetonius and Dio Cassius consistently refer to Tiberius' bride as Agrippina, the imperial family may have addressed her by that name. Tacitus and modern historians call her Vipsania to distinguish her from her younger half-sister, the granddaughter of Augustus who was also called Agrippina. Although we do not know the year of Vipsania's birth, we can calculate it fell between 36 and 32 BCE. Her parents were married in 37 BCE, the year of her father's first consulship; and she was betrothed to Tiberius sometime before Atticus died in 32 BCE.

Vipsania bore Tiberius a son, Drusus Claudius Nero. Although our sources give the date of the boy's birth as October 7, they do not provide his natal year. Very likely this was 14 BCE. This Drusus held his first consulship in 15 CE. Members of the imperial family, who were not successor-designates, occupied this office five years before reaching the requisite age of thirty-three. Drusus would have had to be turning twenty-eight during 15 CE, the year he entered upon the consulship on January 1. The timing of Drusus' birth reveals Vipsania may have accompanied Tiberius, when he joined Augustus' junket to Gaul in 16 BCE. Vipsania conceived a second child who either miscarried or died very young. There is no record of such an individual in the Julio-Claudian dynasty.

Tiberius' brother Drusus espoused the younger Antonia, Octavia's second daughter by Mark Antony. Suetonius maintains only three of the many children she bore to Drusus lived past infancy. All three survivors were born between 15 and 10 BCE. Drusus spent most of this span of years in Gaul, conducting military operations against natives and subsequently against Germans. He did visit Rome during this interval, for he participated in the consecration of the Altar of Peace in 13 BCE and in the funeral of Octavia two years later. We do not know the birthplaces of Drusus' first two viable children. The eldest was Nero, who called himself Germanicus after entering public life. He was born on May 24, 15 BCE. A daughter, Claudia Livilla (Little Livia) arrived sometime during the next four years.

Drusus' third surviving child Tiberius was born at the Gallic capital of Lugdunum on August 1, 10 BCE. In adulthood he would call himself by his *gentilicum* Claudius, and rule as emperor under that name. Since

Augustus spent much of the summer of 10 BCE in Lugdunum, Livia may have been present at this grandchild's birth.

Livia's fierce loyalty to the intractable Tiberius, and her near suicide from grief over the death of Drusus, reveal her intense love for her sons. Their reciprocated affection for her can be sensed from vignettes of information buried in our source material. Drusus appears to have regarded Livia reverentially. He never left her home even after he was married; and he named his only daughter in her honor.

Tiberius' attitude toward his mother appears exploitative by comparison. When Tiberius mounted games in memory of his father and of Livia's, Augustus and Livia financed the project at great expense to themselves. After alienating Augustus and Gaius by retiring to the island of Rhodes without explanation, Tiberius procured rehabilitation with Livia's help. After his accession Tiberius sought to avoid the appearance of being guided by his mother, although every so often he turned to her for advice. Tiberius' independence did not alienate Livia. Even the hostile Tacitus admits that their relationship was amicable until Sejanus compromised it.

JULIA AND TIBERIUS: WHAT WENT WRONG BETWEEN THEM?

Agrippa's death in the summer of 12 BCE prompted Augustus to make a decision that precipitated a family disaster. After considering many candidates, Augustus asked Tiberius to divorce Vipsania and take the widowed Julia as his second wife. The emperor had adopted Gaius and Lucius whom Julia had born to Agrippa, and was preparing the boys to succeed him as *princeps*. Augustus decided no man was better qualified than Tiberius to serve as regent for the princes, should the emperor die before they were old enough to assume his position. Vipsania married an ambitious young senator named Gaius Asinius Gallus. After bearing her new husband six children, Vipsania died in 20 CE, shortly after the trials of Piso and Plancina, and three days after her son Drusus celebrated an ovation for victories in the German and Danubian theaters. Like her father Agrippa, Vipsania was relatively young—in her mid fifties—when she passed away.

The marriage of Tiberius and Julia was solemnized in 11 BCE and worked satisfactorily for at least two years. Julia accompanied Tiberius to Aquileia, the staging ground for his military campaigns in Pannonia. She bore him a son who died in infancy. After the baby's death, Tiberius grew cold. He pined for Vipsania. According to one rumor he followed his former wife with tears in his eyes, after encountering her by chance on the streets of Rome. Tiberius ceased cohabitating with Julia. He subsequently retired to Rhodes, insisting he needed a rest cure. Many people assumed, however, that Tiberius really quit Rome to escape Julia altogether.

Julia and Tiberius could have refused to wed in the first place. Since his natural father was deceased, Tiberius was not subject to a paternal *manus*. Being of age he was free of Augustus' legal guardianship. Tiberius was *sui iuris* (of his own right.) This legal condition allowed him to accept or refuse any contract, including a marriage; he had no guardian to overrule him. Widowhood had rendered Julia *sui iuris* as well. Marriage had freed her from the *manus* of her father, and death from that of her husband.

Once married the pair had the legal right to terminate their union by mutual agreement. Either course of action—a refusal to marry or an amicable divorce—would have left Augustus fuming but without legal recourse. Divorce would not have compromised Tiberius' tenure of the regency for Julia's sons. That position was an extraordinary public office, established by a special senatorial decree. Divorce was an aspect of private law.

Why did Julia and Tiberius neglect to exercise their legal rights to prevent or end their marriage?

If Julia fancied Tiberius as Suetonius asserts, she may have resisted divorce, leaving Tiberius no option but to accuse her of adultery or some other criminal activity. He—and Agrippa before him—may not have had sufficient evidence to do so. Throughout her three marriages, Julia maintained a façade of moral rectitude that kept people guessing about her sexual activities. All five of the children she bore Agrippa resembled him. Augustus touted this fact as evidence of his daughter's chastity; but she provided a far more provocative explanation: "Never unless the hold is full do I accept a passenger." [8]

After Tiberius left her, Julia embarked upon four years undisguised debauchery. She mocked Augustus' morality laws with her unabashed adulteries and blatant displays of licentiousness. We do not know if she flouted her father's regulations to punish him, or to persuade him to repeal the statutes as ineffective.

There was more to Julia's rebellion than orgies of winebibbing and free love. Julia apparently conspired to bring the principate under the control of the dissidents who supported her defiance of the ethics legislation. Her principal paramour was Iullus Antonius, the son of Mark Antony who had married Julia's cousin the elder Marcella. Iullus killed himself rather than face prosecution as Julia's accomplice. Dio Cassius writes that Augustus' investigation into the activities of Julia and her lovers revealed Iullus aspired to the monarchy.

The precise nature of Iullus' plot and Julia's participation therein eludes us. The elder Pliny includes in his list of Augustus' personal vexations, "the adultery of [his] daughter and designs of the parricide overtly made." [9] In addition to describing a murderer of one's parents, the Latin term *parricida* could denote a rebel, a traitor, a betrayer of one's country, or the assassin of a head of state. Pliny's use of this epithet suggests Julia was involved in an effort to overthrow her father. She was nevertheless tried and convicted of adultery, not treason. Perhaps Julia attempted to cajole Augustus, into letting Iullus or another lover replace Tiberius as her husband and the regent for her sons. There is some evidence to support this hypothesis. Julia sent Augustus a letter in which she bitterly denounced Tiberius. Her paramour of many years, the aforementioned Sempronius Gracchus, composed this diatribe for her. Julia also began to maintain she considered marriage to Tiberius Claudius Nero beneath her.

So what drove Julia over the proverbial edge?

Some authors suggest Livia's infertility prompted Augustus to place upon Julia the burden of producing heirs to the throne. According to this premise, Julia rebelled because she could no longer endure life as a brood mare. Augustus drove his only daughter into unhappy prearranged marriages, just so he might retain his own love match with a childless wife.

In ancient Rome it was considered indecent for a couple to separate because the wife was barren. Arranged marriages, however, were a norm, and employed to reinforce political alignments. Even had Livia borne Augustus a dozen sons, he would still have presented Julia's hand to someone of critical importance to his regime.

Foreordained unions were not necessarily dismal. Tiberius was happy with Vipsania, Drusus with Antonia, and later Germanicus with Agrippina. Augustus apparently tried to make Julia's forced marriages as comfortable for her as he could. To forestall her falling in love with the wrong person, he endeavored to shield her from the advances of young men. He sharply berated one youthful nobleman, who had come to call on Julia while she was vacationing at Baiae. On another occasion Augustus urged his daughter to forsake the company of dandies for that of respectable older men. Referring to her companions she snapped back at her father, "And these men will be elderly with me!" [10] Augustus conceivably noticed that Julia was attracted to Tiberius, and considered her feelings when he asked Tiberius to marry her.

Once Tiberius' departure for Rhodes deprived Julia of the mentoring influence of a husband, she succumbed to the persuasions of the dissident party. There is no way to determine her psychological condition. We cannot tell if she became despondent at having been abandoned, euphoric with newly found freedom, or simply fed up with prim and proper appearances. Her family failed to detect and calm her defiant state of mind before it manifested itself in lawbreaking and sedition.

By the time Julia was sentenced in the autumn of 2 BCE, Tiberius must have faced a veritable firestorm of fury. Augustus resented insubordination. Moreover he may have held Tiberius at least indirectly responsible for precipitating Julia's corruption. She did not begin her dissolute career until after Tiberius had left her. Tiberius endeavored unsuccessfully to justify himself, insisting he had actually retired to Rhodes to avoid political rivalry with Gaius and Lucius. This assertion failed to bring about redemption because Gaius had already come to consider Tiberius a threat. His grandson's misgivings, more than anger of his own, impelled Augustus to restrict Tiberius to Rhodes for the three years that followed Julia's disgrace. Gaius' eventual discovery his chief of staff Marcus Lollius had maligned Tiberius prompted Augustus to end Tiberius' confinement.

There is no way, of course, to determine what the Caesars said to one another in private. Still the little available evidence we have suggests poor interpersonal communication between the members of the family precipitated the misfortunes that befell them. Tiberius irritated Augustus and brought suspicion upon himself by retiring to Rhodes without credible explanation. Augustus did not perceive his daughter's growing rebelliousness until her own actions incriminated her. Gaius believed and reacted to distortions of Tiberius' character until these were exposed as Lollius' slanders.

Seven years elapsed between Tiberius' withdrawal to Rhodes in 6 BCE and his return to Rome in 2 CE. During this interval we catch glimpses of Livia caught in the crossfire as she endeavored to repair relations between her husband and son. In 6 BCE she tried to dissuade Tiberius from leaving Rome in the first place. Thereafter she worked to rehabilitate him. To obfuscate the fact Tiberius' voluntary exile had become a forced one, Livia convinced Augustus to designate Tiberius imperial legate to Rhodes. With similar intent, Augustus maintained publicly that he had sent Tiberius to Rhodes to be further educated.

After Gaius' dinner companion offered to decapitate Tiberius, Livia pressed Augustus more urgently for her son's release. Publius Sulpicius Quirinius Cyrenius, who replaced the treacherous Lollius as Gaius' chief of staff, was a kinsman and *protégé* of Livia. His appointment suggests Gaius and Augustus aspired to conciliate Livia, after discovering they had impugned Tiberius in response to Lollius' deception.

The tide of events finally turned in Tiberius' favor. Lucius died in August of 2 CE, and Gaius eighteen months later. The resulting situation enabled Livia to procure Tiberius' reinstatement as a critical member of her husband's regime. Augustus' successor of choice was now Germanicus. He was only seventeen years of age—still undertrained and inexperienced—when Gaius passed away in February of 4 CE. Once again a regent was necessary; and once again Tiberius was the most capable candidate.

Tiberius could not become stepfather to his new charge, as he had been to Gaius and Lucius. Germanicus' widowed mother Antonia staunchly refused to remarry. Livia suggested Augustus adopt Tiberius as son and successor designate, and Tiberius do the same for Germanicus. Since

Germanicus was Augustus' grandnephew, Livia's proposal guaranteed reversion of the principate to the Caesar bloodline. Augustus saw the logic of the arrangement and accepted it.

Several weeks after Tiberius' accession, Julia ended her life by suicide.

LIVIA AND OTHER RELATIVES

There is no way to determine how Livia got along with every single member of her extended family. The historical record nevertheless provides glimpses of her personal interaction with a few relatives apart from her children. As in any family, there were friendships and there were frictions.

OCTAVIA

The younger Seneca reports that Augustus' sister developed a grudge against Livia. When her son Marcellus died of illness, at the age of nineteen, Octavia became inconsolable with grief:

> She chose to have no portrait of her dearest son, nor mention made to her of his name. She hated all mothers and raged mostly against Livia, because it appeared the good fortune promised to hers (i.e. to Marcellus) would pass to the other's son. Most familiar with shadows and solitude, not even showing respect to her brother, she rejected songs composed to celebrate Marcellus' memory and other honors of devotion, and shut her ears against all consolation. From her usual duties drawn aside, and even despising the supremely effulgent fortune of her brother's greatness, she buried herself and withdrew. Surrounded by children, for her grandchildren she would not put aside clothes of mourning, [and] not without contempt for all of hers (i.e., the surviving members of her family), she considered herself bereft although they flourished.[11]

Anyone who has endured the death of a child can empathize with the bitterness Octavia may have felt toward Livia. The prevalence and prosperity of other people's children are all that the bereaved parent seems to notice. Nevertheless, Seneca very likely exaggerated Octavia's antipathy toward Livia. He certainly misrepresented Octavia as a hostile, grief-obsessed hermit.

Marcellus' death deprived Octavia of a certain degree of public stature. Although still the emperor's sister she was no longer the mother of his successor-designate. Ill health may have forced her to curtail her physical activities and public appearances: she would not live past the age of fifty-five. Contrary to Seneca's insistence, however, Octavia continued to interact with her brother and contribute to his regime. In memory of Marcellus she financed and directed embellishments to the portico that Augustus had named for her. She presented the poet Vergil with a large donative, because he had eulogized Marcellus in his **Aeneid**. As late as 13 BCE Augustus named a new theater for Marcellus, who by now had been dead for ten years. The emperor's decision suggests Octavia persisted in influencing him on Marcellus' behalf.

Octavia did not restrict her attentions to commemorations of her late son. Nor did she demand that others celebrate Marcellus in return for her patronage. The military engineer Vitruvius owed his generous pension to Octavia's intervention. He dedicated his comprehensive analysis of Roman architecture to Augustus, rather than to the memory of Marcellus. While Marcellus was alive the Greek poet Krinagoras celebrated him along with other members of Octavia's family. After Marcellus died, Krinagoras and his pupils focused their accolades upon Octavia's last child, the younger Antonia.

If a personal coolness did emerge between Octavia and Livia—whether over Marcellus' death or for other reasons—it did not prevent the two women from cooperating in official matters. Horace depicts the sisters-in-law joyously welcoming Augustus back from Spain; and Krinagoras mentions both in his prayer to Hera for Antonia's forthcoming confinement. The statues of the pair at Glanum attest to their collaboration in honoring that Gallic city. Octavia appears to have participated in the groundbreaking for the Altar of Peace, a structure representative of principles with which Augustus connected Livia. A figure in the badly ruined frieze on the altar's north side depicts a woman of Octavia's years. (She was fifty-three when the edifice was consecrated in 13 BCE.) The figure stands amid identifiable portraits of Octavia's daughters and grandchildren.

Two of Octavia's daughters married relatives of Livia. The younger Marcella wed Marcus Valerius Barbatus Appianus, the son of Livia's uncle Appius Claudius Pulcher. The younger Antonia of course married Livia's son Drusus: their offspring were Octavia's grandchildren as well as Livia's. No evidence suggests Octavia opposed either marriage. If she did the rest of her family obviously overruled her.

Seneca's purpose is didactic. He contrasts the wild and excessive mourning he attributes to Octavia, with the dignified self-discipline he assigns to Livia after the death of Drusus. Both portrayals, we have seen, are distorted. Livia did not face Drusus' demise as calmly—nor did Octavia react to Marcellus' passing as strongly—as Seneca would have us believe.

The Younger Antonia

Octavia's last daughter was born on January 31, 36 BCE—the day following Livia's twenty-second birthday. Antonia was seventeen—relatively old for a Roman bride—when she married Livia's nineteen-year-old son Drusus in the early part of 19 BCE. (Most Roman girls married at fourteen.) Krinagoras describes Antonia preparing in midwinter for the nuptials that were to take place near the time of her birthday. Augustus for certain was not present: the emperor did not return to Rome from his junket to the East until October of the same year. We do not know whether Livia reentered the capital earlier than her spouse so she might attend the wedding.

Drusus and Antonia spent the first three years of their marriage in Rome. After 15 BCE they divided their time between Italy and Gaul, of which Drusus was military governor. While in Rome they lived in Augustus' residential complex on the Palatine. In this venue Antonia chose to rear her children and live out her days, after Drusus perished in September of 9 BCE. She occupied the same room, even the same bed, she had shared with her beloved for a decade. Although Augustus' marital laws imposed heavy penalties upon widows of childbearing age who failed to remarry, Antonia steadfastly refused to take a second husband.

Antonia's decision to remain in her uncle's home was a psychological boon for Livia. The presence of Drusus' widow and children enabled Livia to fulfill the philosopher Areus' recommendation to surround herself with reminiscences of her dead son. Antonia's willingness to contribute to this interaction reveals her fondness for Livia.

Seneca castigates poor Octavia for sequestering herself after Marcellus died. The widowed Antonia, however, appears to have been as reclusive as her mother if not more so. She disappears entirely from narrative sources for Augustus' reign. One epigraphic reference to a *Basilica Antoniarum* (Basilica of the Antonias) suggests Antonia and her older sister may have participated in a building project. This identification of the *Basilica Antoniarum* is not certain; the edifice may date from the reign of Claudius (41 – 54 CE).[12] If the basilica was erected during the reign of Augustus, it connects Antonia with only a single edifice. Livia by contrast was involved with many endeavors of this nature.

During the reign of Tiberius, Antonia supervised the preparations for Germanicus' funeral. She did not attend the actual ceremony.

Antonia's seclusion was very likely the result of health problems. Tacitus admits illness may have kept her from attending the obsequies she arranged for her son. The second century physician Galen writes that Antonia employed the services of several doctors. She was prone to attacks of influenza. We learn from the elder Pliny that she could not spit, from Galen that she used eye salves. Such symptoms are indicative of Sjögren's syndrome. This affliction, common in middle-aged women, is marked by *xerostomia* (dryness of the mouth), enlargement of the parotid glands (the salivary glands at the base of the ears in mammals), and *keratoconjunctivitis sicca* (dry eyes). The condition is associated with autoimmune deficiencies such as lupus, but most frequently with rheumatoid arthritis. The prevalence of either condition would explain why Antonia used one of the liniments Livia favored for stiff joints. There is no direct evidence Antonia was crippled; but an inability to move without assistance could very well have impelled her to forego public appearances.

Throughout her reclusive life Antonia remained alert, resourceful, and sensitive. Inscriptions and papyri reveal she owned and managed vast agricultural properties in Egypt. Like Livia, Antonia took an interest in the royal house of Judaea. She was patroness to Berenice the widow of Aristobulos, a son of Herod who fell victim to family infighting. Berenice's son was the extravagant and reckless Herod Agrippa I, whom Claudius would enthrone in a failed experiment to reestablish the old client kingdom of Judaea. Antonia helped Herod Agrippa pay debts he incurred while living lavishly in Rome. After Tiberius incarcerated him for making some utterances that smacked of sedition, Antonia made sure Agrippa's jailers treated him gently.

Suetonius relates an anecdote, which reveals Antonia and Livia shared concern about ways in which the principate was publicized. Antonia's son Claudius complained he had to break off writing a history of the civil wars between Octavian and Mark Antony. Antonia had joined Livia in berating Claudius for presenting his material too objectively.

Inscriptions and artworks dating from the reign of Tiberius honor Antonia as the widow of Drusus and mother of the heir-apparent Germanicus. The city of Thermis on Lesbos extols her as benefactress. She was divine benefactress at Ilium (Roman Troy), and divine Antonia at Athens. A fragmentary inscription from Ptolemais Hermiou in Egypt (modern El Manshah), associates Antonia with women. Germanicus visited these locales during his Eastern junket of 18 – 19 CE. These Eastern honors have prompted a modern biographer to suggest Antonia accompanied her son on his journey.

It is difficult to believe Antonia, now in her mid-fifties and a victim of continual pain, had much interest in travel. No inscription confirms her presence in Antioch, Germanicus' eastern headquarters. Tacitus details the activities of Agrippina during the trip but makes no mention of Antonia. It seems more plausible Antonia, like Livia, considered petitions from Lesbos, Athens, and Ilium. As Livia was now elderly, Antonia may have begun to assist her in scrutinizing appeals from foreign principalities. The honor at Ptolemais may arise because

Antonia, like Livia and other members of their family, owned lands in the imperial duchy of Egypt.

Dio Cassius and Flavius Josephus credit Antonia with turning Tiberius against his favorite, the praetorian prefect Sejanus. Her task could not have been easy. Not only did Antonia have to get a messenger past the prefect's physical blockade about Capri. She must convince Tiberius that Sejanus was genuinely dangerous. The burden of having to compile persuasive and/or legally sustainable evidence is a likely reason two years elapsed, between the prosecutions of Agrippina and Nero and the exposure of the prefect's malfeasance. Suetonius and Dio attest to the emergence of an anti-Sejanus movement in Rome. Antonia may have taken encouragement from this development, knowing she could rely on opponents of Sejanus to confirm her accusations. Whatever she wrote impelled Tiberius to launch a thorough investigation of the prefect and his activities. The inquiry exposed the murder of Tiberius' son, and Sejanus' intention to destroy the progeny of Germanicus.[13]

Dio Cassius maintains Antonia starved her own daughter Livilla to death, for having been Sejanus' accomplice. Some seven years later—on May 1, 38 CE—the seventy-three-year-old Antonia died by her own hand. Rumor held that her grandson, the deranged emperor Caligula, forced her to commit suicide because she objected to his conduct.

We can detect a sense of humor in the reclusive Antonia. She owned a villa at Baculae (modern Bacoli), south of Baiae on the Bay of Naples. The estate boasted a large fishpond, in which Antonia kept a pet eel. She had the creature festooned with a pair of earrings, and allowed tourists onto the property to see the sight.

GERMANICUS

Nero Claudius Drusus Germanicus, the elder son of Drusus and Antonia, ostensibly excelled at everything he undertook. A courageous and effective soldier, he often slew enemies in hand-to-hand combat. Germanicus was an effective politician as well. He exuded humility, piety, and leniency, even toward his detractors. Suetonius credits him with "a singular benevolence, and for the winning of men's grace and the meriting of their love a wonderful and effective enthusiasm." [14] Germanicus' bearing engendered his immense popularity among soldiers and civilians alike. Suetonius adds that even the king of Parthia went into mourning when Germanicus died.

Germanicus demonstrated competence in his studies of Greek and Roman oratory and academics. He dabbled at writing Greek comedies. His Latin translation of the *Φαινομένα καὶπρογνώστικα— Phaenomena kai prognostica (Appearances and Perceptions)* by Aratus of Soli remains extant today. Aratus, a native of Cilicia, lived in the third century of the pre-Christian era. He was personal physician to the Macedonian king Antigonas Gonatas, a predecessor of Alexander the Great. Aratus' work is a poetic description of astronomical and meteorological phenomena. The piece—now a valuable resource to modern astronomers and historians of science—was immensely popular with the Romans. Cicero translated it years before Germanicus was born. Whether Germanicus aspired to emulate that great orator, made the translation because doing so was a popular fad, or took genuine interest in Aratus' subjects, cannot be ascertained.

To outward appearances at least, Germanicus' association with Livia was harmonious. The prince once asserted that on the night before a battle, Livia offered him spiritual inspiration in a dream. He named two of his three daughters for her—the one Drusilla, the other Julia Livilla. To adorn the temple of Venus on the Capitoline Hill, Suetonius writes, Livia commissioned a statue of the goddess' son Cupid in the likeness of Germanicus' deceased son.

Germanicus was nevertheless leader of the dissident party opposing Tiberius. Its adherents disdained Livia as the evil stepmother whose offspring had usurped the principate from its rightful heirs. Germanicus' association with this group may not have compromised his personal interaction with Livia. Tacitus maintains Germanicus remained on friendly terms with his cousin Drusus, although the latter headed the pro-Tiberian faction rejecting the dissenters' platform. Germanicus' connection with the opposition party nevertheless precipitated frictions, which disrupted the imperial family after his death. As we noted in an earlier chapter, Livia may have neglected to attend Germanicus' funeral because she objected to his public behavior.

CLAUDIUS

The younger son of Drusus and Antonia seemed the antithesis of his elder brother. As a child, Tiberius Claudius Drusus suffered several serious illnesses that left him physically disabled. Weak legs forced him to drag his right foot in a lurching, somewhat comical gait. His head shook, especially when his emotions were aroused. He spoke with a stammer. When angry he slobbered at the mouth and dribbled from the nose. Claudius compounded his bodily deficiencies with uncouth behavioral traits. A dreamy, mind-wandering disposition often made him seem inane and easily confused. His laughter was loud, vulgar, and excessive.

After becoming emperor, Claudius told the Senate that he had deliberately feigned excessive stupidity, "since from a child he grew up amid sickness and immense fear." [15] He also complained in an autobiography, that even after he was old enough to be legally exempt from *tutela* his family subjected him to the care of supervisors. One was a barbarian and former muleteer, "placed in charge of him (Claudius), that he might for whatever reason be punished as savagely as possible." [16]

Claudius had good reason to feel embittered toward his family, being their proverbial black sheep. Everyone—his own mother included—appears to have disliked him; and Livia was no exception.

> Mother Antonia would often call him a monster of a person, not completed by nature but merely stuck together; and if she accused someone of foolishness, she would assert [he was] more stupid than her son Claudius. Grandmother Augusta always held him in utmost contempt, not addressing him except very rarely, usually not admonishing him unless by a bitter and brief note or through intermediaries. Sister Livilla, on hearing that at some time he might rule, openly and clearly execrated so adverse and unworthy a fate for the Roman people.[17]

In adulthood Claudius exhibited symptoms of bulimia. During his youth his conduct at meals apparently so distressed his grandmother, she could not abide having to dine with him. Suetonius has preserved several letters, in which Augustus discusses Claudius with Livia. In one message the emperor declares he will take advantage of Livia's absence, and invite Claudius to dinner every day while she is away.

Although she recoiled at his demeanors, Livia took great interest in Claudius' personal development. Augustus writes to her admiringly of Claudius' proficiency in academic pursuits, and acknowledges an innately noble nature in the youth. The emperor nevertheless deplores Claudius' inattentiveness, his mumbling conversation, and his adherence to friends who do nothing to improve his bearing. Livia seems to have hoped Claudius would someday be able to hold office and participate in public activities without bringing ridicule upon himself and embarrassment to his family. In one letter, Augustus responds to her concerns about this issue. He urges the importance of establishing a firm, family policy with regard to Claudius' public activities:

> For if he is complete, that is to say, sound, what is for us to doubt, if through those same degrees and steps he should be advanced, through which his brother has been advanced? If, however, we feel him to be diminished and hindered in perfection of both the body and the mind, material that might deride both him and us should not be offered to people who are wont to mock and sneer at such things. Indeed we shall always boil, if we deliberate over isolated moments in time, and not determine in advance whether he can manage public offices or not.[18]

The Caesars ultimately pronounced Claudius unfit for an official career, and allowed him to exercise only a few strictly ceremonial functions. Augustus had him invested as an augur. On two occasions during Tiberius' reign, the equestrian order elected Claudius to address the consuls on their behalf: in 14 CE when the equestrians sought the privilege of conveying Augustus' remains from Nola to Rome, and then in 31 CE when they offered congratulations to Tiberius on the overthrow of Sejanus. In 20 CE Claudius accompanied Tiberius' son Drusus to Tarracina, from whence they escorted Germanicus' funeral cortege to Rome. Claudius also attended his brother's funeral. Apart from these occasional public appearances Claudius lived as a private citizen, pursuing intensive studies of history, literature, and languages.

Claudius was betrothed in childhood to Aemilia Lepida, the daughter of Augustus' granddaughter Julia. Suetonius adds that Claudius terminated this arrangement because Aemilia's parents had angered Augustus. It appears the decision to reject Aemilia was Claudius' alone, not a mandate from his relatives. The fact that Aemilia's brother eventually married Germanicus' daughter Drusilla, indicates the imperial family did not hold the misconduct of Julia and her husband against their children. Aemilia herself married Marcus Junius Silanus, a loyal retainer of Tiberius. Claudius turned seventeen in 8 CE, the year of Julia's disgrace and banishment. When he assumed the *toga virilis*—sometime between the ages of fifteen and nineteen—Claudius acquired the right to bind or refuse contracts, including marriage. This legal condition entitled him to repudiate Aemilia without interference from his family or anyone else.

We can detect Livia's hand in the subsequent marital arrangements for Claudius. His next fiancée was Livia Medullina, whose *gentilicum* indicates she was a relative of his grandmother. Medullina boasted another pedigree, which must have appealed to the history-enthusiastic Claudius. Suetonius remarks Medullina bore the second *cognomen* of Camilla because she was descended from the family of Camillus the Dictator. Marcus Furius Camillus was a hero of Roman history. After conquering the city-state of Veii in 396 BCE, Camillus repulsed the invading Gauls who threatened to overrun Rome six years later. Once again, however, plans for Claudius' marriage were frustrated. Medullina became seriously ill, and died on the very day that had been set for the wedding.

Claudius eventually married Plautia Urgulanilla, the daughter of Livia's retainer Marcus Plautius Silvanus, who had been Augustus' colleague in the consulship of 2 BCE. The imperial family apparently hoped Claudius would learn deportment from his bride's family. Continuing his aforementioned comments to Livia, Augustus writes:

At present, concerning the issues about which you seek advice: for him to oversee, at the games of Mars, the banquet of the priests does not displease us, if he will allow himself by Silvanus his kinsman to be advised, so that he does not do what might be caught sight of and derided.[19]

The marriage of Claudius and Urgulanilla produced a son and a daughter. Around 25 CE Claudius divorced the wife Livia had procured for him. We shall see in our next chapter how this breach between Claudius and his grandmother arose from Sejanus' efforts to undermine Livia's influence over her family.

LIVILLA AND THE YOUNGER DRUSUS

Livia's only granddaughter, the middle child of Drusus and Antonia, was very likely born in 14 or 13 BCE. From Tacitus and Dio Cassius we learn Claudia Livilla married Augustus' eldest grandson Gaius. Dio maintains the nuptials took place in 1 BCE, just before Gaius' departure from Rome on his diplomatic mission to the East. Under the terms of Augustus' marital law, a woman had to be at least twelve years of age to be wed. To be capable of fulfilling this requirement, Livilla could not have been born later than 13 BCE. Antonia might have been pregnant when she participated in the consecration ceremony for the Altar of Peace.

Tacitus describes Livilla as a physically ugly girl who matured into a woman of extraordinary beauty. She and her two brothers grew up in the Palatine home of Augustus and Livia, under the tutelage of their widowed mother. For the first three decades of her life, Livilla conducted herself with utmost propriety. No scandal is imputed to her during her childhood or early adult years. Her maternal great-uncle Augustus was fond or at least considerate of her. While on his deathbed he inquired about Livilla, who was ill at the time.

Livilla was respectful of Antonia and of Livia. In a letter to Sejanus, Tiberius writes of Livilla's deference to the counsels of her mother and grandmother. Livilla shared at least two of Livia's prejudices. One was contempt for the bumbling of Livilla's younger brother Claudius, the other the self-aggrandizement of her sister-in-law Agrippina.

As the youthful bride of Gaius Caesar, Livilla may have accompanied her husband on his Eastern junket. Dio Cassius offers this somewhat vague testimony:

> Pressed by necessity, [Augustus] appointed Gaius, gave him the authority of a proconsul and a wife, that esteem might accrue to him, and attached advisers to him.[20]

There is no record of any children born to Gaius and Livilla.

On February 21, 4 CE Gaius died in Asia Minor, from the deleterious effects of the wound he had received in Armenia the preceding September. Within the next decade Livilla remarried. Her second husband was also her first cousin: Drusus Claudius Nero, the son of Tiberius.

The younger Drusus developed a reputation for sexual licentiousness, irascibility, arrogance, and cruelty. He nevertheless had a lighter side. Drusus was a socialite who pursued architectural projects by day and banquets by night. He and Germanicus were the best of friends despite their opposing political positions. Another close friend who shared Drusus' penchant for self-indulgence, was the Jewish prince Herod Agrippa I. Tacitus writes the Romans found, in Drusus' hedonism and conviviality, a refreshing contrast to the self-restraint and inaccessibility of Tiberius his father. We have no idea of how Drusus got on with Livia; there is no record of her interaction with him.

The eldest child of Drusus and Livilla was a daughter, Julia Claudilla. She could not have been born later than 14 CE. By 26 CE Julia had married Nero, the eldest son of Germanicus; hence she was at least twelve as of that year. In 31 CE, two years after Nero's suicide, Julia married an equestrian named Gaius Rubellius Blandus. Eventually Valeria Messallina, the malicious third wife of Claudius, compelled Julia to take her own life in 43 CE.

Livilla bore Drusus a pair of identical sons late in 19 CE. Tacitus avers the brothers' birth helped alleviate the imperial family's distress over the recent death of Germanicus. The one boy, also called Germanicus, was sickly. He died in 23 CE shortly after the decease of his father Drusus.

His brother Tiberius Gemellus (The Twin) was seventeen when his grandfather Tiberius died on March 16, 37 CE.

Tiberius the emperor bequeathed half his assets to this grandson, but conferred the succession along with the balance of his estate upon Gemellus' cousin Caligula. Because Tiberius had adopted Caligula's father Germanicus, Caligula from a legal standpoint was as much Tiberius' grandson as was Gemellus. Caligula was twenty-four. Being chronologically older than Gemellus, Caligula had received more training in government; hence Tiberius deemed him better prepared than Gemellus to assume control of the principate. Furthermore as the son of Augustus' granddaughter Agrippina, Caligula was more directly related than Gemellus to the principate's founder. On becoming emperor Caligula adopted Gemellus and proclaimed him *princeps iuventutis*; but once in the throes of his madness, Caligula had Gemellus executed.

Livilla's outward respectability was deceptive. It concealed a criminal nature that Sejanus eventually unleashed. In 23 CE if not earlier, Livilla committed adultery with the scheming prefect. The pair subsequently colluded to murder Drusus, and convince Tiberius that Agrippina and her sons were plotting to usurp control of the principate.

Although derogatory tradition associates Livia with Gaius' decease it does not implicate Livilla, either as an agent of her grandmother or as an independent assassin. This exemption may result from the fact Livilla had little to gain but plenty to lose from Gaius' death. Since Augustus had indicated Gaius for the succession, his demise scuttled Livilla's opportunity to be empress. Admittedly Livilla created precisely this condition for herself when she helped Sejanus poison Drusus. No suspicion connected Livilla with Drusus' death at the time it occurred. Only the testimony of Sejanus' estranged wife Apictata implicated Livilla, eight years after she helped perpetrate the murder.

MARCIA

Augustus' natural father Gaius Octavius Thurinus died when his son was only five years old. The emperor's mother Atia took for her second husband a man named Lucius Marcius Philippus. His son by his own prior marriage espoused Atia's much younger sister. Their only child Marcia was Augustus' first cousin. She was closer in age to his daughter than to the emperor himself.

Marcia and her mother were dedicated patrons of the literary arts, as was Marcia's husband the urbane Paullus Fabius Maximus (consul 11 BCE). The poets Horace and Ovid were among their *protégés*.

Marcia was related to Augustus by ties of blood; but the first marriage of her daughter, Fabia Numantina, suggests a special alignment with Livia. Numantina espoused the younger Marcus Plautius Silvanus. He was the son of the consul of 2 BCE, grandson of Livia's retainer Urgulania, and eventually brother-in-law of Livia's grandson Claudius.

Camaraderie between Livia and Marcia can be deduced from the story of Paullus Fabius Maximus' ill-fated loquacity. We know from a previous chapter there are two versions of the tale. Tacitus insists Augustus and Maximus evaded Livia's scrutiny to visit the island of Planasia, to which the emperor had banished his deranged grandson Postumus. Plutarch maintains Maximus overheard Augustus bemoaning the fact two of his grandsons were dead, the third living in exile, and the succession destined for a stepson. In both versions Maximus betrays Augustus' secrets to Marcia; she reveals what she has learned to Livia; Augustus confronts Maximus; Maximus atones for his indiscretion by killing himself. The two authors agree Marcia blamed herself for having precipitated her husband's blunder. In Plutarch's account she precedes Maximus in suicide. In Tacitus' rendering she survives her spouse, and berates herself at his funeral for having been the cause of his death.

We find no evidence of a breach between Livia and Marcia or her kindred as the result of this indiscretion—if in fact that entire incident even occurred at all.[21] Silvanus divorced Numantina; but her subsequent marriage to Augustus' grandnephew Sextus Appuleius reveals she retained the imperial family's favor. Since Silvanus eventually proved to be a rake, his repudiation of Numantina was either an act of recklessness or an indication of Livia's growing disfavor toward him.

APPULEIA VARILLA

Augustus' mother Atia was his father's second wife. Gaius Octavius Thurinus' first marriage to a woman named Ancharia produced a daughter. This Octavia married a man named Sextus Appuleius. Because their first son—another Sextus—was consul for 29 BCE, he could not have been born after 62 BCE. A second son, Marcus, held the consulship of 20 BCE: therefore he was born no later than 53 BCE. (Remember, the minimum age for tenure of the consulship was thirty-three.) Atia bore her Octavia in 66 BCE and Augustus three years later.

The ages of these nephews reveal Augustus' half-sister was considerably older than he. Like many second wives among the Romans (Livia included), Atia must have been much younger than Octavius.

The career and marital connections of Sextus the older nephew indicate he enjoyed an amicable relationship with Augustus. Sextus was colleague to Octavian in the consulship of 29 BCE. For the following year Sextus served as proconsul (senatorial governor) of Spain. Twenty years later Augustus appointed Sextus imperial legate of Illyricum.

Sextus Appuleius fathered two children. One was a namesake son. He served as consul in 14 CE and became the second husband of Fabia Numantina. Sextus' other child was a daughter, Appuleia Varilla. Her surname suggests her mother was related to Publius Quinctilius Varus, best known for losing three legions to a German ambush in 9 CE.

Appuleia's derisive remarks about Livia, Tiberius, and the deceased Augustus landed her before the Senate's tribunal in 17 CE. Tiberius and Livia refused to have Appuleia prosecuted for whatever she had said about them. Although Tiberius secured an acquittal from treason charges stemming from her derogations of Augustus, the Senate found Appuleia guilty of adultery.

Augustus' law prescribed banishment for adultery; and that emperor had not hesitated to apply this punishment to his own daughter and granddaughter. For Appuleia, however, Tiberius invoked an ancient tradition that guaranteed a lesser penalty. He remanded her to the custody of her immediate kindred. They removed her to a residence, probably a family estate, 200 miles distant from Rome.

The nature of Appuleia's invectives and her motives for making them remain unknown. The clemency of Tiberius and Livia and the cooperation of Appuleia's relatives, reveal neither side wanted her conduct to become a public display of friction between them. If the Appuleii shared their kinswoman's disaffection toward Livia and the rest of the imperial family, they kept this attitude strictly to themselves.

LIVIA'S FRIENDS

For a Roman politician the Latin word *amicitia*—friendship—carried two meanings. One signified an affiliation based on mutual affection—the concept of friendship the word ordinarily evokes. The other implied the cultivation of people for their loyalty and importance to the politician's party or regime. You would call a political supporter your friend even if you considered the individual personally insufferable.

In earlier chapters we noted Livia had a variety of *protégés*—men and women, Romans and foreigners. But just how intimate were her affiliations with these friends?

Source material about Livia's interactions with male retainers in the prime years of her life is sparse. Publius Quinctilius Varus and Publius Sulpicius Quirinius Cyrenius married her kinswomen. The Plautii Silvani were born into *obsequium* with her, since their family had been clients of the Claudii for centuries. Quintus Ostorius Scapula bequeathed Livia his slaves. Gaius Fufius Geminus and Servius Sulpicius Galba owed their tenures of the consulship to her influence. Livia left Galba a phenomenally generous bequest, if we can believe Suetonius. Her influence protected Fufius from prosecution for derisive remarks about Tiberius. Such information indicates these men were retainers of Livia. It does not reveal her private feelings toward them.

Livia had the orphaned Marcus Salvius Otho raised and educated in her home. After he became an adult she procured his admission to the Senate and marriage to a well-connected wife. The most we can infer from Livia's pursuit of this project is that she respected Otho's potential as a politician and supporter of the principate. The same holds true for the Gallic chieftain for whom Livia sought Roman citizenship.

Quirinius Cyrenius softened Gaius Caesar's attitude toward

Tiberius. This achievement undoubtedly heightened Livia's esteem for Cyrenius; but it does not necessarily imply she liked him personally. Livia valued, or at least heeded, the comments of one Julius Postumus. Tacitus maintains Postumus, at the urging of Livilla, exacerbated the hostility between Livia and Agrippina.

The historic record of Livia's interaction with her female clients is far richer. Nevertheless only one of these women—the Judaean princess Salome—appears with any certainty to have been Livia's comrade as well as her client.

SALOME

Salome was the sister of Herod the Great, who ruled the client kingdom of Judaea from 37 to 4 BCE. When and how she and Livia became acquainted is not known. Livia behaved in the manner of a true patron. She exploited Salome's loyalty to promote Roman hegemony in Judaea, but safeguarded Salome's interests as well.

Around 8 BCE a widowed Salome found herself with two suitors. Her preference was for the Nabataean Arab Syllaeus. He was vizier to Obadas, king of the Nabataeans, whose homeland embraced what is now southern Jordan. Salome loved Syllaeus, and felt their prospective union made sound political sense. Herod, however, wanted her to marry his Judaean retainer Alexas. Salome requested Livia's opinion.

Salome's situation was a familiar one for Livia, whose controversial love match with Augustus became a sound political union. The empress nevertheless told Salome to put aside her feelings for Syllaeus and accept Alexas. The princess complied.

Given the significance of affection in Livia's own marriage, her response to Salome may strike the reader as callously or even cruelly indifferent. It seems to imply that while Livia herself might marry for love, her client must put aside the same inclination for the sake of political expedience. To a certain extent this was true, because Livia was placing Roman interests ahead of Salome's personal desires. But by doing so Livia protected Salome, both politically and emotionally.

Livia would have known the Romans had Syllaeus under

investigation. The Arab proved perfidious toward Roman interests and personally exploitative of Salome. He had undermined Augustus' efforts to finalize a client alliance with the indolent Obadas. Now Syllaeus was wooing Salome for the sole purpose of getting himself close to Herod. Syllaeus planned to utilize that proximity to subvert the alliance between Judaea and Rome. Livia's intervention prevented Salome from making a serious personal as well as political mistake.

The domestic problems of the Caesars paled before those of the Herodians. The Judaean king suffered from a chronic illness—a form of arteriosclerosis, many scholars believe. His condition rendered him often irascible, suspicious, and paranoid. Herod lived in perpetual fear of being overthrown. Furthermore his Jewish countrymen, restive and fiercely nationalistic, resented Herod's submission to Roman suzerainty. The king responded by governing his people with a ruthlessness which made the Romans, who were not above bloodletting of their own, recoil in horror.[22]

To make matters worse for Herod his ten wives, his sons and other relatives, adhered to varying and often opposing political and religious factions. These differences prompted the members of Herod's family, including Salome, to inveigh and conspire against one other—frequently with fatal results. Augustus retained Herod in power because the king was an effective ruler, a loyal client, and the author of a progressive economic policy for Judaea. The emperor nevertheless became increasingly annoyed at the complaints about brutality, and at the Herodians' family squabbles of which he was asked to arbitrate several. "It were better to be Herod's pig than his son," Augustus mused.[23] The emperor's remark refers to the Jewish anathema regarding swine.

One intrigue involved Salome's relationship with Livia. The empress owned a Jewish slave: a woman named Hacme, who may have been a gift from Salome. In 5 BCE Herod's unscrupulous eldest son Antipater bribed Hacme to compose a diatribe against the king in Salome's style of writing. Hacme then sent the critique to Herod with the assertion she had found it among Livia's personal papers. Antipater may have hoped to claim Salome's lucrative patrimony as his reward for revealing her alleged treachery.

Carelessness on Hacme's part led Herod's secret police to uncover the plot. Augustus had Hacme executed. Further investigation revealed Antipater was plotting to seize the Judaean throne after poisoning his father. Herod put Antipater to death in the spring of 4 BCE. Five days later the grieving and ailing Herod died at Jericho.

Geographically the client kingdom of Judaea corresponded more or less with the modern nations of Israel and northern Jordan. The realm was a patchwork of often contentious duchies and city states, which Herod kept united under his iron rule. In his will, Herod divided his dominions among three of his four surviving sons. Antipas inherited Galilee and Perea. Philip received Batanea, Gaulanitis, and Trachonitis (the Golan Heights). Archelaus the eldest acquired the lion's share. His domain extended from Samaria (the West Bank) south to the Herodians' homeland of Idumaea (the region just north of the Negev desert). Between these regions lay the district of Judaea, after which Herod had named his entire realm. The fourth son Herod-Philip was disinherited, because his mother had conspired with Antipater.[24]

Archelaus' administration turned out to be more oppressive and arbitrary than his father's. The new ruler's misgovernment was apparently due to fear and a sense of inadequacy rather than to malice. Nevertheless it was more than his people could endure. Archelaus' subjects dropped ideological feuds with one another and mutual distaste for the Romans, to unite in seeking the intervention of Augustus.

Correspondence between Salome and Livia may well have helped Augustus keep abreast of developments in Judaea. Salome and her husband Alexas gave formal testimony against Archelaus. In 6 CE Augustus deposed the young ruler and converted his realm into the imperial province of Judaea.

The friendship of Livia and Salome persisted, unaffected by the Herodians' political and dynastic problems. The princess died in 10 CE. Her patrimony included Jamnia on the fertile coastal plain south of Joppa (Tel Aviv), a region which to this day produces superlative oranges. The other portions were the regions of Phasaelis, and of Archelais rich in date palms, both lying in the Jordan River valley. Salome could have left this bounty with its substantial income of 60 talents per year to her children or her royal nephews. Instead she bequeathed it to Livia.

Evidence of genuine affection between Livia and Salome comes from a single statement by Flavius Josephus. This great first-century chronicler of the Jews in Roman antiquity writes that when Salome accepted marriage with Alexas:

> She deferred, not only because Julia (i.e., Livia) was
> Caesar's wife, but because she contributed good advice
> in all matters anyway. [25]

These words imply Salome respected Livia as a mentor, in affairs of state and in private situations as well.

DYNAMIS AND PYTHODORIS

The only extant records, directly associating Livia with these two Asiatic client queens, are strictly official. Dynamis was ruler of the Cimmerian Bosporus, Pythodoris of Pontus.

A Pontic city called Liviopolis was located in on the Black Sea coast, near the modern town of Trabzon in northeastern Turkey. The elder Pliny describes Liviopolis as a *castellum*—hence a fortified hill-town like Faesulae (Fiesole) and Perusia (Perugia) in Italy.

An issue of Pontic coins represents Livia as Dynamis' patron goddess Aphrodite. Recall that Dynamis was the first wife of Polemon, King of Pontus. Pythodoris was his second.

From Dynamis' birthplace of Phanagoria, near modern Taman on the eastern side of the Cimmerian Bosporus (Kerch Strait), we have the dedicatory inscription from the base of a statue:

> To Livia the wife of Augustus: from Queen Dynamis the
> Roman-loving to her benefactress. [26]

And from nearby Hermonassa we see on another statue base:

> Pythodoris to Livia her benefactress. [27]

The statue on which Pythodoris' dedication appears could hardly have been the spoil of a war with Pontus. Had the statue originally been erected in Pontus, its inscription would describe Pythodoris as queen, as wife of King Polemon, or as both. Either Pythodoris presented the statue to the Cimmerians as a gift and omitted her titles in a gesture of conciliation, or Dynamis herself requisitioned the piece.

Why would Dynamis allow the installation on her own soil, of a rival's tribute to a common benefactor?

In 8 BCE Augustus confirmed Dynamis as queen of the Cimmerian Bosporus, and Pythodoris as sovereign of the kingdom of Pontus. He required each queen relinquish her claims to the other's jurisdiction and remain steadfastly loyal to Rome. In an earlier chapter we proposed this arbitration was Livia's suggestion.

None of this recondite evidence confirms personal camaraderie between Livia and the two queens. For all we know Livia never actually met either.

Urgulania

Livia's association with Urgulania was an inherited one. The latter's husband was a Plautius Silvanus; his *praenomen* was either Marcus or Aulus. The Plautii Silvani were plebeians of senatorial rank, whose family had originated at the city-state of Tibur. They had been political allies of the Claudii since the third century of the pre-Christian era.

The lawsuit, which Lucius Calpurnius Piso brought against Urgulania in 16 CE, reveals how Livia's exalted public stature could turn an *obsequium* into an awkward political liability. Lucius Piso—brother of Germanicus' enemy Gnaeus Piso—sued Urgulania for recovery of a debt. Tacitus describes the incident:

> Urgulania did not comply, but proceeded to Caesar's house in defiance of Piso; and he did not withdraw, although Augusta complained she was injured and diminished. Tiberius, reckoning it politic to indulge his mother up to this point—that he would betake himself to the praetor's tribunal, and speak Urgulania's defense— left the Palatine, ordering the soldiers to follow at a distance. He was observed, by the thronging people, to

be calm of countenance and with various conversations prolonging the time and the journey until, relatives having pressured Piso without effect, Augusta ordered that the money he sought be handed over. This was the end of the matter, from which Piso was not dishonored, and Caesar was increased in fame.[28]

Urgulania's response to Piso's suit invoked the principles of Roman patronage. Instead of answering the charges in person, Urgulania sought the intervention of her patrons—the Claudii Tiberius and Livia. She approached her benefactors at their home. This was the time-honored procedure by which a client solicited a patron's assistance.

The case stood to have serious political ramifications. Whether Piso won or lost his case, he ran the risk of losing the loyalty and support of other Romans. Many were beholden to Livia as recipients of her benefactions and charities. Others may simply have been reluctant to oppose the imperial family for any reason.

Destruction of a citizen's reputation, especially for the benefit of a personal retainer, would be an abuse of imperial *auctoritas*. Realizing they were in a position to ruin Piso, Tiberius and Livia approached the situation gingerly. Livia offered no more than a verbal remonstrance over Piso's actions. Tiberius responded more concretely: he set out for the praetor's court, there to lend Urgulania his support. Perhaps to emphasize he was appearing as a private citizen—the patron looking after his client—Tiberius kept his bodyguard out of sight. While *en route* the emperor stalled, hoping Piso would respond to the urgings of his family and drop the suit.

In the end Livia capitulated to Piso's demand, and in so doing settled matters to the benefit of all concerned. By paying Piso the sum he sought, Livia fulfilled her obligation as a patron and resolved Urgulania's predicament. At the same time Livia spared Piso the defamation his own actions portended for him. Livia's solution, which kept Urgulania and Piso alike from suffering damage, won the approbation of the Roman people.

Tacitus describes Urgulania as someone "whom above the laws Augusta's friendship had set."[29] This could not have been true in a purely juridical sense, since even the emperor was obliged to obey the statutes and precedents of Roman law. Furthermore were Urgulania beyond the reaches of the legal system, Piso would have been unable to pursue his suit against her. The praetor would have been obliged to throw the case out of court.

Association with Livia may have enlarged Urgulania's *auctoritas*, to the point people who lacked Piso's gumption felt powerless to challenge her. Alternatively, Livia might have procured some sort of special privilege exempting Urgulania from certain legal obligations. Tacitus continues:

> Otherwise Urgulania's power was so extraordinary to the state, that as witness in a certain case, which was being handled in the Senate, she disdained to come: a praetor was sent, who interrogated her in the home; although Vestal Virgins, in the Forum and court were heard, whenever they uttered testimony, the ancient custom was.[30]

None of this indicates whether Livia and Urgulania were intimate friends. The perks and privileges Urgulania and her family came to enjoy could simply have arisen from their long-standing *obsequium* with patrons who had attained unprecedented influence and power. Livia did not consider Urgulania and the Plautii Silvani the most important of her associates. Urgulania's namesake granddaughter was only Livia's third choice as a bride for the empress' grandson Claudius.

MUNATIA PLANCINA

Munatia Plancina was neither a confidante nor valued political ally of Livia. Tacitus exaggerates the pair's intimacy.

We must look carefully, at Tacitus' choice of vocabulary. "Hatred of Plancina," he writes, "was the same [as that toward Gnaeus Piso her husband], but *gratia* was greater." [31] The Latin word *gratia* implies agreeableness, a reward, something for which to be thankful, or indulgence toward an offense. When the Senate brought Plancina to trial in 20 CE for her connection with Piso's subversive activities, Livia requested commutation of the sentence. This is the *gratia* to which Tacitus refers.

Gratia can also indicate the mutual benefits of an *obsequium*: the intervention of a patron on a client's behalf or the client's reciprocal service to the patron. Tacitus wants his readers to believe Livia encouraged Plancina to harass and possibly kill Germanicus. The empress then procured the pardon to reward Plancina while obfuscating their mutual guilt.

We examined in a previous chapter the fallacies of Tacitus' detraction. Plancina had not acted as Livia's agent. The pardon encouraged Plancina to cooperate with the Senate's investigation of her husband's conduct. Moreover it defied critics of the Senate's verdict, aquitting Piso of having murdered Germanicus.

Tacitus describes Livia's relationship with Urgulania as *amicitia*. This term implies a closer bond than *gratia*. Livia esteemed Urgulania as a retainer. The empress secured Plancina's pardon to further the interests of the principate.

Mutilia Prisca

Mutilia Prisca was the wife of Gaius Fufius Geminus. We first encounter her late in Livia's life, after the death of Tiberius' son Drusus. Tacitus describes Mutilia as "Prisca, upon the mind of Augusta influential." [32] He adds that Prisca repaid Julius Postumus for sexual favors by ingratiating him to Livia.

It is hard if not impossible to believe Livia, a pacesetter for chastity, would have condoned an openly adulterous relationship between two members of her personal circle. The couple conceivably kept their affair a secret until after Livia's death—if indeed they had such a liaison in the first place. Postumus and Prisca may simply have been acquaintances—perhaps patron and client—whose relationship gossip embellished. Prisca proved her wifely devotion to Geminus in death. When the Senate indicted Geminus in 29 CE for his derogatory jests about Tiberius,

Prisca joined her husband in suicide. According to Dio Cassius she killed herself before the assembled Senate.

Flavius Josephus is straightforward in his description of Livia's interaction with Salome. He avers Salome followed Livia's counsel in all matters. Tacitus' comment about Prisca's influence upon Livia actually obscures the precise nature the two women's relationship. Did Livia value Prisca as a confidante, with whom innermost private feelings could be exchanged? Or did the empress accept Prisca's advice on purely external issues, such as the potential merits of a new client? We cannot tell.

MUCIA

After reporting the suicide of Mutilia Prisca Dio Cassius, writes:

> Hereafter [Tiberius] destroyed not only Mucia, but also her husband and both daughters simultaneously, because of her friendship for his mother.[33]

We have no idea who Mucia was. The name may be a corruption of Mutilia. Dio's little comment is instructive nonetheless. Livia's influence remained so strong, even after she had died, that Sejanus felt threatened by it. He endeavored to weaken Livia's posthumous hegemony by persecuting her retainers.

NOTES TO CHAPTER VII

1   *Saturnalia* 2.5.2.

2   *Saturnalia* 2.5.5.

3   *Saturnalia* 2.5.8.

4   Suetonius, *Tiberius* 57.

5   Cf. Suetonius, *Tiberius* 43-45. While in residence on Capri, Tiberius surrounded himself with a coterie of academicians, jurists and other intellectuals. Erotic art, intended for the eyes of men, was as much a cultural norm in Roman times as today. Wall paintings in the men's sections of public baths at Pompeii depict *spintriae* (sexual trios) and acts of *fellatio*, both of which Suetonius associates with Tiberius. Children at play in Tiberius' bath were the *delicia* common to most affluent households. Suetonius' assertions that Tiberius raped two boys and subsequently had their legs broken for objecting, and remanded a matron for investigation as a potential traitor because she refused his advances, are either outright apocrypha or distortions of legitimate actions. The naturally reclusive Tiberius eschewed disclosure of innocuous private activities. Much less, then, would he have risked revelation of sexual malfeasance, by afflicting his alleged victims with permanent injury or subjecting them to interrogation that might incriminate him. Suetonius does not allege Tiberius engaged in lascivious conduct during his sojourn on Rhodes. The hostile Tacitus does not mention the aforementioned or any other sexual crimes, and ascribes Tiberius' reputation for lasciviousness to rumor.

6   *Divus Claudius* 1.

7   *Annales* 1.33.

8   *Divus Claudius* 1. *Spoila opima* (superlative trophies) were spoils taken from an enemy chieftain whom a Roman general had killed in hand-to-hand combat.

9   *Saturnalia* 2.5.9.

10   *Historia natura* 7.149.

11   *Saturnalia* 2.5.6.

12   *Consolatio ad Marciam* 2.4.

13. Antonia's son, the emperor Claudius, may have erected the structure, calling it after his mother and the daughter he named for her.

14. See Appendix III regarding challenges to the assumption that Antonia apprized Tiberius of Sejanus' malfeasance.

15. *Gaius Caligula* 3.

16. *Romaïka* 60.2.

17. Suetonius, *Divus Claudius* 2.

18. *Divus Claudius* 3.

19. *Divus Claudius* 4.

20. *Ibid.*

21. *Romaïka* 55.10.

22. See Appendix III with regard to embellishment of rumors surrounding Paullus Fabius Maximus' death.

23. The Massacre of the Innocents described by the evangelist Matthew (2.16), typifies Herod's tactics.

24. *Saturnalia* 2.4.11. Augustus alludes to the traditional Jewish disdain for the pig as an unclean animal.

25. The daughter of Herod-Philip was the Salome who danced for the head of John the Baptist.

26. *Ioudaïke archaiologia* 17.10. Josephus' confusion about Livia's name arises, of course, from the fact that she was known as Julia Augusta after her husband's death.

27. *IGRR* 1.902.

28. *SEG* 39.695.

29. *Annales* 2.34

30. *Ibid.*

31. *Ibid.*

32. *Annales* 3.15.

33. *Annales* 4.12

34. *Romaïkon* 58.4.

29. *Ibid.*

30. *Ibid.*

31. *Annales* 3.15.

32. *Annales* 4.12

33. *Romaïkon* 58.4.

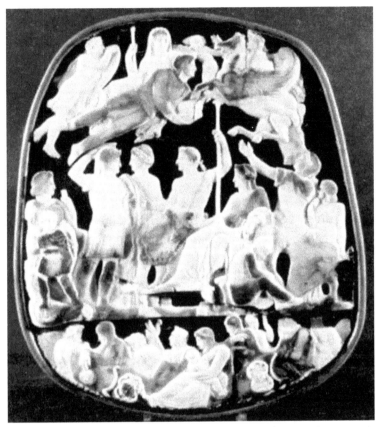

The Grand Camée de France, representing the apotheosis of Germanicus
Tiberius and Livia (seated) are facing from right to left:
Antonia the Younger
Germanicus or his eldest son Nero
Agrippina the Elder with Nero or another son (Drusus or Caligula)
Behind Livia: Tiberius' son Drusus and his wife Livilla
In the heavens:
The deified Augustus
His legendary ancestor Iullus Ascanius (prone)
Drusus the father of Germanicus
The ascendant Germanicus (on winged horse)
Bibliothéque Nationale, Paris
Photo credit: Erich Lessing/Art Resource, New York

CHAPTER VIII

THE TWILIGHT YEARS

The final fifteen years of Livia's life mark the period of her greatest political ascendancy. The same period, however, could not have afforded her much personal joy. Augustus' death on August 19 of 14 CE had deprived her of his love, and of his overwhelming influence upon her life. Two of her three grandsons predeceased her—Germanicus in 19 CE and Tiberius' son Drusus four years later. Her health deteriorated. She fell seriously ill in 22 CE, and then again fatally six years later. Sharply differing political and personal attitudes combined with the subtle intrusion of the praetorian prefect Sejanus, to fracture the imperial family with variance and estrangement.

The Rise of Sejanus

Lucius Aelius Sejanus (Latin spelling Seianus) was of Etruscan extraction. He was born at Vulsinii (modern Bolsena) in southern Etruria (Tuscany), the homeland of the Etruscans. Sejanus' father Lucius Seius Strabo was a member of the Roman equestrian order. Strabo had strong political connections. His mother was sister to Terentia the wife of Maecenas. Strabo's wife—the mother of Sejanus—was related to the senatorial Cornelii Lentuli. The couple had two sons. Adoption by Marcus Aelius Gallus, a wealthy fellow equestrian and former prefect of Egypt, gave Strabo's more famous son the name by which he is known to history. The other son went by the name of Lucius Seius Tubero.

Like many equestrians, Seius Strabo and his sons pursued careers in the imperial services—divisions of the government which reported to the emperor rather than the senatorial magistrates. All three men came to occupy prominent, primarily military, positions.

At the time of Augustus' death, Strabo was prefect of the praetorian guards. These crack units, stationed throughout Italy, constituted the imperial bodyguard. Their principal function was to protect the emperor and his family when they engaged in government business outside of Rome. In 16 or 17 CE Tiberius appointed Strabo to the prefecture of Egypt, a position Srabo occupied until his death five years later. His son Tubero was Germanicus' adjutant during that prince's 16 CE campaign against the Germans.

Sejanus had served on the staff of Gaius Caesar. Tiberius at the beginning of his reign appointed Sejanus co-prefect of the praetorians with Strabo as colleague. Strabo's subsequent transfer to Egypt left Sejanus sole commandant of the imperial guards.

Sejanus proved himself an intrepid commander and a resourceful, conscientious administrator. He was also extremely engaging, capable of charming women and men alike. The prefect exploited his ingratiating demeanor to win the admiration and confidence of people from all walks of life. He endeared himself to soldiers, to ordinary citizens, to senators—and to the imperial family. Tiberius came to esteem and trust Sejanus as a minister, adviser, and special friend—especially after Sejanus with his own body shielded Tiberius from falling debris, when the ceiling of a grotto in which they were dining collapsed.[1] To Sejanus the normally reticent emperor would confide secrets he kept from everyone else.

Beneath their altruistic façade, Sejanus' motives were sinister and destructive. His intent was to control the reigning emperor or become emperor himself; and his method was subtle. He began by strengthening his military power, persuading Tiberius to concentrate the scattered divisions of the praetorian guard into a single barracks at the outskirts of Rome. This consolidation facilitated Sejanus' ability to issue orders, improved the guards' morale, and sent a warning to the populace. With larger numbers on hand the guards were more likely to prevail in a public skirmish. Sejanus socialized with the enlisted men, calling each by name; and he appointed each officer personally.

Turning his attention to the Senate, Sejanus secured privileges and positions of power for his adherents. These appointments were encouraged by Tiberius, who extolled Sejanus to the Senate and general public as his fellow laborer. At the emperor's behest, statues of the praetorian prefect were erected throughout Italy in theaters, municipal forums, and the headquarters of military barracks.

Sejanus' next and greatest obstacle was the imperial family. A plethora of princes must be destroyed, before the prefect could hope to be considered for the succession. After Germanicus died, Tiberius' son Drusus became the anticipated heir to the principate. Next in line were Tiberius' five grandsons—three by Germanicus and two by Drusus. Tacitus avers that Sejanus felt a violent *coup d'état*, directed against all the princes at once, was certain to fail. To avoid arousing the suspicions of the Caesars and of others, Sejanus decided to eliminate his victims secretively and at different times.

He began with Drusus. Tiberius' son was one of the apparently few people who did not like Sejanus. The prefect's growing ascendancy over Tiberius rankled Drusus. By 23 CE the intensity of the prince's resentment drove him to escalate a casual dispute with Sejanus into a fistfight. Although the incident solidified Sejanus' decision to destroy Drusus, revenge was probably not the prefect's primary motive. The removal of Tiberius' only adult male descendant should impel the emperor to select a regent. What better candidate than the presumably loyal and trustworthy Sejanus? Drusus had to be silenced, moreover, before he could change his father's attitude toward the obsequious schemer.

LIVILLA AND THE MURDER OF DRUSUS

Sejanus launched his offensive against the Caesars by slyly and surreptitiously undermining Drusus' marriage. After seducing Drusus' wife Livilla, Sejanus promised to secure from Tiberius permission to marry her once Drusus had been eliminated. The adulterous couple conspired with Livilla's personal physician Eudemus and Sejanus' favorite Lygdus to poison Drusus. The toxin Eudemus provided simulated the action of a natural illness. This ruse worked so well that eight years passed before the imperial family came to understand Drusus had been murdered.

To convince Livilla of his sincerity, Sejanus divorced his wife Apicata the mother of his two children. Likely she was a co-conspirator, because she knew Sejanus had corrupted Livilla and poisoned Drusus. This information Apicata withheld until after Sejanus' treachery was exposed in 31 CE, and just before she took her own life.

Tiberius' sanction of a match between Sejanus and Livilla was not readily forthcoming. The death of Drusus had left Nero, the eldest son of Germanicus and Agrippina, next in line for the succession. Because Tiberius had adopted Germanicus, Nero was legally the emperor's oldest grandson. Although Nero was only seventeen and Tiberius nearly sixty-five, the *princeps* made clear he did not want a regent. Tiberius commended the tutelage of Nero and his fifteen-year-old brother Drusus to the Senate, should his demise impel one of them to the principate before he was ready to handle its demands.

In 25 CE Sejanus yielded to Livilla's pressure and asked Tiberius for her hand. The emperor refused on grounds the marriage would anger Agrippina and heighten rivalries within an already contentious household. Summarizing Tiberius' letter of response to Sejanus, Tacitus writes:

> He (Tiberius) would act more frankly, first regarding the enmity of Agrippina, which for a long time would blaze more bitterly, if Livi[ll]a's marriage as it were should tear apart the Caesar household into divisions. Whenever the rivalry of women breaks forth, the strife disconcerts his grandsons; how much would the contention be exacerbated by such a union?[2]

More than personal jealousy was involved. Livilla and Agrippina represented the opposing political factions that had rallied respectively about Drusus and Germanicus. Drusus had been the focus of Tiberius' hardline supporters, Germanicus of dissenters. A new spouse for either princess would strengthen her particular party by giving it a new champion. If Livilla remarried, Agrippina would maintain her interests were being threatened. If Agrippina took a second husband, she would provide the dissident cause with a new leader.

Continuing his letter, Tiberius raises concern that too quick an elevation of Sejanus' stature will inflame opponents toward the prefect and emperor alike. In conclusion, however, Tiberius offers a note of reassurance. He will not only sanction a marital alliance but also promote Sejanus as far as possible, once an opportunity to do so presents itself.

Sejanus decided to make that opportunity present itself. He must break the deadlock preventing him from marrying Livilla and subduing potential opponents to his advancement. For a time an unwitting Livia became an instrument in this plan.

THE ASSAULT ON AGRIPPINA

Vipsania Agrippina was the second daughter of Agrippa and Augustus' daughter Julia. We do not know the precise date of Agrippina's birth, only that it fell between those of her brothers Lucius (17 BCE) and Postumus (11 BCE). Agrippina married Livia's grandson Germanicus, in 5 CE.

Agrippina grew into a paragon of wifely virtue—chaste, devoted, supportive, resourceful, and fecund. She bore Germanicus nine children. Six survived to adulthood: three sons and as many daughters. One might think these maternal characteristics, which Livia so staunchly endorsed, would have endeared her to the woman who was at once her husband's granddaughter and her grandson's wife. Instead Livia and Agrippina were bitter enemies.

Agrippina was the natural heiress of the dissident party, which had originated among the defenders of her mother Julia. The ideology of this group maintained Tiberius and Livia had engineered the deaths of Julia's sons, the banishment of her elder daughter, and the demise of her son-in-law Germanicus. Now Agrippina and her children were living in imminent danger of suffering similar fates.

Tacitus accuses Livia of harassing Agrippina before as well as after Germanicus died. The historian nevertheless concedes—as does

Suetonius—that Agrippina's tactless condescension and explosive emotionalism provoked frictions within the imperial family. Tacitus also asserts Agrippina did not know how to dissemble. This implies she lacked Germanicus' ability to separate political differences from personal interaction with relatives. When Livia asked the Senate to pardon Agrippina's enemy Plancina, the empress must have anticipated the angry, accusatory response Agrippina's party delivered:

> Now the poisons and artifices, so successfully proven,
> might be turned against Agrippina, against her children,
> that an extraordinary grandmother and uncle with the
> blood of a most miserable family might be satiated.[3]

Livia had nevertheless persevered with her quest for Plancina's reprieve.

Between 24 and 28 CE, Sejanus and his agents contrived to have the Senate prosecute known and suspected supporters of Agrippina and the dissent party. Charges included extortion, misconduct in office, adultery, defamation of Tiberius, and plots against his life. Despite Tacitus' innuendo to the contrary, the arraignments were justifiable. Agrippina's partisans appear to have been intent upon defying Tiberius, and then decrying the consequences as evidence of tyranny. In consequence of the sweep, five men and two women were convicted and sentenced. One of them was Claudia Pulchra, the widow (or daughter-in-law) of Publius Quinctilius Varus and kinswoman to Livia and Agrippina alike. Other partisans of Agrippina were accused, but acquitted or not tried at all.

What if Livia had demanded a Plancina-like pardon for one or more of Agrippina's indicted supporters? Livia would have mollified the dissidents and discredited or at least diminished her evil stepmother reputation among them. Had she intervened in this manner, however, Livia would have lent her support to the very faction which had defied Augustus and now resisted Tiberius. Why should Livia challenge Sejanus' attacks on Agrippina's adherents, so long as his efforts vitiated the strength of the dissent party?

This line of reasoning lends credibility to Tacitus' insinuation, that Sejanus exacerbated hostility between Livia and Agrippina by suggesting the latter aspired to increase her political strength. We repeat a passage earlier quoted:

> [Sejanus] inveighed against [Agrippina's] haughtiness, exciting Augusta's old hatred for her and Livi[ll]a's recent sense of guilt, so they would persuade [Tiberius] Caesar that, proud of fecundity and confident of popular support, [Agrippina] aspired to reign.[4]

The trials of her adherents, especially Claudia Pulchra, enraged Agrippina. More outspokenly than ever she charged Tiberius with aspiring to eliminate her along with her children.

Sejanus worked to heighten Tiberius' misgivings about his daughter-in-law's intentions. Agents of the prefect, posing as Agrippina's supporters, convinced her Tiberius was planning to carry her off by poison. When Tiberius subsequently invited Agrippina to dinner, she refused to eat anything. Noticing her abstinence, the emperor offered her an apple from a bowl of fruit. Agrippina proceeded to distribute the bowl's entire contents among the attendant slaves. Turning to Livia, Tiberius remarked it should not seem surprising if he dealt harshly with someone who insinuated he was a poisoner.

With her implication the offer of fruit was an attempt on her life, Agrippina had committed the treasonable act of disparaging the emperor. At the very beginning of his reign Tiberius had refused to prosecute denigrations of his person. As the dissidents became increasingly outspoken in subsequent years, the emperor began to enforce the law prohibiting vitriolic utterances about the imperial family. He took no action against Agrippina, however, other than to make sure she never again shared his table.

Sejanus began to gather evidence against Nero. The young prince had married Livilla's daughter Julia. Nero had a tendency to talk in his sleep. Julia reported his babblings to her mother, who conveyed them in turn to her paramour.

By the middle of 28 CE Sejanus had managed to convince Tiberius that Agrippina was plotting to overthrow the emperor and enthrone Nero. Tiberius who by now had withdrawn to Capri, prepared written complaints about the mother and son. The emperor forwarded the letters to Sejanus for presentation to the Senate.

Tacitus declares the letters accused Nero of homosexuality, an orientation Augustus' adultery law defined as criminal. Agrippina was charged with "insolence of mouth and impudence of spirit," [5] to quote Tacitus. This terminology for certain described Agrippina's insinuations about Tiberius, so patently displayed in the fruit bowl incident. The vocabulary also supported Sejanus' allegation of Agrippina's intentions to instigate rebellion. Tacitus claims the prefect's agents credited Agrippina with two plans of action. One was to provoke a citizen uprising at the statue of Augustus in the Roman Forum. The other was to induce the armies of the Rhine frontier—once the command of Germanicus—to revolt. Suetonius avers these were the very offenses for which Agrippina was eventually prosecuted.

Sejanus took possession of the letters but held off revealing them to the Senate until Livia was dead. The dowager's influence over the Senate was virtually unassailable, as the immunity of Gaius Fufius Geminus attests. Because Fufius enjoyed Livia's patronage, his jests at Tiberius' expense went unpunished until after her death. There is no evidence to suggest Sejanus poisoned Livia. Reaching her would doubtless have been difficult, since Antonia was her inseparable companion and caregiver. The prefect knew that time was on his side. Livia was extremely old; she could not last much longer.

Livia became ill late in 28 CE. Her condition deteriorated steadily into death, vindicating Sejanus' decision to wait.[6] Tacitus places the indictment of Fufius before the presentation of the letters. Perhaps Sejanus used the attack on Fufius as a test, to ascertain whether Livia's control of the Senate had dissolved at her passing.

Why did Sejanus assume Livia would challenge the letters? Even if she did not believe all of the prefect's insinuations against Agrippina and Nero, Livia could not have denied Agrippina was guilty of slandering the emperor. Livia conceivably felt the legal prosecution of Agrippina and Nero was a step too far. Nero was Tiberius' chosen successor. No one in this position had ever been tried, much less sentenced for a crime. The concept of the principate was still relatively new to Roman political science. What dangerous precedent, what avenue to revolution would arise, from the successful incrimination and conviction of a designated heir to the throne?

An attack on Agrippina stood to validate her assertion Tiberius desired her destruction. The execution or banishment of Augustus' last living grandchild might sully Livia's reputation as well. The dissidents could claim Augustus' only daughter, along with all five of her children, had met with disgrace and/or early death. Is not this the wholesale work of an evil stepmother? Dissident propaganda maintained Livia had sanctioned the death of Germanicus. Would the destruction of Nero not prove this monstrous grandmother now endorsed the ruin of Germanicus' son?

And finally, Livia may have surmised Sejanus was responsible for the frictions that dogged the imperial family. As his reliance on Sejanus had increased, so had Tiberius' hostility toward the influence Livia wielded.

Sejanus and Livia's Estrangement from Tiberius

At the beginning of his reign—in 15 CE to be precise—Tiberius expressed exasperation at some anonymous verses lampooning dissensions between Livia and himself. Tacitus, who reports the incident, does not indicate whether these disputes had any foundation in fact.

Tacitus subsequently reveals in a comment punctuated with sarcasm, that Tiberius' interaction with Livia was cordial as late as 22 CE:

> Around this same time, the terrible health condition
> of Julia Augusta caused a necessity for the *princeps*
> to hasten his return to the City because, so far, of a
> sincere concord between mother and son or else a well-
> concealed hatred.[7]

Tiberius was sojourning in Campania when he received word of Livia's illness.

Over the next three years, according to Tacitus, the relationship between Livia and Tiberius became severely strained. Tiberius once again quit Rome in 26 CE He returned to Campania for some months before retiring permanently to Capri. Tacitus writes:

It is also reported he was driven out by the imperiousness of his mother whose partnership in domination he despised but could not reject, because he had received this very domination as her gift. For Augustus was wavering in resolution to place Germanicus, his sister's grandson and the esteemed of everyone, in power over Roman affairs, but at his wife's prayers he passed up Germanicus for Tiberius, and adopted Tiberius himself. And this Augusta reiterated and reclaimed.[8]

Suetonius likewise attests to the development of friction between Livia and her son:

Annoyed because his mother Livia claimed equal portions of power with him, he avoided frequent conversations as well as and longer, more confidential, discussions, lest by her counsels—which indeed often he was wont to need and utilize—he appeared to be governed. He also was made very indignant by a motion in the Senate, that to his titles, even as Son of Augustus, so also Son of Livia should be added. Consequently, neither to be called Parent of [her] country, nor to receive publicly any consequential honor would he permit; but he also frequently admonished [her] to abstain from important matters inappropriate for a woman, particularly after he became aware that at a fire near the shrine of Vesta she had intervened with the people and solders, encouraging, that they might perform the task more diligently, as she had been accustomed under her husband.

Henceforth he proceeded to the point of enmity—by reason, people say, of this cause. Having been pressed repeatedly to enroll, in a jury, a man on whom citizenship had been conferred, he refused in any way to allow her the enrollment, unless it was clearly noted in the White List (the official list of jurors), that the matter had been extorted from him by [his] mother. Then she, upset, withdrew some old letters to her from Augustus, concerning his (Tiberius') bitterness and insolence of character, from a private shrine and read them publicly. She had kept these so long, and with them spitefully reproached him so vehemently at this time, that some think of the causes for his retirement this was the primary. In the entire three years that his mother remained alive [after Tiberius withdrew to Capri], he saw her only once, and not for more than a few hours of one day; and thereafter he in no way bothered to visit her for illness; and when she died, although he made a promise of coming, after a delay of very many days—whereupon at length she was interred because of the corruption and deterioration of the body—he forbade her to be deified, maintaining that she herself had so mandated. Her testament, moreover, he held as void; and all her friends and familiars—even those to whom she, while dying, had entrusted the care of her obsequies—he struck down within a short time, one of these, a man of the equestrian order, being condemned to the treadmill.[9]

Dio Cassius' testimony strongly parallels the accounts we just considered. Referring to Tiberius, Dio writes:

Furthermore he exhorted his mother to act decorously in all ways, in whatever there was for her to do, not only for the sake of emulating him, but also that she may not be overly proud. For she was great and exalted above all women of old; so that both the Senate and those of the people who wished to greet her, she could receive in [her] house at any time; and this fact was inscribed in the public records. Not only did the correspondence of Tiberius bear her name for a time, but one also wrote to both at once. Except that she never dared enter the Senate chamber, nor in the military camps, nor the public assemblies, she endeavored to direct everything independently. For she had prevailed greatly upon Augustus, and always said she had made Tiberius emperor; and because of this she wished not just to rule equally with him, but to take precedence over him. Because of this, out of the ordinary measures were suggested: many that Mother of the country, and many that Parent, put forth the proposal she be so called. Others moved that Tiberius should be named after her, so that as the Greeks after their fathers are called, so he should be designated for his mother. Vexed by these issues, he would neither sanction what was voted for her except for the minimum, nor allow her to do anything excessive. Indeed, when she dedicated in her house an image to Augustus, and because of that wished to hold a banquet for the Senate and the Equestrians along with the women, he would not acquiesce to any aspect of this until the Senate had voted thereon, and then not to feed the men; but he himself feasted the men and she the women. In the end, he removed her from public affairs entirely, but allowed her to manage matters of the home; and when even in such she became troublesome, he arranged to be away from home and to avoid her by any means, so that primarily on her account he removed himself to Capri.[10]

Tacitus, Suetonius and Dio Cassius all insist Livia attempted to manage affairs of state as if she were Tiberius' equal if not his superior. This reputation may have arisen from Livia's declaration Tiberius owed his tenure of the principate to her. Despite our authors' insinuations to the contrary, Livia was not trying to claim entitlements and privileges from which she was excluded. Tiberius attempted to obstruct his mother's pursuit of public activities Augustus had sanctioned for her. The appeal of Ovid's wife confirms Livia had been receiving citizens in her home, and responding to their petitions years before Tiberius became emperor. Therefore Livia's plea on behalf of the prospective juror was not an unprecedented behavior for her. Tiberius' notation to the White List seems likely to have been an acknowledgment Livia's *plurimum posse* had prevailed on the juror's behalf. Suetonius states outrightly that Livia encouraged the work of fire brigades "as she had been accustomed under her husband." Extant official correspondence from the early part of Tiberius' reign does not bear Livia's name: hence Dio's assertion to the contrary is either exaggerated or outrightly wrong.

None of our writers credits Sejanus with causing the rift between Livia and her son. Their estrangement may well have developed even if had the prefect never intruded upon them. If Tiberius was as much a male chauvinist as our sources suggest, Livia's unprecedented influence and visibility must have grated upon him.

Tacitus' account implies Sejanus exploited the emperor's already escalating disaffection with his mother. The author's chronology indicates Tiberius' relations with Livia started to deteriorate after 22 CE. Within that same frame of time Sejanus perpetrated his scheme to arrogate Tiberius' powers. Tacitus with a malicious twist argues the decision to leave Rome was the emperor's alone, then proceeds to admit other historians of his era maintained Sejanus convinced Tiberius to quit the capital:

> Hereafter, having long contemplated and more often delayed the plan, Caesar at length [went] to Campania, ostensibly because temples were to be dedicated, at Capua to Jove (i.e., Jupiter), at Nola to Augustus, but certainly to live far from the City. Although, following most authors, I have attributed the cause of the withdrawal to the intrigues of Sejanus, nevertheless after his execution [Tiberius] remained for six years equally secluded; and often I am persuaded, that to he himself it is more truthfully attributed, that the savagery and lechery which he betrayed by his actions, may be hidden by location.[11]

Tiberius never saw Livia again. He did not attend her funeral. Tacitus nevertheless insinuates, "compliance with his mother was ingrained in

Tiberius, and Sejanus did not dare exceed the authority of a parent." [12] When writing of Tiberius' death Tacitus adds, "he was simultaneously with good and evil mixed while his mother was alive." [13]

Such comments about Tiberius' habitual obedience to Livia suggest the estrangement between them was not complete.

LIVIA, SEJANUS, AND THE PLAUTII SILVANI

Although Tiberius would not let him marry Livilla, Sejanus still managed to bind himself by marriage to the imperial family's personal circle.

Marcus Plautius Silvanus and his sister Plautia Urgulanilla were the grandchildren of Livia's retainer Urgulania. Silvanus' first wife was Fabia Numantina, daughter of Augustus' cousin Marcia. After divorcing Numantina, Silvanus married a woman named Apronia. Her brother was Lucius Apronius Casianus, an outspoken supporter of Sejanus.

Plautia married Livia's grandson Claudius. The marriage produced two children. Claudius betrothed the elder child—a son called Drusus— to the daughter of Sejanus. This alliance was short-lived. A few days after the betrothal ceremony Claudius' son was found dead, suffocated by a miniature pear that had lodged in his trachea. Claudius subsequently divorced Plautia and disclaimed paternity of her daughter. He then married Aelia Paetina, the daughter of an ex-consul. She was related to Sejanus. As we know, he belonged by adoption to the *gens Aelia*. Tacitus adds Paetina was a relative of the Tuberones. Sejanus' brother bore the *cognomen* of Tubero.

The respective divorces of Silvanus and Claudius dissolved liaisons that had bound the Plautii Silvani to the imperial family. Both remarriages replaced those former unions with marital links to Sejanus. Partisans of Sejanus had infiltrated the closed and privileged clique between the Plautii Silvanii and the Caesars.

Would not Livia have objected to these intrusions, which stood to diminish her influence over her retainers and relatives? It seems hard to believe Livia sanctioned Silvanus' divorce from Numantina, whereby a client of the empress repudiated a member of the imperial family. On the other hand we do not know what transpired privately. Numantina and Silvanus might have been utterly incompatible. Recalling the bitter experience of Tiberius and Julia, Livia may have encouraged Silvanus and Numantina to separate before their disagreement became a public spectacle. Perhaps Livia applied a similar rationale to Claudius' split with Plautia.

Whatever her feelings, Livia had no legal means of preventing Silvanus or Claudius from divorcing and remarrying. She was not a *paterfamilias* to either man; and both were *sui iuris* anyway.

In 24 CE, Apronia died of a fall from her bedroom window. Silvanus insisted she had committed suicide while he was asleep; but Tiberius on investigating the bedroom in person found unmistakable evidence of a struggle and visible ejection. The inevitable conclusion was Silvanus had murdered his wife. Tacitus writes:

> [Tiberius] deferred to the Senate; and after the judges were selected, Silvanus' grandmother Urgulania sent her grandson a dagger. Indeed, this was believed to be a warning from the emperor, in light of the *amicitia* of Augusta with Urgulania.[14]

Silvanus attempted to stab himself with the dagger, faltered, and then had his attendants sever his arteries.

Delivery of the dagger showed Silvanus his grandmother and her imperial patrons were not going to defend him. In other words the Caesars supported Apronia's—and therefore Sejanus'—side. There was no alternative, because the preponderance of evidence incriminated Silvanus. One wonders how much of this was planted by Sejanus' agents. Plautia may have helped her brother perpetrate Apronia's death. Suetonius maintains Claudius divorced Plautia on suspicion of murder as well as adultery.

Silvanus' suicide avenged Apronia, who was Sejanus' retainer. Claudius' divorce and remarriage removed Silvanus' sister from her union with a member of the imperial family and placed a relative of the prefect in her stead. Sejanus profited from the disgrace of Livia's clients the Plautii Silvani; and the dowager had no choice but to accept that consequence.

LIVIA AT THE CLOSE

What does all this information tell us about the private Livia in the sunset of her life?

In some respects her mental faculties remained unimpaired by age. Since Tiberius shared his reaction to the fruit bowl incident with Livia, she must have recognized the implications of Agrippina's posturing. Moreover, Livia continued to understand which privileges she may or may not exercise. She did not challenge Tiberius because she sought new powers or prerogatives, but because he tried to keep her from implementing those already in place. Even as her life was ending, Livia interacted with senators and impelled their decisions. She prevented the prosecution of Fufius Geminus, and was poised to obstruct Sejanus' prosecution of Agrippina and Nero.

After Livia's death, nearly two years elapsed before Antonia apprized Tiberius of Sejanus' treachery. During this interim Sejanus contrived to have the Senate declare Nero and Agrippina public enemies. Tiberius exiled the pair to the Pontine Islands, where they eventually died by their own hands. Agrippina's second son Drusus had accompanied Tiberius to Capri; but Sejanus presently convinced the emperor to send the youth to Rome. There the prefect managed to have Drusus declared a public enemy and incarcerated in the palace. Sejanus apparently achieved his goal of espousing a member of the imperial family. We do not know for certain whether she was Livilla. The portion of Tacitus' **Annales**, which covers the period between the imprisonment of Drusus and the fall of Sejanus, is lost. In a subsequent extant section of his book, Tacitus does describe Sejanus as Tiberius' son-in-law. Dio Cassius asserts Sejanus married Livilla's daughter Julia. Suetonius only states Tiberius enticed Sejanus with the promise of marriage into the imperial family.

The aging Livia possessed sufficient presence of mind to become suspicious of Sejanus—and sufficient persuasiveness to move the Senate against him. Why, then, did her family and her retainer Marcus Plautius

Silvanus fail to accept her reservations about the prefect? Only Antonia, who was deeply attached to Livia, appears to have shared those concerns.

Our evidence indicates Livia only became apprehensive about Sejanus' intentions at the very end of her life. Remember, the prefect was highly engaging. In the early stages of his career, Livia might have considered him harmless and even useful. After all he did vitiate the leadership of the hostile dissident party. Livia's indifference could explain why Sejanus and Livilla relied on Mutilia Prisca—Fufius Geminus' wife—to heighten frictions between Livia and Agrippina. Neither Livia nor Mutilia realized Sejanus was manipulating them.

Furthermore, most of Livia's relatives had become loath to heed her advice. Livilla was not about to countenance criticism of Sejanus, her lover and partner in murder. Always an enemy of Livia, Agrippina must have alienated Nero and Drusus from their great-grandmother. Livia's outspoken dislike for Claudius can hardly have endeared her to him. Moreover Claudius deferred to Silvanus, who at least for a time was Sejanus' ally.

Livia's attitude toward her privileges exasperated Tiberius. She clung to her entitlements with the virulence of a petulant child, without regard for her personal image or for the reputation of the principate. As the wife of Caesar Augustus, Livia had been renowned for her modesty, discretion, and support. By her own admission she had refused to intrude upon her husband's business unless he sought her advice. Now with taunts and embarrassing disclosures, she ridiculed the emperor of Rome in public.

Livia did not discern that in discomfiting Tiberius she was playing directly into Sejanus' hands. Our sources concur: Livia's impertinence was one of Tiberius' cardinal reasons for retiring to Capri and delegating the administration of the principate to the prefect.

Perhaps Livia's years took their toll on her emotional stability. She may have been suffering from a stage of senile dementia, brought on by Alzheimer's disease or a similar age-related ailment. Alternatively, Augustus' incontrovertible hardheadedness may have foiled or controlled an intrinsic psychological weakness in Livia. At any rate as Livia's physique declined toward death, her mind suffered the conflict between a lucid intellect and a fragile psyche. Her emergent uncertainty about Sejanus suggests she died haunted by fears, for the future of her family and of the system of government she had helped develop.

NOTES TO CHAPTER VIII

1.   *Annales* 4.59. I cannot help wondering whether Sejanus rigged the accident.
2.   *Annales* 4.40.
3.   *Annales* 3.18.
4.   *Annales* 4.12.
5.   *Annales* 5.3.
6.   See Appendix III on reconciling the chronologies of Velleius Paterculus and Suetonius with that of Tacitus, in regard to the presentation of the letters and the prosecutions of Agrippina and Nero.
7.   *Annales* 3.54.
8.   *Annales* 4.57.
9.   *Tiberius* 50, 51.
10. *Romaïka* 57.12.
11. *Annales* 4.57.
12. *Annales* 5.2.
13. *Annales* 6.51.
14. *Annales* 4.22.

LIVIA THE ICON OF ROMAN IMPERIAL POWER

Livia with Attributes of the Goddess Ceres
Louvre Museum, Paris
Photo credit: Herve Lewandowski/
Réunion des Musées Nationaux/
Art Resource, New York

CHAPTER IX

THE SYMBOLIC LIVIA

The religious veneration of Augustus' person was critical to his regime. The cult did not imply that the emperor considered himself an actual divinity or expected anyone else to do so. Its purpose was to set Augustus aside in the minds of his subjects, as someone special to be respected, revered and obeyed. The emperor included Livia as a key figure in this objective. An understanding of this program is consequently essential to form a complete picture of Livia's public image.

What follows is a highly superficial examination of this extremely important issue. Two reasons impel such brevity. Firstly the significance of Livia to her husband's religious policy has received thorough treatment, from scholars of Roman history and political theory. Secondly the subject tends to become rather tedious when studied in depth.

Implementation of Augustus' divinization agenda was easily accomplished in the East, where ruler worship had already been conventional for centuries. In the Greek-influenced eastern sectors of the empire, public recognition of Livia emerged during the earliest years of her marriage to Augustus. The cities of Eleusis in Greece and Carthaea in Egypt honored her as the wife of Imperator Caesar before Octavian assumed his more familiar *cognomen* in 27 BCE. Altered to accommodate the new designation, the practice persisted. Epidaurus the healing center of the Peloponnesus, and the city of Lindos on Rhodes, erected statues to Livia wife of Caesar Augustus.

The joint adoration of Augustus and the goddess *Roma*—the personification of the Roman state—spread widely and rapidly throughout the East. As early as 29 BCE the cult emerged in Asia Minor at Pergamon (Bergamo, Turkey). Here Livia was feted along with her spouse. Statues of the imperial couple stood in the goddess' temple. Their birthdays were celebrated: Octavian's on its actual date of September 23, but Livia's on September 21—the vernal equinox—instead of January 30. Some eastern municipalities honored Livia in connection with their patron deities. An inscription from the Cypriot city of Salamina extends the greetings of Olympian Zeus—the chief god—to Livia wife of Caesar Augustus. Coins from Nicomedia in Asia Minor displayed the head of Zeus on their obverses and that of Livia on reverses. Other eastern locales accorded Livia divine honors in her own right. On Samos, throughout Asia Minor, and in Egypt the empress was designated θεά—*thea*. This word means divine as an adjective, goddess as a noun.

The empire's eastern subjects conferred similar honors upon other relatives of Augustus. After realigning their local lunar calendar with the solar year, public officials on Cyprus renamed the months for members of the imperial family. Julia received considerable recognition. As a child she was honored at Eresos on the island of Lesbos. She was addressed as *thea* at Paphos on Cyprus, and in the Thracian Chersonese. At Athens, Julia and Livia shared a priestess with Ἑστία—Hestia the hearth goddess.

Not unexpectedly, many of Julia's distinctions were connected with her motherhood of Augustus' heirs-apparent. One eastern coinage depicted Julia, Agrippa, and their two sons, together with Livia and Augustus. Priene in Asia Minor addressed Julia as θεά καλλιτέχνως—*thea kallitexnos*—goddess of beautiful children. On Lesbos, at Pergamon, at Assos (also in Asia Minor), and in Syria, Julia was identified with Aphrodite. This divinity corresponded with Venus of the Roman pantheon, who was the legendary divine ancestress of the Julian gens. An analogy was implied between Venus and Julia as progenitress of Caesars.

Livia nevertheless held clear predominance over her stepdaughter. Whereas Julia was often represented as Aphrodite, Livia was commonly equated with Hera. The wife of Zeus, Hera was queen of all the gods. She stood for wisdom, strength, and fertility in women; for purity, stability, and affection in marriage. Livia's position as empress paralleled in human affairs that of Hera among the gods.

An inscription from Paphos describes Livia rather than Julia as *véα (nea)* Ἀφροδίτη—New Aphrodite. The client kingdom of Pontus on the shore of the Black Sea issued coins representing Livia with the attributes of Aphrodite. In these cases the association of Livia with Aphrodite also underscores the empress' superiority to any other woman. Aphrodite was the special tutelary divinity of both locales. The highest honor these principalities could offer Livia was to equate her with their divine protectress.

The honors bestowed on Livia and Julia reflect their journeys with their husbands. Augustus' itinerary of 21 – 19 BCE took him through Greece, Asia Minor, and the Near East. While the emperor was in Gaul between 16 and 13 BCE, Agrippa traveled to Judaea, Asia Minor, and the Chersonese.

What had brought Livia such predominance in the East?

The peoples of the eastern empire were accustomed to kingship. Alexander the Great had imposed it on his fellow Greeks three centuries earlier. In Egypt and in areas that had comprised the ancient Persian Empire, the monarchic tradition was even older. To the Easterners Livia was a queen and Julia a princess, both to be honored with a well-established protocol.

Livia, moreover, participated actively in eastern political affairs. Remember she had procured from Augustus entitlements, for the cities of Mytilene on Lesbos and Aphrodisias in Asia Minor. Her designation as εὐεργέτης—*efergetys*—benefactress, in Athens, on the Aegean island of Thasos, and in Pontus, indicates she may have intervened on behalf of these entities as well.

Residents of Thasos acknowledged Julia as *efergetys* but Livia as θεά εὐεργέτης—*thea efergetys*—divine benefactress. Either the Thasians wished to recognize Livia's superior status, or the empress provided more significant benefactions to Thasos than did Julia. The latter may not have intervened in eastern interests to the extent that her stepmother did. Julia seems, in fact, to have kept a relatively low profile during Agrippa's eastern tour. Pregnancy with her fourth child Vipsania Agrippina may have induced her to do so. At one point during the tour, Julia preceded her husband to Ilium (Roman Troy). After almost drowning in the River Scamander during a storm, she found the city utterly unprepared to receive her.

In western portions of the empire, ruler worship was an unfamiliar concept. It threatened to be particularly repugnant in Rome proper, where the very notion of monarchy was so virulently despised. Augustus realized he must introduce the veneration of himself and his family with the same caution and subtlety he had applied to his system of government.

The emperor had begun his western association with the divine at the very beginning of his political career. In 42 BCE as Triumvir he had compelled the Senate to declare the late Julius Caesar a god and Octavian his special priest. Thereafter Augustus encouraged the worship of those deities he considered his special patrons: Venus his legendary ancestress, Apollo (inspiration), *Fortuna* (fortune), *Felicitas* (prosperity), Mars (vengeance through warfare), and the principal god Jupiter (power, paternity, righteous judgment). Other favored divinities represented the cardinal attributes of the principate: *Concordia* (harmony in human relationships), *Victoria* (victory), *Salus* (health, safety, wellbeing), and *Ops* (abundance).

Augustus also associated himself with religious precepts and practices. His person was sacrosanct, his birthday a festal holiday. His name was uttered in the Salian hymn which venerated Mars. Reverses of coins depicted Capricorn, the astrological sign of his conception or lunar sign of his birth.[1] Even his cognomen Augustus, meaning consecrated had a religious connotation.

Marcus Aemilius Lepidus the former Triumvir died early in 12 BCE. Lepidus had been *Pontifex Maximus*—High Priest of the Roman state religion. His death allowed Augustus to enhance his own religiosity. On March 6, 12 BCE the emperor appropriated the chief pontificate for himself.

In the West, Livia's earliest association with a religious concept dates from the Triumvirate. The personal sacrosanctity and exemption from *tutela*, which Octavian procured for both Livia and Octavia, were attributes of the Vestal Virgins. Nevertheless, religious distinctions for Livia were comparatively sparse in western venues prior to the consecration of the *Ara Pacis Augustae*—the Altar of Augustan Peace— in 13 BCE. The southwestern Italian town of Velia (Elea) represented her on a public altar together with Octavia, Julia, Gaius, and Lucius. Velia and Tibur (Tivoli) acknowledged Livia as the wife of Augustus, while Haluntium (Caronia) in Sicily hails her as divine wife of Augustus. As Haluntium and Velia were located in areas of intense Greek influence, their acknowledgment of Livia may well have derived from eastern precedents.

For many years Augustus fretted about the declining population of ethnic Italians. In 18 BCE he began to enact incentives encouraging Roman citizens to marry and raise children. To stress the importance of those policies, Augustus decided to present Livia as a visible epitome of precepts, practices, and deities that extolled Roman women as wives and mothers.

The Augustan Peace had a maternal character. *Tellus Mater* (Mother Earth) is depicted, along with the warrior goddess Roma, on the eastern wall of the *Ara Pacis*. This location has particular significance because it faces the rising sun. On January 30, 9 BCE, the day of the altar's dedication, Livia entered her fiftieth year. The implication here was fertility, since the Romans considered fifty the most advanced age at which a woman was still capable of conception. Like a mother the *Pax Augusta* was benevolent and nurturing. Nevertheless it could not exist without Augustus' government, even as a woman could not be a proper wife and mother without a husband. If Augustus embodied the principate, then Livia must represent the peace his system had engendered.

In Gaul the imperial mint at Lugdunum produced coins that circulated throughout the western provinces. Subsequent to the dedication of the *Ara Pacis*, the mint began to issue coins bearing Livia's likeness with the legend *Pax*. Characterizations of Livia as Peace are strikingly absent from the East, where the empress was so frequently represented as other divinities. A likely reason is that the Greek peace goddess Ειρήνη—Eirene—was customarily portrayed as a young virgin, rather than the nurturing matron Augustus had chosen to epitomize his achievement.

The edifices for which Livia was directly responsible reflected the same nurturing maternalism associated with the Altar of Peace. Individual Roman families venerated the goddess *Pax* in conjunction with *Janus*, *Salus*, and *Concordia*. In her husband's honor, Livia formally dedicated her shrine to *Concordia* on June 11, 7 BCE. This day marked the *Matralia*, the annual feast of the indigenous Italian goddess *Mater Matuta*. As the guardian of ripening seed, *Mater Matuta* was also the protectress of mothers and pregnant matrons.

The oldest living male progenitor of an extended Roman family was the *paterfamilias*. His descendants honored his birthday with great solemnity. They also venerated his *genius* (tutelary life force) as an incarnation of Jupiter in their midst. Around 7 BCE Augustus began to promote the adoration of his *genius* as an aspect of the traditional cult of the *Lares Compitales*. These were benevolent spirits of the dead who guarded crossroads. This practice combined with the celebration of the emperor's birthday to represent him as a paternalistic guardian—in effect the *paterfamilias* of the Roman state. The concept was strengthened on February 5, 2 BCE, when the Senate declared Augustus *Pater patriae*— Father of [his] Country.

The goddess Juno was the wife of Jupiter, and hence queen of the Roman pantheon. Like the Greek Hera with whom Livia was associated in eastern venues, Juno was divine patroness of marital fidelity. She promoted fecundity, successful child rearing, stability and harmony in family relationships. The counterpart of a man's *genius* was a woman's personal Juno, the manifestation of this deity in every woman. Roman families reverenced the Juno of their oldest surviving ancestress, the *materfamilias*.

Archaeological material, although scanty, suggests the veneration of Livia's Juno may have emerged in Rome as early as 2 BCE. It was certainly in practice near Carthage by 3 CE, and in Dalmatia before Augustus' death. The adulation was performed at private altars rather than public places of worship. This suggests Livia's Juno cult arose more from spontaneous actions by individual Romans than from government mandate. Two years before Augustus implemented the public worship of his *genius*, the poet of the **Consolation to Livia** had compared the empress to Juno. The literary device does not confirm the existence of a cult. It does suggest, however, that the Romans had started to consider Livia their national *materfamilias* as early as 9 BCE. The emperor's propaganda, equating his wife with the maternalism of the Augustan Peace, had proven effective.

Augustus had determined he could be more obvious with allusions to his personal divinity in western areas of the empire outside of Italy proper. Along with the veneration of his patron deities and his *genius*, the emperor successfully propagated the cult of *Roma et Augustus*—Rome and Augustus—in Gaul, Spain, Pannonia, and North Africa. Augustus continued to develop Livia's religious image along with his own in the empire's western sectors. In 2 CE the Lugdunum mint began to produce coins that showed the empress seated and holding sheaves of grain. This is the iconography of Ceres the Roman goddess of agriculture.

In his uncompleted *Fasti* (*Feasts*), a poetic calendar of Roman religious festivals, Ovid describes Livia's restoration of the temple to the *Bona Dea*—Good Goddess. The shrine was located on the Aventine Hill. Livia also took an active part in the elaborate rites of this Italian divinity of the earth. The Good Goddess was strictly a woman's deity. No man might enter her sanctuary, witness her rituals, or even utter her name. The *Bona Dea* was patroness of medicinal arts, and special protectress against earthquakes. She promoted the chastity and fertility of girls and women.

Elsewhere in the *Fasti*, Ovid describes the *Porticus Liviae* and the empress' shrine to *Concordia*. Married women invoked the goddess *Concordia* together with Venus (female sexuality) and *Fortuna*. Livia the *princeps* of matrons built and dedicated a temple on the Via Latina to *Fortuna Muliebris*—Fortune of Women. There is no allusion to the temple in the *Fasti*; but a second century inscription, commemorating Septimius Severus' restoration of the building, describes Livia as the daughter of Drusus and wife of Caesar Augustus. The original construction took place, then, between Ovid's relegation in 8 CE and Augustus' death in 14 CE.

Livia continued to be a symbol at Rome, of the principate's commitment to marriage and family life. Sometime between 4 and 10 CE, Tiberius dedicated an altar in Rome to the *numen Augustum*. Literally a nodding of the head, *numen* signified the presence and activity of deific power. Mortals themselves did not possess *numen*, but served as channels through which the gods revealed their divine intentions. *Numen* inhered in harmonious marital and family relationships, of which the imperial family expressing the *numen Augustum* was the model. Although the year of the altar's dedication remains uncertain, its month and day were definitely January 17. This was the wedding anniversary of Augustus and Livia. Knowing the altar was special to Livia in this respect, Ovid admonished his wife to venerate the *numen Augustum* in preparation for her anticipated audience with the empress.

Italians continued to venerate Livia's Juno, now in conjunction with the *genius* of Tiberius as well as that of Augustus. A freedwoman of Falerii (modern Civita Castellana) epigraphically recorded her offering to these three manifestations. For the same religious purpose, Ovid kept silver votive statuettes of each personage.

In one of his letters to his wife, Ovid imputes to Livia the *mores* (character) of Juno. The poet also calls the empress *princeps femina*. This term is more comprehensive than the *princeps Romanae* of the **Consolation to Livia**. *Princeps femina* signifies female *princeps* rather than principal of Roman women. Ovid hereby implies Livia was foremost not only of Roman women but of women throughout the world.

In the same letter Ovid ascribes to Livia the *vultus* (countenance) of Venus. This goddess was the legendary mother of the Trojan hero Aeneas from whom the members of the *gens Julia* claimed descent. Since Livia never bore Augustus a surviving child, Ovid's comparison is meaningless unless it refers to Augustus' adoption of Tiberius. Livia herself emphasized this connection by commissioning a statue of Venus' son Cupid in the likeness of a deceased son of Germanicus.

Livia's fellow Italians began to focus upon her motherhood of the emperor's new heir-apparent. Ticinum (Pavia) and Superaequum (now in ruins) on mainland Italy, as well as Himera Thermae (Termini Imerese) in Sicily, all acknowledged her as the wife of Augustus and mother of Tiberius. The inscription from Ticinum also describes her as the daughter of Drusus, while that from Superaequum recognizes her as the grandmother of Germanicus. An inscription from Segobriga in Spain honors Livia as daughter of Drusus, wife of Augustus, mother of Tiberius, and grandmother of Germanicus and Drusus. The references to Livia's father may have been employed to underscore a sense of family continuity.

Veneration of Livia as Demeter began to proliferate in eastern locales. Tralles, Sardes and Pergamon in Asia Minor, Thessaloniki in northern

Greece, the island of Lesbos, and the city of Panormus in Greek Sicily, all associated the empress with this goddess of agriculture. Demeter corresponded to Ceres, the Roman agricultural goddess with whom Livia was equated in western regions.

By the time Augustus adopted Tiberius in 4 CE, Livia's public stature far surpassed that of other women in the imperial family. Octavia and the elder Julia, whose prominences had once rivaled Livia's, were out of the picture—the former deceased and the latter in exile. Aside from Livia, Augustus' most important female relatives at this time were his youngest niece Antonia and his granddaughter Agrippina. Their significance arose from their connection with Tiberius' heir-apparent Germanicus: Antonia was the prince's mother and Agrippina his wife.

There are no coinages or deific affiliations for either woman. A single, government-sponsored inscription, dating from the reign of Augustus, mentions Antonia. An inscription from Delphi in Greece records the birth of Agrippina. She does not reappear in the epigraphic record until after her marriage to Germanicus in 5 CE. Only two inscriptions honoring Agrippina as Germanicus' wife can be firmly dated to the reign of Augustus. By contrast some twenty-eight captions celebrate Livia.

As Germanicus' grandmother, Livia was *materfamilias* to Antonia and Agrippina alike. Conceivably Augustus felt exaltation of a daughter-in-law would upset the hierarchy of the family, and impugn the familial values that he was striving to promote.

There may be a far simpler explanation for Livia's emergent singularity. Antonia appears in private inscriptions, such as the epitaphs of her slaves and freedmen. She was a recluse who did not even attend the funeral of Germanicus her son. Requiring recognition or veneration of someone who was virtually invisible to the public eye would have been difficult. Official or religious inscriptions honoring Agrippina may have been destroyed and coinages repressed. On discovering the criminality of his niece/daughter-in-law Livilla in 31 CE, Tiberius ordered the eradication of public statues and inscriptions that distinguished her. He may have mandated the destruction of similar epigraphy dedicated to Agrippina when he ordered her banishment two years earlier.

Artists did not always represent Livia as some goddess or political principle. The archaeological record is filled with statues, paintings, and cameos, of Livia simply as Livia. While many of these depict her by herself, others portray her together with Augustus, her sons, or other relatives. Some renderings were private commissions of the imperial family. Other likenesses of Livia, and of the rest of her family, were intended for general consumption. Uniformity in facial expressions and hairstyles, along with well-proportioned bodily features, reveal that such portraits were stylized for public display and purchase. In a similar vein, paintings, photographs, and dolls of modern royals and first families are exhibited in capital cities and offered for sale as keepsakes.

By the time Tiberius became emperor in 14 CE, many eastern and eastern-influenced cities had come to identify Livia with their tutelary goddesses. Utica in North Africa (modern Utique, Tunisia) equated her with the Phoenician goddess-queen Astarte. Livia was Ἑκατή—Hecaté, a goddess of crossroads—at Tralles in Asia Minor, Diana at Ephesus and Corinth, and Aphrodite at Smyrna (Izmir, Turkey). At Cyzicus in northern Asia Minor, Livia shared a priestess with the Roman goddess Minerva (wisdom). Athribes in Egypt venerated Livia as νέα Ἶσσις— Nea Issis—New Isis; while coins of Alexandria represented her as the mother-goddess *Cybele*. In Athens she was Πρόνοια—Pronoia (foresight), Ὑγίεια—Hygiea (health), and Ἄρτεμις Βουλαῖα—*Artemis Boulaia*— Artemis of the City Council, i.e., its divine protectress. Livia was represented divinely elsewhere in Greece as Μνημοσύνη—*Mnemosyne* (memory) at Thespiae near Thebes, as Τύχη—*Tyche* (fortune) at Gythium. Her statue stood beside those of Augustus and Tiberius, in Gythium's temple to Hygeia and her father Aesclepius (healing arts). Thespiae and Gythium celebrated games in Livia's honor, as did Chalcis on the great Aegean island of Euboea and Alexandria in Egypt.

Livia was still recognized as Hera or Demeter—although sometimes as New Hera or New Demeter—throughout Asia Minor, Cilicia, Greece, and North Africa. On the island of Samos Ἀρχηγέτις Ἥρα— *Archetis Hera*—Hera the Progenitress shared a priestess with Livia (the progenitress of the dynasty) and her parents, each of whom is styled as an originator of the world's greatest good. Lampsacus (Lapseki, Turkey), on the Dardanelles north of Troy, adored Livia as Hestia as well as New Demeter. Alexandria honored her as Demeter's attribute Εὐθηνία— *Efthenia*—Prosperity. As goddess of abundance and of the social stability that resulted from successful agriculture, Efthenia may be the closest eastern equivalent to Livia's western representation as nurturing peace (Pax).

An inscription from the Boeotia region of Greece recognizes an Augusta as a harbinger of peace, and fit companion for the nine Muses. Certain identification of the honoree as Livia is nevertheless impossible. The inscription might have described a different woman who held the title of Augusta.

Throughout the east, inscriptions and coinages depicted Livia with Augustus, or Tiberius, or both. Many such honors employ the designation, Σεβαστόι—Sevasti—Augusti. This plural embraces father, mother, and son—the multi-generational royal family. Veneration of the divine Augustus was conducted at special temples, called Σεβαστεῖα— Sevasteia. Such celebrations included homage to Livia, at Pergamon, Ancyra (Ankara), and Attalia in Asia Minor, as well as at Leptis Magna in North Africa.

Antonia and Agrippina emerge a bit. Both women are represented in the imperial family group at Samos, and in the Sevasteion at Leptis Magna. Antonia is benefactress at Thermis on Lesbos, and divine benefactress at Ilium (Roman Troy). At Athens she appears as θεά Ἀντονια—thea Antonia. Agrippina has a single divine representation. Mytilene, the capital city of Lesbos, styled her as θεὰν...ἀιόλιν καρποφόρον—theav...aiolin karpophorov—divine...traveling fruitful one. The inscription celebrates the birth at Mytilene of Agrippina's last child, Julia Livilla. Livia nevertheless continued to outdistance her relatives in an epigraphic sense. Some forty inscriptions from Tiberius' reign do honors to her.

Livia retained in western regions the deific imagery Augustus had developed for her. Coins from the imperial mint at Lugdunum continued to portray Livia as Ceres or as Pax. A statue from the so-called Insula Gaulus (the region around Grenoble, France) represents Livia as Ceres. Livia can be readily identified as Ceres on the *Grande Camée de France*. This immense carved sardonyx, now in the *Cabinet des Medailles* of the *Bibliotheque Nationale* in Paris, depicts the apotheosis of Germanicus. Although other women of the imperial house appear on the cameo, only Livia is portrayed as a goddess.

Like Augustus, Tiberius understood the veneration of a living ruler was prone to be less acceptable in western regions than in eastern. He permitted residents of Asia Minor to erect a temple to himself, Livia, and the Roman Senate, following the successful prosecution of a corrupt governor; but he forbade the construction of a similar sanctuary in Spain.

Tiberius nevertheless enlarged his mother's religious image in the West. Around 16 CE the Lugdunum mint began to produce coins, with Livia's image and the superscription *Pietas* (devotion) on their reverses. Another cameo, now in Vienna, shows Livia seated and contemplating a bust of her deified spouse. Her accoutrements combine the poppies and barley of Ceres with the lion, tabor, and diadem of Cybele. The Romans had come to equate this originally Phrygian goddess with Rhea or Ops, the mother of Jupiter and goddess of abundance. The Cybele aspect of the cameo exemplifies Livia's position as *genetrix*. The cameo allegorically conjoins agriculture (Ceres), with prosperity (Ops/Cybele), and the continuing Augustan dynasty (Livia beholding Augustus).

Inscriptions and coins from Spain employed the epithet *genetrix orbis*—progenitress of the world, i.e., of the empire through its ruling dynasty. This sense of family perpetuity may have inspired the homage to Livia's parents, at Tucci in Spain and Marruvium in Italy.[2]

Sometime between the death of Augustus and his own demise in 17 CE, Ovid produced a poem in Getic. This was the language of the Thracian natives among whom the relegated poet had been forced to live. The poem is not extant: we know of it only from Ovid's letter to a friend. The poet asserts that in this work, he wrote "You, Livia, to be the Vesta of pure matrons."[3] Since Vesta was a virgin goddess, Ovid's terminology is oxymoronic: a matron could hardly be a virgin. We presume Ovid describes Livia's unassailable chastity. This epithet for Livia must have been acceptable to the imperial regime; otherwise Ovid would not have dared use it.

In the East, public commemorations of Livia's birthday had begun as early as 29 BCE. Similar festivals did not emerge in the West until the period we are presently considering. In 18 CE the city council of Forum Clodii erected an altar to the *numen Augustum*, and mandated annual birthday celebrations for the Divine Augustus, Tiberius, and Livia. Individual Roman families honored the birthdays of their *patres*- and *matresfamilias* with religious solemnity. The Forum Clodii festivities suggest this Italian city began to pay public homage to Livia's Juno, along with the *genii* of the two emperors.

Inscriptions from Gaul and Spain, and from Pompeii in southern Italy, reveal the existence of a clergy devoted to Julia Augusta. While some of the inscriptions employ the term *sacerdos* (lay priest), most of the dedications utilize *flamen* and/or *flaminica*. The latter were high priests and priestesses of the most sacred gods in the Roman pantheon. The most important was the *flamen Dialis*, who conducted the veneration of Jupiter. His wife the *flaminica* served Juno. The inscriptions do not attest to the worship of the living Livia. They indicate, rather, that the veneration of her Juno was now practiced in public venues as well as private homes. Coins from Thapsos near Carthage, which specifically honor Livia's Juno, confirm this municipality' observation of the cult.

Livia acquired a new active and significant religious role at Rome. The Senate named her high priestess of the Divus Augustus. She had a college of priests, the *Sodales Augustales*, under her direction. A religious page called a *lictor* was authorized to escort her while she was performing her sacred duties, but not otherwise. Livia used her new sacerdotal position to establish an annual three-day celebration in honor of her late spouse. She reportedly gave a senator named Numericus Atticus a million *sesterces*, because he swore he had watched Augustus ascend bodily to the heavens.

Tiberius and Livia declared the house, in which Augustus died at Nola, a shrine. At Rome they dedicated a temple to the newly deified emperor. While this structure was under construction, mother and son placed a gold statue of Augustus in the temple of Mars. Livia dedicated another image of the deceased in her own home. Tiberius let her commemorate the occasion with a public banquet, but on the conditions that the Senate approved the event, and that she entertained the women while he hosted the men.

In 22 CE, Livia and Tiberius jointly dedicated a statue of Augustus near the Theater of Marcellus. The placement of Livia's name ahead of her son's on the statue's base indicates the importance she enjoyed as the deified emperor's priestess.[4] In her priestly capacity, Livia may have commissioned the ubiquitously famous statue of Augustus wearing armor. The piece was discovered in 1863, at Livia's villa in what is today the village of Prima Porta. The image's bare feet indicate that Augustus had been deified, and that the statue had a votive purpose.

When Livia fell gravely ill later in 22 CE, the Senate consecrated prayers and games to her convalescence. The equestrian order made a financial offering on Livia's behalf to *Fortuna equestris* (Fortune of the Knights). Private citizens erected supplicatory altars to the goddess *Salus* (health).

After Livia recovered, the Senate granted her two new distinctions which rejuvenated her association with Vesta. One was the use of a *carpentum*—a mule-drawn covered carriage traditionally reserved for the Vestal Virgins. The other privilege entitled Livia to sit among the Vestals during theatrical performances.

The senatorial mint in Rome began to produce coins with Livia's portrait on their obverses. This primary position meant the coins specifically honored Livia; on reverses she had been ancillary to whomever was on the corresponding obverses. Superscriptions included *Iustitia* (justice), *Pietas* (devotion), and *Salus Augusta* (Augustan health). The appearance of the last-mentioned legend, at the time of Livia's recuperation, is no coincidence. *Salus Augusta* nevertheless refers to the wellbeing of the regime rather than of the personal Livia; otherwise the combination would read *Salus Augustae*. The phraseology avoided, at Rome, the touchy issue of imputing divinity or divine favoritism directly to Livia.

The *Fratres Arvales* (Arval Brethren) were an ancient and noble order of lay priests, dedicated to the worship of Mars and the Lares. Every January 3rd the *Arvales* offered vows for the welfare of the emperor. In 27 CE—perhaps in honor of her approaching eighty-fifth birthday— the brotherhood began to include Livia in this invocation. Inscriptions reveal that in the final years of Livia's long life, private celebrations of her birthday were prevalent at Rome.

Shortly after his accession—probably in 43 CE the centennial of Livia's birth—the emperor Claudius had the Roman Senate officially declare his grandmother a divinity. Easterners had hitherto venerated Livia as the manifestation of this or that deity, or as a human honoree in the cult of Rome and Augustus. Now they accepted her as a goddess in her own right. At Claudius' instigation the city of Alexandria established a two-day festival, the Ἡμέραι Σεβασταί—Hemerai Sevastai—Augusta's Days—to celebrate the new divinity. Inscriptions from Lydia and Pisidia in Asia Minor describe priests and priestesses to θεά Σεβαστή—thea Sevaste—Diva Augusta. In some eastern locales, Augustus and Livia became virtually one concept. Two inscriptions from Hypata in Macedonia honor ὁί θεοί Σεβαστοί—he thei Sevasti—The Divine Augusti. Another, from Aezani in Asia Minor, describes the deified couple as ὁί μεγάλοι θεοί Σεβαστοί ὁμοβώμιοι—hi megali thei Sevasti homovomii—The Great Divine Augusti Sharing an Altar.

In the West, Claudius clung to well-established representations of his grandmother. An issue from the Lugdunum mint portrayed the Divus Augustus on obverses, with the Diva Augusta as Ceres on reverses. A relief from Ravenna depicts her as the Julian ancestress Venus. Archaeologists discovered a life-sized image of the Diva Augusta in the so-called Villa of the Mysteries at Pompeii. Perhaps there was a connection between the nurturing maternalism of the deified Livia and an elaborate, probably localized, prenuptial rite of feminine fertility. The celebration is magnificently illustrated in the murals that give the house its modern name.

Claudius required the women of Rome to swear oaths in the Diva Augusta's name. He placed a statue of the new divinity in the temple to Augustus, and made the Vestal Virgins responsible for sacrifices to her. These included the annual offering of a cow in celebration of Livia's birthday. Such information, albeit scanty, suggests Livia became in the divine sphere what she had been in the human: a patroness of her sex.

Writing during the reigns of Vespasian and Titus (69 – 79 CE), the elder Pliny indicates that the Romans of his era used Livia to symbolize the quality of material goods. A paper manufacturer advertised his superior product as Augustus paper, and the second-best as Livia paper. The sobriquets reflect prevailing cultural attitudes: a woman no matter how distinguished was still secondary to her husband.

We see the influence of Livia and her example in the public activities and honors of subsequent empresses. In 49 CE the Senate hailed Claudius' wife Agrippina the Younger as Augusta. This Agrippina consequently became the first empress to bear this designation during her husband's lifetime. Hereafter virtually all wives, daughters, sisters, and mothers of living emperors were called Augusta. Tacitus writes that Claudius' funeral rite in 54 CE "was celebrated just as for the Divine Augustus, Agrippina rivaling the splendor of her great-grandmother Livia." [5]

Throughout the first and second centuries, Roman emperors identified their women with goddesses and political concepts that exemplified the principate. Most of these correlations—Juno, Ceres, Venus, Cybele, Pax, Concordia, Pietas, and Salus Augusta—began with Livia. The emperors of the Antonine dynasty (96 – 192 CE) added *Laetitia* (joy), *Hilaritas* (mirth), *Fecunditas* (fertility), *Pudicitia* (modesty), and the Roman hearth goddess Vesta. Here we see nuances of Livia. The poetic **Consolation to Livia** had praised her *pudicitia*. She and her female descendants had enjoyed the privileges of Vesta's attendant virgins at Rome; while in eastern venues, Livia had been associated with Vesta's Greek equivalent Hestia.

Despite the precedent Tiberius had set by forbidding the deification of Livia, emperors began to deify wives or other close female relations who died before or during their reigns. Caligula so honored his sister Drusilla in 37 CE, even before Claudius deified Livia in 43 CE. Nero (54 – 68 CE) consecrated his daughter Claudia in 63 CE and her mother Poppaea Sabina two years later. Vespasian deified his wife Flavia Domitilla, who had actually died before he became emperor.

Female deifications abounded under the Antonines. Trajan (98 – 117 CE) consecrated his sister Marciana who died in 114 CE. Trajan's successor Hadrian (117 – 138 CE) apotheosized his predecessor's widow Pompeia Plotina in 129 CE and his own wife Vibia Sabina in 137 CE. Antoninus Pius (138 – 161 CE) consecrated his Faustina in 141 CE. Marcus Aurelius (161 – 180 CE), Pius' successor and son-in-law, deified Faustina's namesake daughter in 175 CE. Taking their cue from Claudius' deification of Livia, the Antonines paraded images of their immortalized women in chariots drawn by elephants.

The emperors and empresses of the Severan dynasty (193 – 235 CE) took a noticeable interest in Livia. When they restored the temple of the *Fortuna muliebris*, Septimius Severus (193 – 211 CE) and his wife Julia Domna credited Livia with the original construction of the edifice. Septimius and Domna also refurbished Livia's villa at Prima Porta. The couple's elder son, Marcus Aurelius Antoninus Bassianus, is better known to history by his nickname of Caracalla (Hooded One). In an inscription he avers his landholdings near Thyatira in Asia Minor had once belonged to Livia.

Septimius Severus and his successors appended *Felicitas* (prosperity) and *Felicitas Saeculi* (prosperity of generations) to the attributes of the dynasty's women. No direct evidence indicates that Livia was ever represented as Felicitas. Augustus had nevertheless encouraged the worship of this time-honored Roman goddess, as a divine patroness and exemplar of his regime.

The influence of Livia is clearly apparent, in the Severans' acclamations of their empresses as mothers. Titles include *Mater patriae*, *Mater Augusti*, *Mater castrorum* (military camps), and *Mater senatus*. The religiously fanatic and egomaniacal Elagabalus (218 – 222 CE) designated his mother Julia Soaemias—Domna's niece—as *Mater Deum* (Mother of God). All of this terminology derives from Livia's nurturing maternalism.

The Severi duly deified their women. Elagabalus consecrated Julia Domna. Alexander Severus (222 – 235 CE), Elagabalus' cousin and successor apotheosized their grandmother Julia Maesa, Domna's sister.

Livia's cult persisted in pagan circles even as Christianity became the dominant religion of the Roman empire. The fourth century Christian poet Aurelius Prudentius Clemens castigates the veneration of Livia's Juno as hypocritical on the ground her marriage to Augustus was immoral.

NOTES TO CHAPTER IX

[1] The moon may have been in Capricorn at the hour of Augustus' birth. The Romans stressed the lunar sign over the solar for a person born during the night. Hence the first century poet Manilius, in his *Astronomica*, extolls Libra as the birth sign of Tiberius. On Tiberius' birthday—November 16—the sun is in Scorpio.

[2] The Marruvines had another reason to honor Livia's parents: her father had patronized the city. See Chapter I.

[3] *Epistulae ex Ponto* 4.13.29.

[4] Although gossip insinuated Tiberius resented the precedence of his mother's name over his, the fact that he did not challenge the order shows he was willing to accept it.

[5] *Annales* 12.69.

EPILOGUE,
APPENDICES,
BIBLIOGRAPHY,
AND INDEX

Imperial family members on the Altar of Augustan Peace
Museum of the Ara Pacis Augustae, Rome
Photo credit: Nimatallah/Art Resource, New York
Livia stands near to direct center, behind the Asiatic child looking backward.

WHAT DID THEY LOOK LIKE?

We have studied a woman from various perspectives. We observed how she became a formidable public figure, even as she stressed her government's commitment to marriage and the importance of women to the home. We scrutinized her reputation as a criminal—the tradition by which she is best known to the modern world—and determined it is patently false. Delving into her private life we found a loving and much loved wife, a fiercely devoted and forbearant mother, a diligent homemaker, an intellectual, a political adviser, a friend—and at times an emotional powder keg. One element we did not consider, as we examined Livia and those close to her, was physical appearances. What did they look like?

Livia herself was short and stocky. Her face was shaped essentially like a shallow V. She had a high forehead and large hazel eyes. Her aquiline nose was rather large in proportion to the rest of her facial features. Below broad rounded cheeks her face descended to a small mouth. Slightly pursed lips indicate she had closely set teeth. Her chin was round and slightly prominent. She had thick, tightly waved red hair. Her Etruscan coiffeur, with its braided plaits resting against the cheeks, minimized the pudginess of her face. The hair arrangement evoked an air of dynamism and astuteness that fit Livia's personality.

Tiberius strongly resembled Livia, for he had her V-shaped visage. Drusus had a somewhat longer face and slightly broader chin and jaw.

Both sons were tall and broad-shouldered. Tiberius we noted earlier suffered from acne and tended to stoop. His son the sickly younger Drusus strongly resembled his namesake uncle.

Caesar Augustus was small and slender but well proportioned. Self-conscious about the shortness of his stature, he liked to wear boots with thick soles to made him appear taller than he actually was. Beneath a tousle of fair wavy hair and a broad forehead he had merging eyebrows. He made sure this last-mentioned feature, which Suetonius describes, was omitted from his official portraits. Augustus' prominent bluish-gray eyes were bright and penetrating. Their gaze could be intimidating, writes Suetonius, if he stared at you with his head slightly lowered as if to avoid looking at the sun. He had prominent cheekbones and a classic Roman nose. Below his generous mouth with diminutive and stained teeth, he had a small rounded chin. Whether speaking or silent Augustus projected an aura of such mildness, that a Gaul planning assassinate him turned from this purpose upon encountering the emperor in person.

In portraits of Octavia we detect a resemblance to Augustus her brother. She had his broad forehead, large eyes, sharp cheekbones and delicate mouth. Her chin, broader than her brother's, rendered her face U-shaped. Her second spouse Mark Antony was a big and burly man, with a broad round face and head of tightly curled hair. The couple's younger daughter Antonia—Livia's daughter-in-law and soulmate—mingled her mother's large eyes with her father's robust cheeks and chin.

Augustus' daughter Julia had a delicately featured oval face and her father's slight slender build. Her portraits conceal her irregular eyes and prematurely gray hair. Julia's husband Agrippa was a large man with rather rugged facial features. His furrowed brow, closely set eyes, aquiline nose, firm chin, and square jaw projected an air of sober intensity and serious determination. Most of the children Julia bore to Agrippa inherited their father's looks but their mother's delicate physique. Gaius and Lucius were both fine-featured. The circumstances under which they died suggest these brothers had fragile constitutions. The unfortunate Postumus was an exception; he was endowed with great physical strength. The elder Agrippina was a petit woman with an elongated face. She had curly hair which cascaded from her head in ringlets.

Because the kindred of Augustus and Livia intermarried, their descendants assumed a characteristic physiognomy. High foreheads and broad prominent cheeks tapering to small mouths and chins, give the faces of many later Julio-Claudians a distinctly triangular appearance. We see this trait in Germanicus, in his sons, and especially in his brother Claudius. Remember, Germanicus and Claudius were the grandnephews of Augustus and the grandsons of Livia. Germanicus had spindly legs, of which he was extremely self-conscious. He sought to remedy this defect by riding horseback after meals. Portraits of Livilla, the notorious sister of Germanicus and Claudius, are essentially non-existent. Tiberius ordered their destruction after the revelation of her murderous career. Livilla's rare surviving likeness, on the *Grande Camée de France*, represents her as small and lithe. Full hair and regular facial features attest to the beauty Tacitus describes.

And so our study of Livia Drusilla draws to a close. Hopefully we have seen past the cold *façade* of a political institution, beyond the distorted invention of a sinister tradition to find the living, feeling woman who shared the life and career of the founder of the Roman empire.

The Julio – Claudian Dynasty

The use of numbers, to differentiate the Julias who descended from Augustus and/or Livia, is my invention.

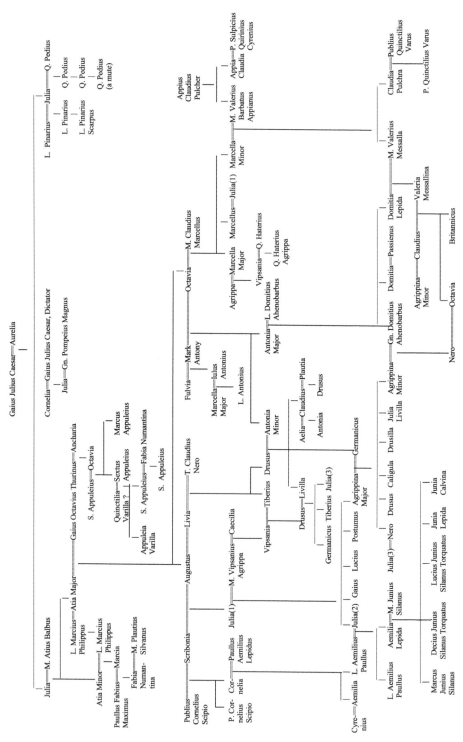

APPENDIX I

THE GENEALOGY OF LIVIA DRUSILLA

The genealogy of Livia's father is disappointingly sketchy. Suetonius writes:

> From this stock (i.e., the *gens Claudia*) Tiberius Caesar drew his descent, and indeed on both sides: the paternal from Tiberius Nero, the maternal from Appius Pulcher, who were both sons of Appius Caecus. He was also intermingled with the family of the Livii, his maternal grandfather having been adopted into it.[1]

A descendant of Appius Claudius Caecus (*censor* 312 BCE, consul 307 and 296 BCE) was Appius Claudius Pulcher, consul for 79 BCE. His progeny, through his son Gaius, became members of the imperial family per the lineage below.

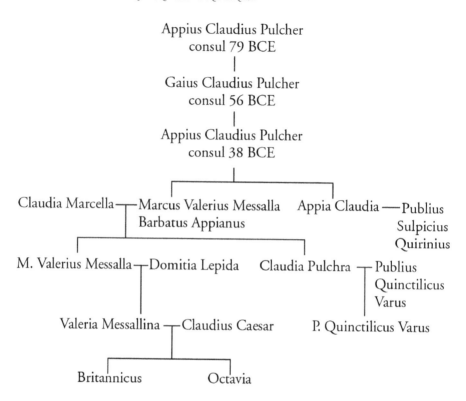

Just how Livia's father was connected to the consul of 79 BCE is not known. I propose this *stemma*:

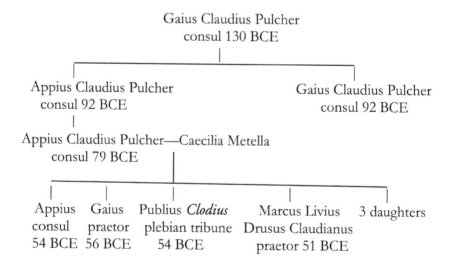

Prior to the Second Triumvirate, forty-three was the minimum age for the consulship, forty for the praetorship and plebian tribunate. Hence the three known sons of the consul for 79 BCE had to be born before 90 BCE. Livia's father was the right age to be a fourth, youngest member of this group. The consul of 79 BCE was an ally of the plebian tribune Drusus. Having numerous sons, Appius Claudius Pulcher could lose one to adoption without jeopardizing his own posterity. Generations of inheritance divisions and the ever-increasing expense of electioneering had straitened his family fortune. Appius and his wife Caecilia Metella might have welcomed the prospect of one less mouth to feed. The parents may also have felt their boy stood a better chance of being educated and promoted into politics as the only son of Drusus rather than as the youngest of Pulcher.

The genealogy proposed above is by no means certain. Drusus the tribune was in the same age bracket as Appius and Gaius Claudius Pulcher. These brothers, who shared the consulship for 92 BCE, were respectively the father and uncle of the consul for 79 BCE. While Livia's father was certainly born no later than 91 BCE, he could have been born earlier. One of the following *stemmae* might apply:

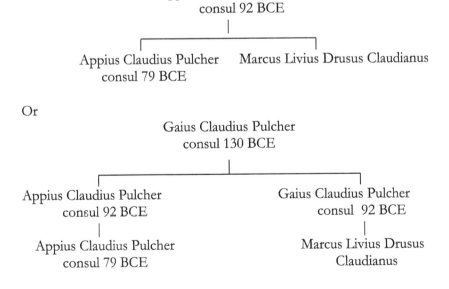

***

The background of Livia's mother is even more elusive than that of her father. Suetonius complains Livia's deranged great-grandson Gaius Caligula,

> ...dared to ascribe low birth to her in a letter to the Senate, as though she originated from a maternal grandfather [who was] a decurion of Fundi, when it is obvious from public monuments, that Aufidius Lurco held the magistracies of Rome.[2]

Suetonius was correct about Aufidius Lurco but wrong about Livia's grandfather.

There actually was a Marcus Aufidius Lurco. He was a senator, a *novus homo* originally from Fundi. There he owned a farm on which he raised peacocks for human consumption. This enterprise may have given rise to his *cognomen* of Lurco which means gourmand.

As plebian tribune at Rome in 61 BCE, Marcus Aufidius Lurco proposed a bill to curb rampant bribery of voters by candidates seeking election to the various magistracies. The Senate defeated the measure which Cicero ridiculed, revealing in the course of his diatribe that Lurco was a cripple. Two years later Cicero called Lurco an "excellent man, my close friend."[3] The comment is most likely facetious. Lurco had testified against Lucius Valerius Flaccus whom Cicero was defending (successfully, it turned out) before the Senate. Flaccus was on trial for allegedly having committed extortion while serving as governor of Asia. Lurco had business interests (the importation of peacocks?) in this province.

Although an intriguing character, Marcus Aufidius Lurco could hardly have been Livia's maternal grandfather. The empress was extremely uncomfortable around her physically disabled grandson Claudius. Such behavior seems anomalous for someone whose grandfather was similarly handicapped. Even if Livia had never actually met her mother's father (for instance, had he died during her infancy), one should think familial stories about him and his condition had prepared her better to accept Claudius.

Furthermore, every extant inscription honoring Livia's mother utilizes the spelling Alfidia—not Aufidia. The *cognomen* Lurco is nowhere connected with this orthography. The Marcus Alfidius who prosecuted Sextus Coelius had no *cognomen*. The imperial legate of Sicily for 4 CE bore the surname Sabinus.

This differentiation led one scholar to propose Alfidia hailed from Marruvium rather than Fundi. An inscription at this site, dating from the reign of Claudius, posthumously honors both of Livia's parents. Alfidia's *gentilicum* is similar in spelling to those of the Alfeni and the Alfii, who do appear at Marruvium. The plebian tribune Drusus had patronized Marruvium as the center of operations for the Italian enfranchisement movement and subsequently for the Social War. By marrying the daughter of a non-Roman Italian newly enfranchised, Claudianus well would have vindicated his adoptive father's efforts on the allies' behalf.

The preponderance of evidence nevertheless favors Fundi over Marruvium as Alfidia's birthplace. Inscriptions confirm the presence of Alfidii in Fundi. Suetonius cites a legend which claimed Tiberius was born there. The author attributes this specious tradition to two particulars: Tiberius' maternal grandmother (i.e., Alfidia) was a native of the town; and the Roman Senate had ordered erection of a statue of *Felicitas* (prosperity) therein. This goddess was an Augustan principle. Its commission by the central government indicates the imperial family had a special regard for Fundi. The Marruvine inscription, on the other hand, was ordered by the local authorities and is formulaic. Similar captions were discovered on the Greek island of Samos and at the town of Tucci in Spain.

The Aufidii (note the spelling) may have been Samnites. Their *gentilicum* seems to derive from the river Aufidus (the modern Ofanto), in the Samnite-dominated region of Apulia (modern Puglia). There was a town called Aufidena, on the western edge of Samnite territory. Today this city is known as Alfidena. Did *Aufidius* corrupt into *Alfidius* and the two clans share a common ancestry?

Marriage to a Samnite would have been grist for Claudianus' political mill. The Samnites were unenfranchised Italians and aggressive combatants in the Social War. Fundi, however, was not a Samnite city. Her founders were an Italian people known as Volsci. Fundi was also one of the allied cities that enjoyed full Roman citizenship. She did not participate in the Social War. Of course this neutrality does not preclude the possibility Samnites resided in Fundi.

The Alfidii and Aufidii were not necessarily related, despite the similarity of their spelling and their coincidence at Fundi. In English the female names Cordelia and Cornelia differ by a single letter. The former is a Celtic epithet meaning jewel of the sea, the latter a patrician Roman *gentilicum* derived from *cornus* the Latin noun for horn. Horace satirized Aufidius Luscus, who was a praetor of Fundi in 37 BCE. The poet depicts Luscus as a pompous inept Poo-Bah incapable even of mixing a proper *mulsum*, the honey-based wine of which the Romans were so fond. Had Luscus been related to Livia, he assuredly would have escaped derision.

The *cognomen* of Publius Alfidius Sabinus tempts one to suppose the Alfidii, like the Claudii, were Sabines. This conclusion is tenuous, because Sabinus was an extremely common Roman *cognomen*. The graffito *Sabinus hic* was the Latin equivalent of *Kilroy was here*. Various *gentes* employed the designation and for various reasons. Publius Alfidius may have had a Sabine mother. He may have been born, owned property, or had patronage interests in Sabine territory—the Apennine highlands northeast of Rome.

We must not overlook the third possibility. Perhaps the Alfidii simply belonged to the Volsci, the indigenous founders of Fundi.

Since we cannot determine Alfidia's ethnic background, we cannot tell whether it impelled Marcus Livius Drusus Claudianus to seek her hand. More likely money and the desire for political advancement brought about the marriage. Marcus Alfidius supplied the wealth, and his son-in-law the necessary connections.

***

Marcus Livius Drusus Libo's combination of names connects him the families of Livia and of Augustus' second wife Scribonia. Precisely how he adhered to either house cannot be determined for sure.

Descendants of Gnaeus Pompeius Magnus did make rather free use of relatives' *cognomines*. His daughter Pompeia Magna married Lucius Cornelius Cinna. Their son called himself Gnaeus Cornelius Cinna Magnus. Lucius Calpurnius Piso Licinianus Frugi (died 69 CE) retained his natal *cognomen* after adoption. He was the natural son of Marcus Licinius Crassus Frugi and Scribonia, the daughter of the aforementioned Lucius Scribonius Libo Drusus.

Because he was consul in 15 BCE, Marcus Livius Drusus Libo could not have been born later than 48 BCE. Many historians assume he was the adopted son of Livia's father, and therefore technically the empress' brother. Ronald Syme proposed the following *stemma*:

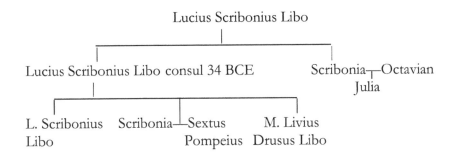

However tempting, Syme's assumption is flawed. The inscription that records Marcus Livius Drusus Libo's consulship refers calls him the son of Lucius. Were he the adoptive son of Livia's father, the inscription would read son of Marcus. There are many potential alternatives to Syme's proposition. Was Drusus Libo Livia's natural brother or half-brother whom a Scribonius adopted? Did Livia have an undocumented sister or half sister who married a Scribonius? Did Claudianus' adoptive father, the plebian tribune of 91 BCE, have a natural daughter who married a Scribonius; or did the tribune adopt two sons, a Scribonius as well as a Claudius?

While we cannot determine *how* Marcus Livius Drusus Libo adhered to the two houses, the fact he did so is made indisputable by his nomenclature.

Sextus Pompeius' daughter Pompeia married her cousin Lucius Scribonius Libo. Augustus' ex-wife was great-aunt to both spouses. The sons of Lucius and Pompeia were respectively called Marcus and Lucius Scribonius Libo Drusus. How and why they acquired the name Drusus is another unknown. Rather significant, however, is that Tiberius conferred upon his son—who was around the same age as the aforementioned sons of Sextus Pompeius' daughter—the *praenomen* Drusus, rather than his own in accordance with time-honored custom. Tiberius produced lavish and expensive games specifically to honor the memory of his maternal grandfather, Marcus Livius Drusus Claudianus. And Tiberius' younger brother Decimus Claudius Nero at some time changed his personal nomenclature to Nero Claudius Drusus. From all this we may infer the Scribonii Libones were in some way related to Livia's father—by blood, marriage, adoption, or a combination of these factors. Moreover the Libones may have been insinuating their respect for the memory and political inclinations of Claudianus exceeded that of his own daughter and grandsons.

The persistent hostility of the Scribonii Libones toward the Nerones must have placed Marcus Livius Drusus Libo in an awkward position. He appears to have remained carefully neutral. The imperial family did not accord him any special honors or promotions. He held a consulship; but so did virtually all other senators.

Complicating matters is the identity of Livia Medullina. She was betrothed to Livia's grandson Claudius, then took ill and died on what was to have been their wedding day. Suetonius indicates she also bore the surname Camilla.

Marcus Furius Camillus (consul 8 CE) adopted a Scribonius who became imperial legate of Dalmatia. Furius Camillus Scribonianus eventually reverted to the antipathy his natal Scribonii held for the Nerones. In 42 CE he led an abortive revolt against Claudius who was now emperor.

Upon this genealogical evidence Syme propounds very plausibly:

Marcus Livius Drusus Libo─┬─Medullina? (the name is my suggestion)

Livia─┬─Marcus Furius Camillus

Furia Camilla Livia Medullina ≈ Tiberius Claudius Drusus

Did Drusus Libo eschew his family's hostility to Livia, and receive in return a marital alliance with the imperial family? Did Camillus adopt a Scribonius to reinforce his connection with his father-in-law's natal *gens*?

The *cognomen* Medullina derives from Medullia (modern Sant' Angelo), a town of Latium lying south of Rome near Lake Alba. Livia

Medullina's name indicates her ancestors were either patrons or residents of Medullia. Nearby is Lanuvium, the town at which the Livii first acquired Roman citizenship in the fourth century BCE. Marcus Livius Drusus Libo was somehow related to Publius Sulpicius Quirinius Cyrenius, who was a native of Lanuvium. Although this information may imply Livia Medullina was related to Marcus Livius Drusus Libo, it does not necessarily signify she descended from him. The Livii Drusi were not the only members of their *gens*. The Augustan historical writer we know as Livy was Titus Livius of Patavia (Padua). Caligula married a Livia Orestilla, whom he divorced after two days. The stepmother of the emperor Galba was Livia Ocellina.

Suetonius does not state Livia Medullina was the daughter of Marcus Furius Camillus the consul of 8 CE, only that Medullina bore the feminine form of Camillus' *cognomen*. She could have been the consul's niece or cousin. Perhaps Camillus—the consul or one of his relations—espoused the daughter of a decurion from Medullia. Another possibility is that Camilla was the name of Livia Medullina's mother. Did the sister of Marcus Furius Camillus wed a decurion named Livius Medullinus?

However she derived it, Livia Medullina could boast a dual pedigree. She was related to the legendary Furii Camilli and was one of the Livii. This heritage explains why our Livia chose Medullina as a bride for Claudius; but it does not confirm Syme's proposed *stemma*. Marcus Livius Drusus Libo and Livia Medullina must both, it appears, remain enigmas.

NOTES TO APPENDIX I

1.   *Tiberius* 3.
2.   *Gaius Caligula* 13.
3.   *Pro Flacco* 87.

APPENDIX II

ISSUES CONCERNING THE IDENTIFICATION OF LIVIA IN AUGUSTAN RELIGIOUS ART

This appendix is ancillary to our chapter on the public symbolism of Livia. Like that chapter the present study is a cursory examination of a very rich topic. Thorough scrutiny of Augustus' use of art to promote the principles of his regime is best left to art historians. My purpose here is to give the reader a sense of Livia's emergence as a religious symbol in the political art of her era.

A PERSONAL TALISMAN?

A tiny *amphoriskos* (beaker) of carved sardonyx, five and one half centimeters in height, depicts the following fable. Venus sits upon a throne. She beckons to Apollo who is holding his lyre, and to his sister Artemis beside him. Hymenaeus the transvestite god of wedding ceremonies also approaches Venus. Cupids the offspring of Venus surround the divinities. The cupids are many because Venus is prolific.

Through her mortal son the Trojan hero Aeneas, Venus was the legendary ancestress of the *gens Julia*. Hence this goddess was the divine advocate of the Caesars' regeneration. Apollo, upon whom Venus gazes approvingly, was Augustus' patron deity. The Roman equivalent of the Greek Artemis was Diana Lucina, the protectress of women in childbirth.

These details raise an intriguing possibility. The little bottle may be a truly private artifact: a personal *memento* of Augustus and Livia, perhaps celebrating their marriage and/or the anticipated birth of a child. The allegory would lend the couple's unorthodox and scandal-ridden nuptials a divine sanction.

The *amphoriskos* is now part of the collection of ancient cameos, in the Hermitage State Museum, Saint Petersburg, Russia.

WHO IS WHO ON THE ALTAR OF PEACE?

The friezes on the *Ara Pacis Augustae* most likely represent the ceremony of consecration to initiate construction of the altar. This observance took place on July 4, 13 BCE.

While some figures in the friezes are easily recognized, most are formidably difficult to identify. The altar is presently in a damaged state. It was repeatedly altered by restoration, in antiquity as well as in modern times. Originally the likenesses were painted to enhance their realism. The portraits were nevertheless idealized. Accustomed to such renderings, Roman viewers would have recognized them with greater ease than those of us who are separated by two millennia. The situation is comparable to that of Americans, distinguishing with less effort than foreigners the presidential likenesses on Mount Rushmore.

The two columns of participants stood either side-by-side or facing one another, on opposite sides of a temporary altar erected for the occasion. Cornerstone-laying ceremonies in modern Italy follow the same patterns.

The first third or so of the altar's south frieze is heavily damaged. We can nevertheless detect Augustus, who is veiled and pouring a libation. Senators, *lictores*, and priests surround him.

The remainder of the south-side frieze is well preserved. A veiled, somewhat elderly man stands behind Augustus. He holds an object now broken; perhaps it was the spiral staff (*lituus*) of an augur. A little boy clasps the hem of the man's toga. The child wears a short tunic, a torque about his neck, and slippers on his feet. He has long hair over which he wears a cap. The boy's costume indicates he is Asiatic, probably a client prince.

The boy looks over his shoulder at a woman. She wears a festal wreath in her hair. Beneath the wreath a diadem is clearly visible upon her forehead. This artifact indicates the woman is a foreign queen. She affectionately rests her right hand on the head of the little prince.

A veiled Roman woman follows the prince and queen. Two toga-clad men follow her. Behind these men a bareheaded woman faces backward. Her hair is gathered at the nape of her neck, in the ponytail style that the women of Augustus' family favored. This woman holds the hand of a very young child, who is crying out of fright at the proceedings. The toddler wears a toga. A *bulla*—the type of locket Roman aristocrats wore in childhood—hangs from the baby's neck. The woman is looking behind her at a man in military dress. Another woman wearing a veil stands in the background between them; only her head is visible. She gazes cheerfully at the soldier and his female companion while holding her index finger to her lips.

A second bareheaded woman stands behind the soldier, and a veiled woman in turn follows her. Beside the veiled woman a young boy holds the soldier's cape. He exchanges mischievous glances with the somewhat older girl who follows him. The veiled woman restrains the boy with her right hand, and the girl with her left elbow. The children resemble each other. Each wears a toga, the traditional costume for young aristocratic girls as well as boys. The boy wears a lozenge-shaped *bulla* similar to the toddler's. The girl's *bulla* is crescent-shaped.

A stooped elderly man stands immediately behind the group of women and children. A middle-aged man follows him, partially obscuring a third, very young man.

The north side depicts three groups of men, veiled or wearing festal wreaths. One man carries a pitcher for the pouring of libations. Others hold boxes containing sacred implements for use in the rites associated with the altar. Since the head of each group holds a *lituus*, the assemblage represents the various colleges of lay priests (*sacerdotes*).

Only fragments remain of the last third of the north-side frieze. A young woman holds her veil against her face. A very young boy precedes her, clinging to the toga of the priest who stands before him. A somewhat older, toga-clad boy follows the woman. A man and woman stand beside the older boy, and a middle-aged woman follows him. Behind this woman a toga-clad man places his hand on the head of a little girl. Still another woman follows the man and girl. Many members of the priestly assemblage are looking over their shoulders, focusing their attention on the group with the women and children. The priests' gaze indicates the familial group consists of significant people.

The women on the north side stand, in that portion of the frieze, which corresponds to the location of the women on the south side. This equivalency suggests the familial groups in both friezes portray Augustus' relatives.

In 13 BCE the imperial family held at least twelve adult women. These included Livia, Augustus' daughter Julia, his sister Octavia, and her four daughters. To this list we must add the emperor's maternal aunt Atia, possibly her daughter Marcia, Tiberius' wife Vipsania, and possibly Augustus' now elderly half-sister (the other Octavia). There was at least two other Vipsanias. The wife of Publius Quinctilius Varus, Tiberius' colleague in the consulship for the year, was also a daughter of Agrippa. Whether she was his offspring by the younger Marcella or by a prior wife is indeterminable. Agrippa and Marcella did have a daughter, who married Quintus Haterius.

Altogether there are five Roman women on the south side and three on the north. The severely ruined condition of the north side may obscure the presence of additional women.

Let us begin with the altar's southern face. This is the more significant wall—the power side, to use a modern euphemism—because it contains the likeness of Augustus.

The veiled augur appears to be Agrippa. Since he had returned from Syria earlier in the year, he may have brought the queen back to Rome with him. Most likely she is Dynamis, Pythodoris, or Salome, since all three were retainers of Livia. While in the East, Agrippa had arranged for Dynamis to marry Polemon King of Pontus. Dynamis conceivably accompanied Agrippa to Rome for finalizing the political arrangements the marriage sealed. The queen on the altar places her hand upon the head of the little Asiatic prince. We do not know whether Dynamis had youthful relatives in Rome at this time. For certain Salome did. Her brother Herod had sent his sons to be educated under Augustus' supervision.

The veiled lady who follows Agrippa must surely be Livia herself. She is the right age, for Livia was forty-five in 13 BCE; and she appears to have Livia's facial features. Furthermore this woman is shorter and heavier than the other women in the scene. Livia in life was diminutive and plump.

Livia's location in the procession underscores her importance to the ceremony. She stands beside the queen and closer to Augustus than any other Roman woman. She also stands frontally facing the viewer, rather than in profile. She is rendered in prominent, high relief which makes her appear somewhat larger than life; and she is directly in the center of the frieze. These nuances foreshadow Livia's eventual association with the completed altar and the principle it represented.

The broad-shouldered man behind Livia appears to be Tiberius, and the soldier his brother Drusus who was military governor of Gaul in 13 BCE. The figures on the altar resemble known portraits of Livia's sons. A consensus among scholars holds that the young woman looking over her shoulder is Drusus' wife, the younger Antonia. The terrified little child who clutches her finger is the right size to be two-year-old Germanicus. There is a nevertheless a significant difficulty with this identification. Roman etiquette demanded married women follow, not precede, their husbands in public. Observe how Livia follows Augustus.

When considered in light of this custom, the woman behind Tiberius could be his wife Vipsania. If the child she is holding is their son Drusus, then he was born in 15 BCE, rather than a year later as historians maintain. The woman is depicted, however, with particular emphasis. Like Livia she stands frontally and in comparatively high relief. This leads me to conclude the backward gazing woman is Julia with a very young Agrippina. The little girl on the north side is the right age to be Julia's namesake daughter who was five in 13 BCE. Her location would have placed her directly beside the backward looking woman during the actual procession.

The young man directly behind Tiberius is a background figure; the prominence of his face is the result of restoration. Beside him stands the woman with her finger on her lips. Her position in the second tier indicates she is of secondary importance; yet she commands sufficient influence to Shht! members of the imperial family. She might well be Augustus' cousin Marcia, and the man her husband Paullus Fabius Maximus. More likely in my opinion—given the proximity of Tiberius—the background woman is his wife Vipsania. Another possibility is Augustus' young aunt Atia.

The two women behind Drusus must be nieces of Augustus: one or both Marcellas or one or both Antonias. The boy is the right age to be Augustus' seven-year-old grandson Gaius. The girl is too old to be either of Julia's daughters. She may be one of Gaius' cousins: Claudia Pulchra the daughter of the younger Marcella and Marcus Valerius Barbatus Appianus; one of the two daughters of the elder Antonia and Domitius Ahenobarbus—Domitia or Domitia Lepida; Appuleia Varilla the granddaughter of Augustus' nephew Sextus Appuleius; Vipsania the subsequent wife of Haterius. This list is entirely conjectural, as we do not know the ages of its members. Whoever the girl is, her parents or grandparents are significant to Augustus.

The decrepit man toward the end of the procession could be Augustus' aging brother-in-law, the elder Sextus Appuleius. Another possibility is the aforementioned Barbatus Appianus. He may have been ailing at the time of the ceremony, since he died early the next year.

Many scholars identify the lead woman on the north frieze as Julia. This woman, whose representation is badly effaced, would have been standing beside Livia in the procession and near but behind Agrippa. The figure, however, is not facing the viewer frontally; nor is she shown in a greater degree of relief than her companions. These characteristics suggest the woman is not Julia but an imperial niece. Conceivably the boy behind her is Augustus' second grandson Lucius, then four and one half years old. In the actual procession he would have been standing beside Livia. Alternatively the boy could be one of Augustus' grandnephews—Lucius Antonius, Gnaeus Domitius Ahenobarbus, or Sextus Appuleius.

The middle-aged woman on the north side, whose frontal stance indicates her importance, very likely seems to be Augustus' sister. Octavia was fifty-three in 13 BCE and therefore the right age to be this figure. We might expect to find her in this location, surrounded by her daughters. Agrippa's sister Polla and Augustus' half-sister Octavia may have been present as well. The women whose likenesses are obscured might be any of the aforementioned.

The identities of the remaining men are equally unclear and the prospects many. They might include Publius Sulpicius Quirinius and Marcus Livius Drusus Libo, both of whom were related to Livia. Sextus Appuleius and the elder Octavia had two sons: Sextus and Marcus. We must also consider Augustus' stepbrother Lucius Marcius Philippus, the husband of Atia and father of Marcia. The emperor's cousins Quintus Pedius and Lucius Pinarius Scarpus present other possibilities. Nor should we exclude Maecenas. Although he was not related by blood or marriage, this particularly close confidant of Augustus may have stood among the members of the imperial family.

As we noted earlier, the deterioration of the north-side frieze has distorted and outrightly obliterated most of the imperial family figures. The little boy who precedes their group is not one of them. He wears a short tunic but no toga, and a neck torque instead of a *bulla*. One interpretation, suggesting the baby is a Gallic princeling, supports the importance of Livia to the altar. We know she was patroness of at least one Gallic chieftain. Alternatively the boy is a Roman plebian. The sacerdotal group preceding the family unit appears to consist of ordinary, non-aristocratic, work-a-day men. Their clothes are shorter and less elegant than those of the senators before them or of the imperial family members who follow.

The identification and interpretative difficulties prompt some scholars to maintain the reliefs are strictly exemplary, illustrating the procedure for the annual sacrifices upon the completed altar. A corporate executive, studying the altar from a layperson's perspective, arrived at the same conclusion. My own spouse proposed that apart from Augustus and Livia, the figures are not meant to be readily identifiable. If the participants are easily recognized the procession represents a particular, chronologically fixed event. Idealized portraits render the pageant timeless, applicable to all ages. The presence of foreign royalty could signify the Augustan Peace extended beyond the borders of the Roman empire. The mingling of patricians with plebeians may imply the peace embraced all Romans without regard to rank or wealth. Idealization would also enable Augustus to evade such prickly questions as *Why is he portrayed standing ahead of me? Why is she in the first tier while I am in the second? Why does her child have better exposure than mine? Do I really look like that?*

THE EMERGENCE OF LIVIA'S CULT

Four freedmen dedicated a small altar, in Rome's *Vicus Sandalarius* (now the Trastevere region), to the *genius* of Augustus and the Lares Compitales. The date is identifiable from the superscription, as the consulship of Augustus and Marcus Plautius Silvanus—2 BCE.

Two men and a woman are depicted in relief on the altar's front face. The man in the center appears to be Augustus. He hands a *lituus* to the man who stands at his right. This figure is generally thought to be Lucius Caesar, whose coming-of-age in 2 BCE included investiture as a pontiff. Remember, Augustus had become *Pontifex Maximus* ten years earlier.

The woman's physiognomy resembles Livia's; but the figure is larger-than-life, barefoot, and wearing a diadem. These are the artistic conventions of a divinity. No Roman would be portrayed with a diadem, the mark of a deity or an eastern monarch. And while gods might be either shod or unshod, mortals were never depicted with bare feet.

The female image is also a hodgepodge of religious iconography. This suggests the devotees either were unsure of the Roman pantheon, or tried to merge several goddesses into one. The torque hanging about the figure's neck is a hallmark of Venus, the legendary progenitress of the Caesars. On her wrist is a bracelet in the form of a snake. This animal was symbolic of Juno as well as of Ceres, the shedding of its skin representing rebirth. Livia was associated with both goddesses. Since venom was a source of medicine, snakes were also sacred to the Bona Dea. Livia restored the temple of this goddess around the time that the altar was erected. The figure holds a *patera* (a small plate used in sacrificial rites) along with a box for incense or medicine. These are accessories both of the Bona Dea and of the goddess Salus (health).

Males should not have erected an image of the Bona Dea who was exclusively a women's goddess. Veneration of *Salus Augusta* did not become official until after 22 CE. Livia's association with Venus cannot be substantiated in western venues prior to the reign of Claudius. This leaves us Ceres and Juno. The imprecise iconography nevertheless keeps us from saying, with certainty, that the figure represents either goddess, much less the specific Juno of Livia.

Official representations of Livia as Ceres did not begin until 2 CE, when the Lugdunum mint began to produce coins depicting her as this deity. Household veneration of Livia's Juno cannot be confirmed before 3 CE. In that year a Roman couple residing near the site of Carthage at what is now El Lehs, Tunisia, inscribed an altar with *Iunoni Liviae Augusti sacrum*—To the Juno of Livia, [wife of] Augustus, sacred.

The uncanny resemblance of *Vicus Sandalarius* image to Livia suggests, however, that some sort of private devotionals to her were emerging in Rome as early as 2 BCE. In the vernacular of my son's generation, the *Vicus Sandalarius* representation is almost Livia but not quite.

The Divinization of Livia in Official Art

Two silver cups, richly decorated in relief, were excavated from the Vesuvian ash near the modern Italian town of Boscoreale. One vessel represents a triumph of Tiberius; the other displays the surrender of the conquered people to Augustus. The cups were comparable in their day to the United States Congressional Medal of Honor. The imperial family or government likely presented them to their owner in recognition of some meritorious service to the state. Today the cups are in the Louvre.

On one side of the Augustus cup the emperor sits upon a *sella curulis*. This was a type of stool on which principal magistrates sat during meetings of the Senate. Although Augustus holds an orb symbolizing Roman dominance of the world, he is toga-clad in the fashion of a magistrate. A goddess standing to his right presents him with a statue of Victory. The naked little Cupid who accompanies the presenter identifies her as Venus. A young man follows, holding a cornucopia. He represents the *genius* of the Roman people. The goddess Roma, in her usual military attire, stands behind the *genius*. At Augustus' left the war god Mars heads a procession of figures who represent the provinces of the empire.

Venus was the divine ancestress of the *gens Julia*. When Augustus designated Tiberius and Germanicus as his successors in 4 CE, Livia became the ancestress of the new dynasty. Some scholars consequently identify the triumph as Tiberius' second (12 CE), and the Venus of the cup as Livia. No extant epigraphic or numismatic evidence confirms, however, that Augustus associated Livia with Venus in Rome or western provinces. Nor is there any telltale indication on the cup itself, of a connection between the Venus figure and Livia.

Like the Boscoreale cups, the *Gemma Augustea* may have been a special gift to a potentate or distinguished citizen. This immense carved sardonyx (9 inches or 22.86 centimeters square and now in Vienna's Kunsthistorisches Museum) also represents a triumph of Tiberius. In the center of the scene, Augustus sits upon a high-backed bench. Beneath him stands an eagle, symbolizing Roman power. Augustus is dressed as Jupiter—naked to the waist with a mantle draped about his hips. The emperor has not been deified; his attire represents the veneration of his *genius*. He holds a *lituus* in his right hand a scepter in his left. His sandaled feet rest on a shield. The goddess Roma, wearing a helmet and quiver and holding a javelin, sits at the emperor's right. Between their heads hangs a medallion which may represent the moon. It is embossed with the sea-goat Capricorn—Augustus' lunar birth sign or (less likely) the sign of his conception.

Tellus Mater (Mother Earth) reclines to Augustus' left, holding a cornucopia. A bearded god stands behind the Tellus Mater. He signifies a body of water—the Mediterranean Sea perhaps or the River Tiber. A veiled female figure stands behind the water-god. Her crown—the *corona muralis* representing the walls of a city—distinguishes her as Cybele. She holds a wreath of laurel branches above Augustus' head. This is the *corona triumphalis*, the emblem of a victorious general.

A young man in armor stands to the right of the goddess Roma. If the cameo represents Tiberius' triumph of 7 BCE, the youth is Augustus' grandson Gaius. If Tiberius' triumph of 12 CE is intended, the young man is Germanicus. Behind the youth are the horses that draw the triumphal chariot. Tiberius—toga-clad, laurel-crowned, and holding a scepter—descends from the car. The goddess *Victoria* (Victory), bareheaded and winged, stands in the chariot behind Tiberius. She holds a whip and the horses' reins.

The cameo's exergue depicts Roman legionaries erecting a commemorative trophy and taking enemy hostages.

Once again we are hard-pressed to equate any of the female figures with Livia. Easterners venerated Livia in conjunction with *Roma* but not *as* this goddess. Livia's association with Cybele cannot be confirmed before the reign of Tiberius.

Since the *Grande Camée de France* depicts the apotheosis of Germanicus, it represents the imperial family as of 19 CE or later. This date helps us to identify the portraits: we know for whom to look.

The Ceres figure enthroned in the middle of the cameo has Livia's physiognomy. She bears a strong resemblance to Tiberius, who sits beside her in Jovian garb. The emperor extends a scepter, aegis, and *lituus* to a young military officer. A middle-aged woman wearing a laurel wreath stands between them. A younger woman, bareheaded and somewhat diminutive, stands behind the commander. She clasps a stripling boy about the shoulders. The boy is dressed in a military uniform.

Perhaps Tiberius is investing Germanicus with the authority for the latter's junket to the East. If so the year is 17 CE, and the boy likely Germanicus' eldest son Nero who was then eleven. Alternatively: the cameo dates from 21 CE and represents Nero's coming of age. Tiberius is commending the legacy of the deceased Germanicus' achievements. The younger boy would be one of Nero's brothers—Drusus or Caligula. Remember the latter's nickname derived from the fact he wore a legionary's uniform in childhood.

In either scenario the woman who holds the boy must be the elder Agrippina, who in life was short of stature. The older woman is surely Germanicus' mother Antonia.

Behind Livia a young woman and a military officer gaze upward at Germanicus, as he rides the winged horse of ascension into Heaven. The man is probably Tiberius' son Drusus with whom Germanicus enjoyed a close camaraderie. The woman would be Livilla, Germanicus' sister and Drusus' wife.

At the top of the cameo a seated, toga-clad, and diademed divine

Augustus welcomes Germanicus. The military commander on Augustus' right must be Germanicus' father, the elder Drusus. The little boy leading the winged horse could be the son of Germanicus who died in infancy. The man in Phrygian dress reclining beneath Augustus might be the legendary Trojan hero Aeneas or his son Iullus Ascanius. The *gens Julia* purportedly descended from Aeneas and his divine mother Venus through Ascanius. In his prone position he is extended above the earth. This suggests the implication that though the sons of Germanicus the Julian house will rule the world.

The cameo's formulaic exergue depicts Roman soldiers taking enemy captives.

This brief examination suggests that despite the emergence of some private devotionals, the Romans were generally reluctant to accept divine attributes for Livia prior to 14 CE. Responding to public opinion, the government art of Augustus obscures or omits Livia from deific pieces intended for Roman viewers.

By the time Augustus died, Roman attitudes toward the divinization of Livia had softened. As a result, Livia's role in religious affairs broadened during the reign of Tiberius. She became *genetrix orbis* in western provinces and priestess of the deified Augustus at Rome.

The *Grande Camée* reflects the evolution of Livia's religious visibility. She is easily recognizable, and associated with a deity. The same characteristics hold true for the Tiberian cameo, which portrays Livia as a Ceres/Cybele hybrid.

Imperial coinage reflects a similar trend. Under Augustus, coins that associated Livia with Ceres or Pax were restricted to Gaul. In 16 CE the Gallic issue was enlarged to include a *Pietas* series. After 22 CE the Senate-controlled mint in Rome began to circulate coins that represented Livia as *Pietas, Iustitia*, and *Salus Augusta*.

APPENDIX III

SOME EXPLICATORY COMMENTS

My computer password for this appendix was, very descriptively, Loose Ends. This section examines issues that are historically significant, but too digressive and distracting for the general narrative.

THE YEAR OF LIVIA'S BIRTH (CHAPTER I)

One narrow possibility could place Livia's birth in 59 rather than 58 BCE. Tacitus records her death as the first significant event of 29 CE:

> Rubellius and Fufius being consuls, of whom both the *cognomen* was Geminus, Julia Augusta met death at extreme age...[1]

After describing events of 28 CE. Dio Cassius writes:

> At this same time Livia died, having lived six and eighty years...[2]

Dio's words imply Livia had passed her eighty-sixth birthday. She had completed eighty-six years of life and hence was in her eight-seventh year. Remember, a person's numeric age reflects the number of years he or she has already lived. We do not say a baby is one year of age at birth, but after the first year of life has elapsed and the child has entered upon the second.

Livia's birthday was January 30. If she died after that date in 29 CE she would have already turned eighty-six. This would indicate she was born in 58 BCE. But if she died in between January 1 and January 30 of 29 CE, she would have been on the cusp of her eighty-seventh birthday. Her birth would have taken place in 59 BCE.

How do we figure?

Let us presume Livia died after January 30, 29 CE. She had already passed her eighty-sixth birthday:

Year of Birth:	58 BCE
+ Year of Death:	29 CE
--	1 compensation for the lack of the year zero
Result:	86

Now let us consider the alternative. Livia died before her 29 CE birthday. She had turned eighty-six on January 30 of the year preceding:

Year of Birth:	59 BCE
+ Year of last birthday	28 CE
--	1 (no year zero)
Result:	86

The Greeks and Romans did not understand the concept of zero as a number. In a temporal sequence such as a succession of days or years, they numbered the present unit as one. We see this precept in Christian theology. Jesus' crucifixion took place on a Friday, his resurrection on a Sunday. Why, then, do the gospels maintain Jesus rose from death on the third day? Because Friday was counted as day one.

Our present Christianity-based system of counting years was

developed in the sixth century. At that time, Europeans still did not know numeric zero. The Moors who overran Spain in the seventh century introduced algebraic calculations with numeric zero and negative numbers.

Lack of numeric zero is the reason we go directly from 1 BCE to 1 CE. The missing zeroeth year must be taken into account when one calculates an interval of years that spans the dateline. You add the BCE and CE dates, then subtract 1 to compensate for the loss of year zero. Think through the logic. A child born in 1 BCE reached his first birthday—not his second—in the following year: 1 CE.

Another illustration can be found in the life dates of Augustus. Suetonius writes that Augustus died a month before his seventy-sixth birthday. We know the emperor was born in 63 BCE and died in 14 CE. Hence we calculate:

$$
\begin{array}{rl}
\text{Year of Birth:} & 63 \text{ BCE} \\
+ \text{ Year of Death:} & 14 \text{ CE} \\
-- & 1 \\
\hline
\text{Result:} & 76
\end{array}
$$

Augustus died on August 19, 14 CE. He would have turned seventy-six on September 23 of that year.

Modern misunderstanding of the missing year zero still prompts millions to presume the third millennium began with the year 2000 rather than 2001.

WHAT ARE THE INFAMOUS IDES OF MARCH?
A DIGRESSION ON THE ROMAN CALENDAR
(CHAPTER I)

The original Roman calendar had twelve months, based upon the phases of the moon. At the beginning of each lunar cycle an augur sighted and announced the new moon. The day of this observation became known as the *Calendae*—Calends—from the Latin verb *calere*—to call or proclaim. From these roots comes our modern English word calendar.

The halfway point of the cycle was marked, of course, by the full moon. The day thereof was called the *Idus*, which we translate as Ides. This word arose from the archaic Latin word *id*, as did *viduus*—separated—and *dividere*—to divide. The Ides, then, was the divisor of the month. *Nonae*—Nones—comes from *novem*, the Latin word for nine. The Nones fell nine days before the Ides.

The Romans reckoned days by counting backwards from one of these benchmarks. An inscription documents Livia's birthday of January 30 as three days before the Calends of February. Remember there was no allowance for zero: February 1 was the first day, January 31 the second, January 30 the third. Suetonius records Augustus' birthday as nine days before the Calends of October. Counting backwards with October 1 as the first day, we arrive at September 23.

The calendar was standardized in 450 BCE, with a year of 355 days. March, May, July, and October each had thirty-one days. All the other months had twenty-nine days, except for February which had twenty-eight. February was shortened because it was the final month: the Roman year began on March 1. The emphasis on odd numbers comes from a very ancient and pervasive superstition which persists to our present day. Even numbers are viewed as unlucky because they can be divided into equal portions. The reference points were also regulated. The Calends remained the first day of each month. In each of the eight shorter months the Nones became the fifth day and the Ides the thirteenth day. In the longer months of March, May, July, and October, the Nones were the seventh and the Ides the fifteenth day. Why were these particular months elongated? Because in an agrarian society, it made most sense to lengthen months that fell during the growing season.

Since the calendar was lunar, it periodically had to be realigned with the solar year. The college of pontiffs accomplished this task by means of occasional and arbitrary insertion of intercalendary months. The process provided a means of manipulating time-sensitive political issues. An intercalendary month could delay an election or rotation of magistrates, or prolong a current term of office.

When Julius Caesar brought Cleopatra and her court to Rome in

46 BCE, the Egyptian entourage included the Alexandrian astronomer Sosigenes. At the behest of Caesar, Sosigenes and his staff set about to reform the Roman calendar. They added ten and one quarter days to the year by lengthening the twenty-nine-day months, some to thirty days and others to thirty-one, and February to twenty-nine days with an extra intercalendary day every four years.

The rationale behind enhancing January and December to thirty-one days is not known. January 1 was the date on which the newly elected magistrates assumed their positions; so the addition of extra days to their first month of office may have helped ease the transition of government. Since the lengthy and festive rites of the *Saturnalia* (December 17 – 26) tended to interrupt normal activities in December, elongation of this month allowed for more regular business to be transacted therein. When the month of Sextilis was renamed for Augustus, it was lengthened to thirty-one days at February's expense. The dates of the Calends, Nones, and Ides were not altered. And so the date Caesar's assassins set for their attack was March 15—the Ides of March.

The new calendar was put into operation, when the magistracies rotated on January 1, 45 BCE. With minor changes implemented in 1582 on a directive from Pope Gregory XIII, the calendar of Sosigenes is the one we use today. When Great Britain adopted it in 1752, she designated January 1—the date on which the calendar was originally implemented—as New Year's Day. The United Nations approved this version as the World Calendar in 1954. The modern names of the months arise from their Roman originals:

January	Ianuarius	from Janus, the Roman god of the passage of years.
February	Februarius	from *februare*—to purify—in reference to a religious rite that was celebrated in the latter half of the month.
March	Martius	from Mars, god of war and father of Romulus, the legendary founder of the city of Rome
April	Aprilis	from *aperire*—to open—in reference to the blossoming of plants

May	Maius	from Maia, the eldest daughter of Atlas, and by Jupiter the mother of Mercury. Maia and her six sisters were the Pleiades. The appearance of this constellation in the dawn sky heralded the start of the sowing season.
June	Junius	from the goddess Juno
July	Julius	from Julius Caesar the Dictator who was born on July 12. The month was originally called Quinctilis from *quinque*—five—because it was the fifth month of the Roman calendar.
August	Augustus	from Caesar Augustus. This month was formerly called Sextilis, from *sex*—six—its place in the Roman year.
September	September	from *septem*—seven—the seventh month
October	October	from *octo*—eight—the eighth month
November	November	from *novem*—nine—the ninth month
December	December	from *decem*—ten—the tenth month

Was *The Banquet of the Twelve Gods* the *cena nuptialis* of Octavian and Livia? (Chapter I)

Efforts of scholars to equate *The Banquet of the Twelve Gods* with the marriage feast (*cena nuptialis*) of Octavian and Livia raise an intriguing but inconclusive possibility. Suetonius does not provide us with a precise date. He only indicates the affair took place during a time of food shortage, and before 32 BCE when Mark Antony used it as propaganda against Octavian. Suetonius writes:

> There was also his (Octavian's) banquet, more secret in gossip, called "Twelve Gods" by the common folk; not only do the letters of Antony, spitefully enumerating individuals by name, reproach the guests for reclining at

table in the dress of gods and goddesses, and he (again, Octavian) himself adorned as Apollo; but also these well-known, anonymous verses:

> After the table of those people secured a *choragus*,
> Six gods Mallia saw and six goddesses,
> While with mendacious impiety Caesar plays Phoebus,
> While he dines amid new adulteries of gods:
> All divine presences then from earth turned away,
> And Jupiter himself fled his golden throne.[3]

In its pristine sense the Greek term χοράγος—*choragos*—implies the leader of a group. At Roman banquets the *choragos* was the leader of the feast, chosen from among the guests by the casting of dice. The principal responsibilities of this individual were to regulate the amount of water was mixed with the wine, and the quantity of drink each person consumed.

Mallia may be a euphemism for the *choragos*. Identification of the Mallia as Livia is unequivocally wrong: the leader of a feast could never be a woman so long as men were present. Attempts to equate the Mallia with Livia's first husband are tenuous. If Tiberius Claudius Nero were present, he stood as much chance of being chosen *choragos* as any other participant. With the exception of Octavian, however, we do not know the identity of any guest. It is also possible Mallia is merely a place name: the designation of a villa or a section of Rome at which the banquet was held.

The ditty deplores *new adulteries of gods*. What were the prior adulteries that rendered the present ones new? If the anonymous poet had legendary tales of divine infidelity in mind, then the new adulteries could mean the scandalous circumstances under which Octavian espoused Livia. On the other hand, if the Caesars' nuptials were the reference point, then the new adulteries represented some subsequent celebration.

The Latin word *adulterium*—like its English cognate adultery—can imply a type of corruption apart from marital infidelity. Criticism of

Octavian's banquet focused more upon waste than on sexual misconduct. Suetonius continues:

> The very great lack and hunger in the city indeed increased the rumors of this dinner; and it was cried out the next day, that the gods had altogether eaten the grain, and Caesar was plainly Apollo, but The Torturer, a *cognomen* by which that god in a certain part of the city was reverenced.[4]

Clad in the sea-green robes of Neptune, Sextus Pompeius sacrificed horses to flaunt his pirates' rout of Octavian's fleet in 38 BCE. For **The Banquet of the Twelve Gods**, Octavian dressed as his own patron deity Apollo. The affair conceivably feted Octavian's conquest of Sextus in 36 BCE. Augustus was never a wasteful man. Moreover he had too much political acumen to elicit criticism from his opponents by squandering food during a famine. Generous portions at the banquet could have celebrated the removal of Sextus' embargo on grain imports, and the anticipated end of shortages at Rome.

WHO MARRIED PYTHODOROS OF TRALLES? (CHAPTER I)

An inscription from Smyrna (now Izmir, Turkey) gives the name of Pythodoros' wife as Antonia:

> The people to Zeno, of mother-loving Queen Pythodoris and King Polemon the son, grandchild of the beneficent Antonia, have extended honor.[5]

The daughter of Pythodoros and Antonia married Polemon, the client king of Pontus. The marriage produced two sons and a daughter. Germanicus installed the younger son—the aforementioned Zeno—as king of Armenia in 19 CE. Antonia Tryphaena the daughter of Pythodoris and Polemon married Cotys, the client king of Thrace. They sent their children—Phoemetalces, Cotys, and Polemon—to Rome. There another

Antonia the widow of Drusus reared the children in the company of her grandson Caligula.

Theodor Mommsen, the great German historian of Roman provincial affairs, concluded the Antonia of the inscription was Mark Antony's eldest known child, born about 52 BCE. At the inception of the Triumvirate, Antony betrothed this daughter to the son of his Triumviral colleague, Marcus Aemilius Lepidus. The troth was broken in 36 BCE, when Octavian expelled Lepidus from the Triumvirate and remanded him to exile.

Six decades later a different authority challenged Mommsen's view. The American Glen Bowersock, specialist in the relations of Augustus with the Greek East, maintains Pythodoros' Antonia was the daughter of a local dignitary, who like Pythodoros himself was Antony's client. It was customary for Greek or Hellenized retainers to demonstrate their loyalty by naming their children after their patrons. A well-known example is the Judaean king Herod Agrippa II, to whom Saint Paul appealed for justice. King Agrippa, of course, was named for Augustus' son-in-law. Paul's Gentile name—Paullus in Latin—implies his own family of tentmakers from Tarsus had a Roman patron.

Both interpretations regarding Pythodoros' wife are plausible. By the time his daughter's betrothal to the younger Lepidus was terminated, Antony considered himself the legal husband of Cleopatra. In 32 BCE he would maintain he had espoused the Egyptian client queen nine years earlier. It is entirely conceivable, that Antony gave his own daughter in marriage to Pythodoros between 36 and 32 BCE. The match could have been the introduction of a political strategy, of solidifying Rome's alliances with vassal powers through marriages between Romans and client nationals. The entry of Antony's daughter into such a union would have enabled him to test Roman and client opinion about this plan, especially before he announced that he had formalized his own liaison with a foreign monarch.

However tempting, the aforementioned idea is purely speculative. No source reveals what became of Antony's early daughter after her separation from Lepidus. For all we know, Pythodoros merely married the daughter of a local magnate with whom Antony or one of his relatives had formed a client relationship. The inscription does not really permit us to extrapolate anything more about this Antonia's background.

TIBERIUS' GAMES
(CHAPTER II)

Suetonius dates Tiberius' presentation of gladiatorial competitions in honor of his father and maternal grandfather between Tiberius' assumption of the toga of manhood and his accession as emperor in 14 CE. This interval spans some forty years! Suetonius then compounds the imprecision by stating the productions took place at different times and in different locations. He provides the venues for some shows: that for Tiberius Nero was held in the Forum, the one for Claudianus in the amphitheater. Still, Suetonius never tells us precisely when the games occurred. He also maintains Tiberius mounted stage plays, but does not indicate either where or when.

Suetonius avers Augustus and Livia underwrote Tiberius' productions at great expense to themselves. Prominent Roman families customarily presented their own privately financed spectacles, to commemorate personal milestones such as comings of age.

For several reasons I suspect Tiberius mounted at least some of these exhibitions during his aedileship in 22 BCE.

Marcellus as aedile had endeared himself to the public by presenting elaborate performances. Tiberius may have deliberately followed a proven successful pattern.

Tiberius' aedileship immediately followed the 23 BCE attempt, by Terentius Varro and Fannius Caepio, to take Augustus' life. Tiberius' successful prosecution of Caepio was certainly reason for celebration. Furthermore the conspiracy gave Augustus motive for advertising the armistice he had made with his opponents. These had included Tiberius' father and grandfather.

A Roman youth usually assumed the *toga virilis* on his fifteenth birthday. Augustus adhered to this age for his grandsons Gaius and Lucius. Tiberius, however, was not physically present in Rome to present spectacles when he turned fifteen on November 16 of 27 BCE. He was on military maneuvers in Gaul until later in 25 or early in 24 BCE. Under Roman custom a young man could wait as late as his nineteenth birthday before he donned the garb of manhood. Caligula did so. And when Tiberius turned nineteen in 23 BCE, he was already aedile-elect. Could there have been a coincidence between the coming of age and the assumption of this office?

We do not know when Tiberius espoused Vipsania; but a wedding was surely an occasion for family festivities. The Caesars did not mount strictly private exhibitions. Augustus often blurred the distinctions between his familial celebrations and those of the Roman state. Sometimes he induced the Senate to mandate public commemoration of a personal event—for example the sacrifices that honored his return to Rome from the East in 19 BCE. In turn, Augustus personally financed many state authorized events. Suetonius reports the emperor bankrolled four exhibitions in his own name, but twenty-three in the names of various magistrates. The implication was that the state was the emperor's family and he its guardian.

The Minimum Age Requirements for Praetors and Consuls (Chapter II)

Under the original provisions of the Roman Republic, a man had to be at least in his fortieth year to be praetor, and his forty-third to serve as consul. By the time Tiberius assumed the praetorship for 16 BCE, the age prerequisites for these offices had been reduced by ten years. One could now be praetor at thirty and consul at thirty-three.

We do not know when this change was put into effect. Pompey the Great held the consulship of 70 BCE at the age of thirty-six; but he seized that position by military force. Thirty-eight-year-old Mark Antony's tenure of the consulship for 44 BCE may have been an exception arising from the favoritism of Caesar the Dictator. Octavian assumed his first consulship in August of 43 BCE—a month before his twentieth birthday; but like Pompey before him, he coerced the Senate by threatening to impose martial law.

The consular lists for the decade in which the Second Triumvirate was in power (43 – 33 BCE) contain the names of men who may have been close to Octavian in age. We see the cousin Quintus Pedius as Octavian's consular colleague in 43 BCE; the friend and legal adviser Gaius Asinius Pollio in the consulship for 40 BCE. Livia's cousin Appius Claudius Pulcher, whose son Barbatus Appianus would marry Octavian's niece, held the consulship in 38 BCE; the confidante and eventual turncoat Titus Statilius Taurus was the twenty-five-year-old Agrippa's colleague a year later. Octavian's stepbrother Lucius Marcius Philippus, who married the younger Atia, was consul in 31 BCE.

Conceivably the Second Triumvirate lowered the age minima in the hope, of eliciting support from the aristocracy by making the upper magistracies more readily available to its members. The requirements may also have been relaxed to obscure the fact Octavian was wielding supreme power at so young an age.

Alternatively, Augustus may have lowered the age prerequisites during the early years of the principate. It behooved the newly established *princeps* to encourage the nobility to join the altered political system. He must obfuscate the reality that senatorial oligarchy was no longer in power. Furthermore early access to the regular magistracies maximized the opportunities, for Augustus' chosen successors to gain public exposure as well as firsthand experience in the art of government.

When Was Cyrenius Governor of Syria? (Chapter III)

We know, from epigraphic evidence as well as the writings of Flavius Josephus, that Publius Sulpicius Quirinius Cyrenius served as imperial legate of Syria in 6 CE. In that capacity he executed Augustus' order for the deposition of Herod the Great's son Archelaus. Quirinius Cyrenius converted Archelaus' territories—Idumaea, Judaea, and Samaria—into the Roman province of Judaea. Coponius the newly installed governor, ordered a census of his jurisdiction. Remember, these events occurred in 6 CE.

Saint Luke writes in words repeated every December:

> And it came to pass, in those days, that there went out a
> decree from Caesar Augustus, that all the world should
> be taxed. (And this taxing was first made when Cyrenius
> was governor of Syria).[6]

Luke's word ἀπογραφή—*apography*—which King James' translators rendered taxing, actually implies a census—the recording of one's identity and assets upon which taxes will be levied.

Continuing, Luke maintains everyone was required to register at the city in which his ancestral family originated. A carpenter named Joseph lived in Nazareth, a city of Galilee the northwesternmost province of Herod the Great's client realm. Joseph had to register in Bethlehem some seventy-five miles to the south, because he was descended from the family of the ancient Israelite king David (ca. 1000 BCE). During their sojourn in Bethlehem, Joseph's wife Mary delivered a son. The couple named their baby Jesus.

Augustus ordered an empire-wide census in 8 BCE. In that year the imperial legate of Syria was Gaius Sentius Saturninus.[7] Publius Quinctilius Varus held the Syrian legature from 6 to 4 BCE. Luke's chronology consequently suggests Cyrenius may have been legate of Syria in 7 BCE as well as in 6 CE. Further, the evangelist's account reveals Augustus included Herod's client kingdom in the general census. Certainly a count of client populations stood to insure accurate and effective exaction of tribute.

Coponius ordered the census of 6 CE after Judaea had been made a Roman province. Her inhabitants must henceforth pay Roman rather than Herodian taxes. A reassessment was appropriate, to establish the base upon which the Romans would calculate their levies. Coponius may have applied the census guidelines originally laid down in 8 BCE to his new jurisdiction. Hence some scholars reject the notion of two Syrian legatures for Cyrenius, presuming Luke confused the universal enumeration of 8 BCE with the specialized census of 6 CE. A fellow evangelist seems to confirm Luke's apparent befuddlement.

Saint Matthew maintains Jesus was born prior to the death of Herod in 4 BCE. To escape the king's persecution, Joseph fled with Mary and the infant Jesus into Egypt. Presumably they presumably hid in Alexandria's

Jewish ghetto—the largest and most prosperous of the ancient world. After Herod died, Joseph prepared to return to his homeland. While Luke's account states Joseph and Mary lived in Nazareth *before* Jesus was born, Matthew's indicates the family settled there *after* they left Egypt:

> But when Herod was dead, behold, an angel of the Lord appeareth in a dream to Joseph in Egypt, saying, "Arise, and take the young child and his mother, and go into the land of Israel: for they are dead which sought the young child's life"…But when he heard that Archelaus did reign in Judaea in the room of his father Herod, he was afraid to go thither: notwithstanding, being warned of God in a dream, he turned aside into the parts of Galilee. And he came and dwelt in a city called Nazareth....[8]

Galilee was by now a separate political entity, the tetrarchy of Herod's son Antipas—*that fox*.[9] Nevertheless the Judaean census of 6 CE could have applied to Joseph if he owned property in Judaea.

Saint Luke avers Jesus started to preach in the fifteenth year of Tiberius' reign. This would be 28 CE.[10] Continuing, Luke specifies Jesus was about thirty years old. He certainly could not have been younger; for according to Jewish custom, thirty was the appropriate age for a rabbi to begin his ministry. Here Luke's chronology parallels that of Matthew, who maintains Joseph returned from Egypt after Archelaus was deposed. If Jesus was thirty or older in 28 CE, he could not have been born as late as the implementation of Coponius' census in 6 CE. Moreover the fourth century bishop Eusebius of Caesarea maintains Jesus' crucifixion took place in the reign of Tiberius. This event would have occurred in the reign of Caligula had Jesus been born in 6 CE. Luke was correct after all, in placing Jesus' birth concurrent with the census of 8 BCE. [10]

Ancient texts no longer extant maintained Jesus was born in the twenty-eighth year of Augustus' reign. The medieval monks who developed our present system of dating on review of these records assumed the reference was to the year in which Augustus received his title.

But dating Augustus' sole rule from the end of the Second

Triumvirate (33 BCE) places Jesus' birth in 5 BCE when Varus was legate of Syria. Luke describes Cyrenius with the adjective 'ηγεμονεύοντος—*hygemoneuontos*—governing, ruling, exercising power. Some Bible scholars have accordingly theorized Cyrenius was deputy to Saturninus or Varus or both. Another possibility is that Varus did not finish his term, and Cyrenius stepped in as interim legate. Or Augustus may actually have accorded Cyrenius two, nonconsecutive terms as imperial legate. From Luke's ambiguous testimony we can neither confirm nor deny Cyrenius was governing Syria when Joseph responded to the census decree of 8 BCE. The evidence is simply too vague.

COINAGE CONVERSIONS
(CHAPTER III)

In Rome's earliest days, livestock was the medium of exchange. The Latin words *peculium*—property—and *pecunia*—cash—both derive from the noun *pecus*—beast. Eventually copper ingots replaced actual animals in fiscal transactions. The size of each ingot represented a specific creature; and the likeness of the appropriate beast was stamped on each bar.

In the fifth century BCE a copper coinage was standardized against a twelve-ounce pound, much like our troy measure of today. Coins of gold and silver in imitation of Greek models were added to the currency two centuries later. The value of the Roman gold piece, the *aureus*, was set at 1/40 of a pound of gold. The silver *denarius* which represented a day's wages was 1/25 of an *aureus*. The smaller silver *sestercius* was one fourth of a denarius or 1/100 of an *aureus*. Large sums of money such as inheritances were generally reckoned in *sestercii*.

The second standard remained in effect for the duration of the Republic and most of the Julio-Claudian years. A devaluation under Nero set in motion a dangerous practice, which wrought a devastation inflation upon the economy of the later Roman empire. Diocletian (284 – 305 CE) restandardized the *aureus* at 1/72 of a pound of gold.

Using the Julio-Claudian standard, one can get a sense of Livia's worth in modern American currency from the following formula:

- Determine the present value of a troy pound of gold
- Divide this figure by 40 to obtain the value of the *aureus*
- Divide the aureus figure by 100 to reach the *sestercis*
- Multiply the *sestercis* figure by 50 million, the amount in *sesterces* Livia received in inheritance from Augustus.

Remember to take into account the purchasing power of inflation-ridden modern currencies as inversely proportional to the price of gold. The higher the present value of gold, the larger Livia's inheritance will be numerically but the lower its actual value.

PLUTARCH, TACITUS, AND THE FATE OF MARCIA (CHAPTERS VI AND VIII)

In his version of the Marcia/Maximus suicide story, Plutarch refers to Paullus Fabius Maximus as Fulvius, and to Agrippa Postumus as Postumius. These substitutions should not be attributed to ignorance or careless research on Plutarch's part. The author of the monumental **Parallel Lives** was an accomplished and meticulous historian; but his purpose in writing **On Loquaciousness** was didactic rather than scholarly. Either Plutarch did not care about the precise spellings of the names, or he purposely altered them to create a *bona fide* work of historical fiction. Alternatively the tract is only attributed to Plutarch, and the actual writer was careless or misinformed about the names.

The Roman historical record of Plutarch's time was replete with stories of wives who shared suicide with their husbands. After the Battle of Actium in 31 BCE, a son of the former Triumvir Lepidus tried to organize opposition to Octavian in Rome. After Maecenas suppressed the effort, the younger Lepidus and his wife Servilia Isaurica took their own lives. Ironically, Servilia had been betrothed to Octavian for a time while they were children. Servilia's father was then an ally of Caesar the Dictator.

The consul Gaius Fufius Geminus took his life in 29 CE, after the Senate indicted him for lampooning Tiberius. Fufius' wife Mutilia Prisca joined him in suicide. So, perhaps, did their two daughters. Pomponius

Labeo and his wife Paexea killed themselves in 34 CE, after the Senate found Labeo guilty of mismanaging the governorship of Moesia (Serbia). In that same year Mamercus Aemilius Scaurus, a former ally of Sejanus, was accused of adultery with Livilla and the practice of magical arts. His wife Sextia took her life after persuading him to take his.

Caecina Paetus was a partisan of Furius Camillus Scribonianus, the imperial legate of Dalmatia who rebelled against Claudius in 42 CE. On receiving word that Claudius had sentenced her husband to die, Paetus' wife Arria stabbed herself. She then handed the dagger to her spouse and assured him it did not hurt.

Nero ordered his former tutor and adviser, the younger Seneca, to commit suicide in 65 CE. Like Paetus before him, Seneca was implicated in an abortive plot to overthrow his sovereign. As Seneca prepared to comply, his young wife Pompeia Paulina insisted on joining him. The couple severed the arteries of their arms with a single dagger stroke. Wishing to minimize the bloodshed that followed his suppression of the conspiracy, Nero had Paulina saved. Tacitus writes she survived Seneca by several years, "praiseworthy to her husband's memory and with face and members white in that pallor, which showed the spirit of life to be greatly depleted." [11]

Plutarch ennobles Marcia by having her precede her husband in suicide. Tacitus degrades her as a grieving guilt-stricken widow, whose indiscretion incited treachery within the Caesar family and drove Maximus to self-imposed death. For all we know the entire loquacity incident never occurred at all. It could simply have emerged from rumors, which arose because Paullus Fabius (not Fulvius) Maximus suffered an unexpected death shortly before the demise of Augustus.

THE CHRONOLOGY OF THE ELDER AGRIPPINA'S DISGRACE (CHAPTER VIII)

Tacitus maintains Sejanus did not disclose the open letters, in which Tiberius incriminated Agrippina and her son Nero, until after Livia had died:

...letters sent against Agrippina and Nero, which the public believed had been delivered earlier and suppressed by Augusta, were certainly read openly not long after her death.[12]

Velleius Paterculus and Suetonius appear to contradict Tacitus, and place the disgrace of Agrippina and Nero before Livia's death. Velleius writes:

How much with noble restraint, because it is greatly tormented, [Tiberius'] breast blazed with fire, because by his daughter-in-law, by his grandson, he was driven to grieve, to be offended, to grow red from shame; whose agony of grief a mother, lost to death, increased.[13]

And Suetonius:

[Caligula] accompanied his father's Syrian expedition. Upon returning, first in his mother's, then she having been relegated, in the residence of Livia Augusta his great grandmother he dwelt; whom having died, although yet underage he eulogized from the *rostrum* (the oration platform in the Forum). He transferred to Antonia his grandmother, and in the summer of his nineteenth year was summoned to Capri by Tiberius...[14]

Suetonius also avers Tiberius relegated Agrippina after she tried to elicit popular and military support:

At length, calumniating her with wanting to take refuge, now at the statue of Augustus, then with the army, he relegated her to Pandataria...[15]

Tacitus claims Sejanus' agents accused Agrippina and Nero of engaging in such tactics before Livia died.

The apparent discrepancy between Tacitus and Velleius can be resolved with ease. Velleius does not maintain Agrippina and Nero were prosecuted. As a member of Sejanus' staff, Velleius was privy to and perhaps a participant in the prefect's efforts to discredit Agrippina and her supporters. Sejanus began this smear campaign several years before Livia's death. Velleius reproduces the hostile propaganda about Agrippina and Nero, which Sejanus was disseminating prior to Livia's demise.

Suetonius is harder to call. Was Agrippina sentenced to *relegatio* before Livia's death? After that event was the penalty was harshened to full *exsilium*, with its lifelong banishment and forfeiture of property and citizenship? Apart from its legalistic sense as a criminal penalty, the Latin word *relegatio* can imply a dismissal. Did Tiberius and Livia become exasperated at Agrippina's behavior, and concerned about its rousing effects on the dissident party? Did they endeavor to silence the princess by separating her from her children and confining her to the island?

Neither explanation is satisfactory. If Agrippina was relegated before Livia died—whether privately by her family or by a court of law—why does Tacitus, Agrippina's ardent apologist, neglect to mention this?

Tacitus maintains Tiberius' letters denouncing Agrippina and Nero, were disclosed soon after Livia's death—not soon after her funeral. Suetonius asserts Livia's mourners delayed her obsequies out of hope Tiberius would attend, until the deterioration of the corpse forced them to proceed without him. If we presume Agrippina's children were installed in Livia's dwelling during this interim, we find Suetonius' chronology does not contradict Tacitus' after all. Remember, Antonia resided in Livia's domicile. In this venue, Antonia must have taken custody of her grandchildren.

Antonia Minor and the Exposure of Sejanus (Chapter VIII)

The Jewish chronicler Flavius Josephus attributes the fall of Sejanus to a single letter from Tiberius' sister-in-law Antonia. Her servants contrived to get the message past the praetorian prefect's blockade about Capri and into the emperor's hands:

321

She (i.e., Antonia) was a very great benefactress of Tiberius; for a substantial conspiracy had been formed against him by Sejanus his friend, and a man who had great power since he was commander of the praetorians; and as many of the Senate and freedmen had joined and the army had been bribed, the conspiracy progressed considerably. The effort would have succeeded for Sejanus, had not Antonia exhibited a deed more daring than Sejanus' villainy. For on learning of the plot against Tiberius, she wrote everything to him accurately; and entrusting the letters to Pallas, the most faithful of her servants, she sent to Tiberius at Capri. He, being informed, executed Sejanus and the conspirators; and Antonia, whom he already held noteworthy, he now esteemed and trusted in all matters.[16]

We do not know if Tacitus described such a letter from Antonia. The portion of the **Annales** which covered Tiberius' decision to overthrow Sejanus is not extant. Suetonius says nothing at all about Antonia's correspondence; but a Byzantine epitomist of Dio Cassius does. Describing Caenis, the concubine of Vespasian, the epitomist writes:

After her mistress Antonia, the mother of Claudius, through her (i.e. Caenis) had secretly written to Tiberius about Sejanus, and immediately ordered her to expunge this, so that none of its contents might remain, "Vainly, O mistress," she said, "you command such; for not only all this, but also whatever else you dictate to me, in my mind I forever bear, and in no way is it able to be erased." [17]

Caenis was Antonia's stenographer.

Dio does not attribute Sejanus' downfall to Antonia's letter but to the Roman populace. He maintains Tiberius invested Sejanus, the prefect's son, and Caligula with priesthoods. Tiberius proceeded to compliment

Caligula, and intimate this youngest son of Germanicus might be the next emperor. These accolades immensely pleased the Roman people, who were still partial to Germanicus' memory; and Tiberius noted this response. The emperor subsequently obstructed the prosecution of an enemy of Sejanus, and restricted the conferral of public honors upon the prefect. These measures increased the people's contempt for Sejanus; and Tiberius considered this reaction as well. Now encouraged by the prospect of senatorial and popular approval, Tiberius decided to overthrow Sejanus.

The lack of attention to Antonia's letter in principal sources for Tiberius' reign has prompted modern speculation this *communiqué* was not the critical impetus which drove Tiberius to overthrow Sejanus. The decisive nature of Antonia's letter is dismissed as propaganda, created either by the Julio-Claudians to reverence Antonia, or else by the Flavians (the family of Vespasian).

Why would the Caesars intentionally create a fiction, alleging a reclusive woman had saved the dynasty? A conceit of this nature imputes weakness to the family's men. Why not credit Caligula or Claudius with the destruction of Sejanus? The later Julio-Claudians did have reason to venerate Antonia as a progenitress. She was the grandmother of Caligula, and mother of his successor Claudius, and great-grandmother of Claudius' successor Nero. But allusions of divinity, not swashbuckling, had set the precedents for tributes to ancestresses. We have no attributions of heroism to Livia who was renowned for her demureness. Her godlike honors nevertheless abounded; and Caligula bestowed all of these upon Antonia.

Was the account of Antonia's letter a Flavian, rather than a Julio-Claudian deceit? Did Vespasian and his sons originate the tale to stress the pusillanimity of their predecessors?

Vespasian loved Caenis, who was his mistress until he married Flavia Domitilla. After Flavia died Vespasian resumed his relationship with Caenis, until her own death around 75 CE separated them once again. Suetonius writes that Vespasian treated Caenis as if she were his lawful wife, even after he became emperor. Their union was not legally adulterous, because Caenis was not a freeborn Roman. Nevertheless she and Vespasian could not wed, because Augustus' law forbade marriages between Roman citizens and freedwomen. Like Livia, Caenis interceded with the emperor on behalf of petitioners and office seekers; but Caenis' motives were far more mercenary than Livia's. Dio maintains Caenis amassed a fortune by selling magistracies, governorships, military commands, priesthoods, and sentences. Did Vespasian endeavor to justify his personal relationship with Caenis, and/or obfuscate her venality by involving her in a tale of heroism?

None of these conclusions is satisfactory either. The outcome of the letter story places Tiberius in a sympathetic light, because it reveals him the innocent victim of a vile deception. Dio's version makes Caenis—Vespasian's beloved intimate—the savior of the unpopular Tiberius and the reprobate Caligula.

Antonia's letter may have received more attention in the Roman historical record than we are able to ascertain. Tacitus' account of the incident is lost. Dio's coverage of Tiberius' relationship with Sejanus is vague and fragmentarily interspersed with Byzantine glosses. Even sketchier is Suetonius' treatment, which serves another purpose. This author represents Tiberius as merciless and sadistic toward everyone—including his family:

> He loved with a father's affection for sons neither the natural Drusus nor the adoptive Germanicus...He strengthened the suspicion [that he had instructed Piso to poison Germanicus], by later afflicting the spouse and also the children of Germanicus in a cruel manner.[18]

Tacitus and Dio alike insist—and quite clearly—that Sejanus tricked Tiberius into believing Agrippina and her sons were plotting against him. Suetonius on the other hand pictures Tiberius as falsely accusing Agrippina, and provoking her sons Nero and Drusus to berating him so he might accuse them as well:

> Indeed, since once during dinner she would not dare taste an apple he offered her, he consequently ceased to invite her, feigning he had been charged with the crime of poisoning her; whereas the whole matter was

prearranged by plan, that he for the purpose of tempting should make the offer, and she should avoid as it were a most certain death. Having charged her anew with wanting to take refuge, now at the statue of Augustus and then with the army, he relegated her to Pandataria... Deprived by death of [his own] children, he commended the elder sons born to Germanicus, Nero and Drusus, to the conscript fathers (i.e., the Senate), and celebrated the day that each entered public life with a gift to the people. But after he learned that, at the beginning of the year, prayers for their wellbeing were offered in public, he importuned the Senate, that this type of honors should not be bestowed except upon those [who were] proven and of mature years. And thereafter, having made plain his inner spirit, he pronounced them guilty of all sorts of crimes; and after they were induced by erratic trickery, so that they may be incited to revile and driven to rebel, he brought accusation in writing most bitterly of collective misdeeds; and after [the princes] were adjudged [public] enemies he killed [them] by hunger, Nero in the island Pontia, Drusus in an lower part of the palace.[19]

Continuing, Suetonius maintains Tiberius promoted Sejanus,

> ...whom he advanced to highest power not indeed out of benevolence, but that through his assistance and deceptions he (Tiberius) might cheat the children of Germanicus, and confirm his grandson through his natural son Drusus to the succession of the empire.[20]

Some paragraphs later Suetonius claims Tiberius

> ...dared to write that he punished Sejanus, because he discovered him plotting against the children of Germanicus his son; whereas he himself slew the one

[grandson] upon suspecting, the other after destroying, Sejanus.[21]

As for the prefect's *débâcle*, Suetonius states simply "Sejanus plotted revolution." The author sneeringly concludes Tiberius "just barely, and by an enchanter's cleverness and fraud rather than by the authority of the principate, overcame him." [22]

Given this portrayal of Tiberius, Suetonius' omission of Antonia's letter is no surprise. The author does not want to admit Tiberius, ignorant or misinformed of Sejanus' intentions, took remedial action upon being apprized of them. Suetonius insists on attributing Tiberius' mistreatment of Germanicus' progeny, as well as Sejanus' eventual downfall, to the emperor's own malevolence.

The fate of Germanicus' family is sometimes cited as reason to diminish the effect of Antonia's letter or reject its existence altogether. If Antonia awakened Tiberius to Sejanus' intentions, why did the emperor persecute Antonia's daughter-in-law and two elder grandsons, and eventually let them perish in prison? Again we must look carefully at our source material. Tiberius was not so wantonly malicious as Suetonius wishes us to believe.

In a passage we quoted above, Suetonius states Tiberius starved Antonia's oldest grandson Nero to death. But the author subsequently maintains Nero's demise was self-inflicted: that the youth was frightened into suicide by the prospect of death by execution. Suetonius' chronology for Nero's death—coincidental with the arousal of Tiberius' suspicions about Sejanus—suggests the young prince took his life before the emperor was able to intervene. Dio Cassius confirms this timing. He writes that Tiberius delivered a letter to a Senate about the death of Nero, just when the emperor was beginning to become ambivalent toward Sejanus.

According to Suetonius and Dio Cassius alike, Tiberius feared his denunciation of Sejanus might precipitate military opposition from the prefect and his followers. The emperor left orders mandating that should such an uprising occur, Germanicus' second son Drusus must be removed from his palace cell and placed in command of the defending imperial forces. Tacitus reveals a subsequent investigation proved Drusus had agreed to cooperate with Sejanus in the destruction of Nero. For this reason Tiberius left the potential fratricide to die of starvation in his dungeon. Antonia may have approved. She purportedly starved her daughter Livilla to death for adultery with Sejanus and complicity in the murder of Tiberius' son.

Suetonius blames Tiberius for atrocities Agrippina suffered during her incarceration on Pandataria. She was transported in fetters. After she verbally execrated Tiberius, a centurion destroyed one of her eyes. But was this brutality perpetrated by Sejanus' agents and kept from Tiberius' knowledge? Furthermore, Agrippina was undeniably guilty of treason. Persistently alleging Tiberius intended to destroy her and her children, Agrippina committed the capital crime of vilifying the emperor. The severities she endured were considered appropriate for such a felon.

There is also evidence to suggest Tiberius tried to minimize the gravity of Agrippina's offense. The prescribed penalties for treason were death or *exsilium*—lifelong banishment and forfeiture of property and citizenship. In two passages, Suetonius clearly states Tiberius relegated Agrippina. Remember, *relegatio* was a milder version of the exile penalty. It entailed removal from Rome for a fixed period of years instead of a lifetime, and retention of legal rights. To keep Agrippina from committing suicide by refusing food, Tiberius had her force-fed. Suetonius represents this intervention as torture; but was that its true intent? Did Tiberius want rather to convince Agrippina her situation was not worth dying for?

After Agrippina eventually managed to end her life by starvation, Tiberius had the Senate add her birthday to the public list of days of ill omen. Was this spite as Suetonius maintains, or an acknowledgement of Agrippina's misfortune? Both Tacitus and Suetonius report Tiberius boasted he had not had Agrippina strangled and dragged down the Gemonian Stairs. The *Scalae Gemoniae* was a set of stone steps that descended the slope of the Aventine Hill to the Tiber. The bodies of executed felons were dragged down the flight on hooks and cast into the river. Tiberius' declaration showed he felt Agrippina did not deserve a criminal's end.

None of this analysis has confirmed Antonia's letter as the specific catalyst which impelled Tiberius into action against Sejanus. Since

Dio Cassius indicates an anti-Sejanus movement was afoot in Rome, Antonia's complaint may not have been the only one Tiberius received. It would nevertheless seem likely a message from Antonia stood the best chance of reaching Tiberius. Sejanus had set a blockade about Capri, to screen correspondence intended for the emperor. Sentries could be persuaded a message from a reclusive relative was devoted to purely domestic issues—the management of estates, for example. A similar claim could not be made for a letter from a senator.

NUMEN AUGUSTUM VS. _NUMEN AUGUSTI_
(CHAPTER IX)

The altar that Tiberius dedicated at Rome on January 17 of an unknown year, was officially called the _Ara Numinis Augusti_. The Latin of this title becomes ambiguous in translation. It could imply either consecrated _numen_ (_numen augustum_) or the _numen_ of [Caesar] Augustus (_numen Augusti_). Fortunately, Ovid unwittingly clarifies this issue by reminding his wife to revere the _numen augustum_. The Roman altar, then, venerated the _numen_ of the imperial office and not that of Augustus' person. The same held true for the altar at Forum Clodii.

The altar at Narbo in Gaul, however, was definitely dedicated to the _numen Augusti_ (my emphasis), and implied the divine essence of _numen_ inhered in Augustus himself. Gaul was a provincial venue, where allusion to the divinity of the emperor's person was more acceptable than in Italy.

THE TRIBUTE OF HONESTUS
(CHAPTER IX)

A valley lying at the foot of Mount Helicon in the Boeotia section of Greece was dedicated in antiquity to the Muses. A statue of a woman bearing title _Augusta_ was erected in the precinct. Only the base of the statue remains; and it bears the following inscription:

> The Augusta, boasting of two sceptered divine Caesars,
> has the double torch of peace illumined. A dance with
> the wise Heliconians (i.e., the Muses) befits her whose
> mind saved the entire world order. From Honestus.[23]

Who was the Augusta and who were the Caesars, to which the inscription refers? What intrepid deed had preserved worldwide stability?

Because it associates the Augusta with the Muses (goddesses of intellect), Honestus' accolade could be a description of Livia. She was renowned for her academic knowledge and her political insightfulness. The Muses were the daughters of Zeus and *Mnemosyne* (memory); and Livia was venerated as this goddess at the Boeotian town of Thespiae. The Caesars of the inscription might be Augustus and Tiberius or Tiberius and Germanicus. The peace may refer to the *Pax Augusta*, with which Augustus had associated Livia. The worthy accomplishment might be some benefaction that Livia provided: for example her contributions in 16 CE to the relief of earthquake victims in Asia Minor.

Biographers of the younger Antonia feel the Augusta was she, and the achievement her awakening of Tiberius to Sejanus' malfeasance. If this be the case, the statue dates from the first two months of Caligula's regime or else from that of Claudius. Antonia did not bear the title of Augusta prior to the reign of Caligula. Upon his accession in March of 37 CE, Caligula bestowed all of Livia's honors upon Antonia because she was his grandmother. She declined the designation of Augusta sometime before she died on May 1 of the following year. When he succeeded Caligula in 41 CE, Claudius restored the title of Augusta to Antonia posthumously.

The identification of the Augusta as Antonia presents, in my opinion, the most plausible interpretation of the dedication. A Greek poet named Honestus was active in imperial circles during the later years of Antonia's life. Claudius issued coins which associated Antonia with a pair of lighted torches. 41 CE, the year of Claudius' accession, marked the tenth anniversary of Sejanus' fall.

If Caligula had the statue erected, the Caesars could be he and his co-heir Tiberius Gemellus—the emperor Tiberius' grandson through his natural son Drusus. If Claudius commissioned the dedication, the Caesars might be he and his brother Germanicus—Antonia's sons.

What if the Honestus who authored the inscription was someone other than the court poet of Antonia's acquaintance? Then the dedication becomes potentially applicable to several other Augustae who were associated with pairs of Caesars. What about the younger Agrippina with Nero and Claudius' son Britannicus?

Under the Julio-Claudians the name Caesar was a family *cognomen*. Subsequent dynasties employed the appellation to indicate an emperor's intended successor. Vespasian's late wife Flavia Domitilla, who received the title of Augusta posthumously, was the mother of two future emperors: Titus and Domitian. Was the tribute dedicated to her? And what of Hadrian's Vibia Sabina? She was associated with two heirs-apparent: Lucius Aelius Verus and Antoninus Pius. Particularly notable for a connection with Caesars and peace was Septimius Severus' Julia Domna. She was an intellectual. When her husband died Domna induced their contentious sons, Caracalla and Geta, to put aside their fraternal feuds and assume the imperial sovereignty.

Lacking a physical portrait of the Augusta we cannot, in the final analysis, ascertain who she actually was. Attempts to extrapolate a firm identity from the recondite accolade inevitably become mired in conjecture.

NOTES TO APPENDIX III

1   *Annales* 5.1.
2   *Romaïka* 58.2.
3   Suetonius, *Divus Augustus* 52.
4   *Ibid.*
5   *IGRR* **1407**=*EE* p. 207.
6   Luke 2:1-2. I use the King James Version of the New Testament for its accuracy, beauty, and familiarity to readers, not to promote or endorse any particular religious persuasion.
7   This man was the father of the Saturninus who was serving as interim legate of Syria at the time of Germanicus' death.
8   Matthew 2.19-23 *passim*.
9   See Luke 13.32. If Jesus uttered this epithet in Aramaic rather than Greek, its meaning more likely signified a jackal.
10 *The Ecclesiastical History of Eusebius Pamphilus, Bishop of Caesarea of Palestine in Ten Books, Translated from the Original by the Rev. C. F. Cruse.* (Philadelphia, 1833), p. 51. Remember, Luke and his contemporary audience did not understand the concept of zero. He counted Tiberius' regnal years with 14 CE as the first.
11 *Annales* 15.54.
12 *Annales* 5.2.
13 *Historia romana* 2.130.
14 *Gaius Caligula* 10.
15 *Tiberius* 53.
16 *Ioudaïke archaiologia* 18.181—183.
17 *Romaïka* 65.14.
18 *Tiberius* 52.
19 *Tiberius* 53, 54 *passim*.
20 *Tiberius* 55.
21 *Tiberius* 61.
22 *Tiberius* 65.
23 *SEG* 13.348.

APPENDIX IV

LIVIAS MEDICINES: THE PHARMACEUTICAL LEGACY OF SCRIBONIUS LARGUS

Scribonius Largus was a personal physician to Livia's grandson, the emperor Claudius. Largus must have been a freedman, as were most palace functionaries; no senatorial Scribonius would practice as a physician. Upon manumission a freed slave assumed the *gentilicum* of his or her former master. A Scribonius had to have been the owner, if not of Largus himself then of one of his progenitors.

Largus accompanied Claudius and the imperial armies to Britain, when the emperor invaded and conquered that island in 43 CE. For five years thereafter Largus devoted himself to the preparation of his **Compositiones medicamentorum—Compounds of Medical Substances**. He arranged this collection, of 271 pharmaceutical formulae according to the parts of the body.

The entries include home produced remedies to which Livia was partial. Largus may have known Livia personally. Since the physician was born around 1 CE, he reached adulthood well before Livia died in 29 CE. Largus could also have discerned Livia's preferences and habits from the written records and oral traditions of Claudius' household.

Largus' work influenced subsequent generations of Roman medical writers. Both Claudius Galen of the second century and Marcellus

Empiricus of the fourth reproduce prescriptions Largus ascribes to Livia and other members of her family.

Please observe the references to lead storage vessels. The Romans did not understand the toxic properties of this metal.

Hopefully the following conversion chart will provide a perspective on the Roman measurements. Like modern pharmacists, Roman apothecaries used balance scales. Coins served as counterweights for small quantities.

denarius	a silver coin, about the size and weight of the American 5-cent nickel piece, approximately 1/4 of an English ounce
victoriatus	a smaller silver coin, half a *denarius*
sextarius	approximately 1 and 1/3 English pints. Like its modern counterpart, the *sextarius* was used for both liquid and dry measurements.
congius	6 liquid *sextarii*
hemina	half a *sextarius*
cyathus	1/12 of a liquid *sextarius*, approximately 1 English liquid ounce
uncia	the Roman ounce
semuncia	half an *uncia*
pondo	the Roman pound: 12 *unciae*. The word *pondo* can also mean weight.
bes	2/3 of a pound, or 8 *unciae*
triens	1/3 of a pound or 1/3 of a *sextarius*, depending upon whether the ingredients were wet or dry
quadrans	1/4 pound, or 3 *unciae*
sextans	1/6 pound, or 2 *unciae*
scripulum	the Roman scruple: 20 grains—288 to a pound or 24 to an *uncia*

Scribonius Largus attributes five of his entries to Livia:

¶ 60 For the most part they employ dentifrice in this way: they pick pellitory when it is already in seed, as much as possible with root; after washing they dry for one day; on the next day they soak in fresh strong brine; on the third day removed, they place it, smashed, in a fresh container, repeatedly with rock salt in layers they intersperse, and so cook in a bath oven until reduced to ash. After it is ground to powder, they mix in spikenard that is sufficient. This is not only that which makes teeth white, but also strengthens them. Augusta always used it.

Marcellus Empiricus, misreading Scribonius' text, mistakenly attributes this dentifrice to Claudius' wife Messallina; cf. **De medicamentis liber** 13.4

¶ 70 This, too, has been beneficial to many, because it is without doubt efficacious and very powerful:

> of costmary, opium, anise, *schoenus* (an aromatic rush with which the Romans often flavored wine) red cassia (a coarse inferior type of cinnamon) each the weight of 2 *denarii*
> of coriander the weight of 1 *denarius*
> of *amomum* (an Indian balsamic shrub) the weight of a single *victoriatus*
> of *besa* which is the seed of wild rue (??; the text is corrupt) the weight of 2 *denarii*
> of crushed alum 1 *semiuncia*
> of oak-apples medium sized the number 5
> of saffron 2 *denarii*
> of saffron scraps the weight of 1 *victoriatus*
> of myrrh the weight of 1 *victoriatus*
> of Greek birthwort (clematis) the weight of 4 *denarii*
> of cinnamon the weight of 3 *denarii*
> of the ash of charred forest swallow chicks the weight of an *uncia*
> of spikenard the weight of 1 *victoriatus*

These whether crushed or sprouted carefully with skimmed Attic honey are all mixed. When it becomes necessary, what should be enough of the same honey is added. This Augusta always had made up.

Marcellus Empiricus clarifies the prescription's purpose: "It indeed works marvelously against quinsy and sore throat," *De medicamentis liber* 15.7.

¶ 175. But among much better plasters this one provides strength, which Augusta hard by for such occurrences kept made up and often applied. We give credit to Trypho our teacher:

of Illyrian iris the weight of 5 *denarii*
of Pontic beaver musk the weight of 5 *denarii*
of the dried sap of a wild fig tree the weight of 5 *denarii*
of the fat of a black bitch the weight of 8 *denarii* (The description
    more likely referred to a breed of dog than mere color)
of her blood the weight of 10 *denarii*
of terebinth resin the weight of 8 *denarii* (The terebinth is a
    Mediterranean tree of the cashew family, from which turpentine
    was originally derived)
of hare's rennet the weight of 4 *denarii*
of ammonium chloride the weight of 2 *denarii*
of Cyrenaican laser the weight of 2 *denarii*, or of Syrian [laser] the
    weight of 4 *denarii* (Laser was a variety of fennel, now extinct,
    favored in the ancient world as a seasoning and a contraceptive.)
of wax of Pontica (modern Isola di Ponza off the Campanian
    coast) the weight of 36 *denarii*
of old oil 2 *cyathi*
of sparkling vinegar 3 *cyathi*

They are dragged dry from the vinegar, (i.e., the vinegar is allowed to evaporate). When they must be liquefied, with the oil by fire melted they are mixed, after having been ground in a mortar and bound in skimmed honey. It is stored in glass.

¶ 268 An anodyne for chilblain, lassitude, as well as pain and tension of the nerves, which applied in winter does not permit any part whatsoever of a limb to chill; this Augusta used. It is made thus:

of marjoram, 1 *sextarius*

of fenugreek, 1 *sextarius*

of rosemary, 1 *sextarius*

of Falernian wine, 1 *congius* (The *Falernus ager*—Falernian field—famous for its wine, was located at the foot of Mount Massicus in Campania.)

of Venafran oil, 5 *sextarii* (Venafrum—modern Venafro—was an ancient Samnite town of Campania, renowned for its splendid olive oil.)

Except for the oil all should in the wine for three days be steeped; on the fourth day the oil mixed in and the medication cooked on a live coal [that is] not intense, until the wine is consumed; thereafter strained through a double linen with the oil still heated, of wax of Pontica 1 *bes* should be added. The medication is stored in an earthenware or lead vessel.

Author's note: I recreated this medication in my own kitchen, substituting commercial cooking wine for the Falernian, extra-virgin Tuscan olive oil for the Venafran, and commercial vegetable shortening for the Pontine wax. All of the ingredients came from the local supermarket except for the fenugreek, which had to be obtained from a spicemonger in Philadelphia. The mixture of the spices with the wine produced a nauseatingly sweet aroma. This was ameliorated to some extent by the addition of the oil and the subsequent cooking process. The concoction nevertheless remained stridently pungent, prompting my family to dub it Livia's Snake Oil, and suggest it might prove an effective deterrent against vermin in our garage. After the liniment was done, I tested it on my own knees. It duly warmed my joints and relaxed some stiffness. Once the unguent had made contact with my skin, its harsh odor dissipated and left a scent akin to that of maple syrup. We stored it unrefrigerated in an aluminum stockpot for about six months. The salve never became rancid or moldy.

¶ 270 An anodyne, which very often Augusta and Antonia used, works on chilblain and all distresses of the nerves; its application does not let limbs become cold, and warms those [already] chilled. It is composed in winter after this fashion:

Take 3 pounds of fat from a sterile young sow, or also the same weight of fat from a goose, then with cold water wash well and in a new vessel add of fragrant old wine (i.e., wine that has become viscous as the result of age—much like modern cooking wine) 1 *congium* or 3 *sextarii*, and these items, not excessively crushed, of this weight:

> of cinnamon wood the weight of a *quadrans*
> of cardamom weight of a *quadrans*
> of sedge weight of a *quadrans*
> of scoenus the weight of a *quadrans*
> of dried rose leaves the weight of an *uncia*
> of *sertulae Campanae* (a type of clover indigenous to Campania)
>   10 crowns

All of these are seethed over coals, then stored chilled in the same cauldron, and on the following day again seethed and laid aside in the same manner; on the third day again reheated and drawn through a linen, or a sieve made for this purpose out of a bulrush. The wine and whatever of the fat remains is placed in a different new vessel; then, when the fat congeals, the bottom of the cauldron must be pierced and the wine drained off altogether; and in the first cauldron the fat again be placed, and the same measure of new wine be added, and these items not greatly crushed nor sifted be poured in:

> of Syrian spikenard the weight of a *sextans*
> of Celtic nard the weight of a *sextans*
> of *amomum* the weight of a *quadrans*
> of cassia the weight of a *quadrans*
> of myrrh the weight of a *triens*
> of cinnamon the weight of a *triens*
> of dried rose leaves the weight of a *sextans*

Then once in early morning, and once at night, this mixture must be seethed; the same must be done the next day. The third day, when all are cooked, they must be strained and transferred to the previously punctured container. But beforehand its opening must be carefully and diligently stopped; and when the fat congeals, the stopper must be extricated and the seal broken, so the wine can flow off altogether. Then when it drains, what remains of the fat is stored in one or more lead vessels well covered and lined.

Author's note: As the mixture cooled it created a vacuum, preventing the wine from draining through the perforations until the stopper was released.

Members of Livia's family in addition to Antonia had favorite prescriptions. Per Scribonius Largus:

¶ 31 This medication works well as Augustus used it:

> of ground alum the weight of 15 *denarii*
> of white frankincense the weight of 10 *denarii*
> of aloe the weight of 15 *denarii*
> of saffron the weight of 15 *denarii*
> of opium the weight of 2 *denarii*
> of oak-apple the weight of 10 *denarii*
> of dry rose leaves the weight of 10 *denarii*
> of plantain the sap or seed, the weight of 10 *denarii*

With Falernian wine these are sprinkled and, after made smooth and bound by skimmed honey; added is a *sextarius* of raisin wine or a *hemina*, and [it is] mixed up afresh. It is stored in a vessel of lead or silver. Marcellus Empiricus indicates the salve was applied to the eyelids, **De medicamentis liber** 8.10.

¶ 59 A dentifrice, which makes teeth splendid. It is made thus: of barley flour 1 *sextarius* must be moistened by vinegar with honey mixed and kneaded a long time, and then divided into six globules; which having been spread out, are mixed with one half *uncia* of rock salt, then cooked by oven until reduced to ash. Then those globules must be rubbed, and mixed with spikenard that would seem satisfactory to create a fragrance; this Octavia, Augustus' sister, used.

¶ 177. An antidote of the doctor Marcian, in which nothing fails; it is called the Grecian ideal; it is perfect. This one works on everything, of all antidotes among the best. It was mixed for Augustus Caesar:

of cinnamon the weight of 8 *denarii*
of *amomus* the weight of 6 *denarii*
of black cassia the weight of 25 *denarii*
of saffron the weight of 26 *denarii*
of *schoenus* the weight of 5 *denarii*
of frankincense the weight of 5 *denarii*
of white pepper the weight of 10 *denarii*
of myrrh the weight of 10 *denarii*
of long pepper the weight of 10 *denarii*
of Indian nard the weight of 10 1/2 *denarii*
of Celtic nard the weight of 16 *denarii*
of dried roses the weight of 6 *denarii*
of white costmary the weight of 2 *denarii*
of balsam sap, the weight of 4 *denarii*
of Cyrenaican laser, the weight of 1 *victoriatus*, or of Syrian [laser]
    the weight of 1 *denarius*
of *storax* (a gum) the weight of 6 *denarii*
of gentian the weight of 5 *denarii*
of the root of pointed trefoil (a type of clover) the weight of 4 *denarii*,
    or of its seed, the weight of 3 *denarii*
of water germander the weight of 12 *denarii*
of polygermander the weight of 5 *denarii*
of hazelwort the weight of 2 *denarii*
of *calamus* the weight of 3 *denarii*
of *phu* (a type of valerian), the weight of 32 *denarii*
of truffle the weight of 2 *denarii*
of the grains of balsam seed the number 20

of parsley the weight of 6 *denarii* and a *victoriatus*

of wild rue the weight of 1/6 *denarii*

of fennel seed the weight of 1/6 *denarii*

of Cretan parsnip the weight of 4 *denarii*

of anise the weight of 2 *denarii*

of Ethiopian cumin the weight of 2 *denarii*

of rape seed the weight of 5 *denarii* and a *victoriatus*

of *navnu* (a wild turnip) the weight of 3 *denarii*

of fresh blood from a female duck the weight of 2 *denarii*

of dried blood from a male duck the weight of 3 *denarii*

of dried blood from a male kid the weight of 3 *denarii*

of dried blood from a sea tortoise the weight of 6 1/2 *denarii*

of Attic honey what suffices.

It works for everything. I myself have this preparation.

APPENDIX V

JUST FOR FUN: WHAT DO THEIR NAMES MEAN?

Our narrative provides the meanings of some of proper names we encountered. Here those are again along with others, for the enlightenment and pleasure of my fellow trivia enthusiasts.

Livius, Livia, Livilla	-	dark blue, indigo
Claudius, Claudia, Clausus	-	lame
Augustus, Augusta	-	holy, consecrated
Tiberius	-	from the Tiber river
Drusus, Drusilla	-	from Drausus, a Gallic enemy whom a Livius defeated in battle
Julius, Julia, Iullus	-	from Iullus Ascanius, son of the Trojan hero Aeneas
Pulcher, Pulchra	-	beautiful
Caesar	-	long or bushy hair
Nero	-	valiant or intrepid, in Sabine dialect
Gaius	-	an ancient Latin name, perhaps meaning law of the earth
Lucius	-	illumination
Marcus	-	hammer

Thurinus	-	from Thurii Copia, more anciently Sybaris, a city on the Gulf of Taranto
Antonius, Antonia	-	from Anton a son of Hercules
Agrippa, Agrippina	-	born feet first
Germanicus	-	German conqueror
Gemellus	-	twin
Quintus, Quinctilius, Quinctilia	-	fifth
Varus, Varilla	-	bowlegged
Sextus	-	sixth
Pompeius, Pompeia, Pompeii Pomponius	-	from Pumpus, an Etruscan *cognomen*
Magnus	-	large, grand
Octavius, Octavia	-	eighth
Scribonius, Scribonia	-	inscribed with a pen
Decimus (the elder Drusus' original *praenomen*)	-	tenth
Cicero	-	chickpea
Balbus (the *cognomen* of Augustus' maternal grandfather)	-	stammering
Appius, Appia	-	from Attus Clausus, the Sabine founder of the *gens Claudia*
Caecus	-	blind
Barbatus (Livia's cousin)	-	bearded
Appuleius, Appuleia	-	from Apulia (modern Puglia), a region of southeastern Italy
Postumus	-	last born
Caligula	-	little combat boot
Domitius, Domitian	-	to dominate or tame

Polla	-	a feminine term of endearment, much like Babe or Dearie in English
Ahenobarbus (the emperor Nero's original *cognomen*)	-	red bearded
Aemilius, Aemilia	-	succoring
Lepidus	-	charming
Caecilius, Caecilia	-	celestial
Servilius, Servilia	-	servile
Terentius, Terentia	-	from Tarentus, the precinct of Rome in which the *Ludi Saeculares* were held
Lurco	-	gourmand
Naso (the *cognomen* of the poet Ovid)	-	nose
Cornelius, Cornelia	-	horned
Flavius, Flavia	-	blond
Maximus	-	greatest
Fulvius, Fulvia	-	tawny
Plancus, Plancina	-	broad footed
Plautius, Plautia	-	flat footed
Silvanus	-	sylvan
Vergilius (the *gentilicum* of the poet Vergil)	-	springlike
Vepasian	-	wasp
Tacitus	-	consigned to silence
Locusta	-	lobster
Caracalla	-	hooded
Empiricus	-	observer, quack physician
Hippocrates	-	cavalry officer
Galen(os)	-	serene

Cleopatra	-	ancestral glory
Dynamis	-	powerful
Pythodoros, Pythodoris	-	given by Apollo
Polemon	-	warlike
Hacme	-	pinnacle
Salome	-	peace

BIBLIOGRAPHY

What is the difference, between primary and secondary source material?

Primary sources belong, culturally and chronologically, to whatever historical period is under consideration. For Livia, primary consist of literary and archaeological materials which have survived from the Roman empire to our present era.

Secondary sources are elucidations and commentaries based upon the analysis and interpretation of primary data. This book is a secondary source for information about Livia.

The following bibliography presents the primary and secondary sources which were consulted in the preparation of this study.

PRIMARY SOURCES FOR LIVIA'S LIFE

The initials *LCL* at the end of an entry indicate the source is published, in the replete and readily available Loeb Classical Library (London: William Heineman, Ltd./Cambridge, MA: Harvard University Press, various dates). This famous series presents each source in its original language, along with editors' comments, and simultaneous English translations on facing pages.

Most of the ancient sources, in their original languages and in translation, are readily available on the Internet.

DIRECT LITERARY SOURCES

These are the works of Roman and Greek writers who actually describe Livia in one fashion or another.

There is no ancient biography devoted specifically to Livia. The closest approximation we have to a work of this nature is the anonymous *Consolatio ad Liviam—Consolation to Livia*. It was written in 9 BCE to commiserate Livia on the untimely death of her son Drusus. The poetic *Consolatio* reveals the intensely emotional side of Livia's character, and the tenderness of her relationship with her family. An anonymous poet offers a prayer for Livia's serenity, in the second of two *Elegiae in Maecenatem—Elegies for Maecenas*. The stylistic similarities between the *Consolatio* and the *Elegiae* suggest the same person composed them. *LCL*: the *Consolatio ad Liviam* is in an Ovid volume, *The Art of Love and other Poems*; the *Elegaiae in Maecenatem* is in *Minor Latin Poets*.

The only other Augustan-era poet, who refers frequently to Livia, is Publius Ovidius Naso (43 BCE – 17 CE). In his *Ars Amatoria—Art of Love* and *Fasti—Feasts*, Ovid mentions public buildings that were constructed under Livia's direction. Ovid wrote his *Tristia—Sorrows* and *Epistulae ex Ponto—Letters from Overseas* to his wife and friends, after his relegation to Thrace (modern Romania) in 8 CE. The Pontus in Ovid's title refers to the preclassical Greek god of the sea, not to the Roman client kingdom of that name. From these anthologies we learn how Livia considered applications of citizens for special intervention from Augustus. The poet instructs his wife to approach Livia with a plea for his recall. Ovid also describes some of the deific characteristics that were imputed to Livia. *LCL*

Horace—Quintus Horatius Flaccus 65 – 8 BCE—penned numerous poetic accolades extolling the achievements of Augustus, Tiberius, and the elder Drusus. This poet nevertheless mentions Livia only once, and without naming her, in his *Carmina—Odes*. The Greek Krinagoras of Mitylene makes a single and nameless reference to Livia, in his prayer for the younger Antonia's success in childbirth. *LCL*: Krinagoras in *The Greek Anthology*.

Gaius Velleius Paterculus served as a military officer in the reign of

Augustus, first under the command of Gaius Caesar,and subsequently under that of Tiberius. The record of Velleius' official career closes with his tenure of the praetorship for 15 CE. Velleius wrote his *Historia Romana—Roman History* to commemorate the 30 CE consulship of his friend Marcus Vinicius. The first book, which exists only in fragments, scantily sketches the history of the Roman people from the legendary fall of Troy (ca. 1200 BCE) to the end of the Third Punic War in 146 BCE. The second book, which covers the period from 133 BCE to 29 CE, focuses primarily on the achievements of Caesar the Dictator and of Augustus. Velleius' treatment of Tiberius must be read cautiously, for it is both abbreviated and excessively laudatory. Velleius' few references to Livia are short and highly complimentary. *LCL*

Long-standing disputes between the Greek and Jewish populations of Alexandria, Egypt often culminated in riots and pogroms. In 40 CE both sides made unsuccessful efforts to secure arbitration from the mad Caligula (37 – 41 CE). A member of the Jewish delegation was the erudite Philo Judaeus. Born at Alexandria about 20 BCE, Philo was highly versed in Greek philosophy and as well as Jewish theology. In his *Πρεσβεία πρὸς Γαῖον—Presveia pros Gaion—Embassy to Gaius*, Philo praises Livia's intellectualism, and her patronage of the Jewish people. *LCL*

Lucius Annaeus Seneca (ca.5 BCE – 65 CE), called Minor (the Younger) to distinguish him from a like-named uncle, was academic tutor and later regent to Nero (54 – 68 CE. In his *De clementia—On Mercy*, a treatise on the advantages a ruler stood to derive from clemency, Seneca describes political insights Livia shared with Augustus. In *De ira—On Anger* Seneca maintains Livia was a target of hostile satire. In 25 CE the treacherous praetorian prefect Sejanus executed a senator and historian named Aulus Crementius Cordus. Seneca's *Consolatio ad Marciam—Consolation to Marcia* addressed to Cordus' daughter, explains how Livia used Greek philosophy to cope with the death of her son Drusus. From the author's *De providentia —On Foresight* we learn of Maecenas' unstable relationship with his wife Terentia. The possibly anonymous *Apocolocyntosis: Ludus de Morte Claudii—Pumpkinification: Farce on the Death of Claudius* is often attributed to the younger Seneca on stylistic grounds. The word *apocolocyntosis* derives from the Greek 'ἀπό—apo—into, and κολοκύνθη—colocynth—pumpkin or gourd. It parodies the word ἀποθέωσις—*apotheosis*. If Seneca did write this highly amusing but bitingly demeaning satire of Claudius' deification, he either published it anonymously or made sure it was not released until after his death; otherwise, the younger Agrippina would certainly have had him executed. The author of the ***Apocolocyntosis***, whoever he or she may have been, mentions Claudius' deification of Livia. *LCL*

One of the several physicians, whom the emperor Claudius employed, was a man named Scribonius Largus. He accompanied his master, when the latter invaded and conquered Britain in 43 CE. Largus' ***Compositiones medicamentorum—Compounds of Medical Substances*** contains formulae for home-produced medical prescriptions Livia and members of her family favored. Latin text: ***Scribonii Largi Compositiones***, edited by Sergio Sconoccia. Leipzig: Teubner, 1983. In German as ***Die Rezeptsammlung des Scribonius Largus—The Prescription Compilations of Scribonius Largus*** translated by Wilhelm Schonack. Jena: G. Fischer, 1912.

Gaius Plinius Secundus (23 – 79 CE) is called Pliny the Elder to differentiate him from his nephew and adopted son. Pliny wrote prolifically on many topics. His lost works include a study of the use of the javelin by Roman cavalrymen, three guidebooks for the training of young orators, eight treatises on grammar and rhetoric, a history of the Germanic wars in twenty-one books, and a thirty-one-book history of Rome from 41 to 71 CE. His only extant work is his encyclopedic ***Historia natura—Natural History*** in thirty-seven books. This compendium of trivia includes data on astronomy, geography, ethnology, anthropology, zoology, botany, horticulture, medicine, metallurgy, and fine art. Pliny incorporates numerous bits of personal information about famous Romans, including Livia. From Pliny we learn of Livia's taste in wine, her partiality to elecampane, the dwarf laurel that grew at her Prima Porta estate, the fig she introduced to Roman markets, her interest in rare collectables. Pliny like Ovid describes some of the public edifices with which Livia was associated. For his vocation, Pliny pursued a career in the imperial service. He was a *praefectus alae* (cavalry officer) in Germany under Claudius, and *procurator* (imperial governor) of Spain under Vespasian (69 – 79 CE). Vespasian's son and successor Titus (79 – 81 CE) appointed Pliny commander, of the fleet that was stationed at Misenum (Miseno) on the Bay of Naples. On August 24, 79 CE, Pliny ordered his sailors to evacuate the residents of Pompeii while the eruption of Mount Vesuvius was burying their city. Although his intervention saved many lives, Pliny lost his own that day. Driven by his fascination and eagerness to observe, he approached the volcano ever closer until suddenly he collapsed and died. Some scholars theorize he suffered a heart attack, others that he inhaled toxic volcanic gas. *LCL*

Youssef Ben Matthias, a Jew of royal and priestly heritage, was born at Jerusalem in 37 or 38 CE. He traveled to Rome, where he was accepted at the court of the emperor Nero. After returning to his homeland Youssef participated for a time, in the great Jewish rebellion against the Romans that began in 66 CE. He evaded execution by prophesying his captor, the Roman general Titus Flavius Vespasianus, would one day become emperor. When the prophecy came true in 69 CE the emperor Vespasian freed Youssef. The latter Latinized his Hebrew forename, adopted his benefactor's family name of Flavius, and became an ardent Romanophile (some say turncoat). Flavius Josephus remained in his homeland as a neutral observer, while Vespasian and his sons suppressed the Jewish uprising. After the Roman sack of Jerusalem in 70 CE put an end to the revolt, Josephus returned to Rome. Supported by the patronage of the Flavian dynasty, Joseph devoted the remainder of his life to writing. He died at Rome around 100 CE. In his seven-book *Ἱστορία Ἰουδαϊκου πολέμου πρὸς Ῥωμαίους—Historia Ioudaïkou Polemou pros Romaious—History of the Jewish War against the Romans*, Josephus seeks to persuade his readers that opposition to the Romans is a guarantee of annihilation. His *Ἰουδαϊκή ἀρχαιολογία—Ioudaïke archaiologia—Jewish Antiquities*, a twenty-book history of his people from the Creation to 66 CE, endeavors to show the prosperity of the Jews was proportional to their adherence to the law of God. Both works describe how Augustus and the members of his family patronized the Herodians. In particular we learn of Livia's interaction with Salome the sister of Herod the Great. *LCL*

The aristocratic Publius (or possibly Gaius) Cornelius Tacitus was born in the middle of the first century. In 78 CE he married the daughter of Gnaeus Julius Agricola, the distinguished and decorated imperial governor of Britain. Tacitus was a senator, whose public career culminated in the consulship for 97 CE. During the reign of Trajan (98 – 118 CE) Tacitus served as governor of Asia. Other biographic information about Tacitus is meager, but sufficient to reveal his bitterness and resentment toward the principate and its founders. Tacitus as a senator observed and perhaps suffered firsthand the pogrom-like efforts Domitian (81 – 96 CE) undertook, to suppress the political power and influence of the Roman senatorial oligarchy. Tacitus blamed Augustus and his descendants for establishing the system that culminated in Domitian's persecution and tyranny. The author's **Annales—Chronicles** is a bitingly sarcastic, muckraking study of the Julio-Claudians. It begins in 14 CE with the final months of Augustus' life, and extends until 66 CE. The portions covering 31CE and the decade following the death of Tiberius in 37 CE are missing; and the work breaks off uncompleted in 66 CE, two years before the suicide of Nero. Tacitus pays meticulous attention to the chronologic narration of events; but he uses hearsay, insinuation, and rhetorical devices to create unsavory representations of Augustus and that emperor's family. Livia is one of Tacitus' principal targets. He portrays her as power-obsessed, homicidal, underhanded, and sadistic. Tacitus insinuates Livia murdered Augustus as well as his grandsons, precipitated the misfortunes that befell the emperor's granddaughters, and condoned the harassment and demise of her own grandson Germanicus. In our narrative we noted Tacitus did not invent this depiction of Livia. He recorded malevolent reports about her which were already in place. **LCL**

A Greek contemporary of Tacitus was Plutarchos (ca. 46 CE – 120 CE). He was born into a wealthy and distinguished family of Chaeronea, a city in the Boeotia region of Greece. Plutarch's privileged status enabled him to attain a superlative education at Athens and subsequently to travel. At Rome where he gave public lectures on moral philosophy, Plutarch attracted the attention of the emperor Trajan. This ruler conferred consular status on Plutarch, and placed him in charge of educating the imperial heir-apparent Hadrian. Plutarch eventually returned to Chaeronea, where he held the office of *archon* (a town administrator). He also served as priest to Apollo at the great sanctuary to that god in Delphi. At Trajan's behest Plutarch undertook his famous *Βίοι παράλληλοι—Vii parallelii—Parallel Lives*, which compares figures of Greek and Roman history. Forty-six of these biographies survive. Plutarch also published treatises on religion, Greek and Roman culture, archaeology, mythology, natural science, and ethics. Particularly affecting is his letter to his wife, consoling her after the death of their five-year-old daughter Timoxena (Hospitality). Plutarch's few references to Livia are brief and non-judgmental. In his life of Mark Antony, Plutarch describes Cleopatra's appeal to Livia for clemency, and Livia's place in the genealogy of the Julio-Claudian dynasty. In his life of Galba, Plutarch writes that this emperor was related to Livia and owed his consulship of 33 CE to her influence. In *Περί τῆς 'Ει τοῦ 'εν Δελφοῦς—Peri tes Ei tou en Delphiis—On the E that is in Delphi*, Plutarch analyzes the philosophic significance of *epsilon*. He mentions that Livia installed a gold rendering of this Greek letter, in the temple of Apollo at Delphi. In *Περί 'αδολεχίας—Peri adolexias—On Loquaciousness*, Plutarch or perhaps his emulator represents Livia as offended by Augustus' failure to tell her of his longing to end the exile of his youngest grandson Postumus. *LCL*

Somewhat younger than Tacitus and Plutarch, Gaius Suetonius Tranquillus was born around 70 CE. Suetonius may have hailed from Hippo, the North African birthplace of Saint Augustine. As *ab epistulis* (personal secretary) to the emperor Hadrian (117 – 138 CE), Suetonius had access to the private archives of preceding emperors. After Hadrian dismissed him in 12 CE for failing to show proper deference to the empress Sabina, Suetonius devoted the rest of his life to writing on a variety of subjects. He died about 140 CE. Suetonius' *De vita Caesarum—On the Lives of the Caesars* is his best-known work, a series of anecdotal accounts of Rome's rulers from Caesar the Dictator through Domitian. These little biographies provide us with considerable personal information about the emperors they describe. Suetonius' representation of Tiberius is particularly derogatory. The author exaggerates this emperor's gravely intense and introverted nature into heartlessness, miserliness, and arcane lechery. Suetonius treats Livia far more kindly. He refers to her in his lives of Augustus, Tiberius, Caligula, Claudius, and Galba. Although a contemporary of Tacitus—and hence familiar with the malevolent traditions that writer recounts—Suetonius does not impute any wickedness to Livia at all. From Suetonius we learn of Augustus' enduring love for Livia, his respect for her opinions and insights, the concerns she shared with him about the development of her awkward grandson Claudius. Suetonius' *De viris illustribus—On Famous Men* includes biographies of the poets Vergil and Horace and the younger Agrippina's second husband Passienus Crispus. *LCL*

Dio Cassius Cocceianus was born sometime between 155 and 164 CE at Nicaea, the capital of the province of Bithynia in northwestern Asia Minor. His father Cassius Apronianus was a Roman senator who served as governor of Cilicia and of Dalmatia. Since Dio's maternal grandfather was the noted orator Dio Chrysostom, his family placed a high priority on education. After his father died around 180 CE the younger Dio repaired to Rome. Here he established a successful practice as a defense attorney and became a senator. Dio was praetor in 194 CE, consul in 220, thereafter governor of Africa, then of Dalmatia, and lastly of Pannonia. His strict enforcement of military discipline earned him the hatred of the imperial bodyguards, who sought his life. The emperor Alexander Severus (220 – 235 CE) protected Dio and elevated him to a second consulship in 229 CE. When this office expired the aging Dio retired to his birthplace of Nicaea, so he could devote all his energies to completing his eighty-book *'Ρωμαϊκα—Romaïka—Roman Matters*, a history of the Roman people from the Trojan War to Dio's second consulship. Dio's occasional comments about divine guidance suggest he was a Christian or at least influenced by Christian doctrines. He writes that he undertook this twenty-two-year-long history project in response to a divine command he had received in a dream. Dio provides little more than an outline of the first millennium of Roman history up to the dictatorship of Julius Caesar. The Triumvirate and imperial period Dio treats in far greater depth. Only fragments of the first thirty-five books are extant. Books thirty-six through sixty are largely complete. They cover most of the Roman Republic's final century, and the emperors from Augustus through Caligula (ca. 80 BCE – 41 CE). Books sixty-one through eighty exist only in the form of summaries, prepared in the twelfth century by the Byzantine monk John Xiphilinos. These span the period from the accession of Claudius in 41 CE to Dio's second consulship in 229 CE. Dio describes Livia's opinions, personal demeanor, and interaction with Augustus. He records the murders attributed to her but questions the validity of these accusations. *LCL*

Pomponius Porphyrio was a second century Roman grammarian, born in Africa. His commentary on the poems of Horace, of which only a fragmentary abridgement remains extant, confirms Livia was pregnant when she married Octavian. Pomponius Porphyrio should not be confused with the third century Neoplatonist philosopher Porphyry Malthus, whose treatise condemning Christianity was burned on orders from the emperor Theodosius II (408 – 450 CE). Latin text: *Acronis et Porphyrionis Comentarii in Quintum Horatium Flaccum—Acro's and Porphyrio's Commentaries on Quintus Horatius Flaccus*, edited by Ferdinand Hauthal. Amsterdam: P. Schippers, 1966. German translation: Diederich, Silke: *Der Horazkommentar des Porphyrio im Rahmen der kaiserzeitlichen Schul und Bildungstradition—The Horace Commentary of Porphyrio in the Context of Imperial Era Educational and Artistic Tradition*. Berlin/New York: de Gruyter, 1999.

The Spaniard Aurelius Prudentius Clemens, born in 348 CE, was educated in rhetoric and law. In his native Spain he practiced as an attorney and subsequently as a judge. In later life the Christian Prudentius retired to a monastery where he died about 410 CE. Prudentius devoted his monastic years to the composition of sacred poems, which he modeled upon the style of Horace. He also wrote diatribes against pagan religious practices. Prudentius condemns the veneration of Livia as the goddess Juno. *Contra Symmachum—Against Symmachus* in *Opera—Works*. Latin text with French translation by M. Lavarenne. Paris: Presses Universitaires de France, 1945.

Sextus Aurelius Victor, another native of Africa, was imperial governor of Pannonia in 361 CE, and urban prefect of Rome in 389 CE. His highly abbreviated *Liber de Caesaribus—Book about the Caesars*, which recounts the lives of Roman rulers from Caesar the Dictator to Constantine I, may well be a condensation of a more detailed narrative. Victor describes Augustus as unlucky in marriage. An anonymous *Epitome de Caesaribus—Summary about the Caesars* strongly parallels Victor's work in content, style, and form. Its nameless author asserts Tiberius Nero willingly divorced Livia so she could marry the passionately enamored Octavian, and confirms some writers attribute

Augustus' death to her mischief. Latin texts: *Liber de Caesaribus, Praecedunt Origo gentis Romanae et Liber de viris illustribus Romae. Subsequitur Epitome de Caesaribus—Book about the Caesars; the Origin of the Roman People and Book about Famous Men of the City of Rome Precede; the Summary about the Caesars follows*, edited by Francis Pichmayr. Leipzig: Teubner, 1970. In English: *The Liber de Caesaribus of Sextus Aurelius Victor*, translated with an introduction and commentary by H. W. Bird. Liverpool: Liverpool University Press, 1994. In German: *Die Epitome de Caesaribus*, translated by Jörg Schlumberger. Munich: C. H. Beck, 1974.

ANCILLARY LITERARY SOURCES

Some ancient writers do not describe Livia *per se*, but delineate people she knew and the environment in which she lived.

Hippocrates of Cos (ca. 460 – 377 BCE) was a scion of the *Aesclepiadae*, a priestly clan devoted to the veneration of Aesclepius the god of healing. Over centuries, the *Aesclepiadae* had gathered and preserved medical formulae, which they transmitted orally from one generation to the next. Hippocrates practiced his art throughout Greece as an itinerant healer. Eventually he settled in Thessaly where he lived until his death. Hippocrates worked tirelessly throughout his long life, at accumulating, recording and systematizing medical practices into a scientific methodology. The many writings attributed to him are not only his own but also those of disciples. Among these were two grandsons, both of whom bore his name. Hippocrates and his school profoundly influenced subsequent generations of Greek and Roman physicians, including those who practiced in Livia's day. Original Greek with French translation: Hippocrates, *Oeuvres—Works*, edited and translated by Jacques Jouanna. Paris: Les Belles Lettres, 2000.

The speeches of Marcus Tullius Cicero (106 – 43 BCE) are all too familiar to second-year students of Latin. Cicero was born into an equestrian family of Arpinum (Arpino) to the southeast of Rome. He and his younger brother Quintus migrated to the capital to study oratory and philosophy. Marcus Cicero's eloquent and persuasive speeches brought him immediate success as a defense attorney. His burgeoning reputation eventually won him admission to the Senate as a *novus homo*—one who was not descended from senators. Toward the end of his consulship in 63 BCE, Cicero exposed the preparations a fellow senator, Lucius Sergius Catalina, was making for a *coup d'état*. Cicero's virulent denunciations of Mark Antony, and his declaration that young Octavian should be used but then set aside, prompted the Second Triumvirate to proscribe and execute him. For two millennia Cicero has been respected and revered for his political and philosophical insights. Cicero's extant correspondence and speeches contain references to Livia's father and to her relatives the Claudii Pulchri. *LCL*

A friend of Cicero was Cornelius Nepos, a native of northern Italy, who lived from 94 to 24 BCE. Nepos predated Plutarch with *De viris illustribus—On Famous Men*, a comparative compilation of biographical information about notable Greeks and Romans in 16 books. Nepos arranged the biographies according to his subjects' vocations, treating the Greeks of each division first and the Romans thereafter. The section on Roman writers includes a biography of Titus Caecilius Atticus Pomponianus, the friend to whom Cicero addressed a considerable volume of correspondence. From Nepos we learn Atticus' daughter married Agrippa, and their daughter Vipsania was betrothed to Livia's son Tiberius. Since the *De viris illistribus* was dedicated to Atticus, Nepos must have completed the work before Atticus died in 32 BCE. This chronology reveals Tiberius was no more than ten when his betrothal to Vipsania was solemnized. *LCL*

Marcus Vitruvius Pollio was a Roman military engineer. After retiring, Vitruvius composed a ten-book treatise on architecture, which he published in 14 BCE. He based his *De architectura* to some extent on Greek sources but primarily upon his own experience. Vitruvius owed his retirement pension, which gave him the leisure to write, to the patronage of Augustus' sister Octavia. *LCL*

Caesar Augustus himself wrote compositions in both prose and poetry. Apart from a few, extremely disparate fragments, the emperor's only surviving piece is his *Res gestae—Matters Accomplished*. Augustus completed this concise and dignified account of his political accomplishments in the year before his death. The brief autobiography was inscribed on the exterior of the emperor's mausoleum in Rome, and on shrines and monuments to him throughout the realm. The most complete version is called the *Monumentum Ancyraneum—Ancyran Monument* because it was discovered with a parallel Greek translation at Ankara, Turkey. Since he omits references to his personal life, Augustus does not mention Livia at all. The *Res gestae* nevertheless provide a firsthand description of the political environment in which Livia lived. *LCL*, in the same volume as Velleius Paterculus' *Historia Romana*.

The Greek geographer Strabo was born at Amaseia in Pontus, about 63 BCE. His interest in geography and history prompted him to undertake long journeys, through Asia Minor, Egypt, Ethiopia, Greece, and Italy. Only a few fragments remain of his forty-seven-book history of Rome from the end of the Third Punic War (146 BCE) to his own time. Virtually complete, however, is his seventeen-book Γεωγραφία— *Geographia —Geography* which he finished about 23 CE. Strabo mentions public buildings in Rome with which Octavia and Livia were associated. From Strabo we learn King Polemon of Pontus married Pythodoris after his divorce from Dynamis, and Augustus recognized Pythodoris as queen of Pontus after Polemon died. *LCL*

Titus Livius was born at Patavia, Italy (Padua) in 59 BCE. We do not know how, or even if, he was related to the senatorial Livii Drusi to which Livia belonged. Livy's family must certainly have been wealthy and well connected; for after a thorough education he was able to establish himself in Rome as a professional writer. Livy was an outspoken defender of Roman Republican traditions and precepts. He nevertheless enjoyed the friendship of Augustus, who teased the historian for being a Pompeian at heart. At the behest of his imperial patron, Livy undertook a monumental history of Rome. The *Ab urbe condita libri CXLII—142 Books from the Foundation of the City* extends from the legendary establishment of Rome in 753 BCE to the death of Augustus' stepson Drusus in 9 BCE. The work is strongly patriotic in tenor, because Augustus commissioned it to rekindle the Romans' pride in their national ancestry. Livy may have intended to continue his history down to the death of Augustus in 14 CE; but the historian's project ended with his own demise at Patavia in 17 CE. Livy published the *Ab urbe condita* in decads (units of ten books). Only the first decad (to 293 BCE), the third, fourth and part of the fifth (218 – 167 BCE) are extant. From Livy we learn of Camillus the Dictator, an ancestor of the bride Livia selected for Claudius her grandson. Livy also describes Gaius Claudius Nero's heroism in the Second Punic War, and the epidemic authorities attributed to a mass poisoning by maddened matrons. *LCL*

Marcus Gavius was a contemporary of Augustus and Tiberius and hence of Livia. His special interest in foods and their preparations prompted him to appropriate the surname Apicius from a Roman epicure who had lived about a century earlier. Gavius' treatise *De re coquinaria—On the Matter Culinary* is the world's oldest extant recipe book. Its entries include gastronomic uses for chickens, laurel, and figs—commodities with which Livia was associated. Like Livia, Gavius was a target of malicious gossip. Rumor held he purchased homosexual favors from Lucius Aelius Sejanus, the hooligan who became praetorian prefect under Tiberius. Gavius was also alleged to have poisoned himself, at a banquet prepared for the occasion, for fear his dwindling assets might force him to forego some of the rare and expensive delicacies he craved. Two centuries late, a gourmand named Coelius appropriated the name Apicius, and added supplemental recipes to Gavius' work. Latin text with simultaneous French translation in *L'art culinaire: De re coquinaria*, edited, with translation and commentary by Jacques André. Paris: C. Klincksieck, 1965. In English as *Cookery and Dining in Imperial Rome*, translated with commentary by culinary chef Joseph Domners Vehling. Chicago: W. M. Hill, 1936.

A contemporary of Velleius Paterculus was Valerius Maximus. He served on the staff of Sextus Pompeius Magnus (great-grandson of Pompey the Great) while the latter was governor of Asia in 27 CE. Valerius' *Factorum et dictorum memorabilium libri novem—Nine Books of Memorable Facts and Sayings*, which he dedicated to the emperor Tiberius, is a somewhat tedious compendium of moralizing anecdotes. From it we learn how Tiberius hastened to reach his dying brother Drusus in Gaul, and how the younger Antonia's devotion to Drusus' memory induced her to live out her widowhood in Livia's home. *LCL*

Lucius Junius Moderatus Columella was a native of Glades, in Spain. He published his twelve-book *De re rustica—On the Matter Rustic* around 60 CE. Columella based this exhaustive treatment of agriculture, not only on extant writings about the subject, but also on his own direct observations of farming procedures in Spain, Asia Minor, and Italy. He describes the luscious red fig named for Livia. *LCL*

Marcus Fabius Quintilianus was born at Calagurris, Spain (modern Calahoora) about 35 CE. He studied oratory in Rome, went home around 59 CE, and then returned to Rome in 68 CE. Here he practiced as a defense attorney, but more successfully as a teacher of rhetoric. Eventually the emperor Vespasian provided Quintilian state funds to open and operate a school of rhetoric. After serving as headmaster for twenty years, Quintilian retired. He turned his energies to writing, and to tutoring the grandchildren of Vespasian's daughter Domitilla. As a reward for these educational efforts, Domitilla's brother—the emperor Domitian—conferred an honorary consulship upon Quintilian. Although materially and intellectually prosperous, Quintilian never considered himself happy, because his young wife and two sons had predeceased him. In his *De institutione oratoria—On Oratorical Instruction*, Quintilian records sayings of Augustus that Macrobius later reproduced. *LCL*

In the middle of the first century, two men wrote similar biographies of their exemplar—a young rabbi from the northern Galilean town of Nazareth. The one author was a Jewish money exchanger called Levi Matthias, the other a Greek physician named Loukas. The gospels of Saints Matthew and Luke yield information about the Herodians, and about Livia's *protégé* Publius Sulpicius Quirinius Cyrenius. For the gospels in their original language: *The Greek New Testament*, edited by Kurt Aland, Matthew Black, *et. al.* New York: American Bible Society, 1968. For English: *The Holy Bible: Containing the Old and New Testaments and the Apocrypha: Translated out of the Original Tongues and with the Former Translations Diligently Compared and Revised, commonly known as the Authorized (King James) Version.* London/New York: Cambridge University Press, 1966.

Decimus Junius Juvenalis, the son of a wealthy freedman, was born around 47 CE at Aquinum (Aquino) near the birthplace of Cicero. He studied oratory at Rome, where he became a member of the equestrian order. Back at Aquinum, Juvenal served as *duumvir* (one of a pair of mayor-like officials), and as priest of the deified emperor Vespasian. He also held a military command in Dalmatia as tribune of a cohort. Juvenal wrote a series of biting satires, in which he glaringly exposes the moral corruption of rich and powerful Romans, particularly in the reign of Domitian. Sixteen of these lampoons are extant today. Juvenal's *exposés* brought about his relegation. As to the location and date of his sentence, our sources vary between Britain and Egypt, and between the reigns of Domitian and Trajan. After returning to Rome, Juvenal lived in poverty until the emperor Hadrian provided him with relief. Juvenal died between 127 and 130 CE at the age of eighty-one. He writes that Augustus banished his granddaughter Julia for her extravagance and immorality, recalled her, but then reinstated her sentence after she failed to mend her ways. Juvenal also mentions the *débâcle* of Tiberius' praetorian prefect Sejanus. ***LCL***

Publius Caecilius Secundus was born to Plinia, the sister of Pliny the Elder, at Novum Comum, Italy (Como) in 62 CE. After Plinia's husband suffered a premature death her brother adopted and helped raise her son, who assumed the name of Gaius Plinius Caecilius Secundus. The younger Pliny studied rhetoric with Quintilian, and began his career as an advocate at the age of eighteen. After serving as a military tribune in Syria, Pliny the Younger became a senator. He was first a plebian tribune, then praetor in 93, and consul in 100 CE. In 112 CE the emperor Trajan (98 – 117 CE) appointed Pliny imperial legate (governor) of Bithynia. Although thrice married, Pliny the Younger died childless in 114 CE. He was well respected for his benevolence and philanthropy, his interest in architectural adornment, and his passionate devotion to the literary arts. None of his poems or speeches has survived, except for a panegyric thanking Trajan for the consulship of 100 CE. Pliny's ten books of letters, to Trajan and other politicians and to notable intellectuals of his day, remain extant. Several letters are particularly famous. In one of these, Pliny in his capacity as governor asks Trajan whether anonymous denunciations accusing Christians of subversive activities are legally acceptable. The emperor replies firmly in the negative. Modern volcanologists study two letters addressed to Tacitus, in which Pliny provides highly detailed eyewitness descriptions of the eruption of Vesuvius. From Pliny the Younger we learn of the heroic Arria Paetina who assured her husband suicide is painless. *LCL*

Next to Hippocrates, Claudius Galenos is probably the most famous medical writer of the ancient world. Galen was born in 131 CE at Pergamon in Asia Minor (Bergamo, Turkey). After an initial education in philosophy, Galen turned to medicine. This he studied in his native city as well as at Smyrna (Izmir, Turkey), Corinth, and Alexandria. In 158 CE Galen returned to Pergamon, where he specialized in the medical treatment of gladiators. In 164 CE he moved to Rome, where he became famous for his successful medical practice and his lectures in anatomy. After the jealousy of rival practitioners impelled him to leave Rome, Galen settled in Pergamon once again. He did not remain there for long. The emperor Marcus Aurelius (161 – 180 CE) recalled Galen to Rome and appointed him personal physician to the crown prince Commodus. Galen died in 200 CE at the age of sixty-nine. He covered every branch of medicine in his prolific writings. About half of these are extant, some only in Latin, Hebrew, or Arabic translation. Galen reiterates the formula for wound plasters attributed by Scribonius Largus to Livia. We also learn from Galen that Antonia tried a variety of eye ointments. In their original language: *Κλαυδίου Γαλενόυ ᾽Απάντα: Claudii Galeni Opera Omnia—Everything by Claudius Galen*, edited by C. G. Kuhn. Hildesheim: Georg Olms, 1964. Only selections have been translated into modern languages. Among the more available are those in *LCL*, and *Corpus Medicorum Graecorum—Collection of Greek Physicians* (Berlin: Akademie-Verlag, various dates).

A second century writer who mentions the Livian fig is the Greco-Egyptian Athenaeus. He was born at Naucratis but educated at Alexandria, where he lived from about 170 to 230 CE. Thereafter he resided in Rome, where he composed his *Δειπνοσοφίσται—Deipnosophistai—Dining Sophists*. The setting is a dinner at which the most learned men of the day share their knowledge and insights. (Galen is among the guests). Remarks about foods include a reference to stuffed grape leaves, a staple of modern Greek cuisine. Athenaeus informs us that at least in his day, the Livian fig was raised in the environs of Rome. *LCL*

Another second-century Greco-Egyptian was Appianos of Alexandria. After a successful career as a trial lawyer in Rome, Appian received appointment as prefect of Egypt from Antoninus Pius (138 – 161 CE). Appian wrote a history of the Roman empire from its inception to the reign of Trajan, concentrating upon the lands and peoples that eventually succumbed to Roman domination. Only eleven of the original twenty-four books remain extant. Appian's work is fraught with mistakes, especially in chronology; but his segment on the Roman civil wars remains an invaluable source for the period and events of the Second Triumvirate. *LCL*

In the later Roman empire, the director of the palace bureaucracies was called the *magister officiorum* (Master of the Offices). The *magister officiorum* to Theodosius I (379 – 395 CE) was one Marcellus, a native of Burdigalia (Bordeaux) in Gaul. About 410 CE Marcellus published his **De medicamentis liber—Book Concerning Medication**. He intended this lengthy handbook of medicinal formulae for use by laymen as well as physicians. Marcellus acquired the somewhat derogatory epithet of *Empiricus* (Observer, or Quack) because he relied upon direct observation and practical experience with proven medical methods rather than on theory and experimentation. He reproduces, almost verbatim, medications Scribonius Largus attributes to Livia and her relatives. Marcellus like Galen records some formulae which Scribonius does not. These include a complex herb-based vitalizing potion both Augustus and Hadrian favored, and a simpler tonic Tiberius utilized for colitis. The **De medicamentis liber** is available with simultaneous German translation as **Über Heilmittel: Corpus medicorum Latinorum—On Remedies: Collection of Latin Physicians—#5**, prepared by Eduard Liechtenhan, translated by Jutta Kollesch and Diethard Nickel. Berlin: Akademie-Verlag, 1968.

The fifth-century Ambrosius Aurelius Theodosius Macrobius was somewhat of an anachronism: a pagan in the now largely Christian Roman empire. His seven-book **Convivia Saturnalia—Saturnalia Entertainments** presents a rich collection of mythological, grammatical, and historical vignettes. Like Athenaeus, Macrobius presents his information as table talk at a festive banquet. Macrobius preserves sayings of Augustus, but more significantly the personality and witticisms of the emperor's daughter Julia. The author mentions Livia's character only once, in a fleeting reference to her demure conduct in public. Macrobius praises the Livian fig. Latin text in **Ambrosii Theodosii Macrobii Saturnalia**, edited by Jacob Willis. Leipzig: B. G. Teubner, 1970. In English as **The Saturnalia**, translated with an introduction and notes by Percival Vaughan Davies. New York: Columbia University Press, 1969.

Non-Literary Primary Sources

Roman Law

On orders of the emperor Justinian I (527 – 565 CE), a panel of accomplished jurists and legal scholars assembled to undertake a monumental project. They organized and codified the morass of Roman laws and legal interpretations, which had accumulated over the preceding millennium. The **Corpus Iuris Civilis—Body of Civil Law** is divided into three sections. The **Codex Iustiniani—Code of Justinian** is a collection of all valid imperial edicts. The **Digesta—Digest**, a compilation of abstracts from the writings of Roman jurists, covers those aspects of the law the **Codex** omits. The third part, the **Institutes** is a concise abridgement of the two aforementioned segments. It was intended as a study aid for students and a ready reference for practicing attorneys and judges. The **Institutes** also provides historians with quick but direct access to the most salient points of Roman law. Our bilingual source was **The Institutes of Justinian**, with English introduction, translation, and notes by Thomas Collett Sandars. London: Longmans, Green and Company, 1922.

Papyri

In ancient Egypt, documents were recorded on sheets of papyrus. The stems of this reed, when unrolled and dried, produced a material much like the modern product that is named for papyrus: paper. Papyri survive admirably in the arid sands and atmosphere of Egypt. Some record government decrees and policies. Others represent the details of ordinary peoples' lives: marriage contracts, commercial correspondence, lease agreements, funerary announcements. Papyri which apply to Livia concern occupants of the estates she owned in Egypt.

Cadell, Hélène, *Papyrus de la Sorbonne*. Paris: Presses Universitaires de France, 1966.

Catalogue of the Greek Papyri in the John Rylands Library. Manchester, England: John Rylands University Press, 1911–1952.

Greek Papyri in the British Museum: Facsimiles. London: Trustees of the British Museum, 1893 – 1907.

Papiri greci e latini: Pubblicazioni della Società italiana per la ricerca dei papyri greci e latini in Egitto—Greek and Latin Papyri: Publications of the Italian Society for Research of Greek and Latin Papyri (periodical). Florence: Felice le Monnier, 1912 – 1979.

Papiri milanesi per cura della Scuola di Papirologia dell' Università Cattolica del Sacro Cuore—Milanese Papyri through the Preparation of the Catholic University of the Sacred Heart. Milan: Università cattolica del Sacro Cuore, 1928.

The Oxyrhynchus Papyri, edited with translations and notes by Bernard P. Grenfell and Arthur S. Hunt. London: Egypt Exploration fund, 1898.

Sammelbuch Griechischer Urkunden aus Ägypten—Compilation of Greek Documents from Egypt. Göttingen: Gedruckt von Hubert, 1952 – 1961.

Large, heavily-used compilations are customarily cited by initials, which precede the entries below.

Epigraphy (Inscriptions)

Acta fratrum arvalium quae supersunt—Acts of the Arval Brethren that Survive, restored and illustrated by G. Henzen. Berlin: Georg Reimer, 1874.

AE L'Année épigraphique—The Epigraphic Annual (periodical). Paris: Presses Universitaires de France, 1888 – present.

CIL Corpus Inscriptionum Latinarum—Compliation of Latin Inscriptions. Berlin: George Reimer, 1862.

Eck, Werner, Antonio Caballos and Fernando Fernández, *Das Senatusconsultum de Cn. Pisone patre—The Senate Decree*

Concerning Gnaeus Piso the Father. Munich: C. Beck, 1996. An inscription of the Roman Senate's decree, condemning Germanicus' enemy Gnaeus Piso for sedition, was discovered in Spain. Historian Eck and his colleagues reconstructed the text with a translation and commentary in German.

EE Ephemeris Epigraphica: Corporis Inscriptionum Latinarum Supplementum—Epigraphic Journal: Supplement to the Corpus Inscriptionum Latinarum. Berlin: George Reimer, 1872 – 1913.

IGRR Inscriptiones Graecae ad Res Romanas Pertinentes—Greek Inscriptions Pertinent to Roman Matters. Rome: "L'Erma" di Bretschneider, 1964.

OGIS Orientis Graeci Inscriptiones Selectae—Select Inscriptions of the Greek East, edited by Wilhelm Dittenberger. Hildesheim/New York: G. Olms, 1970.

SEG Supplementum Epigraphicum Graecum—Greek Epigraphic Supplement (periodical). Alphen ann den Rijn, Holland: Skjthoff & Noordhoff, 1923 – present.

Tansini, Rafaella, *I Ritratti di Agrippina Maggiore—The Records of Agrippina the Elder.* Rome: Giorgio Bretschneider, 1995.

Numismatics (Coins)

CREBM Mattingly, Harold, *Coins of the Roman Empire in the British Museum.* London: Trustees of the British Museum, 1950.

RIC Roman Imperial Coinage, revised edition, edited by C. H. V. Sutherland and R. A. G. Carson. London: Spink, 1984.

SECONDARY SOURCES

As our Introduction explained, reliance on secondary source material was kept to a minimum. To insure that the interpretation of primary sources was as original as it could be, the opinions of modern scholars were avoided as much as possible. Still, the consultation of some secondary sources was essential, for elucidation of specific topics relevant to Livia.

Atlases

Barrington Atlas of the Greek and Roman World, edited by Richard J. A. Talbert, *et. al.* Princeton: Princeton University Press, 2000.

Cornell, Timothy and Matthews, John, *Atlas of the Roman World*. New York: Facts on File Publications, 1982.

Norton, Arthur Philip, *Norton's Star Atlas and Reference Handbook, 19th Edition*, edited by Ian Ridpath. Boston: Addison-Wesley Publishing, 1998.

Dictionaries and Encyclopedias

Brill's New Pauly: Encyclopedia of the Ancient World, edited by Hubert Cancik and Helmut Schneider. English edition prepared by Christine F. Salazar and David E. Orton. Leiden/Boston: E.J. Brill, 2002.

Concordance des oeuvres Hippocratiques—Concordance of Hippocratic Works, edited by Gilles Maloney and Winnie Frohn, with collaboration of Dr. Paul Potter. Montreal/Paris: Sphinx, 1984.

Cruden, Alexander, *Cruden's Complete Concordance of the Old and New Testaments,* edited by A. D. Adams, C. H. Irwin, and S. A. Waters. NewYork/Chicago/San Francisco: Holt, Rinehart, & Winston, 1949.

Daremberg, Charles and Saglio, Edmund, *Dictionnaire des antiquités grecques et romaines—Dictionary of Greek and Roman Antiquities*. Graz: Akademische Druck unter Verlagsanstalt, 1969.

Der Kleine Pauly: Lexikon der Antike/Auf der Grundlage von Pauly's Realencyclopädie, unter Mitwirkung zahlreicher Fachgelehrter bearbeitet und herausgegeben—The Little Pauly: Dictionary of Antiquity/On the Basis of Pauly's Subject Encyclopedia, Under the Cooperation of Numerous Specialists, Compiled and Edited, by Konrat Ziegler, *et. al.* Munich: Deutscher Taschenbuch Verlag, 1979.

DSM IV: Diagnostic and Statistical Manual of Mental Disorders, Fourth Edition. Washington, DC: American Psychiatric Association, 1994.

365

Dorland, W. Newman, *Dorland's Illustrated Medical Dictionary, 26th edition*. Philadelphia: W. B. Saunders, 1985.

The Larousse Encyclopedia of Mythology, translated from the French by Richard Aldington and Delano Ame, and revised by a panel of editorial advisers from the *Larousse mythologie générale*, edited by Felix Guirand. New York: Prometheus Press, 1959.

The Oxford Classical Dictionary, third edition, edited by Simon Hornblower and Anthony Spawforth. Oxford/New York: Oxford University Press, 1996.

RE Paulys Real-Encyclopädie der classischen Altertumswissenschaft— Pauly's Subject-Encyclopedia of Classical Antiquity Knowledge, edited by August Friedrich von Pauly, George Wissova, and Wihelm Kroll. Stuttgart: J. B. Metzler, 1894 – 1963.

PIR Prosopographia Imperii Romani, saeculae I, II, III. Edita consilio et auctoritate Academiae Literarum Borussicae—Biographies of the Roman Empire, for Centuries I, II, III. Edited on the Consideration and Authority of The Academy of Letters of Prussia. Berlin/ Leipzig, Walter de Gruter, 1933.

Seyffert, Oskar, *A Dictionary of Classical Antitqities*, edited with additional translations by Henry Nettleship and J. E. Sandys. London: William Glaisher, Ltd, 1894. Despite its age, a treasure-trove of of Greek and Roman cultural information in a single volume.

Secondary Literature

The decision to offer no more than a selected bibliography, of cogent secondary articles and monographs, was not made lightly. Many analyses of Livia, of her place in history, and of topics relevant to her life, have been written over the past three centuries in a variety of languages. A comprehensive bibliography in which every entry seems important threatens to discourage further study, by creating the impression the reader must master the entire list. This type of bibliography also tends to become obsolete as soon as it is printed, because new material is being published continually.

The abbreviated bibliography here presented aspires to avoid overwhelming the reader, but nevertheless stimulate his or her own interest in exploring Livian topics to greater extent. Most of the entries are available in university or large public libraries. Readers who do not have access to such collections should not despair: smaller libraries can easily acquire the materials through interlibrary loan. Dissertations can be obtained from University Microfilms, Ann Arbor, Michigan.

The following materials are listed according to the subjects for which they were examined.

<u>The Decline of the Roman Republic: The Political and Socio-economic Background of the Principate</u>

Beard, Mary and Crawford, Michael H., *Rome in the late Republic: Problems and Interpretations, second edition*. London: Duckworth, 1999.

Bleicken, Jochen, *Zwischen Republik und Prinzipat: zum Charakter des zweiten Triumvirats—Between Republic and Principate: on the Nature of the Second Triumvirate*. Göttingen: Vandenhoeck & Ruprecht, 1990.

The Cambridge Ancient History, Volume 9: The Last Age of the Roman Republic, 146—43 BC, edited by S. A. Cook, F. E. Adcock, and M. P. Charlesworth. Cambridge: Cambridge University Press, 1934.

David, Jean-Michel, *La République romaine: de la deuxième guerre punique à la bataille d'Actium, 218—31: crise d'une aristocratie— The Roman Republic: from the Second Punic War to the Battle of Actium: 218—31 [BCE]: Crisis of an Aristocracy*. Paris: Éditions de Seuil, 2000.

Gruen, Erich S., *The Last Generation of the Roman Republic*. Berkeley: University of California Press, 1995.

Holmes, T. Rice, *The Architect of the Roman Empire*. Oxford: Clarendon Press, 1928.

Levi, Mario A., *Ottaviano Capoparte: storia politica di Roma durante le ultime lotte di supremazia—Octavian Party Leader: Political History of Rome during the Final Struggle for Supremacy*. Florence: "La Nuova Italia," 1933.

Marsh, Frank Burr, *The Founding of the Roman Empire*. Austin: University of Texas Press, 1922.

Roman, Danièle, *Rome: la république impérialiste: 264—27 av. J-C.— Rome: The Imperialist Republic: 264—27 BC*, with the collaboration of Yves Roman. Paris: Ellipses, 2000.

Scullard, Howard H., *From the Gracchi to Nero: A History of Rome from 133 BC to AD 68, fourth edition*. London: Methuen, 1976.

Syme, Ronald, *The Roman Revolution*. Oxford/New York: Clarendon Press, 1939.

Women in Ancient Roman Society

Balsdon, J. P. V. D., *Roman Women: Their History and Habits*. New York: John Day, 1963.

Chastagnol, A., "Les femmes dans l'ordre senatorial: titulature et rang social à Rome,"—Women in the Senatorial Order: Titulature and Social Rank at Rome—*Revue historique* 103 (1978), 3 – 28.

Dixon, Suzanne, *The Roman Mother*. Norman: University of Oklahoma Press, 1988.

Hopkins, M., "The Age of Roman Girls at Marriage," *Population Studies* 18 (1965), 309 – 327.

The Family in Ancient Rome, edited by B. Rawson. Ithaca: Cornell University Press, 1986.

Frank, Richard Ira, "Augustus' Legislation on Marriage and Children," *California Studies in Classical Antiquity* 8 (1975), 41 – 52.

Friedlaender, Ludwig, *Roman Life and Manners under the Early Empire*, translated from the German by L. A. Magnus, J. H. Freese, and A. B. Gough. New York: Arno Press, 1979.

Grubbs, Judith Evans, *Women and the Law in the Roman Empire: A Sourcebook on Marriage, Divorce and Widowhood*. London/New York: Routledge, 2002.

Kleiner, D, and Matheson, S. B., *I, Claudia: Women in Ancient Rome*. New Haven: Yale University Press, 1996.

Paoli, Ugo Enrico, *Rome: Its People, Life, and Customs*, translated from the Italian by R. D. MacNaughten. London: Longman, 1963.

Raditsa, L. F., "Augustus' Legislation concerning Marriage, Procreation, Love Affairs, and Adultery," *Aufstieg und Niedergang der römischen Welt* 2.13 (1980), 278 – 339.

Schuller, Wolfgang, *Frauen in der römischen Geschichte—Women in Roman History*. Constance: Universitätsverlag Konstanz, 1987.

Treggari, Susan M., *Roman Marriage*. Oxford/New York: Oxford University Press, 1991.

Women in Antiquity: New Assessments, edited by Richard Hawley and Barbara Levick. London/ New York: Routledge, 1995.

Biographies of Livia

Willrich, Hugo, *Livia*. Leipzig/Berlin: B. G. Teubner, 1911, is a sympathetic study, which rejects Livia's criminal reputation but neglects to account for its origin.

Barrett, Anthony A., *Livia, First Lady of Imperial Rome*, New Haven: Yale University Press, 2002, meticulously examines Livia's private life, her public activities, and the development of her unique, unprecedented, yet essential, place in the evolution of the early principate. There is a comprehensive bibliography, as well as a highly useful list of references to Livia in ancient sources. This author declines to tackle Livia's criminality, on the ground it is universally rejected by the scholarly world.

Dennison, Matthew, *Livia, Empress of Rome: A Biography*, New York: St. Martin's Press, seeks the distortions of Livia's character in the writings of Tacitus, and in Livia's position as a public figure which began in her early life and burgeoned to historically unprecedented proportions as the Principate developed.

Smith, Phyllis T, *I am Livia*. Seattle: Lake Union Publishing, 2014. A novel, the plot and accuracy of which are unknown to me. Historical fiction, accurately representing personages and events, can imbue them with a tangibility for the reader that purely academic studies elude.

Livia's Genealogy

Huntsman, Eric Dennis, *The Family and Property of Livia Drusilla*. Ph.D. Dissertation, University of Pennsylvania, 1997.

Linderski, Jerzy, "The Mother of Livia Augusta and the Aufidii Lurcones of the Republic," *Historia* 23 (1974), 463 – 480.

Syme, Ronald, *The Augustan Aristocracy*. Oxford: Clarendon Press, 1986.

Wiseman, T. P., "The Mother of Livia Augusta," *Historia* 14 (1965), 333 – 334.

The Chronology of Livia's Marriage to Augustus

Carcopino, Jerome, "Le mariage d'Octave et de Livie et la naissance de Drusus"—The Marriage of Octavian and Livia and the Birth of Drusus, *Revue historique* 161 (1929), 225 – 236.

Flory, M., "Abducta Neroni Uxor: The Historiographical Tradition on the Marriage of Octavian and Livia," *Transactions of the American Philological Association* 118 (1988), 343 – 359.

Radke, Gerhard, "Der Geburtstag des älteren Drusus" —The Birthday of the Elder Drusus, *Würtzburger Jahrbücher* 4 (1978), 211 – 213.

Patronage

Carcopino, Jerome, *Daily Life in Ancient Rome; The People and the City at the Height of the Empire*, edited by Henry T. Rowell, translated from the French by E. O. Lorimer. New Haven: Yale University Press, 1940.

Dixon, Suzanne, "A Family Buisness: Women's Role in Patronage and Politics at Rome, 80 – 44 BC," *Classica et Medievalia* 34 (1983), 91 – 112.

Eilers, Claude, *Roman Patrons of Greek Cities*. Oxford/New York: Oxford University Press, 2002.

Kleiner, D., "Livia Drusilla and the Remarkable Power of Elite Women in Imperial Rome," *International Journal of the Classical Tradition* 6 (2000), 563 – 569.

Patronage in Ancient Society, edited by Andrew Wallace-Hadrill. London/New York: Routledge, 1989.

Rawson, E., "The Eastern Clientelae of Clodius and the Claudii," *Historia* 22 (1973), 219 – 239.

_____, "More on the Clientelae of the Patrician Claudii," *Historia* 26 (1977), 340 – 357.

Rouland, Norbert, *Pouvoir politique et dépendance personnelle dans l'antiquité romaine: genèse et role des rapports de clientèle— Political Power and Personal Dependence in Roman Antiquity: Genesis and Role of Clientela Agreements*. Brussels: Latomus, 1979.

Livia's Criminality: Acceptances, Rebuttals, and Explanations

Baldwin, B., "Women in Tacitus," *Prudentia* 4 (1972), 83 – 101.

Baring-Gould, Sabine, *The Tragedy of the Caesars: A Study of the Characters of the Caesars of the Julian and Claudian Houses*. London: Methuen, 1897. Beware, but have fun! This clergyman, perhaps best known for his poem *Onward, Christian Soldiers*, bases his conclusions about his subjects' personalities on the once fashionable pseudo-science of phrenology—the study of dimensions and shapes of skulls.

Barini, Concetta C., "La tradizione superstite e alcuni giudizi dei moderni sui Livia"—The Established Tradition and Some Judgments of Moderns about Livia, *Rendiconti dell' Accademia Nazionale dei Lincei* 21 (1922), 25 – 33.

Beulé, Charles-Ernest, *Augustus, seine Familie und seine Freunde, von M. Beulé. Deutsch bearbeitet von Dr. Eduard Doehler—Augustus, his Family and His Friends, by Monsieur Beulé. German prepared by Dr. Eduard Doehler*. Halle: Waisenhauses, 1873.

Blaze de Bury, Henri, *Les femmes de la société au temps d' Auguste— Women of Society in the Time of Augustus*. Paris: Didier, 1875.

_____, "L'impératrice Livie et la fille d'Auguste" —The Empress Livia and the daughter of Augustus, *Revue des deux mondes* 44 (1874), 591 – 637.

Buchan, John, *Augustus*. Boston: Houghton Mifflin Company, 1937.

Burke, Simon, *Domina*, television series for Sky Atlantic Italy and UK, 2021. A stunning example of blatant misrepresentation, this series supports Livia's criminal reputation by distorting the historical record—a travesty not even Robert Graves commits in *I, Claudius*.

Calhoon, Cristina G., *Livia the Poisoner: Genesis of an Historical Myth*. Ph.D. Dissertation, University of California, Irvine, 1994. This study seeks the roots of the criminal tradition about Livia in the characterizations of witches and of politically powerful women in Roman literature and legend.

Charlesworth, Michael P., "Livia and Tanaquil," *Classical Review* 41 (1927), 55 – 57.

_____, "Maiestas and the Power of Sejanus," *The Cambridge Ancient History, Volume 10*, 633 - 634.

_____, "Tiberius and the Death of Augustus," *American Journal of Philology* 44 (1923), 145 – 157.

Deckman, Alice A., "Livia Augusta," *The Classical Weekly* 18 (1925), 21 – 25.

Dessau, Hermann, *Geschichte der Römischen Kaiserzeit—History of the Roman Imperial Era*. Berlin: Weidman, 1924.

Ferrero, Gugliemo, *The Women of the Caesars*. New York: The Century Company, 1911.

Gafforini, C., "Livia Drusilla tra storia e letteratura"—Livia Drusilla in History and Literature, *Rendiconti del' Instituto Lombardo, Classe di Lettere Morali e Storiche* 130 (1996), 121 – 144.

Gardthausen, Viktor E., *Augustus und seine Zeit—Augustus and His Era*. Aalen: Scientia Verlag, 1964.

Grant, Michael, *Greek and Roman Historians: Information and Misinformation*. London/New York: Routledge, 1995.

Graves, Robert, *I, Claudius: from the Autobiography of Tiberius Claudius, Born BC 10, Murdered and Deified AD 54*. New York: H. Smith and R. Haas, 1934. Please remember: this highly entertaining,

Pulitzer Prize winning book is a work of fiction. Although its author boasts that everything he writes can be traced to original sources, he neglects to consider the accuracy of the data on which he relies. He also promotes distortions and outright inventions as historic facts. Graves has probably done more damage, to Livia's reputation, than any writer since Tacitus. Thanks to this famous novel and its electronic offspring—the British Broadcasting Corporation's much touted (if poorly staged and acted) *I, Claudius* television series—the impression of Livia as a criminal has become embedded in modern popular imagination.

Jameson, S., "Augustus and Agrippa Postumus," *Historia* 24 (1975), 287 – 314. This article argues that the absence of Paullus Fabius Maximus' name, from the *Acta fratrum arvalium* for May of 14 CE, validates the story of Augustus' voyage to Planasia.

Kornemann, Ernst, *Grosse Frauen des Altertums: im Rahmen zweitausendjährigen Weltgeschehens—Great Women of Antiquity: in the Framework of a Two Thousand Year Old Setting*. Wiesbaden: Dieterich, 1952.

————, *Tiberius*. Stuttgart: W. Kohlhammer, 1960.

La Romche-Guilhelm, Mlle. Anne de, *The History of Female Favourites: of Mary de Padilla, under Peter the Cruel, King of Castille; Livia, under the Emperor Augustus; Paola Farnesa, under Pope Alexander the Sixth; Agnes Soreau, under Charles VII, King of France; and Nantilda, under Dagobert, King of France*. London: C. Parker, 1772.

Martin, R. H., "Tacitus and the Death of Augustus," *Classical Quarterly* 5 (1955), 123 – 128.

Merivale, Charles, *The History of the Romans under the Empire*. New York: Appleton, 1863.

Perowne, Stewart, *The Caesars' Wives: Above Suspicion?* London: Hodder & Stoughton, 1974.

Pfister, Kurt, *Die Frauen der Cäsaren—The Women of the Caesars*. Berlin: Albert Nauck, 1951.

Questa, C., "La morte d'Augusto secondo Cassio Dione"—The Death of Augusto according to Cassius Dio, *La parola del passato* 54 (1959), 41 – 53.

Rutland, L., "Women as Makers of Kings in Tacitus' Annals," *Classical Weekly* 72 (1978), 15 – 29.

Ryberg, I., "Tacitus' Art of Innuendo," *Transactions of the American Philological Association* 73 (1942), 383 – 404.

Serviez, Jacques Roergas de, *Les imperatrices romaines; ou, Histoire de la vie et des intrigues secretes des femmes des douze Césars, de celles des emperereurs romains, et des princesses de leur sang—The Roman Empresses; Or, History of the Life and The Secret Intrigues of Wives of the Twelve Caesars, of Those of Roman Emperors, and of Princesses of Their Blood*. Paris: Chez Damonneville, 1758.

Stahr, Adolf Wilhelm Theodor, *Romische Kaiserfrauen—Roman Imperial Women*. Berlin: J. Gutentag, 1880.

Syme, Ronald, *Tacitus*. Oxford: Clarendon Press, 1958.

Tarver, J. C., *Tiberius the Tyrant*. New York: Dutton/Westminster: Constable, 1902.

Temporini, Hildegard, Countess of Vitzthum, *Die Kaiserinnen Roms: von Livia bis Theodora—The Empresses of Rome: from Livia to Theodora*. Munich: C. H. Beck, 2002.

The Evil Stepmother Conceit

Barrett, Anthony A., "Tacitus, Livia, and the Evil Stepmother," *Rheinisches Museum für Philologie* 144 (2001), 171 – 175.

Gray-Fow, Michael, "The Wicked Stepmother in Roman Literature and History," *Latomus* 45 (1988), 741 – 757.

Noy, David, "Wicked Stepmothers in Roman Society and Imagination," *Journal of Family History* 16 (1991), 345 – 361.

Watson, Patricia A., *Ancient Stepmothers: Myth, Misogyny, and Reality*. Leiden/New York: E. J. Brill, 1995.

Livia as a Public Figure

Aschbach, Joseph, Ritter von, "Livia, Gemahlinn des Kaisers Augustus: eine historische – archäologische Abhandlung" —Livia, Wife of the Emperor Augustus: an Historico – archaeological Treatment, *Denkschriften der kaiserlichen Akademieder Wissenscheften, Wien* 13 (1864), 36 – 84.

Bauman, Richard A., "Tribunician Sacrosanctity," *Rheinisches Museum für Philologie* 124 (1981), 166 – 183.

_____, *Women and Politics in Ancient Rome*. London/New York: Routledge, 1992.

Fishwick, Duncan, *The Imperial Cult in the Latin West: Studies in the Ruler Cult of the Western Provinces of the Roman Empire*. Leiden/ New York: E. J. Brill, 1987.

Grether, Gertrude, "Livia and the Roman Imperial Cult," *American Journal of Philology* 67 (1946), 222 – 252.

Hoffsten, R. B., *Roman Women of Rank in the Early Empire*. Ph.D. Dissertation, University of Pennsylvania, 1939.

Perkounig, Claudia-Martina, *Livia Drusilla/Iulia Augusta: Das politische Porträt der ersten Kaiserin Roms—Livia Drusilla/ Julia Augusta: The Political Portrait of the First Empress of Rome*. Vienna: Böhlau, 1995.

Purcell, N., "Livia and the Womanhood of Rome," *Proceedings of the Cambridge Philological Society* 212 (1986), 78 – 105.

Sandels, Friedrich, *Die Stellung der kaiserlichen Frauen aus dem julisch-claudischen Hause—The Position of the Imperial Women from the Julio-Claudian Dynasty*. Darmstadt: K. F. Bender, 1912.

Scardigli, B., "La sacrosanctitas tribunicia di Ottavia e Livia"—The Tribunician Sacrosanctity of Octavia and Livia, *Atti della Facoltà di Lettere e Filologia della Università di Siena, Perugia* 3 (1982), 61 – 64.

Seyrig, H., "Inscriptions de Gythion,"—Inscriptions of Gythium, *Revue archéologique* 29 (1929), 84 – 106.

Taylor, Lily Ross, *The Divinity of the Roman Emperor*. Philadelphia: Porcupine Press, 1975.

Winkes, Rolf, "Leben und Ehrungen der Livia"—Activities and Honors of Livia, *Archeologia* 36 (1985), 55 – 68.

Art and Architecture Associated with Livia

Ad Gallinas Albas: Villa di Livia. Bullettino della Commissione archeologica comunale di Roma, Supplementi, #8 — Ad Gallinas Albas: Villa of Livia. Bulletin of the Civic Archaeological Commission of Rome, Supplements, #8, edited by Gaetano Messino, with contributions by L. Calvelli *et. al.* Rome: "L'Erma" di Bretschneider, 2001.

Anderson, M., "The Portrait Medallions in the Imperial Villa at Boscotrecase," *American Journal of Archaeology* 91 (1987), 127 – 135.

Bartman, Elizabeth, *Portraits of Livia: Imaging the Imperial Woman in Augustan Rome*. New York: Cambridge University Press, 1999. Especially valuable: an appendix of all known inscriptions pertinent to Livia, in their original languages with English translations.

Dennis, George, *Cities and Cemeteries of Etruria*. London: John Murray, 1878.

Flory, M., "Sic Exempla Parantur: Livia's Shrine to Concordia and the Porticus Liviae," *Historia* 33 (1984), 309 – 330.

Gabriel, Mabel McAfee, *Livia's Garden Room at Prima Porta*. New York: New York University Press, 1955.

Ghedini, F., "Augusto e la Propaganda Apollinea nell'Amphoriskos di Leningrado"—Augustus and Apollonaic Propaganda in the Amphoriskos of Leningrad, *Archeologica classica* 38 – 40 (1996 – 1998), 128 – 135.

Gross, Walter Hatto, *Iulia Augusta: Unterschungen zur Grundlegung einer Livia-Ikonographie —Julia Augusta: Research on the Foundation of a Livia Iconography*. Gottingen: Vandenhoeck & Ruprecht, 1962.

Lijenstolpe, Peter and Klynne, Allan, *Prima Porta: Villa of Livia*. Website of Uppsala University's 1998 excavations: www.arkeologi. uu.se/primaporta/98Excavations/default98.htm.

Lugli, Giuseppe, *Il Foro Romano e il Palatino* (*The Roman Forum and the Palatine*). Rome: Bardi, 1971.

Megow, Wolf-Rüdiger, *Kameen von Augustus bis Alexander Severus—Cameos from Augustus to Alexander Severus*. Berlin: De Gruyter, 1987.

Moretti, Giuseppe, *L'Ara Pacis Augustae—The Altar of Augustan Peace*. Rome: La Libreria dello Stato, 1948.

Neverov, O., *Antique Cameos in the Hermitage Collection*, translated from the Russian by I. McGown. Leningrad: Aurora Art Publishers, 1971.

Pekáry, Thomas, *Das römische Kaiserbildnis in Staat, Kult und Gesellschaft: dargestellt Anhand der Schriftquellen—The Roman Emperor Image in State, Cult, and Society: An Appendix Offered to the Written Sources*. Berlin: Mann Brothers, 1985.

Romanelli, Pietro, *Il Palatino—The Palatine*. Rome: Instituto Poligrafico dello Stato, 1965.

Simpson, C. J., "Livia and the Constitution of the Aedes Concordiae," *Historia* 40 (1991), 449 – 455.

Taylor, Lily Ross, "Tiberius' Ovatio and the Ara Numinis Augusti," *American Journal of Philology* 58 (1937), 185 – 193.

Winkes, Rolf, *Livia, Octavia, Iulia: Porträts und Darstellung—Livia, Octavia, Julia: Portraits and Representations*. Providence: Brown University Center for Old World Archaeology and Art, 1995.

Zanker, Paul, *The Power of Images in the Age of Augustus*, translated from the German by Alan Shapiro. Ann Arbor: University of Michigan Press, 1988.

Livia's Assets

Huntsman, Eric Dennis, dissertation cited above under Genealogy.

Rostovtzeff, Michael I, *A Social and Economic History of the Roman Empire*. Oxford: Clarendon Press, 1926.

Non-Roman Peoples and Cultures

Applebaum, Shimon, *Judaea in Hellenistic and Roman times: Historical and Archaeological Essays*. Leiden/New York: E. J. Brill, 1989.

Bowersock, Glen Warren, *Augustus and the Greek World*. Oxford/New York: Oxford University Press, 1965.

Chamoux, François, *Hellenistic Civilization*, translated from the French by Michel Roussel, in cooperation with Margaret Roussel. Malden: Blackwell Publications, 2003.

Frank, Harry Thomas, *Discovering the Biblical World*. Maplewood: Hammond, 1975.

Grant, Michael, *Cleopatra*. New York: Simon and Schuster, 1972.

_____, *Herod the Great*. New York: American Heritage Press, 1971.

Kokkinos, Nikos, *The Herodian Dynasty: Origins, Role in Society, and Eclipse*. Sheffield: Sheffield Academic Press, 1998.

Mommsen, Theodor, *The Provinces of the Roman Empire from Caesar to Diocletian*, translated from the German by William Dixon. London: Macmillan, 1909.

Nawokta, K., "The Attitude towards Rome in the Political Propaganda of the Bosporan Monarchs," *Latomus* 48 (1989), 881 – 884.

Rawlinson, Geroge, *The Sixth Great Oriental Monarchy; or, The Geography, History, and Antiquities of Parthia, Collected and Illustrated from Ancient and Modern Sources*. New York: Dodd, Mead & Co., 1901.

Southern, Pat, *Cleopatra*. Stroud: Tempus, 1999.

Tarn, W. W., *Hellenistic Civilization*. London: E. Arnold & Co., 1927.

Suggestions for Further Reading, about Livia, her Milieu, and her Era

Barrett, Anthony A., "The Year of Livia's Birth," *Classical Quarterly* 49 (1999), 630 – 632.

Between Republic and Empire: Interpretations of Augustus and his Principate, edited by Kurt A. Raaflaub and Mark Toher. Berkeley: University of California Press, 1990.

The Cambridge Ancient History, Volume 10: The Augustan Empire, 43 BC – AD 69, edited by S. A. Cook, F. E. Adcock, and M. P. Charlesworth. Cambridge: Cambridge University Press, 1934.

Charlesworth, Michael P., "The Banishment of the Elder Agrippina," *Classical Philology* 17 (1922), 260 – 261.

Corbett, J. "The Succession Policy of Augustus," *Latomus* 33 (1974), 385 – 403.

Eck, Werner, *The Age of Augustus*, translated from the German by Deborah Lucas Schneider, with new material by Sarolta A. Takács. Malden: Blackwell Publishers, 2003.

Ferrill, Arthur, "Augustus and His Daughter: A Modern Myth," *Latomus* 168 (1990), 332 - 346.

Grant, Michael, Aldo Ceresa-Gastaldo, *et. al.*, *Il Bimillenario di Agrippa — The Bimillenarium of Agrippa*. Genoa: Dipartimento di archeologia, filologia classica e loro tradizioni, 1990.

Kokkinos, Nikos, *Antonia Augusta: Portrait of a Great Roman Lady*. London/New York: Routledge, 1992.

Lacey, Walter K., *Augustus and the Principate: the Evolution of the System*. Leeds: Francis Cairns, 1996.

Lear, Floyd Seyward, *Treason in Roman and Germanic Law; Collected Papers*. Austin: University of Texas Press, 1965.

Leon, E., "Scribonia and Her Daughters," *Transactions of the American Philological Association* 82 (1957), 168 – 175.

Levick, Barbara, *Claudius*. New Haven: Yale University Press, 1990.

_____, "Julians and Claudians," *Greece and Rome* 22 (1975), 29 – 38.

_____, "The Fall of Julia the Younger," *Latomus* 35 (1976), 301 – 339.

_____, *Tiberius the Politician*. London: Thames and Hudson, 1976.

_____, "Tiberius' Retirement to Rhodes," *Latomus* 31 (1972), 779 – 813.

Lindersky, Jerzy, "Julia in Rhegium," *Zeitschrift für Papyrologie und Epigraphik* (1988), 181 – 200.

Marsh, Frank Burr, *The Reign of Tiberius*. Cambridge: W. Heffner & Sons, Ltd., 1959.

Nichols, J., "Antonia and Sejanus," *Historia* 24 (1973), 48 – 58. This article challenges the presumption Antonia informed Tiberius of Sejanus' treachery.

Reinhold, Meyer, *Marcus Agrippa: A Biography*. Geneva, NY: W. F. Humphrey Press, 1933.

Richlin, Amy, "Julia's Jokes," *Stereotypes of Women in Power: Historical Perspectives and Revisionist Views*, edited by Barbara Garlick, Suzanne Dixon, and Pauline Allen. New York: Greenwood Press, 1992, 65 – 91.

Rogers, R. S., *Criminal Trials and Criminal Legislation under Tiberius*. Middletown: American Philological Association, 1935.

Rutledge, Steven H., *Imperial Inquisitions: Prosecutors and Informants from Tiberius to Domitian*. London/New York: Routledge, 2001.

Shotter, D. C. A., *Tiberius Caesar*. London/New York: Routledge, 1992.

Southern, Pat, *Augustus*. London/ New York: Routeledge, 1998.

_____, *Mark Antony*. Stroud: Tempus, 1998.

Syme, Ronald, *The Crisis of 2 BC*. Munich: Verlag der Bayerischen Akademie der Wissenschaften: In Kommission bei C. H. Beck, 1974.

_____, *History in Ovid*. Oxford/New York: Clarendon Press, 1978.

Treggari, Susan M., "Jobs in the Household of Livia," *Papers of the British School at Rome* 63 (1973), 241 – 255.`

INDEX

This compendium is far from comprehensive. Were we to cross-reference every element of Livia's life, the resulting table would be as long as our text. Readers seeking material that is excluded from the index, are encouraged to scrutinize the extant entries. Information on Julius Caesar the Dictator, for instance, can be culled from the early political career of Augustus.

Individuals are listed in boldface type by the nomenclature with which modern readers are most familiar. Commas are employed to preserve the proper order of names. For example: Livia's son Nero Claudius Drusus is presented as **Drusus**, Nero Claudius.

Ingram Content Group UK Ltd.
Milton Keynes UK
UKHW010704210323
418913UK00015B/732